St Magnus Cathedral
and Orkney's Twelfth-Century Renaissance

Evan MacGillivray (left) talking to Professor Peter Foote on board m.v. *Orcadia* during the Conference outing to Egilsay. (Stewart Cruden).

St Magnus Cathedral

and Orkney's Twelfth-Century Renaissance

Edited by
BARBARA E CRAWFORD

ABERDEEN UNIVERSITY PRESS

First published 1988
Aberdeen University Press
A member of the Pergamon Group

© The Contributors 1988

*All Rights Reserved. No part of this publication may be reproduced,
stored in a retrieval system or transmitted in any form or by any means:
electronic, electrostatic, magnetic tape, mechanical, photocopying,
recording or otherwise, without permission in writing from the
copyright holders.*

British Library Cataloguing in Publication Data

St Magnus Cathedral and Orkney's twelfth
century renaissance.
1. North—western Europe. Christian
culture, 1100–1299
I. Crawford, Barbara E. (Barbara Elizabeth)
940.1'8
ISBN 0-08-036580-9

PRINTED IN GREAT BRITAIN
THE UNIVERSITY PRESS
ABERDEEN

WITHDRAWN

READING ROOM

Foreword

Many people express surprise when they find a building of the distinction of St Magnus Cathedral in a small group of islands in the North of Scotland, an area which today seems somewhat remote from the mainstream of cultural, architectural and indeed commercial life. It must be remembered, however, that, just as on the old silk road to China, places which nowadays attract comparatively little attention were at one time centres of great importance, so Orkney in mediaeval times was a strategic point on the North–South Sea Lanes from Scandinavia to Scotland, England, Ireland and beyond.

Beginning no doubt as a base for Norse raiders and pirates, the Earldom of Orkney in the twelfth century, the period of the building of the Cathedral, was a semi-independent principality of considerable standing in the North. The Earl held Orkney and Shetland nominally from the King of Norway and Caithness from the King of Scots, though the more powerful Earls had scant regard for either monarch. When either or both Kings were able to exert some authority the consequences could be somewhat embarrassing for the Earls, but this dual role at least meant that the islands were open to influence, good as well as bad, from North and South.

The Earls also had dealings with other monarchs, and we find them making pilgrimages to Rome and meeting the Pope, while one, Earl Rognvald, the founder of the Cathedral, went on a Crusade to the Holy Land. Thus Orkney was by no means a backwater, but was open to the civilising influences of the day.

Bearing this in mind, Orkney Islands Council, as representatives of the owners of the Cathedral, the people of Orkney, decided that as part of the celebrations to mark the 850th anniversary of the founding of the Minster, a Conference should be held to which Scholars interested in the period and in the architectural, cultural and ecclesiastical life of the time should be invited. Dr Barbara Crawford, of the Department of Mediaeval History at St Andrew's University, was invited to organise the Conference, and the Council is grateful to her for undertaking the task. She was able to gather a distinguished team, and the time of the gathering was both informative and enjoyable to all who were privileged to be present. I should like to extend thanks to all who contributed, both to speakers and to those who led the study tours and assisted in numerous other ways.

It was felt that the great mass of knowledge this brought together should be permanently preserved, and this book is the result. Once again our thanks must go to Dr Crawford, who has been reponsible for its publication, a task to which she has devoted herself without stint.

As well as the factual lectures contained in the book, I am glad that it has been possible to print as an epilogue a translation of Swedish Mediaeval Legends of St Magnus by a distinguished Orkney Scholar and former Librarian, Evan MacGillivray. Mr MacGillivray retired to Sweden, to which country his wife belonged, but continued his work on the past of his native islands. He came to the Conference as a guest of honour, but sadly died during its progress. The publication of this volume of studies on St Magnus Cathedral and twelfth-century Orkney will stand as a memorial to him and all he contributed to our knowledge of our history.

I hope the readers of this book will find it as stimulating as the participants in the Conference found the lectures as they were delivered.

Edwin R Eunson
Convener, Orkney Islands Council

Contents

List of Figures

List of Black and White Plates

List of Colour Plates

Acknowledgements

When I received an invitation from the Convener of Orkney Islands Council to organise an International Conference on the occasion of and as part of the celebrations surrounding the 850th Anniversary of the founding of St Magnus Cathedral, I accepted with pleasure. This meant the possibility of gathering together British and Scandinavian historians and scholars for another of those enjoyable occasions which take place from time to time in the Orkney Islands when links across the North Sea are strengthened and renewed. It also provided the opportunity for an analysis of the building which Earl Rognvald's father Kol intended should be 'the wonder and glory of all the North' (*þat er eki se annat dyrligra i þvi landi*), and which could thus be studied in the historical context of the twelfth century by the many scholars of different backgrounds and disciplines who came together at that time. The Conference programme (included below) shows what wide-ranging and diverse areas of history (architectural, ecclesiastical, art, music and literature) were covered. But it was very necessary that such an important collection of studies of the Cathedral and other aspects of twelfth-century Orkney should not be forgotten, and should be made available for all who in the future will want to know more about the islands' past. Due to the generosity of the Orkney Islands Council it has been possible for the papers from the Conference to be published along with a rich and valuable collection of illustrations. I would like to record my thanks to all members of the Council who have supported the plans for publication in the full awareness of the value of their heritage and their responsibility towards the building of which they are the guardians. This book will help to show the wider world what a remarkable monument they have in their care. The Russell Trust and the friends of St Magnus Cathedral have also kindly contributed towards the cost of publication.

Further thanks are due to all those who were involved in the Conference arrangements, and in particular Mr John MacDonald and Dr Raymond Lamb without whom it would never have happened. In the preparation of the book I have relied on Mr William Thomson's good nature and helpfulness over many local matters. Dr Richard Fawcett kindly prepared the Glossary of Architectural terms. Mr Graeme Sanderson, Cartographic Dept., University of St Andrews drew the maps. Mr George MacKay Brown kindly gave permission for the printing of his poem. Finally my thanks are due to all Orkney friends who gave us such a warm welcome to their islands.

Barbara E Crawford
University of St Andrews

ST MAGNUS CATHEDRAL
850th ANNIVERSARY CONFERENCE
24th–29th July 1987

PROGRAMME

FRIDAY 24TH JULY
ORKNEY ARTS THEATRE

8.30 p.m.   Opening Lecture by Professor Emeritus Gordon Donaldson, HM Historiographer in Scotland
'The Contemporary Scene in Scotland'
Chairman: Colonel R A A S Macrae

SATURDAY 25TH JULY
ASSEMBLY HALL, KIRKWALL GRAMMAR SCHOOL

9.15 a.m.   Dr C A Ralegh Radford, formerly Inspector of Ancient Monuments for Wales and Monmouthshire
'St Magnus Cathedral, Kirkwall and the Development of the Cathedral in North-West Europe' (cancelled due to illness)

10.00 a.m.   Professor Donald E R Watt, St Andrews University
'The Church in Scotland in 1137'
Chairman: Mr William P Thomson

11.30 a.m.   Professor Peter Sawyer, Gothenburg, formerly of University of Leeds
'Dioceses and Parishes in Twelfth-Century Scandinavia'

12.15 p.m.   Professor Knut Helle, University of Bergen
'The Organisation of the Twelfth-Century Church in Norway'
Chairman: Dr Christopher D Morris

2.15 p.m.   Dr Kenneth Nicholls, University College, Cork
'Parochial Organisation in Western Ireland and the Scottish Islands'

3.00 p.m.   Dr Per Sveaas Andersen, University of Oslo
'The Orkney Church of the Twelfth and Thirteenth Centuries: a Step-daughter of the Norwegian Church?'
Chairman: Mr William S Hewison

4.30 p.m.   Tour of St Magnus Cathedral
(approx.)   *Guide Lecturers*: Mr Stewart Cruden and Dr Richard Fawcett

5.45 p.m.   Reception—Supper Room, Town Hall

8.30 p.m.   Mr Stewart Cruden, formerly Chief Inspector of Ancient Monuments for Scotland
'The Founding and Building of the Twelfth-Century Cathedral'
Chairman: Mr Edwin Eunson

SUNDAY 26TH JULY

    11.15 a.m.   Service in St Magnus Cathedral

    1.15 p.m.   Excursion on M.V. 'Orcadia' to St Magnus Church, Egilsay

    8.00 p.m.   Professor Eric Fernie, University of Edinburgh
                    'The Church of St Magnus, Egilsay'

    Chairman: Dr Raymond Lamb

MONDAY 27TH JULY

    9.15 a.m.   Professor Peter G Foote, University College, London
                    'Popular and Learned Elements in Orkneyinga Saga'

    10.00 a.m.   Professor Ray Page, University of Cambridge
                    'Runes in the Scandinavian World'

    Chairman: Mr Ian MacInnes.

    11.30 a.m.   Mr Paul Bibire, University of Cambridge
                    'The Poetry of Earl Rognvald's Court'

    12.15 p.m.   Dr Ingrid De Geer, University of Uppsala
                    'Music and the Twelfth-Century Orkney Earldom'

    2.15 p.m.   Dr Hans-Emil Lidén, Riksantikvaren, Bergen
                    'The Romanesque Cathedrals of Norway'

    3.00 p.m.   Dr Martin Blindheim, Oldsaksamlingen, University of Oslo
                    'Representations of St. Magnus in Scandinavia'

    3.45 p.m.   Dr Thelma Jexlev, Rigsarkiv, Copenhagen
                    'The Cult of Saints in Medieval Scandinavia'

    Chairman: Dr Ronald Cant

    8.00 p.m.   Dr Richard Fawcett, Inspector of Ancient Monuments, Edinburgh
                    'An Architectural Analysis of St Magnus Cathedral'

    Chairman: Lady Grimond

TUESDAY 28TH JULY

    9.15 a.m.   Dr Eric Cambridge, University of Durham
                    'The Architectural Context of the Romanesque Cathedral'

    10.00 a.m.   Dr Ronald Cant, University of St Andrews
                    'Norwegian Influences in the Design of the Gothic Cathedral'

    11.30 a.m.   Dr Christopher Morris, University of Durham
                    'Birsay'

    Chairman: Dr Barbara Crawford

    1.30 p.m.   Excursion to St Magnus Church, Birsay and the Brough of Birsay

    7 for

    7.30 p.m.   Conference Dinner in Kirkwall Hotel

WEDNESDAY 29TH JULY (ST OLAF'S DAY)

                 Conference Members dispersed

Songs for St Magnus Day

1   *The ship of Earl Magnus, going to Egilsay for a peace*
    tryst, is struck by a great wave in a calm sea

    'Steer the ship into this one steep wave.
    But nothing matters more.
    We have brought unwanted cargo, a jar of peace'. . . .
    Bailing pans flashed.
    The comber struck the hull, and scattered the
       oarsmen, and flawed the jar.

2   *Magnus foretells his death on Egilsay*

    Sailor, your heart is a stone bowl,
    The wine gone sour.
    A thistle will thrust daggers through that clay
    On the trysted shore.

3   *The sorrows of Magnus in the island of the church*

    If your good angel stands in a door
    With a song of greeting, be sure
    His dark brother is biding, silent, inside.
    Today a long black coat stands at the pier.
    The welcomer
    Folds, with his cup of keeping, at a cold fire.

4   *Magnus passes a night in the church, and a Mass is*
    said for him in the morning

    So cold it is in the kirk
    So dark this April night, in cell and choir
    His hands dovetail
    Like the one stone that locks an arch
    To hold his shaken spirit still.
    So cold it is, so dark.
    Then, soon, the opening rose of dawn.
    Calix sanguinis mei
    One hand unfolds like a bird
    And makes, at matin-time, a cross in the air.

5   *Magnus comes out of the church and stands among*
    his enemies

    Ite: the voyage is over.
    The skipper steps out of the stone ship
    With a blank bill-of-lading.
    A daffodil keeps a crumb of snow.
    A lark
    Soaks the 'isle-of-the-kirk' in a shower of lyrics.
    He offers his clay to wheel and kiln once more.
    Below, a ploughman
    Follows, with a drift of gulls, his dithering share.

6   *The cook Lifolf is summoned by Earl Hakon to*
    execute Earl Magnus in a stony place

    Lifolf the cook had killed a lamb
    And a brace of pigeons.
    A shore-stone flowered with flames.
    Lifolf gave the stewpot a stir.
    Eight hawk-masks stood on the hill.
    'Lifolf,' they sang, 'here's better butchering—
    Come up, come up!' . . .
    'The lords get hungry after a hunt,' said Lifolf.
    He washed his hands in the burn.
    He went in a slow dance
    Up to the blank stone in the barren moor.

7   *Invocation of the blind and the infirm at the tomb*
    of Magnus

    Saint Magnus, keep for us a jar of light
    Beyond sun and star.

                                    George Mackay Brown

The Contemporary Scene

Gordon Donaldson

Bearing in mind the remarkable mobility, not least by sea, of the men who planned the cathedral of St Magnus, it is worth while turning first to geography. The Firth of Forth area, including Holyrood and Dunfermline, is nearly 100 miles closer to Kirkwall than any part of Norway is; Durham is rather nearer than Bergen or Stavanger; London and Oslo are approximately equidistant; and the Straits of Dover are no farther away than Trondheim. True, many of the cathedral's founders knew something at first or second hand not only of north and central Europe but of places as far away as Rome and Constantinople, and in the twelfth century, after the First Crusade had established a Latin kingdom of Jerusalem, excursions to the Mediterranean had become almost commonplace. Such far-travelled men, seeing and no doubt admiring churches in many lands, may have been moved to contemplate imitation. Yet, when it came to inducing architects and masons to work in Orkney it was simpler to bring them from the lands easiest of access. The writers on architecture in this volume are unanimous in accepting the probability which geography dictates, namely that the chief element in the first phase of building at Kirkwall derived from Durham, in part mediated through Dunfermline or other buildings in Scotland. The adjective 'north British' is used appropriately to denote the source of the prevailing influence, but those who look only at the architecture may not always be aware that that term was equally applicable to the political context of the late eleventh and early twelfth centuries. At that time the Anglo-Scottish frontier—if there was one—was not the present Border, Scotland had peculiarly close links with Durham, and southern Scotland, at least, was subjected first to strong Anglo-Saxon influence and then to a Norman Conquest.

It happened that when Scotland was thus potentially a link between Orkney and influences from the south, the personal and dynastic connections between the Orkney earldom and the Scottish kingdom were very close. The details are not always clear, for contemporary Scottish sources, meagre before the twelfth century, show little awareness of what was going on in Orkney, while some saga writers—who, it must constantly be remembered, were not contemporary—had only a sketchy acquaintance with persons and events in Scotland. Amid the confusion, however, certain facts stand out.

The frontier between the earldom of Orkney and the kingdom of Scotland did not in early times lie on the Pentland Firth. There was a land frontier somewhere on the Scottish mainland, in Caithness or farther south, where earldom and kingdom were always rubbing shoulders. As early as about 980, when rival claimants to the earldom clashed in Caithness, one of them had the support of Scottish magnates, styled in the Saga the Scottish king and a Scottish earl. Orcadian power may at that stage have been under some pressure from expansionist Scots, and Sigurd II (c.980–1014) had for a time to defend Caithness against Scottish attacks. As so often happened, judicious matrimony seems to have been pressed into service to ease tension, and in the very last years of the tenth century Sigurd married a daughter of Malcolm II, king of Scots. Their son, Thorfinn the Mighty, sometimes thought of as something like the ultimate Viking, was thus half Scots, and in Orcadian eyes looked like an ugly foreigner, with his black hair, sharp features and swarthy countenance.

The events of Thorfinn's long career brought the Orcadian earldom and the Scottish kingdom together as they had never been before. When Malcolm II, Thorfinn's grandfather, died in 1034, he left no sons. One of his daughters, Bethoc, had married Crinan, abbot of Dunkeld, and they had a son, Duncan; another daughter, whose name is not known, was the mother of Thorfinn (see fig. 1). Transmission of the succession through females was apt to lead to disputes—as was to happen in Scotland in better-known circumstances on the death of the Maid of Norway in 1290—and it would not have been surprising if Duncan and Thorfinn had been rivals. There was another claiment, Macbeth, something of a man of mystery who opens a great field for speculation and around whom fantasies have been woven by writers of fiction among whom William Shakespeare was neither the first nor the last. As Macbeth had the bad luck to be ousted in favour of a dynasty which proved enduring he was vilified as an usurper in much the same way as Richard III, who was ousted in favour of the Tudors.

Historians who have looked at the matter seriously have tended to the view that Macbeth's claim to the throne was in right of his wife, who seems to have been a grand-daughter of a previous king, but there is no reason to believe that even had she been a daughter of a king that would have given her husband a right to the throne, any more than Crinan's marriage to Bethoc gave him a right. The most likely source of any claim Macbeth had was through his mother (wife of Finlay, mormaer of Moray), who may have been a daughter of a Scottish king, possibly even of Malcolm II. Three cousins—Duncan, Thorfinn and Macbeth—might very likely all have considered themselves entitled to the throne. Duncan became king, possibly because he was the eldest or ablest, but just as likely because, on the decease of Malcolm II, he managed to beat his rivals to the place of royal inaugurations at Scone, just as in England in 1110 Henry I beat his elder brother Robert to Winchester.

It would be understandable if Duncan's two cousins, Thorfinn and Macbeth, then ganged up against him and put him out of the way. Duncan, if he was indeed (as I believe) the 'Karl Hundason' of the Saga, had attempted to assert himself in Caithness but was defeated by Thorfinn 'and some say he was slain'. Slain he was, but by the other competitor, Macbeth, and the circumstances strongly suggest that he fell victim to a joint attack by his two cousins, who, after thus disposing of him in 1040, partitioned the kingdom between them. Macbeth got the royal title, but Thorfinn, the Saga says, held nine Scottish earldoms, which by any reckoning looks like a generous share, and he is credited with operating as far south as Fife. A continuing alliance between Thorfinn and Macbeth is indicated by the fact that they both went on pilgrimage to Rome. Macbeth's visit is dated 1050. It is only right to say that they might easily have decided to make this journey independently, for there seems to have been something of a fashion then for rulers to go to Rome: Cnut, the Danish king of England, had gone there, and Edward the Confessor, who was king of England in the very year 1050, intended to go. Yet Macbeth and Thorfinn may have been fellow-travellers.

After a reign of seventeen years, Macbeth was defeated and killed by Malcolm III (Malcolm Canmore), elder son of the deceased Duncan. The Saga says that Malcolm took as his first wife Ingibjorg, Thorfinn's widow. This statement has been challenged since at latest 1899, when Sir Archibald Dunbar published the first edition of his *Scottish Kings*, and I have long believed that Malcolm's wife was the daughter, not the widow, of Thorfinn. But writer after writer has continued to repeat the Saga's statement, and the matter demands examination. The Saga puts Thorfinn's death 'about the end of Harald Hardrada's days' and, as Harald was killed at Stamford Bridge in September 1066, this would indeed point to 1065 or thereby as the date of Thorfinn's death. If he died at that time he had been earl for fifty years, but the Saga credits him with seventy or even eighty years, indicating that he was thought of as a very old man. That does not in itself prove that his widow was an old woman, but the sons of Thorfinn and Ingibjorg were old enough to fight alongside Harald Hardrada in 1066, and the marriage of Thorfinn to Ingibjorg (perhaps not her first marriage) has been placed not later than about 1040. These facts would make it improbable that when Thorfinn died about 1065 Ingibjorg would be capable of producing at least three children in a subsequent marriage.

Looking at the question from the other end, Malcolm's marriage to his second wife, Margaret, cannot have been later than 1070 and may have been a year or two earlier, for by the early 1080s Margaret had produced eight children who grew to adulthood. It is apt to be assumed that Ingibjorg had died, but this is not necessarily so: if she was Thorfinn's daughter then she was Malcolm's second cousin and their marriage was therefore null by the rules of consanguinity which were at that time being tightened; if she was Thorfinn's widow her case was little better, by the rules of affinity. The marriage may well have been terminated by a 'divorce' or decree of nullity, and their eldest son was retrospectively styled a bastard. Now, allowing a decent interval between Thorfinn's death about 1065 and the re-marriage of his widow, and again allowing a decent interval between Ingibjorg's death or divorce and Malcolm's marriage to Margaret not later than 1070, a marriage of Malcolm to Thorfinn's widow could hardly have lasted four years. Yet Ingibjorg is known to have borne three sons to Malcolm, and there may have been other children. There was barely time for all this to happen in the interval between Thorfinn's death and Malcolm's marriage to Margaret.

There is yet another way of looking at the question. Malcolm was born about 1030, and it is difficult to believe that, instead of marrying and begetting an heir to carry on the line of his father Duncan, he remained a bachelor until he was about thirty-five.

While none of those facts, individually, makes a marriage of Malcolm to a widow of Thorfinn impossible, the improbabilities mount, and cumulatively the argument seems conclusive against such a marriage. It is much more plausible that Malcolm, eager to ensure the succession, lost no time, after he had overthrown Macbeth in 1057, in coming to terms with Macbeth's ally, Thorfinn, and marrying Thorfinn's daughter, who may well have had the same name as her mother. Sir Archibald Dunbar placed Malcolm's marriage to Ingibjorg about 1059, without noticing that this was inconsistent with her being the widow of a man who died only in 1065.

The whole problem of the identity of Malcolm's first wife hinges, however, to some extent on the date of Thorfinn's death. It has been pointed out that there is no evidence that Thorfinn survived Macbeth, who died in 1057. This is in no way surprising in view of the paucity of our sources: W F Skene, a hundred years ago, remarked that 'our authorities for the history of Macbeth know nothing of Earl Thorfinn and his conquests. On the other hand, the sagas equally ignore Macbeth and his doings'. If Thorfinn died in 1057 his widow might have married Malcolm and had children by him before Malcolm married Margaret a matter of ten years later. However, 1057, nine years before the death of Harald Hardrada, hardly seems to fall within 'the end of Harald Hardrada's days', the point to which the Saga assigns Thorfinn's death, and Thorfinn's death as early as 1057 is hard to reconcile with the exceptionally long reign attributed to him by the Saga. From the point of view of Scoto-Orcadian relations the precise identity of Malcolm's wife matters less than the fact that she belonged to the ruling house of Orkney, which meant that, whatever other external influences bore on the islands, southern influences continued to be channelled through Scotland.

Scotland itself had long been subjected to external influences. In the late seventh and early eighth centuries the Anglian kings of Northumbria, who controlled the land up to the Firth of Forth, lost the war when their armies were defeated beyond the Tay; yet they won the peace when a Pictish king who ruled beyond the Tay sent to Northumbria for architects to build a church in his dominions—surely the first recorded occasion when English building skills were introduced to Scotland, but by no means the last. In the ninth century the ruling dynasty of the Irish kingdom which had been established in the west of Scotland gained control of Pictland, and Irish influence swept right across the country—a phase to which the round towers of Abernethy and Brechin have been assigned. That phase was short, partly because Scandinavian settlements in the west did a lot to sever Scotland from Celtic Ireland, and Irish influence throughout Scotland ceased for centuries. The eleventh century saw a revival of English influence. In or about 1018 the frontier of the Scottish kingdom was extended to, and beyond, the Tweed and the Solway, which meant that south-east Scotland, the most English part of Scotland, became and remained a spearhead of southern influence. That influence was at first what is loosely called Anglo-Saxon. In the next phase—bearing in mind the substantial Scandinavian settlements in England and the rule there for a time of Danish kings—it can be more accurately called Anglo-Scandinavian. Finally it became Norman. (see Donaldson, 'Scotland's Earliest Church Buildings', printed in revised form in *Scottish Church History* [1985].)

The Normans, in view of their origins, should not have required any introduction to Orkney by way of Scotland. Their 'Northmen' ancestors had settled in France early in the tenth century under Rolf the Ganger, alias Rollo, first Duke of Normandy. If the traditional identification of Rollo is correct—and, like much else, it has been challenged—he was the nephew of the first Earl of Orkney and the brother of the second; thus Thorfinn of Orkney, who seems to have been in a fair way to being a Conqueror of Scotland, and his contemporary William of Normandy, the Conqueror of England, had a common ancestor five generations back. However, the descendents of Rollo and his followers so thoroughly assimilated themselves to their new surroundings that in less than a century their culture was that of those we call Normans and no longer of Northmen. Their influence reached England, and also Scotland, long before the conventionally decisive date of 1066. In 1002 the English king Ethelred, familiarly known as 'the Unready', married Emma, daughter of the Duke of Normandy, and she subsequently married Cnut, the Danish king whose dominions included Norway and England and who also invaded Scotland. Thus Norman and Scandinavian elements came together in the ruling house of England. After the death of Cnut England was ruled briefly by two of his sons, one of them the offspring of Norman Emma. Then in 1042 the English throne went to Edward the Confessor, also a son of Norman Emma, by her first husband the English Ethelred. The Confessor has been characterised as not an English king but a French monk, and he so surrounded himself with Normans that their ascendancy in England can be said to have begun with peaceful penetration in his lifetime rather than with armed conquest after his death.

The stages by which southern—which ultimately meant Norman—influence reached Scotland can be defined. Duncan I, who was the first king to rule all of Scotland down to and beyond the Solway, had found his queen in Northumbria. His supplanter Macbeth welcomed Normans who had to flee when there was a temporary reaction against Norman influence in England in the reign of Edward the Confessor. Such a partiality for Normans perhaps puts a different slant on Macbeth's trip to Rome, an excursion which, as was mentioned, appealed also to the Confessor.

Malcolm III, who defeated and killed Macbeth, was the son of Duncan I and his Northumbrian wife; he was thus half-English before he spent his formative years in the England of Edward the Confessor during Macbeth's reign, and, with an English estate, this son-in-law of Thorfinn was a 'Northamptonshire country gentleman'. It was with armed southern backing that he was able to prevail against Macbeth; he was 'sworn brother' to Tostig, earl of Northumbria (brother of Harold, the king of England who died at Hastings); he visited Edward the Confessor in 1059 in the company of the archbishop of York and the bishop of Durham. And, after the termination of his marriage to Ingibjorg, he married Margaret, a grandniece of the Confessor and like him descended from Ethelred the Unready, but from Ethelred's first, English, wife and not from his second, Norman Emma (see fig. 1). Margaret was thus more English in race than Edward, but she had spent years at Edward's Normanised court. Not only so, but she had spent some of her childhood in Hungary. It has been suggested that Margaret's somewhat ostentatious zeal for the Christian faith owed something to her experience of Hungary, where the Christianity introduced by king Stephen was still an exciting novelty. It has not so often been noted that Malcolm's previous wife, Ingibjorg, was a product of the Scandinavian world, where likewise Christianity was something of a novelty. Perhaps Malcolm suffered from two pious wives. He offset the oppressive piety of his household by four times invading the north of England, where the situation was singularly unstable, and he brought back so many captives that 'there was not a household in Scotland without an English slave' (Anderson, *SAEC*, 93).

Margaret's brother, Edgar the Atheling, had been the native candidate for the English throne in 1066, but William the Conqueror had excluded Margaret's kinsfolk from it, and she gave the first four of her sons the names of former English kings almost as if she saw them as potential pretenders to challenge the Normans. Yet Margaret had fallen under the spell of Norman culture and achievement. She corresponded with Lanfranc, the Norman Archbishop of Canterbury, who sent some Benedictine monks to form the core of a community at Dunfermline, a favoured residence of the Scottish king and queen.

In 1093 Malcolm was killed on the last of his invasions of England, and Margaret, like the dutiful wife she was, expired when she heard the news. It was at once evident that there had been resentment against the southern ways of the late king and queen, for the throne was seized, to the exclusion of their sons, by Malcolm's brother Donald Bane, who seems to have been brought up in the western isles and has been characterised as 'an incorrigible old Celt', but Donald was as likely to have learned Norse as Celtic ways in the isles. Donald was soon confronted by a rival in the person of Duncan, a son of Malcolm by his first wife, Ingibjorg. Duncan had been at the English court for twenty years, as a hostage for his father, and he came north with help from the second Norman king of England, William Rufus, to oust his uncle Donald. Duncan is the first king of Scots of whom we have any depiction: his seal, which shows him as a typical mounted Norman knight, with conical helmet, nose-protector, shield and spear, gives a vivid impression of the Normans riding on to the stage of Scottish history. It may be significant that, while Margaret had given her sons English names, Duncan called his son William after his Norman patrons, the kings of England, and that son figures in history as William Fitz Duncan.

The first attempt, by Duncan, at a Norman conquest of Scotland failed, for the wicked uncle, Donald Bane, soon returned and Duncan was killed. Only three years later, however, Edgar, the eldest surviving son of Malcolm and Margaret, came to Scotland, as Duncan had done, with another army supplied by Rufus. An unnamed battle in 1097, in which Edgar and his Normans defeated Donald Bane, was the Scottish equivalent of Hastings and an important step towards a Norman conquest of Scotland. Edgar ruled the country as a vassal of the Norman king of England.

Edgar and other descendants of Malcolm and Margaret held the throne and intermarried with the families of the Norman kings: one of Edgar's sisters was the wife of Henry I, and his brother Alexander I married a daughter of Henry. David I, before he became king of Scots, was thus at the same time brother of the king of Scots and brother of the queen of England. Normans flocked into Scotland to acquire wide estates and to fill the highest offices in church and state. David brought in monks not only from Norman England but also direct from Normandy.

The links of the Scottish royal family with Durham deserve particular attention. Malcolm III, despite his depredations in England, was on amicable terms with the Bishop of Durham, in whose company he visited Edward the Confessor in 1059. He must have been very familiar with Durham's pre-Norman cathedral, dating from the end of the tenth century, with its tower 'of wondrous size', and shortly before his death he laid one of the foundation stones of the new Norman cathedral, work on which went on until 1133. Malcolm's eldest son, the luckless Duncan II, granted to Durham revenues formerly pertaining to the bishop of St Andrews, and a long series of charters by Scottish kings to Durham runs on through the reigns of Edgar, Alexander I and David. Anyone studying early Scottish charters will find more of them at Durham than in any other repository. Alexander had a very privileged position at Durham, where he was allowed to view the remains of St Cuthbert when they were exposed in 1104 on the occasion of their translation to the new cathedral. It can hardly be doubted that southern Scotland must have been thought of as being in some sense within St Cuthbert's territory.

Thus the rulers of Scotland not merely knew English buildings but were closely associated with them and with their builders. Their own kingdom had plenty of churches in the eleventh century—local proprietary chapels, larger mother churches, some monasteries (probably past their best days), one or two bishops' churches (if hardly yet cathedrals) and establishments of culdees which seem to have been by this time communities of secular priests rather like the old English minsters. Owing to the difficulty of assigning dates to the structures which still survive we know little of what the buildings were like, but it is beyond credibility that their design did not follow that of churches familiar in the north of England. A fluctuating frontier, of which contemporaries can hardly have been aware, could not have curbed the spread of architectural fashions. It does not require great imagination to think of Malcolm Canmore building at St Andrews a tower 'of wondrous size' like that at Durham, or enlarging the culdee church at Dunfermline along Anglo-Saxon lines, with a semi-circular apse; perhaps the captives he brought back from England included masons or even architects.

If Scottish rulers were familiar with the architecture of eleventh-century England they were if anything even more familiar with the Norman architecture which succeeded it. Once again it is beyond credibility that they did not hasten to adopt the new fashion and that any building erected under their patronage could have been of other than Norman type. It is safe to say that the new style was in full flood by the 1120s; indeed no church of other than Norman type can be shown to have been erected in Scotland much, if at all, after 1100 and before the emergence of the First Pointed style.

Any attempt to relate Orkney to those developments in Scotland must not overlook the opportunities which Orcadians had to become familiar with contemporary architecture farther afield than in Scotland. No doubt Thorfinn, perhaps already envisaging a 'minster' in Orkney, would keep his eyes open on his way to and from Rome; yet he—if only when he was campaigning in Fife—and his contemporaries would see the buildings of Scotland. Besides, Orcadians would feel at home among the Anglo-Scandinavian elements in southern Scotland: a piece of land beside Loch Leven in Kinross, which Macbeth gave to the priory of Loch Leven, bore the unmistakeably Scandinavian name of Kyrkenes and in the next generation the first builder of a church in Scotland who is identifiable bore the equally unmistakeably Scandinavian name of Thor—Thor the Long, who built the church of Ednam in Berwickshire.

Earl Paul of Orkney, Thorfinn's son, made an application to an Anglo-Norman archbishop as Queen Margaret did, though he asked not for monks but for a bishop. When Paul's nephew Magnus, the future saint, parted from King Magnus Barelegs, he made his way to the court of that king's enemy, the Scottish king Edgar, a vassal of the Norman king of England to whom he owed his throne. A little later the future saint spent a year at the court of the next Norman king of England, Henry I, brother-in-law of the Scottish kings Edgar, Alexander I and David. Bishop William, the first native bishop of Orkney, who was appointed it seems in 1102, is said to have been a 'Paris clerk', which meant that he was familiar with Norman culture on the continent. Kali Kolsson, the future Rognvald, Earl and Saint, who was brought up in Norway, in his youth visited Grimsby, a place where there was an international trading community. The Orcadian magnate Swein Asleif's son is said to have visited King David at Edinburgh, and David communicated directly with Earl Rognvald, whom he 'directed' (the writ runs *mando et precipio* to protect the 'monks' at Dornoch.

By 1137, when the cathedral at Kirkwall was started, there were already in Scotland a number of churches of Norman type. Work must at least have started on some of the hundreds of parish churches which were built in the course of the century. It may be impossible to assign a precise date to any of them, but Dr Fawcett suggests that masons who worked at Kirkwall included men who had worked on the church of Leuchars, which, in its sophistication, was certainly not an early essay in the new style. The larger structures are more clearly identifiable than the parish churches. David, before he became king, brought monks to Selkirk in 1113 and they were moved to Kelso in or about 1128: in both those places the work must from the start have been Norman. At Dunfermline and Holyrood, both founded by David as king and assigned to 1128, Norman work is still extant, at the former on a large scale. Of David's foundation at Urquhart it can be said only that it was probably established in the 1130s. David's major foundation at Melrose is credibly attributed to 23 March 1136 (probably 1136/7). The dates of some other foundations are more debatable, but the evidence is sufficient to show that a good deal of Norman building was going on in Scotland by the 1130s. Besides, other buildings, which were not started until after Kirkwall had been started, may none the less have influenced it and possibly provided markets where skilled labour could be obtained.

It will be observed that none of the buildings mentioned in the previous paragraph were cathedrals or even bishops' churches. The fact is that this was a field in which Orkney was ahead of Scotland, essentially because Orkney was starting from scratch whereas the situation in Scotland was complicated by the fact that although there was not yet in the early twelfth century a diocesan system there were several places which had been bishops' seats for varying periods of time and there were ancient affiliations and property rights which could not be ignored. Existing churches could serve the modest needs of bishops until chapters were organised. At St Andrews there had of course been a church—very likely a series of churches—for many centuries and there had been a succession of bishops. A Norman bishop was not securely installed until 1127, but even then, it has been argued, all he did was to enlarge and 'Normanise' an existing church; a new church was not started until 1160. At Glasgow, where there had been less continuity, a church was started for the new line of bishops in 1136, but no traces of it remain. It is equally significant that Carlisle, which had been closely associated with Glasgow and which was sometimes at least *de facto* within the Scottish kingdom—David died there in 1153—got its cathedral about 1130. Elsewhere development was slow, but, while Kirkwall, as a cathedral, hardly has a Scottish parallel, at least so far as surviving remains show, cathedrals did make a certain contribution to the outburst of building in Scotland in the 1120s and 1130s.

The Norman church in Kirkwall was not, however, Orkney's first cathedral. There was Thorfinn's 'minster' at Birsay, dating from the middle of the eleventh century, and by the beginning of the twelfth Egilsay was an important episcopal residence with presumably a bishop's church which can be identified with the towered structure still standing there. There are several problems, some of them arising from the fact that many Orkney churches give the impression of being, in Professor Fernie's phrase, 'local and virtually timeless'. Yet an examination of the churches on Wyre, at Orphir and on the Brough of Birsay—the last of them surely dateable on stylistic grounds—is desirable, and the fact must not be ignored that while Egilsay is now *sui generis* in Orkney there were a number of other round-towered churches in the diocese for which dates cannot be supplied. Professor Fernie suggests that Egilsay may have originated when the bishopric of Orkney was connected with Hamburg-Bremen, which would place it very roughly between about 1050 and 1070 and make it almost contemporary with the 'minster' at Birsay. As he says, it would be surprising if the structure now standing at Egilsay was 'being erected at exactly the time when masons skilled in cutting ashlar were at work on the cathedral in the ten or fifteen years after 1137'.

BIBLIOGRAPHY

Anderson, *SAEC* = *Scottish Annals from English Chronicles*, ed. A O Anderson (1908)

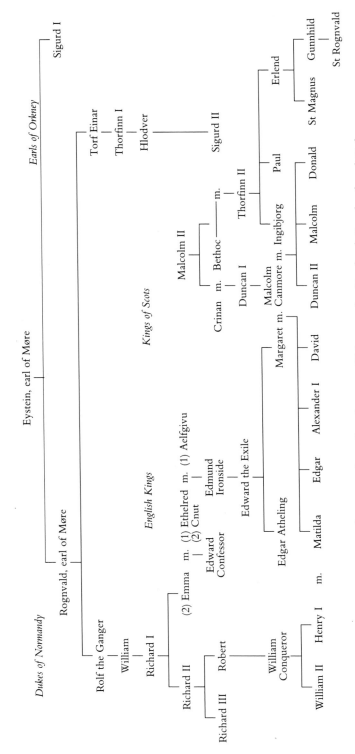

FIGURE 1   Connection between the ruling houses of Normandy, England, Scotland and Orkney.

SECTION I: HISTORY
The Ecclesiastical Background

St Magnus' Cathedral is a symbol of Orkney's place in the Renaissance of culture and learning which flourished in twelfth-century Europe. That Renaissance was partly ecclesiastical, and the history of the medieval Church is basic to our appreciation of what such a Renaissance meant. The peace which the Church had preached for many centuries came nearer to existence than perhaps at any other time; for the power of kings was greatly increased during this century and the royal peace-keeping hand was stretched out wider and wider over their subject territories, whether France, Scotland, England or the Holy Roman Empire. The extension of royal power went hand in hand with the growth of the Church's authority, which benefited from the protection afforded by kings and in return gave religious sanction and the benefits of spiritual ceremonies like crowning and anointing. Of course there were the famous battles between Church and State, between bishop and king—and nowhere more so than in Norway—but in general the Church could never have grown so powerful without the devotion and donations of national kings and their nobility.

The papers in Section I are mainly focused upon the Church's organisation and structures, which developed under these favourable conditions. The establishment of bishoprics was extended virtually throughout the whole of Europe in the twelfth century and the main governmental structure of the Church therefore completed. The hierarchy was also consolidated under the Popes at Rome and this was to lead to a multi-national and highly-organised world empire. At the local level parishes crystalise, based on the myriad numbers of private churches established in previous centuries by pious landowners on their estates. But the way in which this happened throughout Europe varied widely (see Sawyer, below).

The monastic movement was another and very remarkable side of twelfth-century religious development. The desire of pious laymen to found and endow communities of monks who were to devote their whole life to the worship of God, and the desire of many more to go and live in them is a phenomenon not easily understood today. The fact that so many new monastic orders came into existence and so many houses were founded for these orders in the twelfth century tells us a very great deal about the piety and religiosity of medieval men and woman. It also tells us that the age was comparatively peaceful and that incomes were sufficient for the immense outlay invloved. The religious call was also followed by many other members of society who responded to the Crusading movement and

11

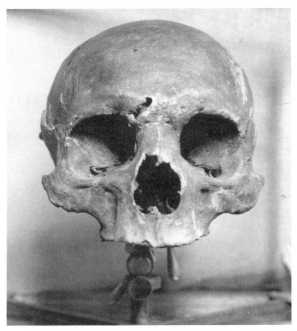

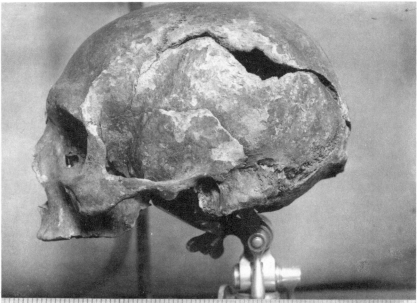

PLATE 1a and 1b   Two views of the presumed skull of St Magnus found in the south pier of the choir in 1919. The damage to the skull visible in 1b may be the direct result of the request made by Magnus that Lifolf strike him on the head rather than beheading him 'like a thief'. (Courtesy of Orkney Library, Photographic Archive).

gave money and very often their lives in attempting to restore Christian control over the Holy Places of Palestine.

The peoples of Scandinavia were fully involved in all these developments. Conversion had come late to Norway and was not yet complete in Sweden. But bishoprics, monasteries and cathedrals all appear in the twelfth century along the lines of the rest of Europe, with strong influence from England and Germany. The kings of Norway were merely the most northerly example of medieval monarchies, and their intention to model themselves on southerly example is quite obvious. In this process the earldom of Orkney was probably a very important point of transmission. Knowledge first of the Christian religion and then of the organisation of the Christian Church must have filtered through the islands back to the homeland more easily than directly across the North Sea. The earls were as concerned with the establishment of a Church in their islands as the kings were in Norway and they were under more direct influence from Scotland as well as England and Ireland. Earl Thorfinn's role here as a trail-blazer in the establishment of a bishopric and as the builder of the first cathedral at Birsay is given full recognition (see Radford, below). But Orkney in turn was going to follow Norwegian example when it came to the matter of creating their own local saint. Olaf Haraldsson's death at the battle of Stiklestad in 1030 against the foreign invader Cnut of England and Denmark, and his subsequent recognition as a saint was an immensely powerful weapon in the hands of his successors, and a potent force in the creation of a national identity. The family of earls in Orkney were going to find the sanctity of a murdered member of the dynasty also very useful. But the growth of local Church structures and the piety of recently-converted populations also lie behind these remarkable developments in kingdom and earldom alike.

CHAPTER 1

St Magnus Cathedral, Kirkwall, and the Development of the Cathedral in Northwest Europe

C A Ralegh Radford

In transalpine Europe the organisation of the church took shape in the fourth century; it followed the secular pattern of the later Roman Empire. The basic unit was the diocese ruled by a bishop; dioceses were grouped into provinces, each under a metropolitan or archbishop. The diocese normally coincided with the area dependent on a 'tribal' centre or *civitas*, in which the principal church, the cathedral of the bishop, was situated. The extent of this identity is illustrated by the later use of *civitas* to denote a town with a cathedral, a normal meaning in the twelfth century.

The establishment of the Christian Empire under Constantine gave the Church access to the wealth and resources of the State. Great cathedrals and memorial churches arose on a scale and of a magnificence commensurate with the importance of the city or *civitas*. In fourth-century Rome the Cathedral of St John Lateran within the walls and the memorial churches St Peter on the Vatican and St Paul on the Ostia road, both in suburban cemetries, (Gunton, 1969, 22, 52, 131 and 135) may be compared with the greatest of contemporary secular buildings. Only the third of these churches remains in recognisable form, largely rebuilt on the old lines after a disastrous fire in 1823. Similar churches in transalpine Europe were on a comparable, though less magnificent, scale.

With the breakup of the Western Empire in the fifth century the building of churches on this scale became difficult, though large cathedrals were not unknown; pre-Conquest Canterbury, basically a building of the seventh century (Taylor, 1969, 108–15), may serve as an example. The great church of the classical world was reborn with the foundation of the Holy Roman Empire under Charlemagne. The early ninth-century Cathedral of Cologne was influenced by St Peter in Rome (Weyres, 1965, 408) and a not unworthy counterpart. But the Carolingian concern with monastic reform determined that many of the new buildings were large abbey churches replacing earlier and humbler shrines, often in rural settings far from the cities and cathedrals. Few great churches of this age survive, but the eleventh-century representation of St Riquier (Clapham, 1930, 78–82) reflects the original appearance of *c*.800, in spite of its seventeenth-century redrawing. In England the monastic reform introduced by St Dunstan in c.940 inspired a number of important churches, of which the eleventh-century Cathedral of Sherborne (Gibb, 1975, 98–102) may serve as an example.

Outside the old imperial frontiers to the north and west, in the regions to which Christianity spread in the fifth and succeeding centuries, there were no cities in the Roman sense nor was the tradition of building in masonry known. But the concept of the *civitas* as the episcopal centre and the site of cathedral remained, reinforced perhaps by the Augustinian ideas of the *civitas Dei*. Kildare, a double monastery founded by St Bridget and Bishop Conlaidh, whose tombs flanked the altar, illustrates the point. An Irish writer of the seventh century mentions the 'numberless wonders of the city (*civitas*) . . . If it be rightly called a city, when it is surrounded by no circle of walls . . . it has received the name of city from the coming together within it of many men.' Here, as often in Ireland, the head of the community took precedence, with the bishop as a necessary officer of the organisation (Radford, 1977, 5–7). It would be difficult to find a better description of the *civitas* in those regions which had never known imperial Rome.

Lacking a masonary tradition the Irish normally built their churches of wood; all were small. A seventh-century tradition (ascribed to St Patrick to confer authority) suggests that the normal length of a major church was 'sixty feet' (18.25m). This is approximately the size of the wooden church, which formed the nucleus of Glastonbury (Radford, 1981, 111–3) and of the earliest stone cathedrals that can be identified in Ireland. Among these is Clonmacnois, which is securely dated in the first quarter of the tenth century (Radford, 1977, 1–7). Architecturally Clonmacnois is a church *in antis*, a building of which the longer side walls project beyond the line of the end walls. This is a common form in early Irish churches. In the eleventh century—and perhaps even before 1000—a new design with a coeval nave and quire and sometimes a western tower began to replace the older form of the church *in antis* (Leask, 1955, 64–72 and 75–8).

The Norse first came into close contact with Christians in Ireland and in the islands off the west and north coasts of Scotland. The *Landnamabok*, based on the family traditions of Norse settlers in Iceland, records that, among the predominantly pagan settlers in that island around 900, many of those who came from 'west of the sea' (Ireland and Scotland) were Christian. Among them was Orlygr the Old, son of Hrapp, who had been in fosterage with Bishop Patrick, probably the refounder of the Christian community on St Patrick's Isle, off Peel, on the west coast of the Isle of Man. A yearning came over Orlygr to go to Iceland and he asked Bishop Patrick to give him an outfit. The bishop gave him timber for a church, a plenarium (a book of the four Gospels to place on the altar), an iron bell, a gold penny and consecrated earth to lay under the corner posts instead of hallowing, for the hallowing of the church to Columcille. The church was built at Esla Rock, where Orlygr set up his dwelling and his descendants, though unbaptised, continued to venerate Columcille (*Landnamabok*, V, 17, 5). The tradition was transmitted through a pagan interlude of at least a century and then passed orally through several generations before it was written down; it illustrates the limited role of the bishop in the earliest stage of the penetration of Christianity.

St Patrick's Isle was the main residence of the Kings of Man and the Isles and later the site of the medieval cathedral of St German, the centre of the diocese of Sodor (the Southern Isles—the Norse name for the Hebrides) and Man. St German's Cathedral was a cruciform building of the later twelfth century, enlarged in the thirteenth century and now long ruined and roofless. To the west of the cathedral is St Patrick's Church, a much smaller building with a round tower of Irish type set axially to the west. Recent excavations have shown that the earliest stage of St Patrick's Church was a rectangular building *in antis*, a smaller example of the type to which the Cathedral at Clonmacnois belongs. This early church is demonstrably older than 1100 and must have served as the Cathedral of Bishop Hrolfr, the first to be named in the fourteenth-century list of bishops of Man in the *Chronicle* of the Kings of Man and the Isles (Munch, 1874, 112–21); he was in office before 1079. The original church of St Patrick had internal dimension of 8.75m (28ft 6ins) x 5.60m (18ft 6ins) and no coeval quire, (Curphey, 1982, 59–62). On the basis of Irish parallels and of the historical record a date between *c*.960 and *c*.985, in the time of the Dublin-linked Kings of Man, Maccus and Guthred Haraldsson (Munch, 1874, 132–6), would seem appropriate.

But the main impulse for the conversion of the Norse lands came, not from Ireland, but from the Empire, through the archbishops of Hamburg, based for much of the period in the safer and more convenient city of Bremen. Master Adam of Bremen, a member of the community, wrote a history of the archbishops down to the death of Adalbert in 1072. His work is based on the records of the church, supplemented by information from the archbishop and from others. Chapter 206 (Adam of Bremen, 366) illustrates the latter source. It gives a list of the bishops consecrated in northern lands by Archbishop Adalbert according to his own account (*ipso narrante*). Adam's History complements and gives precision to the dynastic stories in the Sagas, which provide the main source for early Norse history.

In this period the systematic conversion of a country began with missionary bishops, who followed the court of the Christian ruler. They built and consecrated churches, ordained priests to serve them and performed such other administrative and religious functions as the growing number of Christians required. According to Adam this stage had been reached in Denmark in the time of Archbishop Adaldargus, who died in 988 and was still to be found in Norway and Sweden in his own day (Adam of Bremen, 314, 383). The names of bishops might be known in these circumstances, but not the Sees to which they were consecrated. 'I believe' comments Adam with reference to the earlier Danish position, 'that in places where there are few Christians, no fixed See is allotted to any one bishop, but that each, in his zeal for the spread of Christianity, goes forward, preaching both to his own (flock) and to others.' The account of the foundation of the church on Selje, later the cathedral for West Norway, vividly illustrates this early phase in the conversion of the country. According to the legend, Sunniva, an Irish princess, had taken refuge with her companions in a cave on the island. They were saved from the heathen natives by a rock fall which entombed them inside the cave, and miracles were later recorded from the island, which lies on an important seaway north of Bergen. King Olaf Tryggvasson went to the island with Bishop Sigurd. Sunniva's relics were found and, with the king's support, Bishop Sigurd built a church, in which the relics were enshrined. The date is shortly before 1000, when the king was actively imposing the new faith on his countrymen, both in Norway and in the Norse colonial lands (*Olafs S.* cap. 107, p. 155).

A record of a similar missionary bishop in the Orkneys emerges incidentally in Adam's record of the bishops of Scania. Henry, who was consecrated to the See of Lund in c. 1060, had previously been a chaplain to King Cnut in England and a bishop in the Orkneys (Adam of Bremen, 371). These missionary bishops would have no fixed cathedral; they would officiate, as occasion required, in churches built in royal or other settlements and these chapels would have the status and presumably the architectural form of royal or private chapels.

The earliest record of a fixed See, and therefore of a cathedral, in the Norse lands occurs in the Orkneys. After a description of the islands, based on earlier writers, Adam continues in chapter 243: 'To the same islands of the Orkneys, although they had previously been ruled by bishops of the English and the Scots, our primate (Adalbert), by order of the Pope, consecrated Thorolf bishop of the city of Blascona, who should have charge of all things.' (Adam of Bremen, 384) Lappenberg, editor of Adam of Bremen for the *Monumenta Germaniae Historica*, where the text appeared in 1846 in Volume VII of the Scriptores, was unable to locate Blascona. The solution was provided nine years later by P A Munch, a distinguished Scandinavian philologist and historian, well acquainted with the Norse colonial lands; he prepared a critical and well-annotated edition of the *Chronicle* of the Kings of Man and the Isles, which was published posthumously (Munch, 1874). His 'History of the Norwegian People' includes a footnote, in which he suggests that Blascona was a faulty rendering of Birgsanam or Birsay: the same place where Earl Thorfinn is said in the saga to have built Christchurch for the bishop (see Crawford, 1983, 103, for further discussion of this point). He also identifies the site with the ruined church on the Brough of Birsay (see fig. 5). For nearly a century Munch's solution has been generally accepted by foreign scholars, though the ruins on the Brough of Birsay are seldom referred to.

The use of the phrase 'by order of the Pope' in connection with the consecration of Bishop Thorolf is exceptional. According to the record in chapter 207 of Adam's History (Adam of Bremen, 367; cf. Jaffe, no. 4290 of 1053 Jan. 6) Archbishop Adalbert received from Rome a privilege enabling him to exercise papal rights in the north, including the right to establish dioceses in suitable places and to consecrate bishops chosen from among his own chaplains. The implication is that the consecration of Bishop Thorolf took place before 1053. This early date is borne out by the subsequent consecration to the Orkneys of two further bishops as successors to Thorolf, John, who had been consecrated in Scotland and his namesake another Adalbert (Adam of Bremen, 366). The consecration of Bishop Thorolf in *c.*1050 can hardly be dissociated from Earl Thorfinn's visit to Europe. His 'most famous journey' is recounted in chapter 37 of the Earls' Saga, the first part of the composite *Orkneyingar Saga* (*Icelandic Sagas*, iii, 58–9). The journey culminated in Rome where Thorfinn saw the Pope and 'took absolution for all his sins'. When the Earl returned he 'sat down quietly and kept peace over all his realm. Then he left off warfare; then he turned his mind to ruling his people and land and to law giving. He sat almost always in Birsay (*Byrgisheraði*) and let them build there Christchurch (*Kristskirkju*) a splendid minster (*dyrligt musteri*). There first was set up a bishop's seat in the Orkneys.' The journey took place after the Earl heard of the death of King Magnus of Norway (25 October 1047). Messengers were sent first to the new king, Harald Hardrada, and when they returned Earl Thorfinn went first to Norway and then to Denmark. From Denmark he went to the court of the Emperor Henry III, where he procured horses and set out for Rome. The date of his visit to Rome cannot be earlier than 1048. In that year the Papacy was in dispute. Benedict IX was in Rome from November 1047 till his expulsion on 16 July 1048 by order of the Emperor. Damasus II, elected with the support of the Emperor arrived in Rome on that date and was consecrated Pope the following day; he died on 9 August. His successor Leo IX, also elected with the support of the Emperor, was consecrated in Rome on 12 February 1049 and was in Rome for much of the spring of that year; this is the earliest credible date for the visit of Earl Thorfinn. A date *c.*1050 must be accepted for both the visit and the consecration of Bishop Thorolf.

Leaving aside the small early chapels, there are three important churches in Orkney that should on architectural grounds be older than Kirkwall Cathedral; they make no use of the fine red stone that is so characteristic of the cathedral. The first is the little building on the Brough of Birsay identified by Munch as the Christchurch of Earl Thorfinn. This has a nave measuring 8.70m (28ft 6ins) by 4.70m (15ft 6ins), out of which opens a quire of 3.15m (10ft 4ins) by 2.90m (9ft 6ins) with an apse 2.15m (7ft) deep (see fig. 2). A west tower was planned, but may not have been built. Little detail survives; the doors are plain openings without rebates. The position of the altar is not known, but there is no evidence that it stood against the east wall of the apse. In a second building phase, technically indistinguishable from the first, side altars with raised platforms were set within circular recesses contrived in the eastern angles of the nave, narrowing the arch leading into the quire; at the same time a new door was cut through the north wall of the nave, providing direct access from the added courtyard building to the north. The fullest account is to be found in the Inventory of the Royal Commision (RCAHM(S): Orkney, no. 1); this has been supplemented by notes taken by the writer during the excavations. The Church of St Magnus on Egilsay (RCAHM(S): Orkney, no. 611) has a rectangular nave, opening directly into a vaulted quire with a chamber above the vault. A conjoined round tower at the west end is entered directly from the nave. There is no record of any detail, but the technique is more sophisticated with rebated door jambs. The small monastic church on Eynhallow (RCAHM(S): Orkney, no. 613) originally followed the same model, with the quire opening directly out of the nave and a west tower, in this case rectangular. There are north and south doors to the nave and a narrow window with a widely splayed embrasure remains in the north wall of the quire. Egilsay and Eynhallow are inspired by Irish models of the eleventh century (Radford, 1962, 175–86). The church on the Brough of Birsay is an earlier version of the same type, with the apse and side altars as alien features.

The Shorter Magnus Saga in cap. 13 (*Icelandic Sagas*, iii, 292) states that a church was 'afterwards' built on the place where Earl Magnus was killed on Egilsay. This

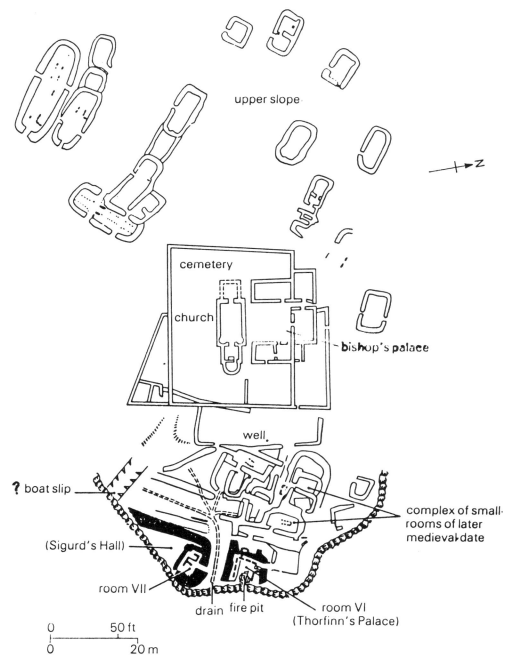

upper slope

cemetery

church

bishop's palace

well

? boat slip

complex of small rooms of later medieval date

(Sigurd's Hall)

room VII

drain   fire pit

room VI (Thorfinn's Palace)

0   50 ft

0   20 m

FIGURE 2   Plan of Norse church site and secular structures on the Brough of Birsay, Orkney (Barbara E Crawford, *Scandinavian Scotland*, fig. 55).

implies a date after 1137, as no memorial church would have been erected between 1117 and 1137, when the Earls Hakon Paulsson and his son Paul were in power. The Saga was written down only in the thirteenth century and should not be allowed to outweigh the architectural evidence. This is borne out by the record in chapter 25 of the Longer Magnus Saga (*Icelandic Sagas*, iii, 264–5) that the church on Egilsay in 1117 was served by a community with at least three celebrants needed for a sung or high mass. Though Eynhallow is first mentioned in the Saga in connection with events that occurred in 1155, (*Icelandic Sagas*, iii, 209), which imply the existence of an ecclesiastical community, the building is closely related to Egilsay. Both should be dated to *c*.1100. The church on the Brough of Birsay must therefore be placed before that date, with both phases dating from the eleventh century; a date *c*.1050 for its foundation is reasonable.

It has been claimed that the parish church of Birsay, alongside the ruined palace of the Stewart Earls (RCAHM(S): Orkney, no. 8), set on the Mainland about 1 km from the Brough of Birsay, is the successor of Earl Thorfinn's Christchurch (Lamb, 1972–4, 201–3). The building has produced no evidence of work earlier than the second half of the twelfth century, the probable date of the masonry of red stone visible in trial holes at the east end of the building in 1982. There is a sketch of the medieval building in the seventeenth-century drawing of the Palace complex published by the Royal Commission (RCAHM(S): Orkney, fig. 68). It is on a small scale, but should be interpreted as a church with an aisled nave and a long aisleless quire and a feature—tower or lantern—over the easternmost bay of the nave. The church was probably of more than one date, with the long quire of the thirteenth century or later replacing a shorter quire, perhaps with an apse. This would indicate a building of the type of St Alban on Selje, which has been ascribed to the second quarter of the twelfth century (Hohler, 1964, 105–9; Nicolaysen, 1892, 3–4). The church would conform to the pattern of an important parish church on the principal estate of the bishop, suitable for use by his familia, when the bishop was in residence. Such a church would be needed soon after the endowment of the See by Earl Rognvald (1137–58).

When considering the position in Orkney it is useful to turn to Norway, of which the king was suzerain of the islands. Developments there ran on a parallel, but rather later course. It was, again, Archbishop Adalbert who began the organisation of fixed Sees in Norway. In chapter 242 Adam refers to the missionary bishops, who still functioned in Norway in his own time (*adhuc*) (Adam of Bremen, 383). He continues: 'Afterwards our metropolitan, at the request of the peoples of the Norwegians, consecrated Thorolf as bishop of the city of Trondheim (*in civitate Trondemnis*) and Siguard in the same region (*in easdem partes*).' These consecrations before 1072 bear out the traditional view that the three earliest Sees in Norway—Trondheim, Oslo and Selje—go back to the time of King Olaf Kyrre (1066–93). It is difficult to establish the plan of the cathedral of Trondheim at the date. The aisled church of St Hallvard at Oslo had a simple apsidal quire, flanked with chapels; it has long been destroyed and only the plan is known (Fett, 1909, pl. 19). This has been claimed as the cathedral of Olaf Kyrre's day. But the Icelandic annals state that St Hallvard in Oslo was burnt in 1137 (Storm, 113). The church of which only the plan is known should more probably be seen as the rebuilt cathedral dating after the fire; Olaf Kyrre's cathedral was perhaps of wood.

Selje, the site of the third of the late eleventh-century Norwegian Sees, is an island flanking a frequented sea route a little north of Bergen (see fig. 4). The early fourteenth-century episcopal list in Cod. Arn. Mag. 415 includes a number of bishops of Selje; it continues with Bishop Pal, whose See is given as Bergen. The original from which Ar. Mag. 415 was copied was connected with the See of Skalholt; it also includes the Annales Vetustissimi (Storm, VII–X). Later lists attribute the whole succession of bishops to Bergen, but there is no reason to reject the early connection with Selje. There is a lacuna in the Annales Vetustissimi from 999 to 1270, but there are relevant entries in the Annales Regii, which were connected with the See of Holar. The death of Sigurd, Bishop of Bergen, one of the predecessors of Bishop Pal is recorded in 1156; in the older list he figures as Bishop of Selje. In 1170, in the time of Bishop Pal, the translation of the relics of St Sunniva to Bergen (from Selje) is noted. Bishop Pal's death is dated to 1194 (Storm, 115–21). The translation of the relics to Bergen clearly marks the consummation of the transfer of the See from the island of Selje to the growing city of Bergen, which had been founded a century before. The change forms a close parallel to the transfer of the See from rural Birsay to the growing settlement at Kirkwall a generation earlier.

The fullest account of the ecclesiastical remains on Selje was published in 1892 (Nicolaysen) with detailed drawings of the standing ruins made before the works carried out in the present century (see fig. 3). According to the legend Sunniva and her companions were found entombed in a cave, where a rockfall had hidden them from the heathen. The cave, from which King Olaf Tryggvasson and Bishop Sigurd collected the relics lies at the head of a cleft running into the hillside; they built a church, in which the relics were enshrined, shortly before 1000. The cave is surmounted by ruined walling identified in a recent guidebook as the church of St Michael (Djupedal, 1967, 29). The remains as described in 1892 are too fragmentary for identification or dating (Nicolaysen, 1892, 2–3); they could be of much more modern date. But churches named in honour of St Michael are often early; the cave itself may well have served as a memorial chapel and may be compared with the early sanctuary of St Michael in a cave in Telemark (Fett, 1909, 3). Below the cave and the ruins attributed to the church of St Michael two artificial terraces fill the narrow cleft; the church of St Sunniva stands on the upper terrace, which must have been consolidated before it could serve as the base for a masonry building; it could however have served as the site of a wooden church based on horizontal beams. It may be suggested that the terraces are the work of Olaf Tryggvasson and Bishop Sigurd and that the lower terrace in front of the church served for the assembly of the faithful on festival days, particularly on 8 July, 'the festival of the men of Selje'.

St Sunniva's Church has a rectangular nave (8.50m x 5.50m) with a quire (5.25m x 3.50m). The masonry is faced with squared stones, having small rectangular fillings set into the corners of some of the larger blocks, probably a technique imposed by the nature of the material. There is no west door, but doors in both the side walls

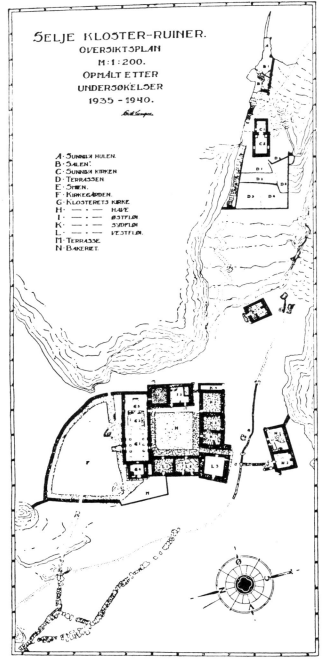

SELJE KLOSTER-RUINER.
OVERSIKTSPLAN
M:1:200.
OPMÅLT ETTER
UNDERSØKELSER
1935 - 1940.

A · SUNNIVA HULEN.
B · SALEN.
C · SUNNIVA KIRKEN
D · TERRASSEN
E · SMIEN.
F · KIRKEGÅRDEN.
G · KLOSTERETS KIRKE
H · — · — · HAVE
I · — · — · ØSTFLØI
K · — · — · SYDFLØI
L · — · — · VESTFLØI.
M · TERRASSE
N · BAKERIET.

Kloster og kyrkjer på Selja. Oversynsplanar teikna av Cato Enger. A. Sunnivahola. B. Salen eller Mikalskyrkja. C 1: Koren i Sunnivakyrkja. C 2: Skipet i Sunnivakyrkja. D 1-6: Murane og jordvollane. E. Smia. Sør for smia ligg Sunnivabekken. Ved utgravingane i 1930-åra minka vatnet i kjelda. F. Kyrkjegarden. G. Albanuskyrkja som og vart kalla Kristkyrkja og Mariakyrkja. H. Klosterhagen.

I. Austfløyen. K. Sørfløyen. L. Vestfløyen. M. Murvollen framfor Albanustårnet (G 4). N. Eldhuset (bakeriet). Nordvest for klosteret går Sjøvegen som fører frå klosteret ned til naustet og vorrane.

FIGURE 3   Plan of Selje monastery and early church site, West Norway (plan by Cato Enger in Djupedal, 1967.

of the nave, an unusual feature that has been compared with English pre-Conquest planning. Altars are set in the eastern angles of the nave, from which three steps rise 90cm to the level of the quire. The main altar stands centrally some 1.20m (4ft) from the east wall of the quire. The space to the east was a further step higher, the raised level projecting to form the base of the altar. The whole eastern area was filled with a shelf rising above the altar and designed to carry relic holders or shrines. (Nicolaysen, 1892, 3). The layout suggests that the altar was designed for a celebrant facing west to the congregation, the early Christian rite still used by bishops in the twelfth century, and that the high shelf was a later insertion, though the point is not commented on by Nicolaysen. The only ornamental fragment recorded is a drum from an attached column, probably the shaft of a doorway. On architectural grounds St Sunniva falls into place in a group of early Norwegian churches of *c*.1100. The group includes Vaernes and the ruined church at Naero (Fett, 1909, 14–5). A date in the time of Olaf Tryggvasson, which has been suggested, must be ruled out both on architectural grounds and by reason of the impossibility of building in masonry on an unconsolidated terrace.

Lower down where the narrow cleft containing the early structures opens out is the church and cloister of St Alban. The developed plan dates from *c*.1300 and later. But the church is of two periods with an earlier aisled nave, which survives as a ruin, and an aisleless quire, which was destroyed when the east end was enlarged in *c*.1300. The older building has been claimed as contemporary with the church of St Sunniva, mainly on the basis of the masonry technique (Nicolaysen, 1892, 3–4). But this is a dangerous criterion. The developed Romanesque detail and the plan point rather to a date in the second quarter of the twelfth century (Hohler, 1964, 105–9). There is no trace of a claustral layout of this date, though wooden buildings alongside the early church are a possibility.

Historically and architecturally Selje provides an interesting parallel to the Brough of Birsay and the more advanced character of the Church of St Sunniva strengthens the case for the mid eleventh century dating of the Orcadian church.

These small early Norse cathedrals, in form little more than palace chapels, serve to bring out the immense advance, liturgically and architecturally, represented by the Cathedral of St Magnus at Kirkwall. This building incorporated the results achieved in Norman England, which in the early twelfth century stood in the forefront of church building in western Europe. Trondheim, from the middle of the century the metropolitan cathedral of Norway, benefited by the experience of Kirkwall, but the great design was never completed.

BIBLIOGRAPHY

Adam of Bremen, M Adami, *Gesta Hammaburgensis Ecclesiae Pontificum usque ad annum 1072*, edente Jo M Lappenberg. *Monumenta Germaniae Historica, Scriptores* VII, 267–389. (Hannover, 1846)

Clapham, A W, 1930, *English Romanesque Architecture Before the Conquest*

Crawford, B E, 1983, 'Birsay and the Early Earls and Bishops of Orkney, *Orkney Heritage*, 2

Curphey, R A, 1982, 'Peel Castle', Isle of Man Natural History and Antiquarian Society, IX, 1, 59–94

Djupedal, R, 1967, *Klosteret paa Selje.* Selje

Fett, H, 1909, *Norges Kirker i Middelalderen.* Christiania/Oslo

Gibb, J H P, 1975, 'The Anglo-Saxon Cathedral at Sherborne', *Arch. Jnl*, cxxxii, 71–110

Gunton, L, 1969, *Rome's Historic Churches*

Hohler, C, 1964, 'The Cathedral of St Swithin at Stavanger', *Jnl. Br. Arch. Assocn*, III, 27, 92–118

Icelandic Sagas, Rolls Series, LXXXVIII. *The Orkneyingar Saga*, i, texts, G Vigfusson ed., 1884, iii, translation, G Dasent, 1894. These volumes include the Earls' Saga (capp. 4–38) and the Story of Earl Magnus (capp. 39–60), which together with the Story of Earl Rognvald (capp. 61–118) form the composite *Orkneyingar Saga*. The volumes also include the Saga of Magnus the Longer and the Short Magnus Saga and other illustrative material.

Jaffe, P, *Regesta Pontificum Romanorum ab condita ecclesia ad annum post Christum natum* MCXCVIII. 2nd edn, Leipsig, 1885

Lamb, R, 1972–4, 'The Cathedral of Christchurch and the Monastery of Birsay', *Proc. Soc. Ant. Scotland*, 105, 200–5

Landnamabok, G Vigfusson and F York Powell, eds, *Origines Islandicae*, i, 2–236. Oxford, 1905

Leask, H G, 1955, *Irish Churches and Monastic Buildings I. The First Phases and the Romanesque*, Dundalk

Munch, P A, 1855, *Det Norske Folks Historie*, Christiania/Oslo

Munch, P A, ed., 1874, *Chronicon Regum Manniae et Insularum*, Manx Society, 22

Nicolaysen, N, 1892, *Om Ruinerne paa Selje, Foreningen til norske Fortidsmindesmaerker Bevaring.* Christiania/Oslo

Olafs S, The Saga of King Olaf Tryggvasson, trans J Sephton, London, 1895

Radford, C A R, 1962, 'Art and Architecture, Celtic and Norse', in *The Northern Isles*, F T Wainwright, ed., 163–87

Radford, C A R, 1977, 'The earliest Irish Churches', *Ulster Jnl Arch.*, III, 40, 1–11

Radford, C A R, 1981, 'Medieval Art and Architecture at Wells and Glastonbury', *Brit. Arch. Assn., Conference Trans.*, IV, 110–33

RCAHM(S), Royal Commission on Ancient and Historical Monuments in Scotland: *An Inventory of the Ancient Monuments of Orkney.* Edinburgh, 1946

Storm, G ed., *Islandske Annaler intil 1578.* Christiania/Oslo, 1888.

Taylor, H M, 1969, 'The Anglo-Saxon Cathedral Church at Canterbury', *Arch. Jnl.*, cxxvi, 101–30

Weyres, W., 1965, *Der Karolingische Dom von Koln, Karl der Grosse: Lebenswerk und Nachleben*, III, 385–423, Dusseldorf

CHAPTER 2

The Church in Scotland in 1137

D E R Watt

As we consider developments in Kirkwall from 1137 onwards, we need to be aware of what was happening in the church at large at that time, and more particularly in the province of the church which lay nearest to Orkney, indeed within sight across the Pentland Firth. Of course the church in Scotland had had a very long history before the early twelfth century, from the heroic days of St Ninian in the fifth century, St Columba and St Kentigern in the later sixth century, and St Cuthbert in the seventh century. The arrival of pagan Vikings from the North in the ninth century seems to have cut most of the old links between Ireland and Western Scotland, so that control and development came to be concentrated on the area between the rivers Forth, Clyde and Tay (see fig. 4). Some long-traditional cult-centres retained especial respect—for example St Andrews, Abernethy, Dunkeld, Culross, Glasgow, Brechin and Rosemarkie—these were places where relics of saints were venerated, where groups of clergy formed organised communities supported by the endowments of the faithful, and from where ecclesiastical authority in matters of faith and order was exercised. The clerical caste in Scottish society seems likely to have become largely an hereditary one, and so the late eleventh-century campaign directed from Rome for a celibate clergy organised hierarchically under the pope as Christ's vicar on earth cut little ice. The papal efforts to reduce royal control over the clergy by attacks on what were now denounced as simony and lay investiture also made little impact, and it was the twelfth-century kings themselves who were to lead the Scottish church into new ways, with new leaders and new organisation. Alexander I and more especially David I brought both clergy and laity enthusiastically into a new era. The surviving evidence is slight at first; but by 1137 much had been achieved which must have been well-known and well-discussed in Orkney.

The key to understanding why so much happened rather suddenly is the decision taken under David I (1124–53) at some unknown date to bring Scotland into line with other countries by enforcing the annual payment of teind (or tithe) to the church by everyone in the country (*RRS*, 1960, 65–66). This had been compulsory in England since the tenth century (Deanesly, 1961, 307–11), but cannot be traced back before 1124 in Scotland. In 1137 therefore it was probably still something new. On the one hand the sheer size of a tax to the value of one-tenth of farm production or of business profits for the support of (say) just one or two thousand

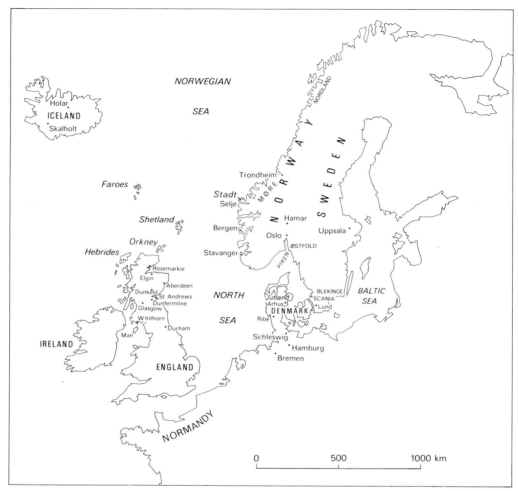

FIGURE 4   Map of Scandinavia and Britain showing places mentioned in the text.

clergy takes some comprehension: it opened up church developments on a very large scale indeed (a scale which in modern terms is in the same league as a Defence or National Health budget). But then who out of these clergy were to share in this and other traditional endowments, and in what proportions? The fashions of centuries were by 1137 changing. In place of groups of clergy led by an abbot or a bishop who served a wide area from some central point, only a small proportion of the clergy were now being maintained in communities, and the majority, with the active support of local landowners, were being settled as separate 'parish priests', with many of the new parish units co-extensive with lay estates (Cowan, 1961, 43–51). It now for the first time became vitally important to define both parish and diocesan boundaries, for it had to be clear where teind was to be paid. Furthermore it was the intention from the start of this new tax that it was to be used not only for the support of the local priest but also for other fashionable clerical activities, and so its collection made possible (among other things) the support of episcopal administration, the building of cathedral churches, and the foundation of abbeys on a scale previously unimaginable. The years just before 1137 therefore were a time when revolutionary changes were being developed at a remarkable rate.

At the same time throughout the whole western church the theme of centralisation of authority was being emphasised, and Scotland was beginning to respond to the novel demands made by the pope in Rome for obedience as well as respect. In a lesser way the local bishops, who in Scotland for centuries appear to have played a subordinate role to monastic abbots (performing essential ceremonial functions but without powers of jurisdiction), began to emerge as replacements for these old-style abbots as figures of authority with territorial responsibilities (Donaldson, 1985, 19). As dioceses came to be defined on the ground, so did bishops come to be regarded as necessary officers of the church in new ways. It was the bishops who were needed to organise the local network of parish priests, to decide on how these local priests were to conduct themselves, and to offer general leadership to both clergy and laity within the bounds of their dioceses. As late as the first years of the twelfth century there seem to have been lengthy gaps in the episcopal succession in some parts of the country, apparently without too much inconvenience. But by 1124 the need for a more consistent approach was clear to the king. How far, then, had things advanced by 1137 in the various regions of the country?

The extensive diocese of Glasgow running from the head of Loch Lomond to the English border had already before 1124 seen a major revival of episcopal authority. Before he succeeded to the throne Prince David had carried through a restoration of ancient endowments which had been diverted from the bishop's hands (*ESC*, 1905, 44–47). He had taken a personal interest in successive appointments of bishops to this ancient see after a period of vacancy; and in particular he had secured the election of John, a monk by training, who had been his own chaplain and who remained his particular friend, and who was to hold this see for thirty years *c*.1117 to 1147 (Dowden, 1912, 294–6).

In 1133, apparently by general agreement, the southern boundary of his see was fixed at the Anglo-Scottish border by the erection of a new English see based on

Carlisle (*SAEC*, 1908, 168–9). Such a rationalisation of political and ecclesiastical boundaries was certainly a feature of the period. The episcopal headquarters over the centuries may not always have been sited at Glasgow the pilgrimage centre containing the shrine of St Kentigern (Shead, 1969, 220–5); but Bishop John made it his business to attract new endowments for the church there in association with the erection and dedication of a new church building on 7 July 1136 (*ESC*, 1905, 82, 85; *Chron. Holyrood*, 1938, 119). This must have been a well-known example for the men of Orkney in the following year, even if no trace of this probably quite modest building survives for us to see today. By 1137 Bishop John had in fact temporarily withdrawn from his responsibilities at Glasgow to live as a monk for a while in a French monastery for reasons which will be examined later; but a year afterwards the king was agreeing to ask him to return to Scotland (*SAEC*, 1908, 211), and the two friends resumed their close co-operation in affairs of both church and state.

To the north and east of Glasgow, ecclesiastical boundaries in 1137 were less clear-cut. There were two main centres of traditional leadership, St Andrews and Dunkeld. Both places had had over the centuries continuing communities of clergy including at least occasional leaders identified by the title of bishop (or sometimes chief bishop) (Donaldson, 1985, 15–17). The boundary between the areas influenced by these two places in the early twelfth century, however, was not a simple one on the ground, and as parishes emerged with loyalty to one see or the other, old ties which may well have dated back for centuries to early missionary days were stronger than any suggestions of administrative tidiness (*Atlas*, 1975, 138, 141). Thus Blairgowrie, Methven and Luncarty adhered to St Andrews while surrounded by parishes belonging to Dunkeld diocese; and Dunkeld itself included more than twenty parishes scattered through Angus, Fife and the Lothians (with even two in Berwickshire), right in the midst of St Andrews territory. The situation had its parallels in other parts of western Christendom, especially in Italy (Brentano, 1968, 62–63), but contrasted strikingly with the dioceses consisting of solid blocks of territory with very few detached parishes which had grown up in England (*Monastic Britain*, 1978), or were being deliberately set up in contemporary Ireland (Moody, Martin and Byrne, 1984, 26–7). It does make east-central Scotland very different from the rest of the country. By 1137 the two bishops of St Andrews and Dunkeld must, like bishops elsewhere, have been taking an interest in establishing precise parish boundaries for teind purposes; but there were probably still grey areas where episcopal authority in a legal and administrative sense was not yet clear, for within twenty years the position became even more complicated with the emergence of two other permanent bishoprics based on Brechin and Dunblane respectively (Watt, 1969, 39, 75). Both these bishoprics too were to attract the loyalty of a scattering of churches among others loyal to St Andrews or Dunkeld (*Atlas*, 1975, 141), and the explanation is probably the same in all four cases—the pull of long-standing ties dating back to missionary days. There may well have been bishops from time to time at Brechin and Dunblane in earlier centuries; but the fact that there is no trace of them in the 1130s suggests that such appointments had lapsed for the time being, and that it was to be in the light of a reaction against vigorous expansionist moves from St Andrews and Dunkeld that King David was persuaded at the end of his life to confirm two exceptions to his earlier policy and approve permanent bishoprics at Brechin and Dunblane as well.

Certainly by 1137 there had been a major effort to revive and develop the authority of the bishop of St Andrews, though not—interestingly enough—along the same lines as David had earlier encouraged at Glasgow under his friend Bishop John, for the traditions at the two centres had been different. King Alexander had experimented with attracting two successive Benedictine monks from England as bishops at St Andrews, but with disappointing results (Watt, 1969, 290). Just before his death in 1124 therefore he arranged for Robert, an Augustinian regular canon whom he had brought from Yorkshire *c*.1120 to be prior of his new monastery at Scone, to be elected to the see of St Andrews, and Robert was to be bishop there for more than thirty years (ibid.; Barrow, 1973, 171–2). King David, therefore, from 1124 was served in the two largest sees of Scotland by two men who remained long in office. At St Andrews Bishop Robert developed the small church with the tall square tower known nowadays as St Rule's (Fawcett, 1985, 28–29; Cruden, 1986a, 14–19; Cruden, 1986b, 7–9). The ancient endowments attached to this holy site had come to be divided among thirteen Culdee priests, each with a separate income held by hereditary right, and five 'persons', i.e. laymen who enjoyed further shares of the endowments on an hereditary basis in return for offering hospitality to pilgrims (*Chron. Picts–Scots*, 1867, 188–9; Barrow, 1973, 222; Anderson, 1976, 9). As at Glasgow the problem was to secure the return of these endowments so that they might be used for the support of the bishop and his staff, and with King David's active and generous help Bishop Robert must have been busy with this in 1137. The general plan was to become clear in 1144 when a community of Augustinian canons was introduced to St Andrews with another Robert from Yorkshire as prior (*Chron. Picts–Scots*, 1867, 191–3, and it was this community who from 1160 were to find it possible to start erecting their great new cathedral church, planned from the beginning as the largest church building in Scotland (Cruden, 1986b, 11, 15). In planning for the introduction of a monastic community to serve his cathedral Bishop Robert was probably reacting against the way in which his predecessors had allowed church endowments to become too much the personal family property of individual clerics. He would have seen the advantages of a community who held things in common—a development which Bishop John had apparently not found possible or necessary at Glasgow, where the future was to bring a community of secular canons with separate prebends. But Augustinian canons were not inward-looking monks: strengthened by their communal life, they were by their rule authorised to go out and about as priests to serve the people in the parishes. Indeed as an order of priests they 'represented the very vanguard of the Gregorian reform and of the new ideas at work in the western church' (Barrow, 1973, 171). A model for the plans which king and bishop were maturing at St Andrews in 1137 had been agreed only four years earlier at Carlisle. They were fully in harmony with reformist thinking in the church as a whole at that time.

The see of Dunkeld in 1137 still retained responsibility for the parts of the old Scottish kingdom of Dalriada which had not become part of the Norwegian diocese

of the Isles (i.e. mainland Argyll), as well as for the area around Dunkeld itself and
the parishes scattered eastward from there. The tradition of an hereditary abbot as
head of an endowed religious community was strong at Dunkeld; but King
Alexander appears to have diverted at least some of the old abbacy endowments
for the support of a line of bishops (*ESC*, 1905, 11; Donaldson, 1985, 20), and a
man with the native name of Cormac was in office before the accession of King
David in 1124. He was certainly still active in the 1130s (Watt, 1969, 94). It has
been suggested that King Alexander planned for a community of Augustinian
canons to be established at Dunkeld Cathedral as was later to happen at St Andrews
(*MRHS*, 1976, 91). If so, this would have been the intention still in 1137, even if
c.1160 the plan was in fact to mature rather differently. The Augustinians were then
established in another part of the diocese (on the island of Inchcolm in the Firth
of Forth), and at Dunkeld a community of secular canons on the Glasgow model
was to be developed from the later twelfth century onwards (Watt, 1969, 101). But
in 1137 the probable intention was for Dunkeld to be as much in the van of reform
as St Andrews.

   Moving further north to Aberdeen, Moray and Ross, we encounter in 1137 three
dioceses of the more usual territorial type. Of these Ross, centred on Rosemarkie
on the north side of the Moray Firth but convenient for communications on both
sides of the water, was the site of greatest antiquity in Christian terms, famous since
the days of a bishop called either Curetan or Boniface *c*.700 (*Chron. Wyntoun*, 1906,
122–3; Smyth, 1984, 127–8). A bishop called by the native name of Macbeth is
known to have held office between 1127 and *c*.1136 (Watt, 1969, 266). He was
styled after the parish of Rosemarkie, whilst his successors from the thirteenth
century onwards were to be styled after the wider province or earldom of Ross.
It is not known whether his cathedral in 1137 was on the site of the later parish
church of Rosemarkie or already situated one mile to the west at Fortrose in the
same parish, where the thirteenth-century cathedral was certainly to be built.
Equally nothing is known of the group of clergy who supported him, though later
it was to be one of secular canons like Glasgow.

   The area to the south of the Moray Firth may well have looked to Rosemarkie
for leadership in earlier days; but from at least the eleventh century it was being
governed by its own *mormaer* (Celtic provincial ruler) and seems likely to have had
its own bishop by then (Smyth, 1984, 219–20; Donaldson, 1985, 21). We certainly
know of the existence of Bishop Gregory of Moray from *c*.1120 into the 1130s
(Watt, 1969, 214). His name is probably a Latinised form of a native name such
as Giric (Donaldson, 1985, 18), and clearly he was in office before the big effort
was made after 1130 by King David to bring this independent-minded province
under central royal control. An unusual feature was the fact that this bishop's see
was not associated with any particular place of hallowed antiquity. Instead the
twelfth-century bishops are known to have moved their headquarters between
three small churches in the neighbourhood of Elgin as they thought fit—Birnie,
Spynie and Kinneddar (*Moray Reg.*, 1837, 40). We do not know which of these was
favoured by the bishop in 1137. In 1206 an attempt was to be made to fix the
cathedral at Spynie, but this was superseded by the final move to Elgin in 1224

(ibid., 39–43, 19, 63–65). It is interesting that for at least a century before then no settled see was thought necessary in Moray, with of course the implication that a cathedral did not require a special building or an endowed community of clergy to serve it. Birnie kirk remains today a simple twelfth-century parish church, though whether anything of the present structure dates from quite as early as 1137 is not quite certain (Shepherd, 1986, 17, 117).

Rather to the east of Moray near the modern Dufftown in Banffshire lies Mortlach. There is a believable tradition that the Scottish kings established a line of bishops there as an extension of royal authority north of the river Dee in the early eleventh century, following a victory over some Norwegian forces in the district (*Chron. Fordun*, 1871, 182–3); and certainly there was an endowed community of clergy there (*Abdn. Reg.*, 1845, i, 3, 6). But with the emergence of the nearby see of Moray by the early twelfth century this site lost its logic; and so sometime in the late 1120s Bishop Nechtan of Mortlach (another native) moved his see to a site near the mouth of the river Don near the royal castle and burgh of Aberdeen at the mouth of the river Dee (ibid., ii, 125; Watt, 1969, 1). This was clearly done with King David's encouragement, for in 1136 the king was to provide a major endowment for the new church of Aberdon (which we usually call Aberdeen!) (*Abdn. Reg.*, i, 3–4). But by 1137 the bishop was still making a slow start. Twenty years later his successor was to obtain papal encouragement to establish either monks or canons in his cathedral (ibid., i, 5–7). In the end the choice was for secular canons as at Glasgow; but at the date which interests us the matter was apparently an open question. Aberdon may not have been exactly a 'greenfield site', for veneration of St Machar had probably been practised there for centuries; but the move to a site not previously associated with monastic or episcopal activity did presumably permit more untrammelled planning than at some other places. The necessary funds, however, were accumulated only slowly, so that no impressive start was possible as at Kirkwall in 1137 or at Elgin in 1224.

The deliberate setting up of a see at Aberdon deprived St Andrews diocese of its traditional influence north of the Dee in the same way as the erection of the see of Carlisle in 1133 deprived Glasgow of its influence south of the Border. Such major adjustments point to positive planning and action by King David. And something similar is likely to lie behind moves in this period in two other areas, both at the extremities of the kingdom, which have not yet been mentioned—Galloway and Caithness. There had been a succession of bishops associated with Whithorn in Galloway (famous for its shrine of St Ninian) while south-west Scotland had been ruled by Anglians as part of Northumbria in the eighth century (*HBC*, 1986, 222–3); but once political circumstances changed in that region as a result of Viking expansion, there was a long gap in the episcopal succession until the appointment of Bishop Gilla-Aldan (another native name) in 1128, and it was he who still held office in 1137 (Watt, 1969, 128; Somerville, 1982, 39). There is some debate whether the initiative for the revival of this see came from an independent-minded Fergus lord of Galloway as part of his resistance against the centralizing pressures of King David, or whether David master-minded the scheme as part of a settlement of various matters made in 1127 between him and the archbishop of York (cf.*SAEC*, 1905, 162–3; *ESC*, 1905, 63–5). Certainly a price was paid whereby alone of the Scottish bishops the bishop of Galloway from 1128 onwards acknowledged the superior metropolitan authority of York. For a region long accustomed to links over the Irish sea with Ireland and the Isle of Man, it was convenient enough to communicate over the Solway Firth with England as well as over the moors and up the valleys with the Scottish government: we need not assume that this link with York was unwelcome. But we really know very little about Gilla-Aldan, and certainly have no knowledge of the arrangements he made for serving his cathedral church. All we can be sure is that this diocese was in 1137 regarded as a part of the Scottish kingdom, and so was assuredly under the watchful reforming eye of King David.

The position in Scotland north of the Kyle of Sutherland has certain parallels with Galloway. This was an area where the traditional control by the Norse earls of Orkney was to suffer from some intrusion by King David before the end of his reign (Crawford, 1977, 97–101; *RRS*, 1960, 44); and we know that by the late 1140s Andrew, a Benedictine monk of Dunfermline, was active at the king's court as bishop of Caithness, and that he was not just a pretender to this office, for he obtained recognition from Harald Maddadson when he was sole earl of Orkney (Dowden, 1912, 232). But in 1137 the king's expansionist policy in this region had probably not yet taken active form, and there is no evidence to contradict the assumption that it was the bishop of Orkney who still had jurisdiction there. Like Galloway, however, the area was one which looked two ways. At least since the treaty of 1098 between the Norse and the Scots this area was implicitly part of the Scottish kingdom (Crawford, 1977, 97). In practice ecclesiastical authority was probably still exercised from Orkney across the Pentland Firth; but this tardiness in the rationalisation of political and ecclesiastical boundaries was something which King David was unlikely to accept for long.

If this was the position in each Scottish diocese in 1137, what about their relations with each other and with the rest of the western church? Though in earlier centuries there had been a hint that one bishop (usually that of St Andrews) was in some way regarded as superior to the others, this was not in the early twelfth century interpreted as implying the kind metropolitan authority which under Roman Canon Law an archbishop might be given by the grant of the symbolic pallium by the pope. The Scottish bishops were equals, recognising no superior authority apart from Rome. This did not prevent them sometimes finding it convenient to make use of the services of the neighbouring archbishop of York to secure the consecration of a new bishop of Glasgow between 1109 and 1114 or of St Andrews in 1127 (Watt, 1969, 144, 290)—just as York sometimes helped in this period over the consecration of bishops for the Norwegian sees of the Isles or Orkney (ibid., 198, 248). Particularly from 1119 onwards, however, there had been pressures from York in the light of the novel tighter discipline which was being enforced from Rome on the whole reformed church for acceptance by the Scottish bishops of the duty to seek consecration by a metropolitan archbishop in return for a formal acknowledgement of their duty of obedience to him as an authority intermediate between them and Rome (Somerville, 1982, 7–10). It was a campaign conducted by York in the Roman Court for many decades before the dioceses which comprised the Scottish province of the church (excluding Galloway) were in 1192 confirmed as exempt from metropolitan authority. At one time in 1125 there was an abortive proposal that St Andrews be erected into a metropolitan archbishopric (Hugh the Chantor, 1961, 126), and this idea was to be broached again in 1151, when interestingly it was proposed to bring Orkney and the Isles under St Andrews despite their different political affiliation (John of Salisbury, 72)—though of course this led to a reaction which in a year or two was to lead to their alternative subordination to the new Norwegian metropolitan see of Trondheim (Watt, 1969, 247). The details of the ups and downs of this defence of the independence of the Scottish church do not concern us here; but some general consequences of the struggle are important. There is nothing like a good legal battle for building up *esprit de corps*: in resistance to York's machinations at Rome both the Scottish church as a whole and the Scottish state must by 1137 have been developing their sense of identity and purpose. Galloway may have been surrendered to York, but Caithness was not to go under Trondheim.

More important were the regular contacts which the Scottish church now had with Rome. Earlier in the century there had been some correspondence between the bishop of St Andrews and the pope when for the first time (so far as we know) the king in Scotland wanted to obtain definitions from Rome on a variety of detailed matters of ecclesiastical order and liturgical practice, so that Scotland might fall into line with the generally approved customs of the church as a whole (Somerville, 1982, 19–22). But the York controversy brought Roman pressures to bear in Scotland in much more positive and unwelcome ways. Not only did Scottish envoys have to go to Rome to counter the campaign conducted there in the interest of York, but the year 1125 had seen the arrival in Scotland of the first known papal legate commissioned to compel the bishops to attend a council held within the bounds of the country under his authority (ibid., 28; *SAEC*, 1908, 158–9; Brett, 1975, 22–23). In the event he was probably not allowed by King David to do this, and he seems to have been treated more as just a diplomatic envoy; but it was a new era for the Scottish church to have Roman authority brought to Roxburgh in this way.

The continuing York dispute also meant that Scotland could not stand aside from the problems raised by the schism in the papacy of 1130–38. At first Scotland appears to have supported Innocent II; but when, after the death of King Henry I of England in December 1135, Innocent supported Stephen against his rival Matilda for the English throne, King David veered towards the alternative pope, Anacletus II, for a couple of years (*Historians of York*, 1894, 63, 66–67; Brett, 1975, 26–27). Thus in 1137 the Scottish king and church were being reviled as schismatics by the pope who in the following year was to end up as the one undisputed pope; this means that in 1137 Scotland was for political reasons out of step with most of Europe, and judging by the behaviour of Bishop John of Glasgow already mentioned (cf. Barrow, 1973, 176), it appears that the Scottish church was divided and unhappy. It was to take a visit from another legate from Rome in September 1138 to reconcile David and his bishops to Innocent as the one true pope (*SAEC*, 1908, 210–12). 1137 had been a traumatic year for the church in Scotland.

We have been considering dioceses, bishops and their cathedrals, and clearly in Scotland in 1137 these features of the church were under active development at the urging of the king. The clergy who inspired and helped David in his reforming enterprises were partly of native stock and partly Anglo-French. It was presumably they who encouraged him also in his introduction of new ways of practising the monastic way of life to replace outmoded ways which had fallen into disrepute. Already before 1137 there had been important moves in this direction. As heir to the throne David had in 1113 brought French monks from Thiron near Chartres to Selkirk, and once he was king he moved them to Kelso beside the major royal castle and burgh of Roxburgh (*MRHS*, 1976, 70, 68). Some of the new church buildings there must have been erected by 1137, though not the part which still survives (Cruden, 1986a, 44). He also took an interest in developing the traditional Benedictine house at Dunfermline in Fife with which his mother Queen Margaret and his brother Alexander had been associated, by having it raised to the full status of an abbey in 1128, arranging for Geoffrey prior of Canterbury to come there as its first abbot (*MRHS*, 1976, 58; *SAEC*, 1908, 166). Again buildings on a new scale must have been started by 1137, though probably all that survives dates from rather later (Cruden, 1986a, 27, 31). And it may have been *c.*1136 that David helped to endow a daughter house in the form of Urquhart priory near Elgin as part of his plans for a new order in the recently subdued province of Moray (*MRHS*, 1976, 55, 61). We have seen how there were plans for introducing Augustinian canons (already established at Scone) to serve St Andrews and Dunkeld Cathedrals as well as Carlisle. Further advanced was the king's foundation of an Augustinian abbey at Holyrood near the royal castle and burgh of Edinburgh in 1128, with Alwin its first abbot brought from Merton in Surrey (ibid., 90; Barrow, 1973, 178). And then in 1136 a group of monks was brought by the king from the recently-founded Cistercian abbey of Rievaulx in Yorkshire to start a daughter-house at Melrose in Roxburghshire (*MRHS*, 1976, 76). Thus a variety of examples of the latest fashions in religious practice had been introduced into Scotland before 1137 by two successive kings who with at least some of their bishops were committed to experimenting with what was commended by foreward-looking circles in the western church. Not only was there no cultural time-lag in a Scotland that was readily open to the latest ideas from England and the Continent, but leaders for the new monasteries were recruited from houses which were themselves recent foundations where the inspiration was strong. It was a good time for monks to be alive! The necessary resources were found in Scotland, and both bishops and abbots were recruited as reforming leaders in their respective spheres—all with the active backing of kings who were prepared to make large investments out of crown revenues for the support of bishops and cathedrals, abbots and abbeys. New life was being given to old structures. It would be no wonder if some of this new-found enthusiasm crossed the Pentland Firth to Orkney.

BIBLIOGRAPHY

Abdn. Reg., 1845, *Registrum Episcopatus Aberdonensis*

Anderson, M O, 1976, 'The Celtic Church in Kinrimund', in *The Medieval Church of St Andrews*, D McRoberts, ed.

Atlas, 1975, *An Historical Atlas of Scotland c.400–c.1600*, P McNeill and R Nicholson, eds

Barrow, G W S, 1973, *The Kingdom of the Scots*

Brentano, R, 1968, *Two Churches: England and Italy in the Thirteenth Century*, Princeton

Brett, M, 1975, *The English Church under Henry I*

Chron. Fordun, 1871, *Johannis de Fordun, Chronica Gentis Scotorum*, vol. i, W F Skene, ed.

Chron. Holyrood, 1938, *A Scottish Chronicle known as the Chronicle of Holyrood*, M O Anderson, ed.

Chron. Picts–Scots, 1867, *Chronicles of the Picts: Chronicles of the Scots*, W F Skene, ed.

Chron. Wyntoun, 1906, *The Original Chronicle of Andrew of Wyntoun*, vol. iv, F J Amours, ed.

Cowan, I B, 1961, 'The Development of the Parochial System in Medieval Scotland', *Scottish Historical Review*, xl, 43–55

Crawford, B E, 1977, 'The Earldom of Caithness and the Kingdom of Scotland', *Northern Scotland*, ii, 97–118

Cruden, S, 1986a, *Scottish Medieval Churches*

Cruden, S, 1986b, *St Andrews Cathedral*

Deanesly, M, 1961, *The Pre-Conquest Church in England*

Donaldson, G, 1985, *Scottish Church History*

Dowden, J, 1912, *The Bishops of Scotland*

ESC, 1905, *Early Scottish Charters prior to 1153*, A C Lawrie, ed.

Fawcett, R, 1985, *Scottish Medieval Churches*

HBC, 1986, *Handbook of British Chronology*, 3rd edn, E B Fryde, D E Greenway, S Porter and I Roy, eds

Historians of York, 1894, *The Historians of the Church of York and its Archbishops*, vol. iii, J Raine, ed.

Hugh the Chantor, 1961, *The History of the Church of York 1066–1127*, C Johnson, ed.

John of Salisbury, *Memoirs of the Papal Court*, M Chibnall, ed., 1956

Monastic Britain, 1978, Ordnance Survey Maps

Moody, T W, Martin, F X and Byrne, F J, 1984, *A New History of Ireland*, vol. ix, *Maps, Genealogies, Lists*

Moray Reg., 1837, *Registrum Episcopatus Moraviensis*

MRHS, 1976, *Medieval Religious Houses Scotland*, I B Cowan and D E Easson, eds

RRS, 1960, *Regesta Regum Scottorum*, vol. i, *The Acts of Malcolm IV King of Scots 1153–1165*, G W S Barrow, ed.

SAEC, 1908, *Scottish Annals from English Chroniclers 500 to 1286*, A O Anderson, ed.

Shead, N F, 1969, 'The Origins of the Medieval Diocese of Glasgow', *Scottish Historical Review*, xlviii, 220–5

Shepherd, I A G, 1986, *Exploring Scotland's Heritage: Grampian*

Smyth, A P, 1984, *Warlords and Holy Men: Scotland AD 80–1000*

Somerville, R, 1982, *Scotia Pontificia: Papal Letters to Scotland before the Pontificate of Innocent III*

Watt, 1969, *Fasti Ecclesiae Scoticanae Medii Aevi ad annum 1638*, second draft

CHAPTER 3

Dioceses and Parishes in Twelfth-Century Scandinavia

Peter Sawyer

By the end of the eleventh century Christianity had been accepted officially in most parts of Scandinavia. Rulers and leading members of society accepted the exclusive claims of the Christian God, and were encouraging priests and building churches. A start had also been made in establishing the ecclesiastical organisation that would integrate these priests and churches with the Universal Church, but progress was slow. The Danish dioceses were all founded by about 1060 but it was another century before the diocesan organisation was complete in Norway and Sweden.

At the same time as the dioceses and parishes of Scandinavia were being formed, the western Church as a whole was undergoing a fundamental reformation one aim of which was to resolve the contradictions and uncertainties in the canon law. An important stage was the completion, in about 1140, of Gratian's *Concordia discordantia canonum* but it was not until 1234 that the corpus of canon law was for the first time defined officially in the *Decretales* of Gregory IX. A great variety of local customs remained. Some were accepted as legitimate, for example, the election of priests by their parishioners in some Italian and German dioceses (Kurze, 1966), but others, including clerical marriage, were condemned as abuses. Canon law was not static or fossilised; it was developed as circumstances changed. So, for example, in the eleventh century reformers sought to ensure the right of bishops to three-quarters of the tithes of the parishes within their dioceses but by the thirteenth century Popes were insisting that tithes belonged to the church of the parish in which they were collected (Boyd, 1952, 119–46). This change of emphasis is clearly relevant in any consideration of the efforts made by Scandinavian bishops in the twelfth and thirteenth centuries to gain control over part of the tithes collected in their dioceses, although there was, of course, a fundamental difference between the role and rights of a bishop in Italy, where there were 250 medieval dioceses, and Sweden, Norway and Denmark, with 19 (Boyd, 1952, 49; *KHL* i, 618–9).

In the eleventh and early twelfth centuries there was, naturally, an even greater variety of local customs; liturgical practices differed as well as forms of organisation. The men who then began to organise the church in Scandinavia came from areas with very different traditions and this may well explain some of the distinctive

36

features and local peculiarities of the Scandinavian church. The fourfold division of Icelandic tithes in the twelfth century, for example, contrasts with the triple division common in France and England but is similar to the fourfold division that was customary in Germany and Italy (Constable, 1964, 43–56; *KHL* xviii, 287–8). It is therefore possible that the first Icelandic bishops, who were consecrated in Germany, followed a German model, but an alternative source was in Celtic Britain, for a similar division is attested in Ireland and in Argyll (ex inf. Kenneth Nicholls). Ireland also provides a parallel to the head-tithe, a sort of inheritance tax, that is found in Iceland, Norway and in Västergötland (*KHL* xviii, 280, 290, 295). No parallel, however, appears to be known for the Icelandic custom of tithing property rather than produce (Jóhannesson, 1974, 171–2; *KHL* xviii, 287).

Whatever the local customs, it was the bishops who had ultimate responsibility and authority within their dioceses, and until the ninth century these continued to be called *parochia* (Fournier, 1982, 526–7). Some functions, such as baptism were delegated, but others, including confirmation, the consecration of churches and the ordination of clergy, remained exclusively episcopal. The first bishops to visit Scandinavia were either like Ebbo and Anskar, who had sees elsewhere but were authorised to act as missionaries, or, more commonly, were ordained as missionary bishops without dioceses. Adam of Bremen recognised that this was the situation in the tenth century; 'With Christianity in a rude state, none of the bishops was yet assigned to a fixed see (*certa sedes*), but as each pushed out into the farther regions in the effort to establish Christianity, he would strive to preach the word of God equally to his own and to the others' people' (Adam of Bremen ii, 26). That remained the situation in Norway and Sweden when Adam wrote, about 1075, for, as he explained; 'because of the newness of the Christian plantation among the Norwegians and Swedes, none of the bishoprics has so far been given definite limits, but each one of the bishops, accepted by king or people, cooperates in building up the church, going about the region, drawing as many as he can to Christianity, and governs them without envy' (Adam of Bremen, iv, 34).

The first regular Scandinavian dioceses were apparently founded by Cnut the Great, and Danish diocesan organisation was completed by about 1060, a century after the conversion of Harald Gormsson. The only major pre-reformation change in Denmark being the elevation of the see of Lund to an archbishopric in 1104. There was a similar delay in the creation of dioceses in other parts of Scandinavia. Iceland accepted Christianity in 1000 but the see of Skálholt was not established until 1056 and the second see, at Hólar, fifty years later. The first three Norwegian sees were founded early in Olaf Kyrre's reign, some 70 years after Olaf Tryggvason was confirmed as a Christian in England, and two others were added later; Stavanger in about 1125 and Hamar in 1153. By then Nidaros (Trondheim) had been made an archbishopric independent of Lund and with authority over the Norse colonies in the Atlantic where sees had been founded at Kirkwall, in the Faroes, Greenland and the Isle of Man (Kolsrud, 1958, 179–82, 188–90). The early history of the Swedish dioceses is most obscure, as is the history of the Swedish conversion, but it is likely that the five sees that existed in 1164 when one of them, Uppsala, was made an archbishopric, had all been founded shortly before or after

1100 (Kumlien, 1962), while the youngest pre-reformation Swedish see, Växjö, was created in about 1170.

This consistent pattern has been obscured by the claims of the archbishops of Hamburg-Bremen. These make it appear that three Danish bishoprics were already established ten years or more before the conversion of Harald Gormsson, an extraordinary reversal of the normal order of events. In 948 bishops of Schleswig, Ribe and Ärhus were consecrated as suffragans of Hamburg-Bremen. This was however, not an act of missionary zeal; the intention was to defend the status of Hamburg-Bremen; an archbishop had to have suffragans and in 948 Hamburg-Bremen had none (Refskou, 1987). There was no need for these men ever to set foot in Denmark, but one of them, a Frisian called Liafdag, did. He was, however, not a diocesan bishop but a missionary who worked in Sweden and Norway as well as in Denmark (Adam of Bremen, ii, 26). Harald would have been most unlikely to welcome German bishops at any time, and Hamburg-Bremen certainly had no part in his conversion. The only bishops who appear to have worked in Denmark during his reign, apart from Liafdag and Poppo, who became a bishop after persuading the king to convert, was Odinkar, a Danish noble who evangelised in Sweden as well as in Fyn, Sjælland and *Skåne* (Adam of Bremen, ii, 36) and at a synod at Dortmund in 1005 was the only bishop without a see (Thietmar, 295–6 = vi. 18). His nephew, also called Odinkar, was the first certain bishop of Ribe, and was consecrated by Libentius II, archbishop of Hamburg–Bremen from 1029 to 1032, apparently after having been educated in England under Cnut (Adam, scholion 25; Adam of Bremen, ii, 36 confuses the two Odinkars and this Libentius with his namesake, who was archbishop 988–1013). Cnut had earlier had Gerbrand consecrated for Roskilde by Æthelnoth, archbishop of Canterbury (Adam of Bremen, ii, 55).

It is hardly surprising that under Cnut the Danish church was closely connected with England. Already in his father's reign an English bishop, Gotebald worked in Skåne (Adam of Bremen, ii, 41). English influence is even clearer in Norway. It began early in the tenth century under Harald Fairhair and was powerfully reinforced under both Olaf Tryggvason, who was confirmed in England in 995, and Olaf Haraldsson, whose leading bishop, Grimkell, was English (Kolsrud, 1958, 126–60).

English influence is vividly illustrated by the fragments of liturgical manuscripts that have been recovered in Scandinavia. There are, for example, several leaves from English service books of the eleventh and twelfth century in Norway, as well as some copies of English books that were apparently made in Norway (Gjerløw, 1970; 1974). Remains of at least 20 fine twelfth-century service books have been recovered from Swedish archives, giving substance to the traditions about the role of English missionaries in the early Swedish church (Schmid, 1933; 1934). This evidence is clearly relevant in any discussion of early church organisation in Scandinavia. English influence in Norway and Denmark has long been recognised (Taranger, 1890; Jørgensen, 1908)) but, until recently, little attention has been paid to the contribution of the English in Sweden (Toy, 1983).

By the end of the eleventh century there were numerous churches in most parts of southern Scandinavia. Adam of Bremen's claim (iv. 7) that there were 550 in Skåne, Sjælland and Fyn should, perhaps, not be accepted as an accurate enumeration, but there is no doubt that church-building was already on that scale. Excavation has revealed many eleventh-century timber churches that were later replaced by stone buildings. In a few cases dendrochronology can provide firm dates; the earliest church in Lund, for example, was built before 990, and by 1100 there were at least nine churches in that town (Nilsson 1985; Andrén, 1985, 36, 164, 207–10, 218–21), while in Västergötland there are at least eight stone churches that have structural timbers dateable before 1150 and there can be little doubt that all replaced wooden buildings (Bråthen, 1983).

Churches were certainly built by rulers for their bishops and some of these eventually became cathedrals; Jelling is a conspicuous exception (Krogh, 1982). There are good reasons for thinking that most other early churches were similarly built by substantial landowners (Ferm and Rahmqvist, 1985). Proprietary churches of this kind were common in eleventh-century Europe; in England, for example, Domesday Book, a survey compiled in 1086, recorded churches together with mills among the appurtenances of manors, and as such they could be bought, sold, divided or even used as pledges (Barlow, 1963, 183–208). The proprietary character of the early churches in Iceland is undoubted (Jóhannesson, 1974, 165–78, 227; Skovgaard-Petersen, 1960) and there are various indications that this was also true elsewhere in Scandinavia. The fact that some churches were placed well away from the main centres of settlement is one sign of their non-communal character. Some were, indeed, close to important farms that were later held by men of great wealth and high status (Ferm and Rahmqvist, 1985). The tendency in Denmark and Sweden for churches to be named after farms, not districts, also suggests that they were founded by individuals rather than communities; only in Södermanland do parishes regularly have district names (*KHL* xvi, 385–95; Ståhle, 1950).

It is true that the earliest churches were timber structures that could have been made by local craftsmen, but by the end of the twelfth century many had been rebuilt in stone. As Scandinavians were unfamiliar with that technique, foreign masons must have been employed for a generation or more, and that is more likely to have been done by rich landowners than by their tenants or the less affluent farmers. What is more, most early churches, whether of wood or stone, were far too small to accommodate large numbers of people; they appear to have been intended for private rather than communal use. In England, similarly, the naves of most tenth-century churches were small, typically in the range 20–30 square metres, although some were less than 14 square metres (Morris, 1988). A few Scandinavian churches have inscriptions naming the builders. These all give prominence to one or two individuals who could, perhaps, have been mastercraftsmen but they could alternatively have been the men who made it possible for the builders to work (Svärdström, 1963; Olsen, M., 1951, nos 110, 121; Jansson and Wessen, 1962, no. 119). The others named in these inscriptions may have been tenants or neighbours who cooperated in the enterprise, but they did not necessarily do so voluntarily. One twelfth-century English charter that has been cited as evidence for communal responsibility in church building records the endowment of Keddington church, in Lincolnshire, with an acre given by each of the tenants of that manor (Stenton, 1920, lxx–lxxi). Such uniformity seems rather to imply compulsion than the voluntary generosity of many individuals.

Communal responsibility for the erection of churches is rendered even more unlikely by the fact that tithe was not paid until the last years of the eleventh century, and then only in Iceland. It was introduced in other parts of Scandinavia in the twelfth century. Tithe was first enforced in Europe by the Carolingians in the eighth century, and compulsion must commonly have been needed; there are many indications of resistance. In 1199, for example, the bishop of Vercelli complained of resistance in his and in neighbouring dioceses; some landowners deducted the expenses of cultivation and tithed the net product, others took tithe from their tenants and gave it to the poor or to churches of their own choice, some refused to pay because of the immorality of the clergy, while others simply claimed exemption (Boyd, 1952, 169–70). Such problems encountered in the heart of Christian Europe should be borne in mind when considering the Scandinavian evidence, most of which consists of laws prescribing tithe payments; there is very little evidence for the tithe that was actually paid and it would be unrealistic to assume that the law was obeyed in Scandinavia any more than elsewhere.

Adam of Bremen says explicitly that Scandinavians did not pay tithe in the 1070s, when he wrote. He complained that 'baptism and confirmation, the dedication of altars and the ordination to holy orders are all dearly paid for among the Norwegians and the Danes. This, I think, proceeds from the avarice of the priests. As the barbarians still either do not know about tithes, or refuse to pay them, they are fleeced for offices that ought to be rendered for nothing. Even for the visitation of the sick and the burial of the dead—everything there has a price' (Adam of Bremen, iv. 31).

Tithes were introduced into Iceland in 1096 or 1097 and in Denmark by 1135, the date of the earliest reference. In Norway tithe is said to have been first levied in some areas under Sigurd, who died in 1130, and made general later in the century by Magnus Erlingsson, while in Sweden it was apparently being collected by the end of the century (*KHL* xviii, 280–99). As already noted, there is little information about the payments that were in fact made; normally we have to rely on statements of what should be paid. In some laws a proportion was kept back by the tithe-payers 'for the poor', and this, together with the portion due to the fabric fund, could be used as a reserve in times of need. The Older Law of Västergötland, of the thirteenth century, defines the priest's share of tithe very vaguely as depending on the church's consecration, apparently implying that an agreement was made when the church was consecrated (*KHL* xviii, 296). The first indication of actual tithe payments are agreements or compositions made in the fifteenth and sixteenth centuries in Sweden. These show that much less than ten *percent* of produce was paid, and that the burden was heavier near the centre of dioceses than in remoter parts. After the reformation tithe was taken over by the crown as a royal revenue, with a third reserved for the priest; the records of these levies show that the burden was then greatly increased, and so too presumably was the efficiency of collection (Larsson, 1966).

Only in Iceland did bishops have a share of the tithe from the outset. Elsewhere they faced serious opposition when they claimed part of the tithes paid within their dioceses. In Gotland, which formed part of the diocese of Linköping, the bishop never had a share of the tithe, while in north Jutland episcopal tithes were only imposed on the eve of the reformation. It appears that tithe was originally introduced locally, no doubt at the behest of the lord who 'owned' the church, and it seems likely that it was these men, rather than the tithe-payers themselves, who initially resisted episcopal encroachments.

The payment of tithe is reflected in the word used throughout Scandinavia for a parish, *sokn*. It is commonly asserted that this word, related to the word 'seek', refers to the choice of a church by its parishioners and defines the district whose inhabitants all 'sought' the same church (*KHL* xvi, 374). A more likely explanation is that it refers to the church as the centre of a district within which tithe was collected, or 'sought' (cf. German *suchen* 'look for, gather'). It was in a very similar sense that the Danes used the word when they settled in England in the ninth century. Royal, or formerly royal, estates or lordships that were in other parts of Britain known as shires or lathes were called 'sokes' by the Danes. The characteristic duty of a 'sokeman', or his equivalent elsewhere, was to render goods and services to a centre that either was, or had been, royal (Barrow, 1974; Sawyer, 1983).

The term *sokn* was later used loosely for annexe-churches that were not entitled to tithe but were served by priests based on central churches to which tithe was in fact paid. In Västergötland these 'main' or 'parish' churches were called *gäll-*churches and the district belonging to such a church, including its annexe-churches, was in medieval Swedish a *prästagiäld*, 'priest-*gäll*' (*KHL* xvi, 381). Similar words were used elsewhere in Scandinavia, and all are cognate with the English word yield, or the Old English *geld*, confirming the importance of tithe payments as the unifying factor. Normally there was only one priest in a *gäll*, and mass can only have been celebrated rarely in distant annexe churches. These churches did however have cemeteries and many fonts of the twelfth or thirteenth centuries (Sawyer, 1987, 85). Baptism was supposed to be restricted to parish (initially episcopal) churches, but even in Italy this rule was breaking down at this time (Boyd, 1952, 157–8).

The status of a particular church was not immutable; some annexe-churches became mother churches, and examples of the reverse process are known. It does, however, seem likely that most late medieval annexe-churches were originally private churches that were incorporated in the parochial system by the end of the thirteenth century, but were too poor to support a priest. This seems to have been an especially acute problem in Västergötland where the proportion of annexe-churches (4:1) was much higher than elsewhere in Scandinavia. In 1234 Pope Gregory IX reassured the bishop of Skara that he was entitled to join together churches on the grounds of poverty which suggests that regular parishes or *gäll* were being formed at that time (*Diplomatarium Suecanum*, no. 286).

It was tithe that created the need for parish boundaries, which are consequently not necessarily ancient. The assumption, made by some legal historians and archaeologists, that medieval parishes preserved the structure of pre-Christian units, is therefore fallacious (Hafström, 1949). When parishes were formed in the twelfth or thirteenth centuries their bounds may well have been the same as those of estates or administrative units that then existed. These may have been centuries-old, but it would be wrong to assume that they were. There is the additional complication that few of these bounds can be traced in any detail before the sixteenth century and for many the earliest evidence is in nineteenth-century maps. As it can be shown that some boundaries were altered in the later middle ages, we cannot assume, in the absence of evidence, that the original limits were preserved unchanged (Rahmqvist, 1982).

The possibility that many churches were built on the site of pagan temples has been much discussed, but there is little evidence for any pre-Christian buildings under churches (Olsen, O., 1966; 1986). There are, however, indications that many cathedrals and some important parish churches were built in places that had previously been places of assembly, even cult centres. This is implied by the place names Odense 'the *vi* or holy place of Odin' and Viborg 'hill(s) by the holy place' (Hald, 1965, 189, 251) and a similar association is suggested by archaeological evidence found at Mære, in Norway, and more recently at Frösö in Jämtland (Lidén, 1969; Hildebrandt, 1985). More commonly it may be observed that churches stand near large prehistoric mounds. Some were built on the eve of conversion, or even after it; the north mound at Jelling has recently been dated 958, less than a decade before a church was built at its foot, and the south mound was completed even later, in 970. Others, including the mounds at Uppsala are much older. The suggestion that some of these mounds were centres of assembly for people living in the neighbourhood can be no more than speculation, but it may be significant that in Västergötland the churches close to mounds (none of them securely dated) tend to be *gäll*-churches (Sawyer, 1987, 85); this would at least be consistent with the interpretation of the annexe churches as private, while at least some of the *gäll*-churches had a more public character from the outset. It is interesting to note that only two of the Västergötland stone churches that can be dated dendrochronologically earlier than 1150 were *gäll*-churches, the others were annexes that have apparently never needed any major rebuilding (Bråthen, 1983; cf Lundahl, 1961, *s.n.*).

The attitude of many people towards the local church and their sense of communal responsibility must have been affected by the imposition of tithe as a general obligation. One sign of the growing involvement of the church with the community is the development of the office of churchwarden. This first appeared in Italy in the mid twelfth century and by 1300 had spread throughout Europe (*KHL* 8, 410–11; Drew, 1954). This alone makes nonsense of the claim that in Scandinavia the office of churchwarden is as old as the conversion itself (*KHL* 8, 415–6). A sense of community was, of course, not a novelty, but it was encouraged and reshaped around the churches in which people were baptized and buried. When all, or even most, people paid tithe, the parish church became in a very real sense the church of the community. And when that happened, there was a natural tendency to assume that it had always been so, and to believe that churches were from the beginning communal enterprises. This firmly-held belief has tended to distract attention from the many indications that most churches were founded, and built, by rulers and landowners. Royal churches naturally tended to be under direct episcopal control, but other churches long remained in private ownership, although the bishop would be expected to consecrate them and ordain the priests who served in them. Bishops were only gradually able to extend their rights, above all to a share of the tithe, which itself must have been exacted under pressure from secular lords who in this way contributed to a sense of communal responsibility.

Evidence for early church organisation in Scandinavia is slight and any generalisation must allow for the existence of a great variety of local customs and abuses, most of which are beyond discovery. Church laws were promulgated, and many have been well preserved, but it is impossible to say how well they were observed. The establishment of parishes, and the extension of episcopal control over them was, like Christianisation itself, a slow process. In the twelfth century and long afterwards most of the clergy must have been ill-educated and the imposition of any form of effective episcopal discipline was hampered by the huge size of many dioceses, especially in Sweden and Norway. In interpreting the slight evidence from Scandinavia it is perhaps salutary to note that in the late twelfth century Gerald of Wales, a well-informed observer, complained that in England, that had been Christian for 500 years, the clergy were illiterate, and that 'the houses and hovels of parish priests are full of bossy mistresses, creaking cradles, new-born babies and squawking brats' (cited by Cheney, 1956, 137). The demand of the western church for clerical celibacy was not easily enforced; it was even more difficult to impose church law on laymen who were most likely to obey when it suited them.

BIBLIOGRAPHY

Adam of Bremen, *History of the Archbishops of Hamburg–Bremen*, trans F J Tschan (New York, 1959)

Andrén, A, 1985, *Den urbana scenen: städer och samhälle i det medeltida Danmark* (Melmö)

Barlow F, 1963, *The English Church 1000–1066*

Barrow G W S, 1973, 'Pre-feudal Scotland: shires and thanes', in G W S Barrow, *The Kingdom of the Scots*

Boyd, C E , 1952, *Tithes and Parishes in Medieval Italy* (Ithaca).

Bråthen, A, 1983, *The Tree-ring Chronology of Western Sweden* (Dendrokonologiska sällskapet, meddelanded 6; Stockholm)

Cheney, C R , 1956, *From Becket to Langton*

Constable, G, 1964, *Monastic Tithes from their origins to the twelfth century*

Diplomatarium Suecanum, 1, J G Liljegren, ed. (Stockholm)

Drew, C, 1954, *Early Parochial Organisation in England. The Origins of the Office of Churchwarden* (St Anthony's Hall publications, no. 7)

Ferm, O, and Rahmqvist, S, 1985, 'Stormannakyrkor i Uppland under äldre medeltid', *Studier i äldre historia tillägnade Herman Schück 5/4 1985*, R. Sandberg, ed. (Stockholm), 67–83

Fournier, G, 1982, 'La Mise en place du cadre paroissial et l'évolution du peuplement', *Cristianizzazione ed Organizzazione Ecclesiastica delle Campagne nell'alto medioevo: espansione e resistenze* (Settimane di Studio del ·Centro Italiano di studi sull'alto medioevo, xxviii; Spoleto), 495–563.

Gjerløw, L, 1970, 'Missaler brukt i Bjørvin bispedømme fra misjonstiden til Nidarosordinarier', *Bjørgvin bispestol [2] byen og bispedømmet*, P Jukvam, ed. (Bergen), 73–127

Gjerløw, L, 1974, 'Missaler brukt i Oslo bispedømme fra misjonstiden til Nidarosordinariet', *Oslo bispedømme 900 år*, F Birkeli, A O Johnsen and E Molland, eds (Oslo), 73–142

Hafström, G, 1949, 'Sockenindelningens ursprung', *Historiska studier tillägnade Nils Ahnlund 23/8 1949*, S Grauers and Å Stille, eds (Stockholm), 51–67

Hald, K, 1965, *Vore Stednavne*, 2nd edn (Copenhagen)

Hildebrandt, M, 1985, 'En kyrka bygd på hednisk grund?', *Populär arkeologi*, iii: 4, 9–13

Jansson, S B F and Wessén, E., 1962, *Gotlands Runinskrifter*, i (Stockholm)

Jóhannesson, J, 1974, *A History of the Old Icelandic Commonwealth*, trans H Bessason (Winnipeg)

Jørgensen, E, 1908, *Fremmed indflydelse under den danske kirkes tidligste udvikling* (Copenhagen)

KHL = Kulturhistorisk leksikon for nordisk middelalder, 22 vols (Copenhagen etc.)

Kolsrud, O, 1958, *Noregs kyrkjesoga 1 Millomalderen* (Oslo)

Krogh, K, 1982, 'The Royal Viking-Age Monuments at Jelling in the light of recent archaeological excavations: a preliminary report', *Acta Archaeologica*, liii, 182–216

Kumlien, K, 1962, 'Sveriges kristnande i slutskedet—spörsmål om vittnesbörd och verklighet', *Historisk Tidskrift* (Stockholm), lxxxii, 249–94

Kurze, D, 1966, *Pfarrerwahlen im Mittelalter, Ein Beitrag zur Geschichte der Gemeinde und des Niederkirchenwesens* (Köln)

Larsson, L-O, 1966, 'Kyrkans tionde och kronans. Studier kring reformationens återverkningar på tiondebeskattningen', *Scandia*, xxxii, 268–313.

Lidén, H-E, 1969, 'From Pagan Sanctuary to Christian Church. The Excavation of Mære Church in Trøndelag', with comments by W Holmqvist and O Olsen, *Norwegian Archaeological Review*, ii, 3–32

Lundahl, I, 1961, *Det Medeltida Västergötland* (Lund)

Morris, R K, 1988, *Churches in the Landscape* (forthcoming)

Nilsson, T, 1985, 'Drottenskyrkan och dess föregångare. Nya arkeologiska rön i Lund', *Kulturen*, 173–82

Olsen, O, 1966, *Hørg, hov og kirke. Historisk og arkeologiske vikingetidsstudier* (Copenhagen)

Olsen, O, 1986, 'Is there a relationship between pagan and Christian places of worship in Scandinavia?', *The Anglo-Saxon Church: Papers . . . in honour of Dr H M Taylor*, L A S Butler and R K Morris, eds, 126–30

Olsen, M, 1951, *Norges Innskrifter med de Yngre Runer*, ii (Oslo)

Rahmqvist, S, 1982, 'Härad och socken—världslig och kyrklig indelning i Uppland', *Bebyggelsehistorisk tidskrift*, iv, 89–97

Refskou, N, 1986, 'Det retslige indhold af de ottonske diplomer til danske bispedømmer', *Scandia*, lii, 167–210, summary, 349–50

Sawyer, P, 1983, 'The Royal *Tun* in Pre-Conquest England', *Ideal and Reality in Frankish and Anglo-Saxon Society: Studies presented to J M Wallace-Hadrill*, P. Wormald, D. Bullough and R. Collins, eds, 273–99.

Sawyer, P, 1987, 'The process of Scandinavian Christianization in the tenth and eleventh centuries', *The Christianization of Scandinavia*, B and P Sawyer and I Wood, eds (Alingsås), 68–87

Schmid, T, 1933, 'Smärre Liturgiska Bidrag, v. Sancta Sexburga', *Nordisk tidskrift för bok-och biblioteksväsen*, xx, 31–4

Schmid, T, 1934, *Sveriges Kristnande: från verklighet till dikt* (Stockholm)

Skovgaard-Petersen, I, 1960, 'Islandsk egenkirkevæsen', *Scandia*, xxvi, 230–96

Stenton, F M, 1920, *Documents illustrative of the Social and Economic History of the Danelaw*

Ståhle, C I, 1950, 'Sockenbildningen i Törens prosteri', *Namn och Bygd*, xxxviii, 100–12

Svärdström, E, 1963, 'Birgitta i Rådene', *Fornvännen*, lviii, 246–63

Taranger, A, 1890, *Den angelsaksiske kirkes indflydelse paa den norske*, Christiania/Oslo

Thietmar = *Thietmari Merseburgensis Eiscopi Chronicon*, R Holtzmann, ed. (Monumenta Germaniae Historica. Scriptores Rerum Germanicarum, nova series, ix; Berlin, 1935)

Toy, J, 1983, 'The Commemorations of the British Saints in the Medieval Liturgical Manuscripts of Scandinavia', *Kyrkohistorisk Årsskrift*, 91–103

CHAPTER 4

The Organisation of the Twelfth-Century Norwegian Church

Knut Helle

Christian beliefs and practices began seriously to seep in to the coastal districts of Norway in the Viking Age of the ninth and tenth centuries. In return for the viking expeditions, Norway, like the rest of Scandinavia, was laid open to European cultural influences, and Christianity was by far the most consequential of these. By the mid tenth century foreign missionaries were probably at work both in east and west Norway. But the official conversion of the country did not start until the decades about the year 1000. It was set in motion by the landings of two viking kings who had both of them accepted the new faith abroad. Under Olaf Tryggvason (995–1000) and Olaf Haraldsson (1015–28), the later St Olaf, Christianity was established among the larger part of the population to the exclusion of other beliefs, and the first elements of a church organisation were introduced.

My theme is the Norwegian church organisation as it had developed by the first half of the twelfth century, when the building of the St Magnus' Cathedral of Kirkwall started. I shall also very briefly touch upon the important changes which took place throughout the rest of that century. But it is impossible to do justice to this subject without looking back to the missionary period of the late tenth and early eleventh centuries and the foreign influences at work in that period.

The pioneer of historical research in nineteenth-century Norway, Professor Rudolf Keyser, in his comprehensive history of the medieval church of Norway stated that this church 'was entirely the daughter of the English church' (Keyser, 1856, 33). This was to put it rather strongly. Missionaries from northern Germany were active in the Viken or Oslofjord area of east Norway. In the latter part of the eleventh century the archbishop of Hamburg-Bremen succeeded in making good his claim to metropolitan rights over the church of Norway. We know that architectural impulses over the Continent made an early imprint on Norwegian church-building, and they were presumably accompanied by other ecclesiastical influences as well. Broadly speaking, however, Keyser's words still hold good. Later research, notably that of Taranger (Taranger, 1890) and Birkeli (Birkeli, 1960, 1973), has substantiated the view that the main stream of early Christian impulses flowed to Norway from the British Isles and that the first elements of a Norwegian church organisation were introduced mainly from England (research discussion recapitulated by Birkeli, 1982, 24–39, 49–56).

There is no reason to doubt the traditions that King Haakon the Good, who had been brought up at the English court of King Athelstan, sent for a bishop and priests from England to help him in his abortive attempt to establish Christianity in his homeland. Olaf Tryggvason was accompanied by a bishop and priests when he left England for Norway in 995. St. Olaf brought with him several bishops and priests from England in 1015. Among them was the English-born Bishop Grimkell who is mentioned at his side as an initiator of the oldest Christian laws of Norway. King Harald III Hardraadi was accused by Archbishop Adalbert of Hamburg-Bremen of having his bishops—some of them English—ordained in England and Gaul (Taranger, 1890, 142–202; Birkeli, 1960; Sveaas Andersen, 1977, 103, 108, 113, 124–28, 189–91; cf. Stenton, 1947, 456–57; Barlow, 1963, 233).

In 1066 Harald's son, Olaf III (Kyrre) followed his father to England together with his relatives, the earls of Orkney. This was the expedition that ended in the battle of Stamford Bridge. Before Olaf went back to rule Norway he spent the winter in Orkney (*Orkneyinga saga*, chap. 34). Back at home he started to build Christ Church cathedrals in the towns of Trondheim (Nidaros) and Bergen and established the first permanent episcopal seats of Norway there (Helle, 1982, 90–92). Generally the habit of dedicating Norwegian cathedrals and other churches to Christ (and the Holy Trinity) must have been introduced from England (Taranger, 1890, 219–20). But in this particular case we can guess that King Olaf was more immediately influenced by his experience of Orkney. Here, in about 1050, Earl Thorfinn the Mighty had erected his Christ Church in Birsay and attached the first episcopal seat in Orkney to this church (*Orkneyinga saga*, chap. 31). This is an instance which ought to remind us of the fact that Orkney was not only a stepping stone for vikings going abroad from western Norway. The islands may also have functioned as a bridgehead by which some of the early Christian and ecclesiastical impulses passed to Norway from the British Isles.

It is easy enough to recapitulate single events which bear testimony to the important part played by the English church in the conversion and early ecclesiastical development of Norway. Still, the most telling evidence does not lie in such incidents but in the numerous details which reflect English influences on ecclesiastical terminology, ritual and organisation in Norway. This is what Taranger termed 'Anglo-Saxon influence on the constitution of the Norwegian church' and on its 'practice' (Taranger, 1890, 203–412). Not least was it of lasting importance that the members of the English clergy who went to Norway brought with them the habit and art of writing in the vernacular. Hence the framing of laws and religious literature in Old Norse.

The evidence available for a study of the early twelfth-century church of Norway is far from complete. Certain main features and numerous details are bound to remain obscure. Still, the overall impression which emerges from such a study is quite unambiguous. It is that of a Germanic 'national' church under the authority of the monarchy and at the same time strongly dependent on the peasant society into which it had been incorporated.

The most detailed and reliable evidence for this situation is supplied by the oldest 'Christian' laws of Norway, that is, laws regulating the observance of Christianity and the relations between church and society. Typically enough such regulations were incorporated into secular law so that they formed separate but not strictly exclusive sections of the codes of the four main law-provinces of Norway. The Christian laws reflect agreements reached between king and bishops on one hand, the initiators of this type of legislation; and on the other, the freemen of the representative 'law-things' or assemblies of the respective law-provinces. It was with the representatives of peasant society that the final legislative authority rested. That this authority was more than formal is revealed by the fact that the legislative programme of monarchy and church was modified in different ways from law-thing to law-thing before it was recorded in the vernacular of the provincial law-books. There was, in this early phase, no internal ecclesiastical legislation in accordance with generally recognised canonical principles. The church had to approach the law-things, supported by the authority of the king, in order to have its religious programme and organisation accepted by the representatives of a legally free peasantry.

The results of this procedure are the extant Christian law sections of the provincial codes of the Gulathing of West Norway (G), of the Frostathing of Trøndelag and adjacent districts further north (F), of the Eidsivathing of the inland area of east Norway (E), and of the Borgarthing of the Viken region (B) (all printed in *Norges gamle Love*, i, iv). Most of these regulations probably originated before c. 1150. Part of them seem to go back even to the eleventh century, but only a few of them can be dated more precisely, such as a small nucleus of provisions attributed to St Olaf and Bishop Grimkell. On the other hand the Christian law sections contain—to varying degrees—amendments from the latter part of the twelfth century, datable to the days of King Magnus III Erlingsson (1161–1184) and Archbishop Eystein (1161–1188). The Christian laws of the Frostathing code probably represent the results of a more total revision by Archbishop Eystein himself (for further details, see Rindal, 1983, 9–10, 16).

The king was head of the early twelfth-century church. His predecessors had established Christianity in Norway, and not for religious purposes alone. In their viking days abroad, notably in England, they had become acquainted with a pattern of close cooperation between monarchy and church under royal leadership. And they were hardly blind to the political benefits that might be reaped from the application of the same pattern to Norway. The bishops of the missionary period had been members of the royal *hirð* or body of retainers. In the early twelfth century they were still appointed by the king. The Eidsivathing code (E I 31) prescribed that the bishop was to be selected and placed in his seat by the will of the king. The code adds that he should also be 'rightfully elected' and here probably alludes to the old canonical form of election by the clergy and people of the diocese. But, as had earlier been the case in Anglo-Saxon England and other Germanic kingdoms (Barlow, 1963, 99–113), the popular election was hardly much more than an acceptance of the candidate nominated by the king (cf. Sveaas Andersen, 1977, 332). In the 1070s Adam of Bremen may have allowed for this type of procedure when he wrote that the bishops of Norway and Sweden were accepted *a rege vel populo* (Adam of Bremen, 1918, lib. iv, cap. xxxiv). At the end of the twelfth century the so-called 'Oration against the Bishops', inspired by King Sverre, maintained that bishops had formerly been chosen by the kings and installed in the various dioceses without any consultation of the clergy. As late examples of this practice are cited two appointments to the see of Bergen in the 1150s (*En tale*, 1931, 14–15).

The Eidsivathing code finally adds that the bishop should be consecrated before taking over his office. As I have already mentioned, King Harald Hardraadi (1047–1066) refused to accept the metropolitan rights of the archbishop of Hamburg-Bremen in this respect and had his bishops consecrated elsewhere. But it seems that his son, Olaf III, came to terms with the metropolitan of Bremen and respected his right of consecration without giving up his own right of appointment. After 1104 the metropolitan rights over the church of Norway were in the hands of the Danish archbishop of Lund (Sveaas Andersen, 1977, 311–13, 333).

The first bishops of Norway had been ambulant; they followed the king or went on their own missionary expeditions. In the latter part of the eleventh century can be glimpsed the rudiments of a diocesan arrangement within the framework of the secular judicial and administrative system. The main law-provinces became the fields of episcopal activity, and gradually this activity came to centre on one or a few residential churches within each province. The last stage of this development was reached when the bishop took up permanent residence in a town or town-like settlement. The first permanent episcopal seat of Norway was established in Trondheim in the reign of King Olaf III (1066–1093). At the turn of the century it appears that the bishop of the Gulathing province had become resident in Bergen. The see of Oslo may also go back to the late eleventh century; in its early days it served both of the east Norwegian law-provinces. In the 1120s, at the latest, the diocese of Stavanger in southwestern Norway was separated from the bishopric of Bergen. And in 1152 or 1153 the fifth and last medieval see of Norway was established at Hamar, for the inland Eidsivathing province of east Norway (Sveaas Andersen, 1977, 313–14, 329–30; Helle, 1974, 48) (see fig. 4).

According to the Eidsivathing code the bishop should be present at the annual summer meeting of the law-thing, listen to the readings from the law-book, say the canonical hours, and preach to the people (E I 10). The other bishops probably also quite frequently attended the meetings of the law-things of their bishoprics, not least in order to initiate new Christian regulations. But—as I have already touched upon—they had no legislative authority. Nor are there indications of any participation on their part in the judicial decisions of the things, be it the law-things or the local things of lower rank. The provincial codes ascribe to the bishop all the lesser fines and varying parts of the heavier fines and confiscations for violations of the Christian laws. Hence the right of the bishop and his lay stewards to prosecute. But it belonged to the freemen of the things to pass judgement. Other public courts did not at this stage exist in Norway (Seip, 1942, 13–26). The church had to content itself with its jurisdiction through the *forum internum*, the confessional. It is true that the power of granting absolution for sin through penance was a potential point of departure for the development of external jurisdiction as well. Moreover, the trend towards private settlements between parties to a conflict, including cases initiated by the bishop or his stewards, would in the long run tend to blur the distinction between such settlements and judgement proper and open the way for external ecclesiastical jurisdiction. But by the early twelfth century the Norwegian church hardly yet possessed the administrative apparatus necessary to exploit such possibilities to any large extent (Seip, 1942, 26–46, 53–67; Gunnes, 1970, 125–29; Bagge, 1981, 135–40).

Part of the explanation for this state of affairs lies in the economic basis of the early church. The first cathedrals of Norway were built by the kings on or nearby royal urban estates. In most cases they were probably also endowed with land by the monarchy. There is no evidence for the rights of the bishops in the administration of the economic affairs of their churches before the mid twelfth century. But it is doubtful whether they had obtained full jurisdictional rights in that respect, and even less likely that private donations of land to the bishops' churches had so far assumed more than modest proportions. Even after they had become resident in the episcopal towns the bishops would have to go on exploiting their rights to demand food, lodging and transport from the clergy and the peasantry when travelling about their dioceses. For the rest they must have been heavily dependent on various other dues from the inhabitants of their bishoprics: a fixed annual contribution in the form of a light head tax (reiða), fees charged for services rendered, such as the consecration of churches and graveyards, and not least the fines derived from violations of the Christian laws (Sveaas Andersen, 1977, 329–30, 334–37).

The conclusion to be drawn from this survey of episcopal rights and authority is fairly evident: The conditions for a strong and independent episcopate were as yet lacking in Norway by the early twelfth century. The leaders of the church were under royal authority and dependent on peasant society. Their economic basis was too slender and their political, judicial and administrative powers too weak to allow them much leeway even in the government of ecclesiastical affairs.

It is now time to turn to the local church organisation: The Christian laws of all four law-provinces take for granted a smaller number of 'head-churches' (Old Norse hǫfuðkirkjur) or county churches (fylkiskirkjur) of higher rank. Originally there appears to have been one of these churches in each of the small counties of Trøndelag as well as of the far larger counties of west Norway (F II 7, 10, VII 26; G 10, 19). In east Norway there was one head church for each third of the old and large inland districts or 'folklands' which came to be called counties (fylki) in the twelfth century (E I 32, II 28; Norges gamle Love, i, 393). In the Viken area are named two county churches in each of the counties there (B I 8, II 16, III 11; cf. Smedberg, 1973, 34–48; Sveaas Andersen, 1977, 319–21).

It seems that the head or county churches had much in common with the 'old minsters' of Anglo-Saxon law, even though they were not, as their English

1   St Magnus Cathedral, nave interior, looking west. (Gunnie Moberg).

2   St Magnus Cathedral, nave bays and piers with trifocrium above. (Gunnie Moberg).

3   Figure of St Magnus from the altarpiece from Lurøy Church, Nordland. (Courtesy of Historical Museum, Bergen).

counterparts, collegiate establishments. In both cases the original parishes can be explained in terms of old secular boundaries (Taranger, 1890, 257–61; Stenton, 1947, 148–9; Barlow, 1969, 183–4). According to the later saga tradition the first churches of Norway were built on royal initiative (Taranger, 1890, 120–41), and Olaf Tryggvason and St Olaf are credited with the establishment of the county church system (*Olafs saga hins helga*, 28, 43). Modern research has tended to accept the view of Taranger (1890, 257) that the head churches were the original baptismal and burial churches of the country and that they functioned as mother establishments for larger districts. It appears that they were generally built on royal land, but it is more doubtful whether they were further endowed by the kings (Smedberg, 1973, 63, 126–28; Sveaas Andersen, 1977, 320–21). At least in Trøndelag this seems not to have been the case (Sandnes, 1969). The Christian laws make it perfectly clear that the responsibility for the upkeep of these churches rested on the peasantry (G 10, B I 10, II 16, F II 7, E I 34).

In the early twelfth century the head churches were crowded by a rising tide of churches of lower rank. So-called 'churches of ease' or 'convenience' (*hægendiskirkjur*) are mentioned in all the law-provinces. They were originally proprietory churches of the common Germanic type (*Eigenkirchen*), built by kings and other prominent persons on their private estates and farms. There was by now obviously in motion a process of converting such churches into ordinary parish churches with graveyards (E I 40, F II 10, 17; cf. Smedberg, 1973, 37–40; Sveaas Andersen, 1977, 322).

In Trøndelag and the inland districts of east Norway, where the number of head churches was comparatively high, there was presumably no need for defining legally other parish churches than the head or county churches and the converted private churches. In the Viken area, however, are mentioned a group of so-called *heraðskirkjur* of intermediate rank, between the county churches and the private churches. They probably functioned as parish churches within the old and smaller administrative districts called *herð* (sing. *herað*) in this part of the country (B I 8, II 17; cf. Smedberg, 1973, 41–45; Sveaas Andersen, 1977, 322). *Heraðskirkjur* are also referred to in the western law province of the Gulathing, but now in the more general meaning of local parish churches. They are grouped together with churches for quarters and eighths of counties (*fjórðungs-* and *áttungskirkjur*) in what appears to have been largely an intermediate class of churches, between the head churches and the private churches (G 12; cf. Smedberg, 1973, 45–48; Sveaas Andersen, 322). In the extensive and topographically divided counties of west Norway parish churches in addition to the single head church of each county must have been required at an early stage. In the diocese of Bergen the restricted number of original head churches would seem to explain the fact that both a higher rank and certain administrative functions were later attributed to the 'quarter churches' (*fjórðungs-kirkjur*) (Tryti, 1987, 419–28).

Very largely, then, the local churches of Norway in the early twelfth century may be grouped in a tripartite system of head or county churches, lesser parish churches and privately owned churches. This system has been shown to have had certain features in common with the ranking of various classes of churches in late

Anglo-Saxon law (Taranger, 1890, 257–59; cf. Stenton, 1947, 148; Barlow, 1969, 187). The parishes of the lower-ranking parish churches had apparently been carved out of those of the first rank, if they had not indeed been established at an early date, more or less at the same time as the parishes of the head churches. One should beware of too systematic historical reasoning in these matters. A spontaneous growth of churches, founded by both private persons and local peasant communities, may have coincided with more methodical attempts to establish a system of local churches from above. And the Christian laws of the twelfth century may well reflect the efforts of the legislators to adapt themselves to a rather fluid situation.

It is at any rate difficult, by this time, to trace fundamental differences of rights between the various parish churches of the country. They had in common the collective responsibility of the parishioners for the upkeep of the church and the maintenance of its priests by means of an agreed annual contribution (*prestreiða*, *prestgipt*) and of fees charged for some of the services rendered by the priest, for instance a burial fee corresponding to the old English soul-scot. At this stage of development the parish churches and their priests could presumably not to any large extent be maintained by the income of landed endowments. Such endowments would probably not at any rate be controlled by the priests themselves. Parish churches were apparently considered the collective property of their parishioners; they were in a sense proprietary churches alongside the private churches of single persons or families. Such private churches were regarded as the property of the founders and their heirs, who were, on the other hand, responsible for the maintenance both of church and priest. Private royal churches are not mentioned in the Christian laws, but we know from later sources that they existed both on rural estates and in urban palaces (Smedberg, 1973, 129–37; Sveaas Andersen, 1977, 320–23).

The Borgarthing code granted the parishioners in the Viken area unlimited right to appoint priests to the parish churches of lesser rank (*heraðskirkjur*) (B I 12, II 23). In the rest of the country the right of appointment of parish priests had by the early twelfth century come to rest with the bishop, on the condition that he would find candidates fit for rendering proper service to their congregations. This was an ecclesiastical programme ascribed to St Olaf and Bishop Grimkell back in the 1020s, and it was probably only gradually implemented in the various law-provinces (G 15, E I 31, F II 12; cf. Sveaas Andersen, 1977, 323–4). The priests of the private churches were still in the first part of the twelfth century appointed by the owners. The Christian laws of the Gulathing code laid down the principle that priests should have the same legal rights as other freemen, perhaps because they had originally had a lower status. The same laws take for granted that the priests were tied to the local peasant society by marriage bonds (G 15).

In general, then, the main features of the local ecclesiastical organisation bear witness to the incorporation of the church and its clergy into lay society. They strengthen the impression of a national church dependent on the peasantry of the country.

There were, however, in progress certain movements away from this situation. One of these I have already mentioned: the establishment of urban episcopal sees within better-defined dioceses. Earl Rognvald and his father may have been influenced by this part of their Norwegian background when they started the building of the St Magnus' Cathedral with the intention of moving the episcopal seat of Orkney to Kirkwall (*Orkneyinga saga*, chap. 69, 76).

Another important development was the introduction of tithe. The origin and early development of tithe as an annual payment to the church in Norway is rather obscure. There is, however, no reason to doubt the essence of the saga tradition that King Sigurd the Crusader put his authority behind this regular church tax some time before his death in 1130. It appears that it was first paid in the diocese of Trondheim, but it was not made legally binding on the inhabitants of all the main law-provinces until the days of King Magnus Erlingsson in the latter half of the twelfth century (Johnsen, 1945, 26–7; Helle, 1974, 46, 63, 237–8). To the degree that the payment of tithe was made effective before that time, it would strengthen the financial basis of the church and make it less dependent on day-to-day contributions.

Finally, the first part of the twelfth century saw the origin and early development of the monastic movement in Norway. Three Benedictine houses were established in the early years of the century, two of them close by the sees of Trondheim and Bergen and the third one attached to the bishop's church of Selja north of Bergen. It is quite possible that they functioned in support of the sees mentioned, before the establishment of cathedral chapters. Three Benedictine nunneries were founded in the following decades. In the 1140s the Cistercian movement reached Norway. The bishop of Bergen and probably also his colleague in Oslo were involved in the establishment of the first religious houses of this order. The monastic foundations did of course by their very nature contribute to the trend towards a church more separate from and independent of lay society. They also helped to bring the Norwegian clergy into closer contact with the European reform movement and its programme of liberation of the church from all kinds of lay influence (Johnsen, 1945, 27–30; Helle, 1974, 238–9. Sveaas Andersen, 1977, 314–15, 330).

To a certain extent, then, the ground was prepared for the most important single event in the history of the medieval church of Norway. This was the establishment of a separate Norwegian church province in 1152 or 1153, under the authority of the new metropolitan see of Trondheim, and covering also the six dioceses of the Norse island societies west-over-sea, from Greenland to the Hebrides and Isle of Man. By this epoch-making event the Norwegian church took its first and most important step away from its subordination under the monarchy and its heavy dependence on peasant society, to become more firmly incorporated into the universal church under papal leadership. By means of its new national and hierarchic organisation it started its development into an almost state-like public authority at the side of the monarchy.

The more independent church continued to collaborate with the monarchy, and in the days of King Magnus Erlingsson and Archbishop Eystein was granted further concessions from the crown. The new rights of the church were partly contested in its bitter clash with King Sverre at the end of the twelfth century, but this was, after all, a passing conflict. It showed that there was not room for a politically autonomous church in the Norwegian society of the High Middle Ages. But in the long run the monarchy showed itself willing to respect the bulk of other rights obtained by the church in the third quarter of the twelfth century.

Time does not allow me to go into details about the important organisational reforms of this period. But it brought the church a high degree of internal autonomy in the form of ecclesiastical elections, episcopal appointments of priests to all types of churches, and jurisdiction over the clergy. The central organisation of the church was strengthened by the establishment of cathedral chapters. Its chances of acquiring landed endowments were greatly enhanced by the right of all people to give away freely one tenth of inherited and one quarter of self-acquired property. The proprietry church system was dealt its deathblow by the right of the bishops and other clergy to administer the finances of the churches and their property. Finally, various attempts were made to separate the clergy from the rest of society, including the first, cautious steps towards celibacy (Helle, 1974, 45–53, 57–69).

For the church of Orkney the establishment of the metropolitan see of Trondheim meant closer connections with Norway. From now on the bishops of Orkney were consecrated in Norway and often attended both ecclesiastical and political meetings there. One concrete result of the closer ecclesiastical ties between Orkney and Norway are the traces of architectural influences from the cathedral of Trondheim on the building of the St Magnus' Cathedral in the late twelfth century. Corresponding influences from the early Romanesque cathedrals of Norway cannot—as far as I know—be traced in the oldest, Anglo-Norman parts of the St Magnus'. But this is a theme I shall leave to more expert speakers in this conference.

BIBLIOGRAPHY

Adam of Bremen, *Adam von Bremen, Hamburgische Kirchengeschichte*, 1917, B Schmeidler, ed. Scriptores rerum Germanicarum in usum scholarum

Bagge, S, 1981, 'Kirkens jurisdiksjon i kristenrettssaker før 1277', *Historisk Tidsskrift* [Oslo], lx, 133–59

Barlow, F, 1963, *The English Church 1000–1066, A Constitutional History*

Birkeli, F, 1960, 'Hadde Håkon Adalsteinsfostre likevel en biskop Sigurd hos seg?', *Historisk Tidsskrift* [Oslo], xl, 113–36

——— 1973, *Norske steinkors i tidlig middelalder*

——— 1982, *Hva vet vi om kristningen av Norge?*

En tale mot biskopene, 1931, A Holtmark, ed.

Gunnes, E, 1970, 'Kirkelig jurisdiksjon i Norge 1153–1277', *Historisk Tidsskrift* [Oslo], xlix, 121–60

Helle, K., *Norge blir en stat 1130–1319*, Handbook i Norges historie, iii

—— 1982, *Bergen bys historie*, i

Johnsen, A O, 1945, *Studier vedrørende kardinal Nicolaus Brekespears legasjon til Norden*

Keyser, R, 1856, *Den norske Kirkes Historie under Katholicismen*, i

Norges gamle Love, 1846–1895, R Keyser *et al.*, eds, i–v

Orkneyinga saga, 1913–1916, S Nordal, ed., Samfund til udgivelse af gammel nordisk litteratur [xl]

Rindal, M, 1983, 'Introduction', *King Magnus Håkonsson's Laws of Norway and other Legal Texts*, Corpus codicum Norvegicorum medii aevi, quarto ser. vii, 9–25

Sandnes, J, 1969, 'Fylkeskirkene i Trøndelag i middelalderen', *Årbok for Trøndelag*

Seip, J A, 1942, *Sættargjerden i Tunsberg og kirkens jurisdiksjon*

Smedberg, G, 1973, *Nordens första kyrkor, En kyrkorättslig studie*, Bibliotheca theologiae practicae [Uppsala, xxxii]

Stenton, F M, 1947, *Anglo-Saxon England*, 2nd edn, The Oxford History of England

Sveaas Andersen, P., 1977, *Samlingen av Norge og kristningen av landet 800–1130*, Handbok i Norges historie, ii

Taranger, A, 1890, *Den angelsaksiske kirkes indflydelse paa den norske*

Tryti, A E, 1987, *Kirkeorganisasjonen i Bergen bispedømme i første halvdel av 1300-tallet* [thesis, University of Bergen]

CHAPTER 5

The Orkney Church of the Twelfth and Thirteenth Centuries—a Stepdaughter of the Norwegian Church?

Per Sveaas Andersen

In the year of grace 1890 a Norwegian historian of some eminence, Absalon Taranger, published a book on the relationship between the Anglo-Saxon and Norwegian churches — *Den angelsaksiske kirkes indflydelse paa den norske*. His main conclusion is unequivocal: the Norwegian church in its early phase was in many essential traits as regards ritual and organisation a genuine daughter of the Anglo-Saxon Christian institution (Taranger, 1890, 1).

The title of *this* paper is quite simply a paraphrasing of Taranger's introductory sentence applied to the relationship between the Orcadian and Norwegian churches. Due reservation has been taken by prefixing a specific — 'step' before 'daughter', as the Norwegian motherhood may be in doubt. I will limit my discussion to a presentation of the more essential features of the church *organisation* in the Orkney islands with some comparative references to the Norwegian organisation. The main emphasis within this study of the Orkney church will be on the rise and development of the bishopric as a permanent institution and more briefly on the local kirks and chapels.

Only scanty sources are available for an examination of the Orkney church organisation of the twelfth and thirteenth centuries. They are undoubtably more copious as regards the contemporary Norwegian institution (see Helle above). Storer Clouston in his *History of Orkney* outlined the difficult source situation for the student of the early Orkney church, and perhaps in a too optimistic way.

> One is dealing here with a period of the Orkney Church's history, and with a phase in the development of the land, both entirely without written records. Everything is a matter of inferences. Yet the facts on which the inferences rest are so certain, so fully proved by rentals, actual chapel sites, good and consistent tradition, and authentic records of what happened in other parts of the Norse dominions; . . . that it seems quite safe to say that the order of events must have been this. (Clouston, 1932, 146 f.).

Then he goes on to sum up how the local church system, based on the urisland/eyrisland unit, originated. In his enumeration of sources Clouston has

somewhat haphazardly mentioned all the main categories for the present subject—
rentals, church archaeological material (and sites), traditions in a broad sense, and
contemporary records from other parts of the Norse-speaking area. But he refrains
from a critical evaluation of their qualities and usefulness, and he seems to make
no distinction between contemporary and later sources; and, what is more interesting from our point of view, is the way in which scholars of Clouston's generation
and most of his successors have used these sources, exploiting them to throw light
on the Orkney church both as a central and local organisation. It is probably fair
to say that most scholars who have dealt with this subject, have been more interested in the bishop's church than in the church at the local level.

The main problems inherent in the early history of the central Orkney church,
(and they are probably applicable to the origins of all central church organisations
in northern Europe), are:

1. The question of transition from a more or less peripatetic existence for the
    bishop to the establishing of a permanent residence, a bishop's seat.
2. The questions of the bishopric's economic basis and organisation and its rela-
    tions to lay power.

By way of preamble, even if it is possible to expatiate on these questions to some
extent, it appears highly doubtful whether any definite conclusion can be reached.
The posing and the discussion of the problems mentioned above, and the questions
connected with the local kirks and chapels outlined below, are in themselves sufficient ventures into a hazy unknown.

Scholars who have studied the early bishopric in Orkney, have been more interested in its incumbents, their period of office, and their obligation of obedience to
some archbishop, be it of York, Canterbury, Hamburg-Bremen, Lund, or Nidaros.
But some historians (Munch, 1849/1971, 436 f; Dowden, 1912, 252 f; Kolsrud,
1913, 198f; Brøgger, 1929, 151, 158; Storer Clouston, 1932, 141; Ralegh Radford,
1964, 179; Watt, 1969, 249; Cant, 1972, 4; Crawford, 1983, 104 f.; Seip, 1984,
126, 260; De Geer, 1985, 85 f.; Cowan, 1987, 1) have discussed briefly the establishment of a permanent bishop's seat as a matter of some interest. Most of them,
however, have not attached too much importance to this problem. A study of the
origin of an independent ecclesiastical organisation is conceivably of some significance to the understanding of the bishop's political engagement in the following
period.

The discussion has naturally been concerned with the bishop who might be considered the first *resident* incumbent of a permanent seat, the first independent bishop
of Orkney. Two main views are represented: those who think the presence of a
consecrated bishop in Orkney more important than the establishment of an independent and permanent bishop's seat, and a smaller group of historians who attach
more weight to the bishop's *material basis with a fixed seat* (or seats), an organisation,
and landed property. Representative statements by adherents of the former view,
are the following: 'The first *recorded* . . . bishop of the York succession was Ralph
(Radulphus). Consecrated at York on 3 March 1072-3 . . . .' (Dowden, 1912, 253);

FIGURE 5   Map of Orkney and Shetland showing places mentioned in the text.

'Thurolf . . . Appointed by abp. of Bremen as bp. to the Orkneys . . . , more specifically he was consecrated to the see of Birsay . . . .' (Watt, 1969, 247); 'Whatever the order of succession, the first consecrated bishop of Birsay is traditionally accepted to have been Thurolf, appointed *c*.1050 by the archbishop of Bremen on the specific authority of the pope.' (Cowan, 1987, 1). In a middle position we find three scholars who seem to regard a consecrated bishop and a permanent seat as equally important. P.A. Munch was the first historian to see a connection between an archaeological find in St Magnus Cathedral in 1848 and a short statement in the Orkneyinga Saga ch. 52: ' . . . hann [Vilhialmr] var þar [i Orcneyium] fyrstr byskup.' (He was there the first bishop). The find of the same bishop's coffin or stone cist with his presumed bones and a leaden plaque with his name inscribed, during the repairs to the cathedral in 1848, was accepted by Munch as a confirmation of the saga text. The text on the plaque is well known: 'Hic requiescit Willialmus senex, felicis memoriæ. Primus Episcopus.' Munch, however, interpreted the reference to Bishop William the Old as the first of Orkney bishops *not* as the first bishop *in* the isles, but as the first bishop with clear Norwegian support (Sigurd the Crusader) and the first bishop at the seat in Kirkwall (Munch, 1849/1971, 437; 1855, 622 f.) To Munch the first consecrated bishop *of* Orkney was Thorolf, whose seat was established by Earl Thorfinn in Birsay (1855, 217). Two modern scholars have adopted Munch's position and seem to consider a consecrated bishop and a permanent seat as equally important: ' . . . the earl's [Thorfinn's] main residence was indeed the seat of the first Hamburg-appointed bishop' [Thorolf] (Crawford, 1983, 104), and ' . . . there is no way of naming a first bishop of Orkney', but 'a bishop's seat in Birsay' was erected 'at some time during the first half of the 11th century . . . .' (De Geer, 1985, 78, 85).

Storer Clouston was the first historian to recognise the importance of a permanent seat for the Orkney church. It implied eventually the establishment of a central and local organisation: 'The first Bishop of Orkney resident in the islands and recognised by the Orkney chapter was William, styled "the old", ...' (Storer Clouston, 1932, 141). He has later been seconded by two eminent specialists in different fields: 'These extensive alterations and additions [in the church on the Brough of Birsay] mark a change in the use of the site. This can most easily be associated with the establishment of the bishopric at Birsay, which must have taken place some time during the long episcopate of Bishop William, who died in 1168.' (Ralegh Radford, 1964, 179). And finally a quotation from a classic article on the church in Orkney and Shetland: 'He [Earl Hakon Palsson] could conceivably have been founder of the bishopric of Orkney as a regular and permanent institution, but this honour would seem to belong rather to King Sigurd, ... The bishop concerned in this process was William "the old", ...' (Cant, 1972, 4).

To sum up the discussion a comparison with the contemporary Norwegian development might be of some interest. In Norway there seems to have been an establishment of the Christian church through three phases: During the ninth and tenth centuries the Christianisation of Norway was carried out by missionary priests and bishops. During the eleventh century came the introduction of Christianity as a state religion (Olav the Saint *c*.1024) and along with it some sort of organisation. It was marked on the higher ecclesiastical level by the introduction of the office of *hirð*-bishop and later in the second half of the eleventh century by the establishment of regional bishops without any *formal* residential seats, evidently one for each of the three (or four) main law-provinces of Norway (Vikin/Uppland, Gulathingslaw and Frostathingslaw). The bishops were changing from a peripatetic existence in company with the kings (as *hirð*-bishops) to a less peripatetic life within the above-mentioned provinces. The last phase is marked by the establishment of permanent bishop's seats at Nidaros, Bergen and Oslo towards the end of the eleventh century, the bishops then receiving their own cathedral churches.

Let us return to the Orkney scene. Is it possible to visualise a similar development for Orkney and Shetland? The religious situation during the first centuries of Norse presence in the islands is quite complex. The pre-Norse, Pictish, Christian population and certain Papa centres must have survived the invasions from the North to some extent. But the dominant Norse population element was chiefly pagan until the end of the tenth century. We know the names of seven bishops connected with Orkney before the episcopate of William the Old, three of whom are termed 'missionary bishops', Henry, Jón *irski*, and Adalbert (Kolsrud 1913, 198). We do not know, however, whether they came to these islands or not . If they did, and one or two from Britain and /or the Continent probably did, they would be entirely under the protection of the earl. It is therefore reasonable to assume that in this first phase they accompanied the earls as (court-) *hirð*-bishops and as important figures in the earl's *hirð* or entourage at least until the founding of Christ Church in Birsay.

Whether Orkney and Shetland ever went through a second phase of half-peripatetic bishops (that is, bishops with special *veizlu*-seats), is dependent on how we define these seats as permanent or non-permanent. But if we accept as a fact that the bishops had seats on certain farms near more prominent churches, this might have been a development between *c.*1050 and 1137. (cf. Clouston, 1927, 43 f.). There are a few indications of such a transitional stage both in the *Orkneyinga Saga* and possibly in archaeological church site material from both Orkney and Shetland. In the *Orkneyinga Saga* (ch. 66) there are references to two prominent residences for the bishop during the first half of the twelfth century (and before 1137). One of these seats must have been on a farm near the church on Egilsay (possibly *Skaill*, see Marwick, 1952, 72); the other may have come into existence in or near present-day Kirkwall, where there was already a church dedicated to St Olaf, possibly established some time in the late eleventh century (O.S. ch. 57, post 1117). Two other important churches to which the bishops might have preferred to be attached for some time during the pre-cathedral period were the Orphir Round Church and in Shetland the church on St Ninians Isle off the west coast of Dunrossness (Cant, 1972, 4. note 4) (see fig. 5).

The final and last stage in Orkney was reached when the bishop became the earthly guardian of a saint in the cathedral at Kirkwall. Although William the Old may have stayed frequently at his seat in Birsay, it was not until he became stationary at Kirkwall (*Kirkjuvágr*) that he was in a position to establish a central and local church organisation in a more systematic fashion. And it is almost certain that he created a group of supporting clergy to assist him in his office. Storer Clouston would prefer to term this group a chapter (1932, 141), but a proper chapter is not documented until 1247 (*DN*, I, no. 42).

This brings us to the second important question in connection with the central church organisation in Orkney: its material and economic basis. And I would like again to quote your great historian Storer Clouston:

> An original and princely endowment undoubtedly formed the first source of the Bishopric's wealth, ... The vast growth of its estates must, however, be attributed, mainly, to three causes: — purchase of land as an investment, acquisition of land through lending money on wadsets which were never redeemed, and fines and penalties for breaches of canonical law. There may of course have been occasional gifts, . . . (what in Norway was termed *proventkjøop*). (1932, 149).

Clouston did not find much documentation for last-will bequests or dispositions of land; and he does not seem to have mentioned whether the Scottish practice of appropriation of parish church revenue had taken root in Orkney during the thirteenth century. In Scotland this practice had taken great proportions at that period. It has been defined as follows: 'It involved the transference of the income of the church derived from its endowed land and its tithes, to the corporation to whom the gift was made' (Cowan, 1975–9, 207).

There are extant in Rome and Edinburgh two important early documents on the Orkney church which may throw light on economic aspects of its central (and also local) organisation during the thirteenth and early fourteenth centuries: a taxation roll of annates 1327–8 from the Papal archives (Vatican Archives, Collectorie 227, fol. 99; cf. Cowan, 1971, 8), and a bishop's rental of the Orkney bishop's land in and revenue from Caithness, datable to *c*.1500 (or earlier?) (Adv. MS. 49.7.19 [IV], Nat. Lib. of Scotland). The tax roll of 1327–8 confirms the charter of 1247 showing that a chapter existed at St Magnus Cathedral during the thirteenth century. It also gives the valuable additional information that prebends[1] were a constituent element of the cathedral's economy by this date. Four prebends appear in the list: 'prebenda de scons-ay [Stronsay] . . . , vicaria de scronsay [Stronsay], . . . , prebenda de sandwik . . . , prebenda ecclesie sancte crucis de Be [Sanday], . . . , prebenda domini Rikardi . . . .' (See Cowan, 1971, 11). The document implicitly indicates that there were more than four prebends at the cathedral, the above-mentioned being the vacant benefices for the years 1327–8. And it is tempting to add some of the following: St Augustine's (the 'song school' 'stouk' or prebend), St Peter's (the 'Grammar School' prebend), St Ninian's, St Katherine's, St Barbara's, St Andrew's, St Ola's, St John's, St Lawrences's, St Nicholas', and the Lady altar. (See Clouston, 1926, 33 f.). Furthermore it is legitimate to assume that this source gives us the first clear evidence of the appropriation system in Orkney. 'Prebenda ecclesie sancte crucis de Be' refers to one of the three parish churches of Sanday, Cross Kirk. Ruins of the church with a cemetery still in use are situated between Bea Loch and Backaskaill Bay (Cowan, 1971, 8; Thomson, 1987, fig. 3). Here is the first extant documentation of a church's income (rental dues and teinds or tithes) being transferred to a central institution, the chapter of St Magnus Cathedral. And it probably was not the only church appropriated at this time. Hoy, Orphir, and Stronsay (with its Lady or St Nicholas Church), all mentioned in the tax roll of 1327-8, may have become appropriated churches during the fourteenth century (see Cowan, *Parishes*, 1967, 221). Otherwise, the common source of income for bishop as well as members of the chapter would be the same as in Norway—food rents from farms and parts of farms, in Orkney assessed on the basis of the pennyland/urisland land registration, and bishop's tithes (one quarter of the total annual tithes). In Shetland the bishop's share of the annual tithes amounted to 50 per cent of the cornteind with a few exceptions (Cowan, 1967, 5 et passim).

In Norway the appropriation system was not quite unknown, but it remained a relatively rare phenomenon during the thirteenth century (*DN*, II, no. 15; III, nos. 10, 13; V, nos. 7, 8). It became more common in Nidaros (Trondheim) arch-bishopric during the later middle ages (Hamre, 1958, 197).

Clouston in his enumeration of sources which might throw light on the early bishopric's economic resources, emphasises the 'princely endowment' of land by the earls. Then he goes on to elaborate on the 'vast growth of its estates' through different procedures, purchases of land, acquisition of land 'through lending money on wadsets which were never redeemed, and fines and penalties for breaches of canonical law.' Although he admits that there might have been 'occasional gifts . . . in return for provision and support in old age . . .', he seems to reject the possibility of last-will bequests. (Clouston, 1932, 149.) But undoubtedly the Orkney people on their deathbeds would hardly be less pious than their fellow-beings in Scandinavia, although few or no charters remain to substantiate such bequests.

The rental of the Orkney bishopric's lands and revenue in Caithness presents both palæographic and dating problems.[2] According to Professor Emer G Donaldson the script of the rental seems to represent a hand from about 1500 or even somewhat earlier (personal comm. 1984). Most of the rental denominations used are clearly Scottish, but there are also some interesting ancient terms which seem to be traceable to a Norse background. The townships are assessed in pen-nylands (*d land*) and skatlands (*skaitland*), and we also find *skait malt* and *skait silver*.[3] With regard to the dating of the *imposition* of rents and dues, it is tempting to infer that the bishop of Orkney could hardly have received these townships or been granted the earl's revenue in skat malt and skat silver *after* the constitution of the Caithness bishopric at Dornoch about 1238. (Watt, 1969, 62). There is naturally a possibility that a few of the *touns* might have been willed to St Magnus after this date, but hardly the skat silver and skat malt of two of Caithness' northeastern parishes, Dunnet and Canisbay. A further confirmation of the great age of the Orkney bishopric's landed property in this country is a statement by Bishop Graham, in 1642, that 'They [Lord Caithness, Lord Rae, the Laird of Murchill, the Laird of May] hold of the bishopric [of Orkney] but little parcels of land, serving for the bishop's sojourning there when he stayed at the Pentland Firth' (St Clair, 1911, 18; cp. Peterkin, 1820, III, 21 f.). The different assessment values of the townships (originally single farms) between 24 pennylands (Dounray) and one pennyland (Thuray) render it probable that they represent early bequests from the owners to the bishop (to St Magnus).

Shetland with half its corn-teinds from the churches paid to the bishop, Caithness with some of its land rents, skat malt and skat silver bequested or granted to the same bishop, show the wide range of the resources of the Orkney bishopric during the high middle ages. Finally there is a city outside the confines of the bishopric which contributed to its income. There are at least six references in the official Scottish records about a due or payment from the City of Aberdeen to St Magnus/the bishop of Orkney. In 1328 it amounted to 118s. 4d. In 1341 it had been converted into a cask of wine and three chalders of corn (value: 100s.). (See *RN* IV, 1979, nos. 566, 595, 753, and V, 1979, nos. 560, 561, 648).

We may conclude this section about the development of the bishopric's central organisation and economic basis with the somewhat slanted characterization given by Bishop George Graham of his former bishopric in pre-Reformation days: ' . . . the old bishopric of Orknay was a greate thing, and lay sparsim thro'out the haill parochines of Orknay and Shetland. Besyde his lands, he hade the teynds of auchtene kirks. His lands grew daylie as adulteries and incests increased in the countrey.' (Peterkin, 1820, III, 21). This description, apart from its moral tenor, might just have well have applied to the bishopric of the thirteenth century.

In conclusion it is essential to point out some conspicuous features of the relationship between the earl and the bishop. The physical neighbourhood of the two political leaders became almost an everyday reality after the establishment of the bishop's and the earls' residences at Kirkwall about 1137. St Magnus Cathedral remained as long as the Norse earldom existed, and even longer, the family 'chapel' of the earls. In the partnership between earl and bishop the earl always seems to have had the political leadership at least in all matters concerning the lay government of the islands.

A comparison of the Orkney central church organisation with those of Norway and of Scotland might generally be summarised as a development from the Norse model (see Helle above) to the acceptance of the Scottish pattern (see Cowan, 1961, 43 f. and, 1975–9, 203 f.) during the late twelfth and thirteenth centuries. The main clue to this change is to be sought in the feudalization of the Orkney church through the instrument of appropration. It brought about the disintegration of the old Norse system.

It is hardly possible to give a full picture of the Orkney church of the twelfth and thirteenth centuries without a more thorough treatment of the local church. It is in the local church organisation with its kirks and chapels, its territorial divisions into parishes, that we may find the more 'democratic' features of the early Orkney church, in the sense of a church created by laymen for laymen and dependent on laymen for its sustenance and perpetuation. Initially all churches were the private property of individual families or in collective ownership of a local community. (*Eigenkirche* is the German technical term for this type of church or chapel). Is it at all possible to recreate a plausible picture of the local church in Orkney during the early Norse period? The written sources are practically non-existent, and the remaining archaeological and toponymical material hardly yields direct information on the subject. Neither has it been very much in the focus of earlier and more recent research. To my knowledge, only two historians have studied the *early* local church in Orkney and Shetland at close range. They have both succeeded in reconstructing the main features of its organisation before the thirteenth century—Storer Clouston and Ronald G. Cant. Clouston has given us the classic picture of an early, pre-parochial organisation of the Norse church and the doctrine of the *urisland/eyrisland* chapel system. According to him and his learned friend Hugh Marwick, this system was based on an earlier regular lay division into *eyrislands*, possibly adopted from the pre-Norse, Pictish population of Orkney. The corresponding terms in Gaelic would have been *davach* or *tiruinge* and are actually documented along the coastal areas of Northern and Western Scotland. Clouston assumes that this lay territorial division was introduced into Orkney before the Norse settlers became Christian, and that it facilitated the introduction of a district church organisation by offering an already existing lay system. In his *History of Orkney* he clearly operates with two phases in the development of the local church system—an early period of small urisland districts with a chapel in most urislands ('protoparish churches') and then in the twelfth century the break-through of a more sophisticated ecclesiastical organisation with parishes proper.

> . . . the order of events must have been this: First, a grouping of 'towns' on a geographical basis to form eyrislands for the purpose of skat. Then, for the same reason of geographical convenience, the employment of the same districts as units for early ecclesiastical purposes; the first churches (in the form of private chapels) being erected in them, usually one in each district; though occasionally a couple of families might each build a chapel, or there might only be one chapel for a couple of districts. (1932, 147)

In an earlier publication on 'The Old Chapels of Orkney' (1918, 231 f.) Clouston had given a more specific explanation of the background to the origin of the urisland system: ' . . . districts of a sort—groups of odal kinsmen roughly expressed in land—must have existed from the very beginning [of the Norse settlement], and what Earl Hákon [Pálsson] (if it were he) presumably did, was to redress to some extent inequalities in these [districts] and distribute the legislative and judicial power among a greater number of the "best" families . . . .' It is in such districts with an urisland basis that Clouston finds his *urisland chapels*.

Cant in his article on 'Settlement, Society and Church Organisation in the Northern Isles' has shown some scepticism regarding the pre-Norse roots element in Clouston's theory; that is, to the idea that the territorial divisions of Orkney, both lay and ecclesiastical, should be sought in a Pictish-Gaelic-Christian society. As he puts it: 'It . . . must remain a matter of doubt' that 'the actual units employed were related to an older pattern of territorial divisions . . . .' (1984, 175). It is not difficult to share Dr. Cant's scepticism, but it should probably be extended to comprise the whole concept of an urisland chapel system. Clouston's hypothesis should either be further substantiated by detailed research or discarded entirely.

A chief objection to accepting Clouston's theory, is the lack of contemporary evidence for the term *eyrisland* in the early Norse period. The first direct documentation of the word is to be found in the *Hákonar Saga Hákonarsonar*, ch. 328: 'King Hákon then made a list of the urislands (*eyrislǫnd*) for his *lendirmenn* (barons) and *sveitarhǫfdingjar* (company chiefs) for their sustenance (*vista-taka*).' The date of the king's measure is 1263 shortly before he died in Kirkwall. The only earlier reference in the records to terms of territorial division is the well-known description in the *Orkneyinga Saga* (ch. 76) of how Earl Rognvald and his father Kol ran out of means when building the cathedral:

> Then the Earl sought advice from his father; and Kol proposed that the Earl should bring in a change in the laws. The Earls had in the past inherited all the odal lands from their owners, but the heirs might redeem them; and that was thought rather hard. Then Earl Rognvald had a thing summoned and bade the bonder buy their odal lands once for all, so that there would be no need for heirs to redeem. And that they agreed to, in such a way that all were well pleased. But one mark was to be paid to the Earl for each plough-land (*plógsland*) throughout the isles. And from that time on there was no lack of money for the building of the church.

Plógsland is a rare word in Old Norse literature, only used a couple of times by Snorri in his *Edda* and in *Heimskringla* (see Fritzner, II, 943, and Ynglinga-saga, ch. 5). As plough-land does not appear elsewhere in the *O.S.* or in any Orkney record, it has been suggested that *plógsland* is a scribal error for *penningsland* (pennyland), originating from a manuscript-contraction of pennyland (*pland*; A. Bugge, 1916, 173, and O.S., ed. Taylor, 1938, 387, note 4). Now plough-land is a well-known term of land-measurement in England (*plowland*) as well as in Scotland (*pleuchland* or *plewland*). The Icelandic author of the O.S. is supposed to have written his story shortly before 1200; and from his knowledge of the Orkneys and especially of Caithness, he must have stayed in the earldom for some time. Under these circumstances it is remarkable that the author should be completely ignorant of the Orkney territorial divisions of urislands and pennylands at Earl Rognvald's time (about 1140). It is tempting to infer that no such territorial organisation existed at that time and that it was introduced in connection with the establishment of a parish organisation and the introduction of annual tithes, as being an assessment of the production capacity of a landed property. It goes without saying that this imposition of an ecclesiastical due also offered an excellent opportunity for the earl to take a similar step, introducing some sort of skat malt and skat silver taxation.

An important feature of the early Norwegian church was its private proprietary status. Every church was built on private property and belonged to some lay person or persons, be it the king, a chieftain, a leading farmer or a group of farmers. Even the first so-called head-churches (ON *hǫfuðkirkjur*) must be regarded in their origin as private churches, as they were built on landed property granted by the king: only gradually were they converted into more 'official' churches. Thus churches for greater administrative districts were generally termed head-churches and in some parts of the country county churches (ON *fylkiskirkjur*). Many of the private churches were converted into parish churches before 1153 (when the Nidaros archbishopric was established). But the process took place gradually and was hardly completed until the end of the twelfth century and resulted in the establishment of a fully-fledged parish system. Thus head-churches and parish churches were not created to fit into an already existing lay district division, but they were introduced to meet the religious and political needs of the king and the local people. Hence the Old Norse general term for a parish church is *sóknarkirkja*, meaning the church to which people *sought* for religious edification (*at soekja*—to seek). In conclusion I would like to endorse Helle's conclusion (see above): 'A spontaneous growth of churches, founded by both private persons and local peasant communities, may have coincided with more methodical attempts to establish a system of local churches from above.' Before the parish system was introduced into Orkney, the local church was left to *organise itself*; and it must to a great extent have followed the Norwegian pattern (See also Cant, 1972, 10 f., 1984, 175 f.).

NOTES

1 Prebends were the portions of revenues (from a Cathedral's landed estates) granted to canons as their stipend [editor's note].
2 The rental is in the National Library of Scotland (Adv. MS.49.7.19 [iv]) and has been transcribed by Dr P Anderson of the Scottish Record Office.
3 Skat (ON *Skattr*) was the tax paid in Orkney (and evidently Caithness) to the earl, and in Orkney and Shetland to the King of Norway. It was paid in malt, butter or money [editor's note].

BIBLIOGRAPHY

Sources:
Manuscript:
'The rentale of the bischop of Orknayis landis within Cathnes', Adv. MS. 49.7.19 [IV], National Library of Scotland

Printed sources:
Anderson, A O, ed., 1922, *Early Sources of Scottish History*, ii
Clouston, J S, ed., 1914, *Records of the Earldom of Orkney 1299–1614*
Cowan, I B, ed., 1971, 'Two Early Scottish Taxation Rolls', *The Innes Review*, xxii, 11
DN = *Diplomatarium Norvegicum*, ii, iii, v, 1852, 1855, 1861, C C Lange and C R Unger, eds, Christiania/Oslo

Edda Snorra Sturlusonar, 1926, Finnur Jónsson, ed., Copenhagen

Hákonar saga Hákonarsonar, 1887, G. Vigfússon, ed., Rolls Series (88/2)

Heimskringla, 1941–51, B. Aðalbjarnarson, ed., Íslenzk Fornrit xxvi–xxviii, Reykjavik

Johnston, A W et A, eds, 1907–13, *Orkney and Shetland Records (Diplomatarium Orcadense et Hialtlandense)*, Old-Lore Series, vii

Munch, P A, ed., 1864, *Pavelige Nuntiers Regnskabs- og Dagbøger . . . 1282–1334*, Christiania/Oslo

Orkneyinga saga, 1938, A B Taylor, ed.

Peterkin, A, ed., 1820, *Rentals of the Ancient Earldom and Bishoprick of Orkney*

RN = *Regesta Norvegica*, iv, v, 1979, E Gunnes and H Kjellberg, eds, Oslo

Literature:

Andersen, P S, 1977, *Samlingen av Norge og kristningen av landet 800–1130*, Oslo (Handbok i Norges historie, ii)

Brøgger, A W, 1929, *Ancient Emigrants*

Bull, E, 1914, 'The Cultus of Norwegian Saints in England and Scotland', *Saga Book of the Viking Society*, viii, 135–148

Cant, R G, 1972, 'The Church in Orkney and Shetland and its Relations with Norway and Scotland in the Middle Ages', *Northern Scotland*, i, 1–18

Cant, R G, 1984, 'Settlement, Society and Church Organisation in the Northern Isles', *The Northern and Western Isles in the Viking World, Survival, Continuity and Change*, ed. by A Fenton and H Palsson, 169–79

Clouston, J S, 1918, 'The Old Chapels of Orkney', *Scottish Historical Review*, xv, 89–105, 223–39

Clouston, J S, 1926, 'The Old Prebends of Orkney', *Proceedings of the Orkney Antiquarian Society*, iv, 31–36

Clouston, J S, 1927, *The Orkney Parishes*

Clouston, J S, 1927, 'The Orkney "Bus" ', *Proceedings of the Orkney Antiquarian Society*, v, 41–9

Clouston, J S, 1932, *A History of Orkney*

Cowan, I B, 1961, 'The Development of the Parochial System in Medieval Scotland', *Scottish Historical Review*, xl, 43–55

Cowan, I B, 1967, *The Parishes of Medieval Scotland*, Scottish Record Society, xciii

Cowan, I B, 1975–9, 'Some Aspects of the Appropriation of Parish Churches in Medieval Scotland', *Records of the Scottish Church History Society*, xiii, 203–22

Cowan, I B, 1987, *The Cathedral of St Magnus and its Medieval Bishops*, paper given at the St Magnus Easter Conference, MS

Craven, J B, 1901, *History of the Church in Orkney from the introduction of Christianity to 1558*

Crawford, B E, 1983, 'Birsay and the Early Earls and Bishops of Orkney', *Orkney Heritage*, ii

De Geer, I, 1985, *Earl, Saint, Bishop, Skald—and Music, The Orkney Earldom of the Twelfth Century. A Musicological Study.* Uppsala

Donaldson, G, 1984, 'Some Shetland Parishes at the Reformation', *Essays in Shetland History*, ed. by B E Crawford, 143–60

Dowden, J, 1912, *The Bishops of Scotland*

Fritzner, J, 1883–96, *Ordbog over Det gamle norske Sprog*, i–iii, Christiania/Oslo

Hamre, L, 1958, 'Domkapitel', *Kulturhistorisk Leksikon for nordisk* middelalder, iii, 195–98

Helle, K, 1974, *Norge blir en stat 1130–1319*, Oslo. (Handbok i Norges historie, iii)

Keyser, R, 1856, *Den norske Kirkes Historie under Katholicismen*, i, Christiania/Oslo

Kolsrud, O, 1913, 'Den norske Kirkes Erkebiskoper og Biskoper indtil Reformationen', *Diplomatarium Norvegicum*, xvii B 2

Marwick, H, 1952, *Orkney Farm-Names*

Mooney, J, 1947, *The Cathedral and Royal Burgh of Kirkwall*

Munch, P A, 1849/1971, *Lærde brev fraa og til P.A. Munch*, iii, ed. by T Knudsen and P S Andersen, Oslo

Munch, P A, 1855, *Det norske Folks Historie*, part ii, Christiania/Oslo

Radford, C A, Ralegh, 1962, 'Art and Architecture: Celtic and Norse', *The Northern Isles* ed. by F T Wainwright

St Clair, R, 1911, 'The Bishopric of Orkney. References to Lands in Caithness', *Old-Lore Miscellany of Orkney, Shetland, Caithness and Sutherland*, iv

Seip, E, 1984, *Bispegodset på Orknøyene fra ca.1100 til reformasjonen*. (Hovedoppgave i historie, graduate thesis, 1984–ii)

Taranger, A, 1890. *Den angelsaksiske kirkes indflydelse paa den norske*, Christiania/Oslo

Thomson, W P, 1987, *History of Orkney*

Wainwright, F T, 1962, *The Northern Isles*

Watt, D E R, 1969, *Fasti Ecclesiæ Scoticanæ Medii Aevi ad annum 1638*

Section II: Buildings

The Architectural Achievements of the Age

Architectural achievements are material evidence for the spirit of an age, and the cathedrals of medieval Europe are our most memorable monument of that period of history, giving us insight into the strength of belief which led the patrons, architects and masons to build such magnificent houses for the worship of God. They are all inspired by a common west European culture, reaching back in origin to the style and plan of Roman basilicas, with influences in design traceable from country to country and sometimes from building to building. The cathedrals of Norway have their roots in more southerly examples, so it is not surprising that St Magnus also drew its inspiration from earlier cathedrals and great churches in Scotland and England. Several of the lectures in this section painstakingly traced the links and pinpointed the ultimate source of the design and sculptural detail of the building. Such analyses vividly display the involvement of the patrons of St Magnus' Cathedral with southern culture as known from the architectural developments of Scotland and northern England, and moreover the best and most advanced in technical terms, of that Romanesque culture. When one realises that it was primarily the kings of Scotland or prince-bishops of Durham who were the patrons of this building revolution then the earls of Orkney—in particular Earl Rognvald Kolsson and his father—move into the front rank as patrons of the age. Nowhere north of the central political heartland of Scotland is there a Romanesque building of this quality, but in Kirkwall.

As regards the historical circumstances surrounding the building of St Magnus' we have in Orkney unique and precious knowledge about the background to its founding and construction. In very few places in northern Europe is it actually known why great cathedrals were built and who was responsible for their construction, and if it is then it is usually only the name of a great cleric who is recorded in the cathedral charters as being the inspiration as founder. But for St Magnus Cathedral we actually know why and when and by whom it was founded, from a narrative and nearly contemporary source, the saga of the earls (*Orkneyinga Saga*). This vivid account provides us with a glimmer of understanding of the politics and passions which lay behind its building. That glimpse clearly indicates that its inception and birth was a result of political rivalries in the earldom family (Crawford, 1983, 114–15). Such rivalries were endemic, for the earldom could be claimed by more than one son—primogeniture was unknown—and it was sometimes divided between two or even three sons. Moreover the right to claim the earldom could pass through the female line so that sons of earls' daughters had as much right as sons of sons. It was this custom which enabled Rognvald Kolsson to come from Norway and launch his claim on the earldom through his mother, Gunnhild (see Genealogical Tree following).

Rognvald's claim was a particularly valid one, for he was the male representative of the line of Earl Erlend, one of the two sons of Thorfinn the Mighty who divided the earldom between themselves, and whose sons' quarrels had resulted in the martyrdom of Magnus Erlendsson. As nephew of the martyred earl Rognvald's duty was to press the claim of his line to Erlend's half of the earldom which had been swallowed up by Hakon Paulsson and his two sons in the years since Magnus' death. Twenty years after the event this was a most difficult thing to achieve, especially since the attempt came from outside the islands, and Rognvald needed all the help he could get. That help came from the spiritual support he derived from his murdered uncle whose posthumous fame was steadily increasing. The saga is quite clear that the driving force behind Rognvald's venture and the association of his claim with his holy uncle's name was his father, Kol 'a man of exceptional intelligence' (OS, chap. 58). He it was who suggested that Rognvald make a vow to build a stone minster at Kirkwall 'more magnificent than any in Orkney', dedicate it to the holy Earl Magnus, provide it with endowments, and move to it both his uncle's relics and the episcopal seat (see Cruden, below). Here is a master plan, not only for providing Rognvald with a sacred banner to operate under, but for providing a new earldom political centre and powerbase to operate from once he had succeeded in winning control of his family inheritance and his uncle's legacy.

This was a revolutionary and deliberate political plan, for it involved the setting-up of a rival earldom base to the older power-centre on the Brough of Birsay at the north-west tip of the Orkney Mainland. That had been the main earl's seat since Earl Thorfinn's time in the mid-eleventh century, and an earldom residence possibly since the founding of the earldom in the late ninth century. Earl Thorfinn had brought together the secular and ecclesiastical authorities in his earldom by establishing the first bishop there and building Christchurch for him (see Radford and Andersen, above). When however the earldom was divided between Thorfinn's sons, Paul and Erlend, the latter took the northern and eastern half of the islands and Kirkwall lay just inside his territory, on the important geographical isthmus which provided passage from the waters leading in from the northern Orkney islands to Scapa Flow and the southern sea-roads (see fig. 5). This was also the area of Magnus Erlendsson's rule and a vein of loyalty to this half of the earldom family must have been deep-rooted in the eastern Mainland and northern isles of Orkney (as well as in Shetland) (Crawford, 1984, 71). By the time Kol chose Kirkwall for the site of the new cathedral it had become a small urban centre, with a church dedicated to St Olaf, and was the place where Earl Rognvald held an assembly with the farmers in 1136 (OS, chap. 76). There were probably sound economic reasons as well as political ones for the choice of Kirkwall as the new political centre of the earldom.

The building of a cathedral at Kirkwall was therefore intimately bound up with the political ambitions and aspirations of Earl Rognvald and his father. Once the wily Bishop William had been won over to this plan and become the prime mover in encouraging recognition of Earl Magnus' sanctity, the saint's relics could be moved from their resting-place at Christchurch, Birsay, and brought to their new home at Kirkwall, eventually being housed in the magnificent Romanesque building constructed especially for them. As the private resting-place of the family saint—and of his heir and successor in the earldom, Rognvald, who was also considered to be a holy man after his death—St Magnus' Cathedral is as much a monument to that dynasty and its claims to power as it is to the saint who rested in it. Few royal dynasties were able to achieve as much (see Cambridge, below).

DESCENDANTS OF EARL THORFINN

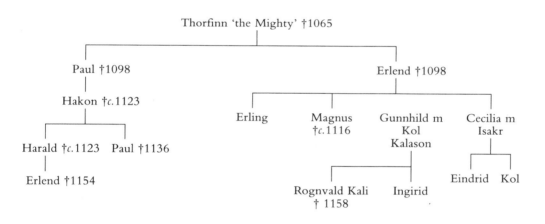

ritage,

·d, ed.

CHAPTER 6

The Romanesque Cathedrals of Norway

Hans-Emil Lidén

The christianisation of Norway (in the broadest sense of the word) took place in the period from the tenth century to approximately 1150 when the archbishopric of Trondheim was established and the Norwegian Curch for the first time became a fully integrated part of the universal catholic church. The process can be divided into three phases:

1. The mission period lasting up to 1030.
2. The establishment of the first form of church organisation and the building of a first group of churches which, without exception, seem to have been built of *wood*. This period lasted from, say, 1030 to 1070.
3. The continuing development of the Norwegian Church, transforming it from a national Church controlled by the king into a part of the universal Church. This final phase which lasted from 1070 to 1150 is characterised by the establishment of permanent episcopal seats and the building of the first bishops' churches (which were the first *stone* churches to be erected in Norway). These early churches differed in some respects from the later cathedrals, which is why I have preferred to call them 'bishops' churches', and their later history shows how the churchmen and architects of the twelfth and thirteenth centuries tried to adjust them to an architectural form common to cathedrals all over Europe.

The British Isles seem to have been involved in each stage of the process. The first missionaries were British, and the primary Norwegian church organisation was probably modelled on an Anglo-Saxon pattern. The third phase, from 1070 to 1150, also shows signs of being influenced from the west, and here the Orkneys seem to have played a very significant role. After having witnessed the death of his father, Harald Hardråde, in the battle at Stamford Bridge in 1066, the king to be, *Olav* (later nicknamed *Kyrre* or 'the Gentle') proceeded to the Orkneys with the rest of the Norwegian army. Here he spent the winter of 1066/67 at Birsay, where Earl Thorfinn a few years previously had started to build a Christ Church at his residence, probably in connection with an attempt to establish a bishopric on the islands. Almost certainly Thorfinn's initiative was inspired from Ireland where the Norse kings had founded bishoprics and built Christ-churches at their residences in Dublin (around 1040) and Waterford (around 1050). The Norse bishoprics in

Ireland did not become part of the Irish church, but were placed directly under Canterbury. Christ-church, Canterbury, also seems to have provided the inspiration for their church dedications.

When King Olav Kyrre returned to Norway in 1067, he brought with him from the Orkneys a priest whom he installed as the first bishop of *Nidaros* (Trondheim) (*DN* V, XVII p. 199). He also started to build *two* Christ-churches, both of which were to become cathedrals later: one in Trondheim, next to the royal residence there, the other in Bergen in the same area where a royal residence was established a few years later. Obviously the building of these churches had something to do with the establishment of permanent episcopal seats. According to Adam of Bremen, in his *Gesta Hammaburgensis* which was written around 1070, the Norwegian bishops travelled around together with the king, 'sharing everything between them in a most brotherly fashion' (*Gesta Hammaburgensis*, 4. Chap. XXXIV). From now on, the country was divided into three sees or dioceses which corresponded to the three main legal districts or *lagdømmer*. The bishops were based in Oslo and Trondheim, and, for western Norway, first at Selje, and then, a little later, in Bergen.

The first Christ-church in Trondheim must have been under construction during the time of Olav Kyrre (he died in 1093) and up to around 1140 when the building of the present cathedral was begun. Remnants of this early church building were noticed in the 1870s when the choir and the transepts of the present church were investigated. Excavations showed that the central piers of the choir rested on the foundations of the original outer walls of the nave of King Olav Kyrre's church. Beneath the octagon to the east of the choir the remains of the earlier chancel with two lateral chapels came to light, and in the crossing, beneath the present tower, the foundations of an older tower, presumably with lateral wings or chapels, were also revealed, (Fischer, 1965, 23ff.). There is some difference of opinion as to the interpretation of this western part of the building. Gerhard Fischer (the great authority on the history of Trondheim cathedral) thought it was a *central* tower with dwarf transepts—an idea which implies that a nave was planned to the west of it. Another suggestion is that it might represent some sort of a *westwork*. Fischer is probably right, assuming that the western part is a secondary addition, a first attempt to enlarge and modernise the original building, a plan which soon was to be replaced by the building of a full-scale transept.

At Selje, a small, barren island on the west coast between Bergen and Trondheim, the ruins of a small church can still be seen (see fig. 3). The church was rebuilt around 1300 when the chancel was enlarged and a west tower was added. The fame of Selje as a holy place goes back to the early eleventh century when the bones of the *Seljemen* (later known as *Sunniva and her followers*) were spotted in a cave on the island. Around 1100 a Benedictine abbey was founded here, probably of English origin since it was dedicated to St Alban. The monks took over the church and built their monastery next to it, but the church had probably been built for the *bishop* who, according to the *Series Episcoporum* resided on the island before he moved permanently to Bergen. It was dedicated to Christ, St Mary and St Alban—the latter dedications probably dating from the time when the monastery was founded.

The early church at Selje had an aisled nave, but was not a regular basilica. The whole structure was covered by a single roof. The walls of the central nave rested on six slender columns with corresponding buttresses in the outer walls which were very thin (approximately 80 cm), and dressed with ashlar. A small chancel terminated the church in the east, (Enger, 1949, 54ff.). Of King Olav Kyrre's Christchurch in Bergen nothing remains. The church was probably completed by 1160. We know that King Magnus Erlingsson was crowned there in 1163. Later in the Middle Ages it was enlarged and rebuilt. In 1530, however, the whole building was torn down with such a thoroughness that even the foundations were obliterated. In Stavanger, on the other hand, the Romanesque fabric is still standing, apart from the original chancel and western tower, both of which were replaced by larger structures at the end of the thirteenth century. Like the churches in Bergen and Trondheim mentioned above, Stavanger was dedicated to Christ and the Holy Trinity. It was, however, also dedicated to St Swithun of Winchester, but this dedication is probably secondary, (Fischer, 1964; Hohler, 1964). When the see of Stavanger was actually founded, is hard to say. The first bishop mentioned is *Reinald*. According to the sagas, he was an Englishman who was hanged in Bergen in 1135, but he is probably the same man who is mentioned as bishop of Stavanger in 1128. As far as we know, the see of Stavanger represents a secondary division of an early, very large West-Norwegian see. It comprised the southern part of this earlier see plus, strangely enough, the two isolated valleys of Hallingdal and Valdres on the other side of the central mountain range. The division of the see may have taken place around 1120 or a little earlier.

The cathedral church as it now stands is a regular basilica of six bays with a long, aisleless thirteenth-century choir to the east, and a decapitated tower, covered by an extension of the nave roof, to the west. The walls of the nave rest on ten cylindrical piers rising from square plinths and carrying square, chamfered abaci. There is no triforium, but clerestorey windows are set directly over the piers, indicating that *vaults* were not planned. These windows, as well as the original aisle windows (the present aisle windows are nineteenth century), were double-splayed without any decoration. The first building campaign in Stavanger included the building of the original chancel (with a crypt), the outer walls of the nave and the lower parts of the first west tower. The easternmost pair of piers in the nave with their arches also belong to this primary building phase. The chancel was a very small structure, approximately square, with sides the same width as the central aisle of the nave. Until 1869 it was cut off from the nave by a narrow chancel arch flanked by two roundheaded openings with their sills some 6 feet above the floor. These openings were probably for doors leading to a rood loft. The original west tower was narrower than the present one. An arch opening, also narrower than the present one, led from the nave into the base of the tower.

The second building campaign saw the erection of the piers and the upper walls of the central nave, and the insertion of two side doors in the aisles. Judging from the details of these doorways, the church was nearing completion around 1150. But when did the work start? The design of the pier capitals and their decoration may give us a clue as to *when* the work started and also by *whom* it was started. The two eastern capitals and their responds in the east wall of the nave are very old-fashioned, compared to the scalloped capitals on the columns of the two doorways. They must be characterised as Norman or early Anglo-Norman and I think they would be dated to around 1070 if found in a church in Normandy or England. Examples of capitals similar to the Corinthian-derived capital in Stavanger include the one surviving capital from archbishop Lanfranc's cathedral at Canterbury and capitals in the crypt of la Trinité in Caen, Normandy. The other capitals may be described as *multicubical* capitals of various shapes. Some of them have been given an embellishment which at least in some cases seems to be secondary. The most conspicuous example is the capital of the pier just inside the south doorway, the lunettes of which are decorated in a manner which shows a close resemblance to the famous carved capitals in the crypt of Canterbury Cathedral from around 1120. The pier capitals, as well as the scalloped capitals of the doorways and the chevron moulding on the voussoirs of the arcades and the doorway arches, demonstrate beyond doubt that English masons must have worked in Stavanger right from the start and up to the completion of the building. Certain details show, however, that masons from other parts of Europe may have worked there as well. The classical mouldings on the pilasters in the west wall of the nave are most uncommon in Anglo-Norman architecture, and so is the character of the figure sculpture on the capital of a respond facing the south doorway. It is generally assumed that this sculpture is ultimately of Lombardic origin, and that it found its way to Stavanger via Bergen and Lund in Sweden. It is tempting to regard the unadorned double-splayed clerestorey windows at Stavanger as another manifestation of Continental influence. Windows of this kind are almost without parallel in Anglo-Norman architecture, but frequent enough in contemporary German and Lombardic buildings. The nearest parallel to the Stavanger windows can be seen in St Mary's in Bergen.

In Oslo, only traces of the medieval Cathedral of St Hallvard have survived. The church was demolished in the seventeenth century. Only the foundations were still intact when Gerhard Fischer excavated the building in 1929–1933, showing a church of a quite different form from that in Stavanger. The most conspicuous novelty was the transept with a central tower over the crossing, placed between a short chancel and an aisled nave of presumably four bays. To the west, the church was probably terminated by a twin-towered front (Fischer, 1950, 94ff.). According to the sagas, St Hallvard's was at least under construction in 1130 when King Sigurd was buried in the south wall of the choir. The church-plan, as we know it, could be the result of a rebuilding after the fire which ravaged the church and the town in 1137.

The see of Hamar was established in 1152. Consequently the building of Hamar Cathedral must have started after that year. Today, the church stands as a ruin, but the south wall of the nave with its three stocky piers is still standing more or less intact. The church was obviously modelled on St Hallvard's in Oslo. As in the Oslo cathedral, the eastern part of the building was extended later in the Middle Ages, but we find the same original short chancel, transepts and tower over the crossing, an aisled nave of four bays and a twin-towered west front with a gallery. The six cylindrical piers in the nave are crowned with foliated capitals which, together with the framing of the west doorway, suggest a date of completion around 1200. As in Stavanger, there is no triforium but clerestorey windows set above the piers in a way which render impossible any vaulting of the central nave. The side-aisles, however, seem to have been covered from the outset by longitudinal barrel-vaults intersected by transverse arches corresponding with the arcading, (Nordhagen, 1908, 211).

In Trondheim ambitious plans for a new cathedral were launched around 1140. They may have something to do with the fact that Trondheim became the seat of an archbishop in 1152. Typically, the building operations started with the erection of a full-scale transept with a central tower. This transept still exists as the oldest part of the present cathedral. The Trondheim transepts were not aisled, but two large, two-storeyed chapels were added to the east walls. It is worth mentioning that chapels of this kind, which—as far as I know—are without parallels in English cathedral architecture of the period, were copied in St Magnus in Kirkwall when the transept chapels were rebuilt after 1160. Originally, the Trondheim transepts were planned with two storeys only; a third storey was added some 40 years later. The details show that English masons—probably from Lincoln—must have worked in the church. The doorways leading to the chapels are sumptuously decorated with chevron mouldings, scalloped capitals etc. In the upper storeys Transitional and Early Gothic forms are introduced.

As was mentioned earlier a distinction is being made between 'bishops' churches' and cathedrals proper—reserving the latter word for churches with transepts. Let me explain why I make this distinction. There are several reasons why the early churches should not be called cathedrals, even if they were built to be used by a bishop. Firstly, more than one bishop's church seem to have existed, or at least to have been planned, within a diocese: for instance, the churches of Selje and Bergen, both of which were situated within the West-Norwegian diocese. This could even be the case with Stavanger if the building of this church was started before the separate diocese of Stavanger had been established. This is inconsistent with canon law.

The churches were not *built* like ordinary cathedrals. It is difficult to understand how, say Stavanger, could have functioned as a cathedral. From the outset there was simply no room in the church for the clergy, who staffed it, to sing the office. A diminutive chancel was cut off from the rest of the church by a narrow chancel arch and, as the lateral openings suggest, a rood loft. Thus, there was no possibility of choir stalls extending into the nave. Only after the rebuilding of the chancel in the last quarter of the thirteenth century was ample room provided for the singing of the Mass. Ordinary cathedrals, in the European sense, were introduced in Scandinavia by the building of the cathedral in Lund in Scania, now a part of southern Sweden (see fig. 4). Lund became the seat of an archbishop in 1103, and soon afterwards the building of a new, appropiate church started. As can be seen from the ground plan, the transepts formed a significant part of the structure. East of the transepts a rather tiny chancel was built. There was no central tower over the crossing, but a twin-towered west front was added to the aisled nave.

I am quite certain that Lund served as a type model for the cathedrals at Oslo and Hamar in Eastern Norway, although the central towers and the cylindrical piers of these two churches suggest another source of architectural influence than Lund. It is perhaps worth-while noticing that when the rebuilding of Christ-church, Trondheim, was determined, they started with the building of the transepts.

What we are witnessing here is, in my opinion, a change of architectural form which must be interpreted as a visible sign of an underlying process, namely the 'internationalisation' of the early national churches of Denmark and Norway. The first archbishop of Lund, Archbishop Asker, was an ardent advocate of Cluniac reform, and in Norway, Archbishop Eystein (1160–83) became the first church leader who really opposed the king. If we now turn to the Orkneys, it seems quite clear that a parallel process took place there. With St Magnus Cathedral the fully-developed European cathedral—admittedly on a modest scale—was introduced to the islands. St Magnus certainly represents a big step forward, compared to the bishop's church on Birsay. So far, the parallel holds good. But if we look at the architecture of St Magnus, no sign of any reciprocal influence between it and the Norwegian monuments can be traced. The pedigree of St Magnus includes Durham and Dunfermline, while the two Norwegian churches which still can be studied, reveal influence from other centres within the Anglo-Norman region.

BIBLIOGRAPHY

DN = Diplomatarium Norvegicum. Vol. I–XX, Christiana/Oslo, 1847–1915
Gesta Hammaburgensis = Adam av Bremen, Gesta Hammaburgensis Ecclesiae Pontificum. Transl. by Carsten L Henrichsen, Cop.h. 1968

Enger, C, 1949, 'Helligdommen på Selja', *Fortidsminneforeningens årbok* 1946, 5ff
Fischer, G, 1950, *Oslo under Eikaberg*, Oslo
Fischer, G, 1964, *Domkirken i Stavanger*, Stavanger
Fischer, G, 1965, *Domkirken i Trondheim*, Vol. I–II, Oslo
Hohler, C, 1964, 'The Cathedral of St Swithun at Stavanger in the Twelfth Century', *Journal of the Archaeological Association*, Third Series, Vol. XXVII
Nordhagen, O, 1908, 'Hamar domkirkes ruiner', *Fortidsminneforeningens årbok* 1907

CHAPTER 7

The Founding and Building of the Twelfth-Century Cathedral of St Magnus[1]

Stewart Cruden

In *Orkneyinga Saga* it is related how, after an unsuccessful attempt to recover his Orkney heritage from Earl Paul Hakonsson, the nephew of Earl Magnus, Rognvald Kolson, makes a long and eloquent speech in Norway proclaiming his intention to do or die in a second attempt. His speech is applauded heartily and he is promised help for another expedition. Then up stood Kol (his father) and said

> we have heard from the Orkneys that all men there wish to rise against thee, and defend thy realm against thee along with Earl Paul; they will be slow to give over their emnity when once they have taken up arms against thee, kinsman. Now my advice is to seek for help where it is abundant, for I think that he may grant thee thy realm who had it by right—I mean St Magnus the Earl, thy uncle. I desire that, to provide for his granting thee the ancestral lands that are thine and were his, thou make a vow to have a church of stone built in Kirkwall in the Orkneys, when thou gainest thy realm, so that there be not a more magnificent in the land; and let it be dedicated to St Magnus the earl thy kinsman. And let it be endowed so that the foundation may increase and that to it may be brought his relics and with them the Episcopal seat. (*Orkneyinga Saga*, ed. Taylor).

This passage is often quoted or paraphrased in histories of the cathedral which commonly say it was founded in memory or in honour of St Magnus. That is true enough, but does not get to the heart of the matter. The foundation was much more than a pious gesture of remembrance. It was the fulfilment of a contract. 'Seek help where it is abundant', said Kol, 'for I think that *he* may grant thee thy realm who had it by right. I mean St Magnus the Earl, thy uncle.'

That was said in 1136, and Earl Magnus had been dead for about 20 years, yet he is spoken of as though alive and effective still. This last-minute advice of the shrewd and practical Kol is a striking illustration of that medieval belief in the power of relics and the continuing presence of the saints which is so difficult for us to understand today. The dead saints were among those present still, to give counsel, lend their aid, receive presents, even to sign documents, and in their relics resided their awful power. Every church was eager to possess them, and every king. They influenced the very design of churches. The influential part they played in

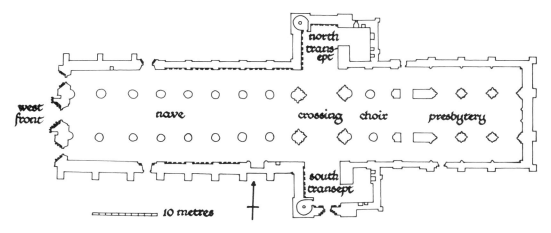

FIGURE 6   Plan of St Magnus Cathedral (Richard Fawcett)

the founding and building of St Magnus Cathedral in Kirkwall is of great significance in the interpretation of its architecture (pl. 2; fig. 6).

The style of the architecture, the characteristics of its plan, the details of design and construction, and its known building history, all agree with the saga story, and allow us to acknowledge 1137 as the formal foundation date and probable beginning of the work.

'The work on it went on faster for the first three years than during the four or five years following', continues the narrative, and we are reminded of the building of Canterbury Cathedral in the early twelfth century: 'You do not know which to admire the most,' wrote William of Malmesbury about it, 'the beauty or the speed.' Praise of a good start was probably literary convention, but it proclaims a virtue in speed and indicates a real possibility that initial impetus could raise the choir of a church a great deal faster than average building progress of other parts. At Kirkwall they did indeed run quickly out of funds. Ambition outran resources, and the interruption was so severe that it was rectified only by legislation permitting the outright sale of odal land rights to the people, with a building tax deducted from the proceeds, 'and thenceforward there was no lack of money for the building of the church and it became a magnificent structure' (*Orkneyinga Saga*, ed. Taylor, 261).

Like so many notable ancient monuments in this remarkable country, the richest archaeological area in the British Isles, it is more than a good example of its kind, it is absolutely outstanding. The choir, which is the earliest part, is the finest Romanesque work north of Durham which inspired it, while contrasting red and white stones in alternate courses, voussoirs and arch rings, must have invested the building with an almost eastern splendour. This is not so fanciful as it sounds. In sunshine Orkney sea and sky have an extraordinary brilliance.

The later twelfth-century nave and the thirteenth-century extension of the choir are also notable, but it is the original choir which really distinguishes the church

PLATE 2 St Magnus Cathedral from the south–east (Crown copyright, HBM Directorate).

PLATE 3   St Magnus Cathedral, the choir *c.*1140 (Crown copyright, RCAMS).

(pl. 3). It stands as a lasting memorial to the Norse dominions west-over-seas, to remind us that they were not the cultural backwaters they are too often assumed to be, but in the full stream of European cultural and artistic development. It was founded by a Norseman, named after a Norseman, for the veneration of Norsemen, but the architecture suggests that it was designed and built by masters and masons from Durham Cathedral whose main walling was up to the wall-heads about 1130. They came it seems by way of Dunfermline Abbey which has even more persuasive Durham indications. The dates are right for an exodus of the Durham workforce to the north, in the years following 1130.

No dedication or consecration date is known which would signalise the completion of at least the east end, but in 1151 the founder and his bishop departed from Orkney on a two-year crusade to the Holy Land and back, an adventure which had been discussed with the King of Norway in 1148. It is unlikely that they would leave before the choir was completed and the relics of St Magnus enshrined within it. With the work advancing as rapidly as the saga says it did an eastern limb of three bays with Durham-style apses could have been completed by 1142 or thereby (figs. 7; 11).

It is interesting to recall the observations of the monk Gervase of Canterbury in his well-known and illuminating account of the rebuilding of that church after the great fire of 1174. He relates how the first year was preparation, 'and in the following year . . . . . . before the winter he (William of Sens) erected four columns, that is, two on each side, and after the winter two more were placed, so that on each side were three in order, upon which and upon the exterior wall of the aisles he framed seemly arches and a vault . . . . . . with these works the second year was occupied' (Willis, 1845). For St Magnus that would give us vaulted aisles and the main arcade of three bays up to the level of the triforium, in two years, and in the third year the triforium and clerestorey. Allow another year or two for the apse and the return of the aisle walls into the transepts, and a certain urgency in exhibiting the relics, and we have a possible dedication date of c.1142/45. The transepts up to triforium level, three bays of the north wall of the nave up to the wall-head, plus half a window and a complete wall arcade of the fourth bay, with similar although not identical progress on the south side, and with columns to correspond, is the visible surviving extent of the first-period style (fig. 8). It is characterised by exceedingly heavy window-heads with label-mouldings, and eight-sided cubical capitals for the principal piers.

Nothing of the original crossing remains, unless re-used in the new crossing which was boldly inserted probably about 1170, presumably after a collapse of the original crossing-tower. Although notably pointed, with deep mouldings and water-leaf capitals, the new work did not disdain the old, and the arches adjacent to the crossing were carefully refashioned, for example in the first bay of the nave on the south side, where incised chevron ornament represents the original arch which has been half-demolished and rebuilt without it.

The polychrome treatment of the architectural elements, by a counterchange of red and white building stone (not just painted decoration) is worth a special mention for it has never received due recognition, probably because some of it is

4 St Magnus Cathedral, the west facade. (Gunnie Moberg).

5   St Magnus Cathedral, the west window designed by Crear McCartney for the
850th Anniversary of the founding. Its theme is Light, flooding over the islands and
cliffs of Orkney. At the top is the battle-axe, symbolising St Magnus's martyrdom
and sanctified by the dove, symbol of the Holy Spirit.

FIGURE 7   St Magnus Cathedral, end of phase 1, *c*.1137 to *c*.1142 (Stewart Cruden).

FIGURE 8   St Magnus Cathedral, end of first period style, *c*.1145 to 1150 (Stewart Cruden).

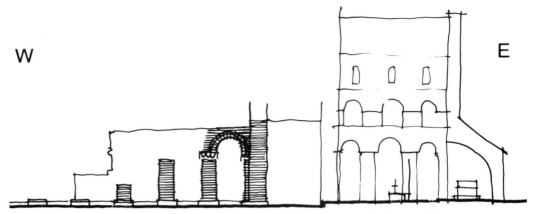

FIGURE 9   St Magnus Cathedral, progress westwards after *c.*1145 to 1150, north arcade of the nave (Stewart Cruden).

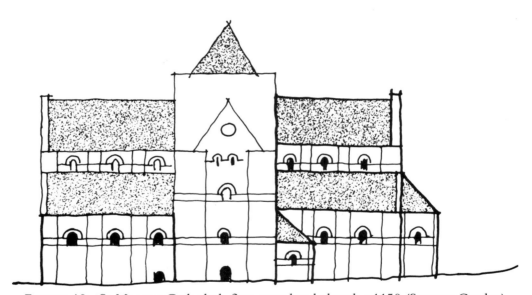

FIGURE 10   St Magnus Cathedral, first completed church *c.*1150 (Stewart Cruden).

not too easy to see, the choir having been, at one time rendered hideous by pews, galleries, whitewashed, pinkwashed and yellow-ochred pillars. It is a very remarkable scheme, especially so in a country where freestone is scarce, and it is thorough. The banded masonry of the east transept walls turns into the choir aisles and the very jambs of their windows. It lies over a wide diapered string-course such as Dunfermline has, and this returns into the choir aisle also, as does the plain flagstone walling below it, which would be plastered. The arch-rings of the main and triforium arcades, and of the windows, exhibit all variations of red and white counterchange.

The end of the Romanesque church was a completed east limb with the transepts and three east bays of the nave up as high as the window-heads (figs. 8; 9). The first piers next the crossing were completed and arched to buttress the crossing. The second were completed but not arched, the third were half-built and the fourth pair was started, all their bases having been laid, and the bench for the wall arcade, before building in height began. It is this sort of picture, therefore, which we should have in our mind's eye when we think of St Magnus Cathedral about 1150 (fig. 10).

It is singularly unfortunate that the apse of the east end was demolished in the early thirteenth century to make way for the additional choir, good though it is, for the surviving evidence suggests the influence of the cult or relics upon its plan and design. The eastmost bays of the Romanesque choir, whose arches on north and south spring from massive rectangular piers, is uncommonly narrow, the arches noticeably small and underscaled. The sudden change in size suggests a passage across the choir between the apse and the reredos of the high altar. No better explanation suggests itself for this unusual deviation from the regular rhythm of a main arcade. But the suggestion of a passage across the choir, passing behind the altar and in front of the apse, recalls the saga and the cult of relics (fig. 11).

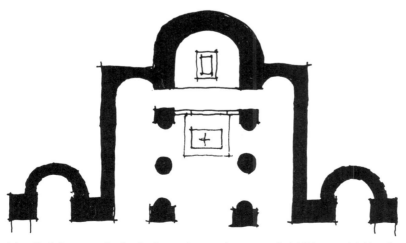

FIGURE 11 St Magnus Cathedral, conjectural east end 1137 to c.1142, showing altar, cross passage and shrine in the apse.

Earl Magnus' remains were first interred in Christ Church, on the Brough of
Birsay, which had been founded for the bishop by Earl Thorfinn in the mid-eleventh
century. Some twenty-one years later the relics of the sainted Magnus were
disinterred, enshrined, and taken to Kirkwall and the shrine 'set over the high altar
in the church that was there.' (*Sette skrin ufir altari*) In Old Norse *skrin* is a loan-word
from the Latin *scrinium* which at this date would have the meaning of portable shrine
or reliquary. It is so used by Honorius of Autun in a near-contemporary record,
*arca testamenti a sacerdotibus portabatur et scrinium vel feretrum cum reliquiis a protitoribus
portatur*. Later in the Middle Ages the meaning was extended to include the permanent architectural shrine which was a separate erection behind or to the east of the
high altar.[2]

Many men and women from as far as Unst in the Shetland islands now came to
the shrine, and among them were two who despoiled it by stealing gold from it.
The saga narrative is circumstantial and we may conclude from it and the foregoing
indications that the shrine was an enriched casket containing if not the whole body
then at least representative bones. This accords with the early twelfth-century practice of placing reliquaries in prominent places, frequently upon a beam over an altar,
as Gervase of Canterbury describes in a vivid passage in his account of the great
fire and rebuilding there, to which reference has already been made. 'And now the
people ran to the ornaments of the church, and began to tear down the *pallia* and
curtains, some that they might save, but some to steal them, the reliquary chests
were thrown down from the high beam and broken, and their contents scattered;
but the monks collected them and carefully preserved them from the fire.'

When the new cathedral was begun in Kirkwall in the name of a saint to whom
the founder felt a personal obligation the shrine would inevitably be the most
important thing about it and it would have been in accordance with the custom
of the time to erect a permanent shrine of fitting splendour in the great eastern apse
which St Magnus Cathedral may be presumed to have had. There is good reason
to believe that this is what was done.

Such an arrangement ingeniously adapted and prolonged the life of the traditional apse which had been the usual termination since the early Christian times
when it contained the benches of the clergy round its wall with the bishop's throne
in the middle. With the development of the cult of relics and the consequent need
to provide circulation for pilgrims within the church the apse ceased to be the synthronon and became the repository of the shrine. The east end of Durham, which
was probably the model for Kirkwall, was sanctified by the shrine of St Cuthbert
in just this position, which was one of great convenience. At Kirkwall a passage
behind the altar screen would provide easy access to the apse by way of the side
aisles of the choir and would ensure no distractions at the altar and choir stalls. This
is good planning. From the cult of relics there thus developed a division of the
eastern limb of the greater churches. The arrangement is still preserved in
Westminster Abbey, but few examples survive because the original Romanesque
apses have everywhere been demolished to make way for the inevitable later expansion of the choir, which happened at Kirkwall too.

The last historical reference to the relics in Kirkwall is for the winter of 1263, when the remnants of the Norse fleet returned to Kirkwall, after its defeat at Largs and the great King Hakon died in the adjacent Bishop's Palace. Shortly before he died, thinking that a cure might be effected by the sanctity of the relics of St Magnus, he walked to the cathedral and round the shrine. But his sickness steadily increased. For consolation he had Latin works read to him, but finding this too great a strain books in the familiar Norse tongue were read instead, both night and day; first the *Lives of the Saints* and then the *Sagas of the Kings of Norway*, one after the other. By the 15 December 1263 he was too weak to speak, 'near midnight Sverri's Saga was finished, and just as midnight was past Almighty God called King Hakon from this world's life'. Until winter was over he was temporarily laid to rest in state before the shrine of the saint in the adjacent cathedral, presumably in the new choir. On Ash Wednesday the 5 March 1264, his coffin was solemnly lifted and carried to his flagship in Scapa Flow and sailed back to Bergen for final burial in Christ Church there, a symbolic departure of the Norse power west-over-seas.

St Magnus Cathedral was founded and endowed by the Norse earls. As Earl's property it came into the possession of James III who took over the Earldom of Orkney in 1470. As royal property it was granted to the people of Kirkwall in 1486. Since then it has belonged to the Magistrates, Councillors and inhabitants of Kirkwall. Their right to ownership has been challenged from time to time by powerful forces. The various attempts which have been made to deprive the town of its most splendid possessions are but repetitions of similar challenges to other Norse medieval private churches, especially in Iceland, where they have been likewise stoutly resisted.

For ten years (1844–1854) the church totally ceased to be a place of worship and was an Ancient Monument. The Crown's claim of ownership was finally defeated and the £3,000 it had so recently spent on repair and renovation was gratefully acknowledged as a donation towards maintaining an object of public interest.

NOTES

1. This paper is an abbreviated version of an account recently advanced in *Scottish Medieval Churches*, 113–26 (1986). I have dealt in greater detail with the relics in 'The cathedral and relics of St Magnus, Kirkwall', in M Apted, R Gillyard-Beer and A D Saunders (eds) *Ancient Monuments and their Interpretation* (1977), 85–96.
2. For those two quotations and their interpretations I am wholly indebted to the generous scholarship of Dr C A Ralegh Radford.

BIBLIOGRAPHY

Willis, R, 1845, *The Architectural History of Canterbury Cathedral*

Chapter 8

Kirkwall Cathedral: an Architectural Analysis

Richard Fawcett

Kirkwall Cathedral is a stimulating building to study, at a variety of levels: perhaps not least because of its appearance of being an essentially Romanesque building of very great scale, despite this appearance being at least partly misleading on two counts. On the count of scale the cathedral can hardly compete with the great Anglo-Norman cathedrals, such as that of Durham with which it has so often been compared. In its original form Kirkwall was only about half the size of that cathedral, and very much in the same league as Dunfermline Abbey; yet it is a measure of the skills of the master masons of both Kirkwall and Dunfermline that they have been able to convey a sense of scale out of all proportion with real size. On the count of being a Romanesque building, architectural subtlety is again a factor, since much less of the building is in fact Romanesque than first appearances might suggest. The later masons of the cathedral took the architectural forms estab-lished by their first predecessors as the guide for their work and, despite the inor-dinate length of time it took to complete, the end result is a building of remarkable homogeneity.

The sense of architectural unity which the cathedral offers makes the attempt to distinguish between the phases of its construction particularly intriguing, and it is on this aspect that I intend to concentrate. I shall also be looking sideways at com-parable buildings elsewhere in order to clarify the relative dating of the constituent parts, although it is for others to place it within its precise architectural context.

The progression of the architectural detail suggests that, when Earl Rognvald began construction of the cathedral in 1137, he started, as was more common, at the east end. Thus the high altar, the focus of the building's liturgical life, could be accommodated as soon as possible, along with the shrine of St Magnus. However, although much of the first eastern limb of three bays still survives, there is a great deal that we do not know about it, including the form of its eastern ter-mination. The ground levels within the choir have been so extensively disturbed in the various restoration projects from the 1840s onwards, that it now seems very unlikely that sufficient archaeological evidence will have survived for the plan ever to be determined with absolute confidence. Nevertheless, it must be seen as prob-able that previous writers have been correct in assuming that the central part ter-minated in a semi-circular apse as a foil to the high altar and the shrine. In addition, some evidence suggests that the flanking aisles terminated externally in straight walls (Mooney, 1924–5, 74). On this basis we can assume that the choir had the configuration still to be seen in several of the greater churches of Normandy, with a tall central apse projecting from straight walls.

If so much is likely, a remaining question is how the aisles were finished internally. At Durham, for example, excavation has shown that the straight external walls enclosed semi-circular apses, as was also the case at a number of churches in Normandy. It is a possibility that a similar arrangement was planned at Kirkwall; however, the surviving details indicate that such flanking apses were not in fact built here, since the decorative string courses on the eastern respond of the south arcade extend further east than would be expected if there were to be sufficient space for an enclosed apse (pl. 4a).

Nevertheless, it is possible that what we now see represents a change from the plan as first laid out. In particular, the curious arrangement of an eastern half bay after the two full bays of the choir arcade could point to such a change. Although this half bay was built with arches of a similar form to those in the full choir bays, it is most unusual in the way it rises from straight sided jambs rather than on more orthodox piers or responds. I know of no precise parallel for such an arrangement, and it could be that there was originally intended to be a continuous wall on each side flanking enclosed apses in the aisles, as at Durham. Certainly the half bay width would be of an appropriate size for this purpose, and the present arrangement may be thought to have some of the hall marks of an *ad hoc* change of design made after the footings and lower walls had been laid out, but before work had progressed far.

Turning to the internal elevation of Rognvald's choir, its design places the cathedral within the northern British context, including of course, mainland Scotland. The three-storeyed elevations, with cylindrical piers and relatively simple tiering of arches in each bay, is comparable with such as the fragmentary nave of Carlisle Cathedral, where work was in progress in the earlier 1130s. Comparisons may also be made with the rather more sophisticated work at Southwell, in Nottinghamshire, where work had begun on the collegiate church in about 1108, and was still in progress when Kirkwall was started. But the closest analogies for the first phase of the work are with Dunfermline Abbey, with which a comparison of scale has already been made. Dunfermline was probably started in, or soon after, 1128, which was an opportune moment for giving employment to some of the Durham masons who had been displaced following the death of Bishop Ranulf Flambard in that year. However, the surviving nave can only have been started a little before the commencement of work at Kirkwall.

Comparison of the details of Kirkwall and Dunfermline suggests that it was Dunfermline which started off with the more lavish funding, but which eventually had to be completed with much penny pinching. By contrast, the start of Kirkwall suggests a tighter budget, which became less restricted as the work progressed. The similarities between the two churches are particularly striking in the arcades and aisle windows, in which the shared use of bands of billet mouldings across the outer arch orders is perhaps most notable. But at this stage of the operation Kirkwall was not attempting to copy the full range of decorative effects seen at Dunfermline. One only has to note the absence of wall arcading compared with Dunfermline where

PLATE 4a St Magnus Cathedral, south choir aisle looking west showing the half bay to the east of the two full bays of the arcade, and the two tiers of string courses on the eastern respond (Crown copyright, HBM Directorate).

PLATE 4b   St Magnus Cathedral, south choir aisle looking east (Crown copyright, HBM Directorate).

PLATE 5 St Magnus Cathedral, choir and presbytery from the north-east, showing the exposed arch of the transept gallery at the west end of the aisle roof. The changes at clerestory level are also evident. (Crown copyright, HBM Directorate).

PLATE 6   St Magnus Cathedral, the south flank of the choir showing the early thirteenth century form of the aisle corbel table: it can be compared with the corbel table of the heightened clerestory. (Crown copyright, HBM Directorate).

there is also use of full wall shafts to divide the aisle bays and provide visual support for their vaults. Further comparison with Dunfermline reveals an even more significant omission in the choir flanks of Kirkwall in their final form. Whereas at Dunfermline, as also at Durham, the outer walls of the gallery stage above the aisles were originally raised high enough to allow the provision of windows at this intermediate level, at Kirkwall the walls were only carried up high enough to clear the aisle vaults. This is remarkable, since the gallery openings into transepts are of the same size as those in the choir, and thus call for a gallery roof high enough to clear them. Without a high roof these arches are awkwardly left partly exposed on the exterior, and there can be little doubt that this must represent another change from the first intentions (pl. 5). Further support for this comes from the evidently early thirteenth century character of the south aisle wall head corbel table (pl. 6), and from the way in which the twelfth-century heads of the north corbel table show all the signs of having been re-set. Together this evidence points to the choir aisle wall heads having either been rebuilt or left unfinished in the first campaign, and only completed when the fashion for high galleries had generally passed.

Apart from later modifications in the roof form of the galleries it should be mentioned here that there is a significant change in design between the gallery arches on the two sides of the choir. Whereas the piers of those on the south are of simple rectangular section—except for the western respond which was rebuilt with the crossing piers—those on the north are of stepped profile, corresponding to the profile of the supported arches.

The first building campaign extended from the choir, through the transepts, and into the eastern parts of the nave. The structural problems of building to any great height without adequate abutment probably meant that the lower masonry of the transepts and eastern nave walls was under construction even before the choir itself was complete. It has already been said that the work became more detailed as it progressed. This is seen initially in the introduction of a simple external plinth course in the transepts—although it was omitted on the north side of the nave—and in the elaboration of the internal lower walls by the provision of intersecting wall arcading below the windows. It is a tantalising possibility that this greater richness of detail might be linked with Rognvald's re-establishment of the building finances on a firmer footing, as recorded in the *Orkneyinga Saga*. (*Orkneyinga Saga*, 1981, 142).

The use in the nave of intersecting wall arcading carried on twinned shafts has naturally suggested comparison with the similar feature at Durham. However, whilst Durham could have been the ultimate inspiration of this and other ideas, there is a different sense of scale at Kirkwall, which may indicate the transmission of the idea through an intermediary. Intersecting arcading is found in many of the better endowed building operations of the period, but potentially significant analogies may be drawn with such as Leuchars church in Fife. At both Leuchars and Kirkwall there is the motif of a triangular spur between the paired shafts, albeit at Leuchars it is used in association with the simple arches of the apse rather than the intersecting arches of the choir flanks. Both the detailing and scale may be taken as pointers to the likelihood of continuing reliance on masons who reached Orkney through Lowland Scotland as the work progressed.

PLATE 7 St Magnus Cathedral, wall arcading in the nave. (Crown copyright, HBM Directorate).

It is the wall arcading which provides one of the clearest clues to the extent of the first building campaign in the nave (pl. 7). On the south side it continues into the fifth bay from the crossing, and in the sixth bay the rear arch of the processional doorway at this point is also clearly Romanesque, although the external jambs and arch date from a late rebuilding. Above the wall arcade the evidence is confused by harsh restoration on the exterior. But, internally, it is clear that no more than the first two south aisle windows were part of the first operation, and the easternmost of those was itself later rebuilt. Turning to the north aisle, the fully Romanesque wall arcading extends no further than the fourth bay from the crossing, and above the arcading only three and a half of the aisle windows are part of the Romanesque campaign. Even less of the main arcades of the nave can be attributed to this part of the construction. Only the first of the great cylindrical piers on the north and the first two on the south are entirely of this campaign, on the indications of their scalloped capitals. However, other piers may have been at least started at the same time, since the first five piers on each side do have essentially similar bases.

The walls of both the choir and the transepts seem to have been taken up to the full intended height at their points of junction with each other against the tower

PLATE 8 St Magnus Cathedral, the eastern limb from the south, showing the extended presbytery, the rebuilt transep. chapel, the raised clerestory and the thirteenth-century tower. (Crown copyright, HBM Directorate).

in the first campaign (although the way in which the transept gables were eventually completed may suggest the north and south walls had only reached gallery height in this operation). The internal transept elevations were largely conditioned by what was designed for the choir and nave. Tall arches led into the aisles, and above them were the large openings into the ends of the choir and nave galleries which have already been discussed in connection with the choir gallery roofs. Additionally on the east sides of the transepts, arches similar to those opening into the choir aisles were constructed to give access to the transept chapels. These chapels are generally assumed to have been first laid out to an apsidal plan, although nothing now remains of them in their original form and it is by no means certain that they had been completed. Above these were smaller arches to the wall passage which corresponded to the galleries in the choir, whilst at the highest level were the clerestorey windows, through which a second mural passage passed.

However, before the transepts were completed, and in advance of the main effort of raising the central vessel of the nave, the decision was taken to make major changes in the design of the building. This must have called for the demolition of considerable masses of masonry which had been raised only a little earlier. Slight changes of design in the nave aisles, which will be discussed later, suggest that, for a few years before this major campaign of alterations, work had been progressing in a rather faltering manner. The new effort therefore indicates both a new infusion of funds at a critical stage of the work, and also perhaps the intervention of a more dynamic driving force. Could this new impetus correspond with the election of Bishop Biarni Kolbeinsson after the death of William II in 1188? His long episcopate would cover much of an important building period, and he would seem to have been a man of some energy. (Dowden, 1912, 256: and see Cant, below).

From the evidence it appears that a new crossing, enlarged transept chapels and a greatly extended eastern limb were all started virtually simultaneously—an act of great optimism which reflected the changed architectural and ecclesiastical ideas of the time (pl. 8). If we are to look for reasons, it may be that the transept chapels were rebuilt because the old ones were outmoded and cramped, and their new plan is of some interest. As newly set out they were rectangles which were originally joined in their full height to the rest of the church only towards the transepts, albeit with lower connecting sections on the flank next to the choir. It is possible that in adopting such a plan for the remodelled chapels the earlier rectangular transept chapels at the mother church of the province at Trondheim were a factor. Yet it must also be said that similar chapels are to be found in England at about the same date as Kirkwall, as for example in the two-storeyed transept chapels at Chichester Cathedral of about 1187 to 1199.

Although the justification for the eastward extension of the choir was presumably to provide an enlarged presbytery and to permit the removal of the choir stalls eastward from the crossing and nave, its planning at this stage of the operation may suggest that augmentation of the cathedral establishment was under consideration. On the evidence of the base heights, three full bays appear to have been intended for a slightly elevated presbytery, though the decorative wall arcading of the lower east wall suggests the altar itself may have been placed a little way to its west. (The intended position of the shrine of St Magnus in the extended presbytery is unknown, but it may well have been transferred to the area behind the altar, a favourite position for an important shrine.) In considering the plan of the new eastern limb it should be remembered that the turn of the twelfth and thirteenth centuries saw many such rectangular eastward extensions to the greater churches of the British Isles, which allowed them to hold the clergy in a more dignified manner within an architecturally distinct part of the structure, and again this suggests that it was Anglo-Scottish influences which were paramount in this phase of the work at Kirkwall.

From the similarity of their base courses it is clear that the transept chapels and the presbytery were laid out at the same time as each other. Yet the carving on the decorative capitals in the two parts shows that the main brunt of work on the presbytery was postponed until the crossing area and transept chapels were well advanced. In the crossing and the chapels water leaf foliage was widely used. That on most of the high crossing pier caps, with the exception of those at the north-east corner, is of relatively stereotyped form, and calls for little comment. By comparison the caps which embellish the transept chapels are more interesting (pl. 9).

PLATE 9   St Magnus Cathedral, a water leaf capital on the east window of the south transept chapel.

In the deep undercutting between the angle leaves, their strong ribbing and intermediate leaves, they show similarities with caps in the transepts of Ripon collegiate
church in Yorkshire, which were probably carved in the 1180s. Related carving
of around the 1190s is also to be found in northern England on such as the west
door of the Cistercian abbey church of Byland in Yorkshire, or in the choir of the
Northumbrian Benedictine priory of Tynemouth. On the basis of these comparisons a date around the last decade of the twelfth century seems most likely for
the transept chapels and crossing area of Kirkwall.

Turning to the upper parts of the crossing area, its remodelling can be seen to
have called for considerable rebuilding of the high walls on those three sides which
must have reached an advanced stage by that point of the operation. The water leaf
capitals of the windows at clerestorey level in the bays of the choir and transepts
next to the tower show that they were certainly reconstructed at that time, whilst
the corbel tables and roof mouldings can also be seen to have been rebuilt. In some
areas the reconstruction of the clerestorey was more far-reaching than might have
been expected. On the east side of the south transept, for example, the original

PLATE 10   St Magnus Cathedral, gallery arch on the east side of the south transept. At the
back of the arch can be seen the inserted sub-arches (the central pier of which has a water
leaf capital). (Crown copyright, HBM Directorate).

outline of the second window from the crossing is clearly to be seen around the inserted window.

Construction of the north transept gable from clearstorey level upwards as part of this campaign is also plainly detectable—and the same is probably true in the south transept, although the total restoration of this part in the nineteenth century makes certainty impossible. It would similarly appear likely to have been in the same operation that it was decided to reduce the external impact of the choir galleries by sloping down their roofs to the level of the aisle tops in the way to which attention has already been brought. So that the roofs could be swept down in this way, pairs of subordinate arches were rather awkwardly placed on the outer plane of the transept gallery arches, and where the lean-to aisle roof passed over the opening one of the arches was blocked (pl. 10). The use of water leaf caps within these openings would certainly seem to link their subdivision with this stage of operations as also would the form of the aisle head corbel table on the south side. One other part of the operation on the crossing and transepts was the piercing of a new door at the base of the south transept gable wall. The outside caps of this door are so wasted that detailed comparison is impossible, although some of them may not have been unrelated to the more elaborate high caps of the north-eastern crossing pier. Internally the rear arch caps of the door are of handsomely enriched crocket forms, similar in form to such as the less corinthianesque west door caps at Jedburgh of around 1180.

These south transept door caps can be seen in some ways as a stylistic bridge to the work on the presbytery, where construction was probably re-started once the alterations to the transepts were largely completed. Building of the three bay presbytery on the new plinth course appears to have been a rather protracted operation. The design for the internal elevation was dictated by a wish to make the new sit happily with the old in its ranks of simple undivided arches. But its piers were made more elaborate, presumably to emphasise the high altar, and the shrine area of the cathedral's patron saint. I know of no precise parallels for the pier section, although the constituent parts were all used widely in the buildings of northern England and Lowland Scotland. The combination of keeled shafts on the main axes, and lesser shafts within a stepped profile, is the same formula as in the arcade responds of Holyrood, of about 1210, for example. More unusual is the way in which the subordinate shafts are linked by a curve, although a similar detail may be seen in a number of Scottish contexts. The arch of the night stair doorway at Arbroath Abbey, which is probably datable to the years around 1200, provides a possible comparison.

The variety of capital types in the presbytery is very wide. They range from rather crocket-like stiff leaf foliage (pl. 11) through curiously flattened corinthianesque, to multiple moulded bells. It also has to be said that the quality is very variable. Two capitals, including the eastern respond of the north arcade, have dragon-like beasts which may suggest (like the plan of the transept chapels) links with the mother church of the province at Trondheim. But it must be remembered that such fabulous creatures were also a part of the Scottish repertoire. Despite being later, some of the beasts which once lurked in the darker recesses of Elgin

PLATE 11   St Magnus Cathedral, a capital of the presbytery arcade, with sprigs of stiff leaf
foliage. (Crown copyright, HBM Directorate).

Cathedral, for example, appear closer in type to those at Kirkwall than anything
to be seen at Trondheim. For some of the crocket-like sprays of foliage northern
English parallels can be found as at Cartmel Priory in Cumbria, which was under
construction from about 1190 to 1220. In the same area comparisons for the
crudely over-simplified sprigs on the north side of the south-east respond caps at
Kirkwall can be found at St Bees of about the same date and also in Cumbria—
although the degree of simplification in both examples may make this particular
comparison rather unsafe.

One of the most puzzling parts of the new presbytery is the great east window
(pl. 5), which has been so grossly over-restored that one is tempted to dismiss it.
But close inspection shows that the reveals, the sub-arches and the central oculus
are all basically contemporary with the presbytery, as are the smaller areas of
tracery in the spandrels between the sub-arches and oculus. Early views of the
cathedral point to the paired lights within each of the sub-arches as not existing
in the eighteenth and early nineteenth centuries, as may be seen in a drawing on
a map of 1769 in the Scottish Record Office. (Scottish Record Office, RHP 6096).
Nevertheless, there could have been some basis for their restoration, since the

sub-arches are so large that they might be expected to have contained some sub-division in this way. The tracery within the oculus is similarly modern, although its basic wheel design seems to have been based on what was there.

From the surviving details in the spandrels, and from the date around the second quarter of the thirteenth century suggested by the capitals of its reveals and central mullion, it is certain that the window must have been of the plate-traceried type. This gives it a special importance, despite its mutilated state, since large windows of plate tracery are now extremely rare. In its arrangement of two paired lights with a central circle occupying the main tracery field, the window is of what must have been one of the stock patterns of such tracery. But at Kirkwall the central oculus is given particular emphasis, and to achieve this the containing arch of the window is greatly stilted after a fashion which was perhaps more common in France than in England, although this would not appear to be a reason for claiming an exotic inspiration. Assuming that the restored tracery in the oculus is to be trusted the one remotely comparable window now surviving in Scotland is a fragmentary wheel window found at Elgin Cathedral, the original position of which is unknown, and which probably represents a stage of design beyond Kirkwall in the detailing of the inner band of trefoils.

The east window must have been completed along with the presbytery clerestorey, even though it may have been designed at an earlier stage. Unlike the presbytery arcade and gallery stages, which followed the lead of those in the choir in having round arches, the clerestorey windows were built with pointed heads. This is perhaps the most immediately noticeable of the various changes which took place as work on the eastern extension progressed, although it should be remembered that round and pointed arches still seem to have been regarded as virtually interchangeable in the architecture of northern Britain at this period. Indeed, in roughly contemporary work at Elgin Cathedral, pointed arches pre-date round-headed ones.

Other changes are seen in the different mouldings employed for the two sides of the gallery. But, architecturally, the most significant change in the presbytery is in the wall shafts which divide it into bays. At the level of the arcade these shafts were single and very slender. Up to the arch springing of the gallery stage they were given more substantial section, although they still seem to have been designed essentially as decorative wall shafts rather than vaulting supports. However, from the gallery arch springing and up into the clerestorey they became triplets of shafts, and as such they appear to represent a major change of design, in which preparations were being made for a stone vault above the presbytery. If so, this must have been the first time that stone vaults were contemplated for any of the high main spaces of the cathedral, and it represents a most daring initiative.

Nevertheless, there are considerable difficulties in deciding at just which stage of the operation the decision was taken to vault the eastern limb. It seems certain that when the outer skin of the presbytery clerestorey was being built there was still no thought of vaulting, since the wall was at first only constructed to the same level as that of the existing choir clerestorey, and that could hardly have afforded enough headroom for the abuttal of quadripartite vaulting. Unequivocal pointers to this initial intention to extend the existing choir wall head through into the presbytery are seen on the north side, where the masons went as far as to build the cornice corbel table—albeit apparently using earlier head corbels which had presumably been cut for use elsewhere (pl. 5). Beyond this, there is unquestionable evidence for the subsequent heightening of the outer wall on both sides of the clerestorey in a change of stone colour from red to white (pls. 5 and 8). Thus, externally, the evidence for a first low clerestorey in the presbytery is beyond doubt; but internally, the evidence is more confusing. Not only is there a lack of such clear physical evidence for heightening, but, as has been said, vaulting seems to have been under consideration even while the upper part of the gallery stage was being finished. Presumably the solution to this apparent contradiction is to be found in the 'thick-wall' construction of the clerestorey, in which the outer skin of the wall outside the passage at this level could be at least partly constructed before the inner skin. It must be assumed that the decision to vault was taken after this outer skin had been built, but at a stage at which it was still feasible to construct—or reconstruct—the inner skin with the modified provisions necessary to receive a vault.

Having decided to vault the presbytery, it was also necessary to vault the earlier choir. Again, the external change in stone colour clearly shows the extent of the consequent heightening of the choir clerestorey walls (pls. 5 and 8). The original wall head height is also indicated by retained fragments of corbel table near the junctions of these walls with the transepts (pl. 6). It may be added here that, as an extension of this same operation, it was decided to raise the wall heads of the transepts—so much is evident from the use of the same characteristically thirteenth-century corbel type for both the eastern limb and transepts.

It appears that the work of vaulting the whole of the eastern limb was pressed ahead vigorously (pl. 12). Comparison of the rib types shows that the choir was vaulted before the presbytery, and presumably whilst the presbytery clerestorey was still being completed. To receive the new choir vault, triplets of wall shafts were let into the clerestorey walls, although insufficient thought was given to the problems which would be created by constructing a continuous vault over two sections set out with differing bay lengths. When the vault was eventually continued from the choir into the presbytery, in which the springing points had to be at a lower level because of the greater bay width, the vault of the third bay had to be reconstructed in order to make an effective transition. But, with a commendable sense of economy characteristic of many areas of the cathedral, parts of the earlier ribbing were re-used. One area in which economy was not allowed to detract from the effect, however, was in the new vaulting bosses of the presbytery in which delightfully spreading foliage knots give emphasis to the intersections.

The architectural and sculptural details of the latest work in the presbytery suggest that it was probably not until well into the second quarter of the thirteenth century that it was eventually completed. In all these years the main architectural effort of the cathedral masons must certainly have been concentrated on the more sacred parts of the building east of the nave. Nevertheless, at the same time there is clear evidence that work on the nave was also advancing, albeit sometimes with

PLATE 12   St Magnus Cathedral, choir vault. (Crown copyright, HBM Directorate).

masons of lesser calibre than those engaged on the choir and transepts. It is in the fifth bay of the north aisle from the crossing that there is the first significant change from the design established at the start of the work on the nave. In that bay the designer of the wall arcading rejected cushion or volute caps in favour of handsome water leaf caps. These carvings, in their spirited undercutting and convoluted profiles, appear to be significantly similar to examples in the south transept of Byland Abbey, of the last years of the twelfth century. On this basis they are unlikely to be far in date from the great change of design in the transepts and eastern limb, of around 1190.

The mouldings and carvings of the internal rear arches of the aisle windows provide further pointers to the rate of progress of the nave. Having completed the wall arcade up to the sixth bay from the crossing on the south, and up to the fifth bay on the north, it was the south aisle windows from the third to the sixth bays which received the next attention, and these were given capitals with rather heavy crockets, which suggest a date of around 1200. Work then moved back to the north aisle in the early thirteenth century, where the fourth window from the crossing was completed, having been left in a half-built state in the first campaign. In finishing this window there was no attempt at compromise, and shafts with stiff leaf foliage on the west side were opposed to the existing cushion-capped shafts on the east, whilst the window opening was bridged by an arch with early Gothic mouldings. A window continuing these same early Gothic themes was then built in the next bay, and in the sixth bay from the crossing a handsome doorway of three orders was installed. This doorway was presumably intended to serve as a principal lay entrance, but its carvings have now been so over-restored that it is difficult to pin down its date. Once this bay was completed the wall head of the six aisle bays on the north side was capped by a corbel table with trifoliate pendants, which has no parallel in other parts of the building.

It seems to have been the intention to bring work to a temporary halt after the sixth bay of the aisle walls on both north and south sides. Presumably construction of the three-storeyed elevations of the central vessel was also being pressed ahead to near the same point, although the very limited quantity of carved detail in the central part of the nave makes it difficult to gauge the progress of the work. It has been pointed out earlier that only the first arcade pier on the north and the first two on the south were completed in the first campaign, and everything above and beyond them—with the exception of some pier bases—is later. The rest of the piers, up to the sixth from the crossing on each side, are of essentially identical design with moulded capitals, and there is no way of determining their relative dating. It appears, however, from the character of the mouldings, that the first bay on each side was arched over before the others, incorporating some earlier work, and the aisle vaults of this bay, which are differentiated from the rest by the absence of a central boss, are also likely to be earlier than those to the west.

Although other changes of detail can be seen, such as the use of different arcade arch mouldings on the two sides of the nave after the first bay from the crossing, these are of relatively little value in determining the chronology of the work. Nevertheless, it does seem likely that the completion of the arcade and gallery stages was pressed rapidly ahead up to the sixth bay, to a design which was still dictated in its essentials by that established in the choir at the start of the first campaign. But, as in the choir, a major stock-taking effort had to be made when the decision was taken to place a vault over the high central vessel.

As in the choir, the determination to vault was accompanied by a most helpful change of stone colour in the clerestorey. On the clues provided by the masonry on the south side it seems that a low clerestorey wall had already been started at the junction of nave and transept before it was decided to construct the vault, but from that point onwards the clerestorey was raised to a sufficient height for a vault along as far as the middle of the sixth bay from the crossing. Since it is inherently implausible that the idea of vaulting the nave was taken up before the decision had been reached to vault the more important eastern limb, the likelihood is that this stage was not reached until well into the thirteenth century, and such a general date is supported by the character of the individual lancet windows along the clerestorey.

The problem of how, and at what point, the nearly complete first six bays of the nave were closed off from the Orcadian elements before the final two bays were raised is one which has intrigued some writers on the cathedral. At few other buildings is there such definitive evidence for a neat pause in the operation, where at the same time there is every indication that more was still to come. The suggestion has been made that a substantial temporary gable must have been constructed on completion of the sixth bay, (RCAHMS, 1946, 114), although there seems to be no archaeological evidence to support this idea. On balance, such a wall seems unlikely, and perhaps the signs of westward settlement within the sixth bay might point to a less stable form of closure. Possibly something like the timber and slate screen which still finishes off the incomplete nave stump of the French cathedral of Beauvais—started in 1225 and left unfinished in 1573—is closer to what may have been provided at Kirkwall. A supporting argument against a stone wall being built across the open end of the nave is that this would have diverted resources from the completion of the work, at a time when it was certainly intended to push it ahead with energy. The west front on the existing line must have been started before either the first six bays of the nave or even the presbytery were complete, and it was evidently under the control of a mason of greater standing than the one in charge of the central parts of the nave.

There is no doubt that when work started on the western facade it was intended to provide a frontispiece of great magnificence. With three portals opening onto the central nave and its flanking aisles it was firmly in the grand tradition of European west front design—in conception if not scale. Indeed, we know of nothing of similar date in mainland Scotland or northern England which might have rivalled it. The two side doors were firmly subordinated to the main portal at the centre (pl. 19). Each has an engaged order framing the opening, followed by three orders carried on detached shafts. These side doors are contained within the wall thickness, unlike that at the centre, which is altogether more ambitious. Immediately around the central opening is an engaged order with jambs which were originally intended to be carved entirely in undercut relief; although only the jamb tops were to be

PLATE 13a   St Magnus Cathedral, north doorway of the west front, capitals of south jamb.

PLATE 13b   St Magnus Cathedral, south doorway of the west front, capitals.

PLATE 13c   St Magnus Cathedral, central doorway of the west front, triplet of capitals
below pinnacle on south side.

carved in the event, it may still be seen that all of the stones below are hollowed
out as a prelude to the surface carving. Following this engaged order are no less
than seven staggered orders of detached shafts carrying highly elaborated arches
which, like the jambs, were designed to be deeply undercut—in this case the carving
was executed, but has largely fallen away. Framing the splayed flanks of the
doorway are three detached shafts in front of a solid core, which were intended to
carry lofty shafted pinnacles. A combination of lack of resources to finish what had
been intended, and the present state of advanced decay, have robbed this door of
a great deal, but the magnificence of its first conception and execution is still abun-
dantly clear.

   Perhaps the most individually remarkable feature of the doorways is their foliage
carving. That on the north door was the simplest, with relatively plain but well
carved sprays on each cap (pl. 13a). the carving on the central and southern doorways is more closely inter-related whilst still showing some diversity of form
which may suggest the presence of two distinct hands. The leading characteristic
of the foliage on these two doors is its density; indeed, on the south door, and on
the outer caps of the central door jamb, it is so concentrated that there is no break
between the caps (pl. 13b). On the main jambs of the central door there is less
density, although the trails still run across from cap to cap (pl. 13c). Foliage of this
type is very unusual, and must be seen as the personal mannerisms of individual
masons. One of the few possible parallels for it may be seen on the west side of

the south-east processional door at Dryburgh Abbey, which is probably of the first decade of the thirteenth century, and thus a little earlier than the Kirkwall doors. It should perhaps be mentioned here that foliage trails do seem to have enjoyed considerable local popularity in Kirkwall. Much simpler horizontal trails had already been carved for the rebuilt western respond of the north choir arcade, of around 1190. Reference should also be made to caps built into a garden gate at Trumland House on Rousay, which have foliage trails which may well have been a product of the cathedral workshop, albeit they cannot be linked with any specific part of the operation (Lamb, 1982, 11).

It is the most unfortunate aspect of the Cathedral's building history that the entrance front which was started so magnificently in the first quarter of the thirteenth century was eventually to be finished so feebly. The architectural evidence suggests that, towards the middle of the thirteenth century, work on the cathedral must have virtually ground to a halt and, following the completion of the central tower around that time, there is little sign of renewed activity before the later fifteenth or sixteenth centuries. Of course, it was by no means unusual for medieval building operations to be halted for lengthy periods, and Kirkwall was at least fortunate that the resources were eventually found to achieve something approaching completion. However, the blank areas of walling on the west front, and the strangely limping intersecting tracery of its central window, could hardly be seen as worthy successors to the inventiveness of the earlier masons. The dating of the later parts cannot easily be fixed on stylistic grounds. Dietrichson and Meyer have pointed to Thomas Tulloch, who was bishop between 1461 and 1477, as the individual who re-started building operations, (Dietrichson and Meyer, 1906, 55), although apparently without any particularly good reason. There is, however, some heraldic evidence which may possibly supplement that of the architecture. A coat of arms carved on the gablet of the central west door, seems very likely to be that of Bishop Andrew, known as Pictoris, who occupied the see between 1477 and about 1506, (Marwick, 1929–30, 45; Owen and Smith, in press). Such a date would certainly be stylistically acceptable for the continuation of work on the front. Beyond this, the remodelled doorway in the third bay of the south aisle from the west end is said to have been associated with Robert Reid, who was bishop between 1541 and 1558 (MacGibbon and Ross, 1896, 289). Whether or not this tradition is correct the mouldings certainly point to a date into the sixteenth century, and such polygonal door heads in Scotland are usually no earlier than the second half of the fifteenth century and frequently much later.

The architectural clues to the very late completion of the western bays of the nave are more evident externally than internally. So far as the outside is concerned, there seems to have been only a partial effort to continue the design established further east. There are clear changes in the treatment of the aisle wall heads of the two western bays, whilst small unmoulded lancets rather than shafted round-headed windows were provided to light the aisles, and an ogee section base course was formed at the wall foot. Between the bays large buttresses were constructed instead of the light pilasters which had apparently proved structurally inadequate in the earlier bays of the nave. However, since it may have been in this same campaign that some of the supplementary buttresses were added to the earlier pilasters along the south aisle, this change at least was unlikely to have attracted attention. At clerestorey level the break was signalled by little more than a change in stone colour from white back to red, and a slight difference in the corbel type at the wall head in the two and a half western bays.

Internally, greater efforts were made to preserve the cathedral's architectural unity by continuing the three stage elevations of the central space as they had been started in the thirteenth century. It is only in relatively slight modifications to the cap and base mouldings of the arcade piers that the extent of the later work in the main elevations is readily seen. But in the aisles the last phase is more easily identifiable in the absence of decorative wall arcading, in the simpler windows and in the characteristically late Gothic design of the triplet vaulting shafts. These shafts in the aisles, however, along with the vaulting corbels in the three western bays of the central vessel, were not destined to receive the stone vaults which had been intended for them. Indeed, it was only in the 1840s and the 1970s that vaulting of the form, if not the intended materials, was eventually constructed. Once the walls had been completed and roofed in the sixteenth century, events appear to have intervened to prevent further progress; if the south door is indeed attributable to Bishop Reid, who died in 1558, this intervention seems most likely to have been the Reformation.

The later history of the cathedral is essentially the story of its adaptation to new forms of worship after the Reformation, and its eventual restoration, as renewed appreciation of its superlative architectural merits began to re-emerge. But that is outside my present remit.

ACKNOWLEDGEMENT

In preparing this paper I have greatly benefited from discussions on site with Professor Eric Fernie, although I must bear responsibility for the opinions offered.

BIBLIOGRAPHY

Dietrichson, L, and Meyer, J, 1906, *Monumenta Orcadica*, Christiania/Oslo
Dowden, J, 1912, *The Bishops of Scotland*
Dryden, H, 1878, *Description of the church dedicated to St Magnus at Kirkwall*
Lamb, R, 1982, *The Archaeological Sites and Monuments of Scotland*, 16; *Rousay, Egilsay and Wyre*
MacGibbon, D and Ross, T, 1896, *The ecclesiastical architecture of Scotland*, vol III
Marwick, H, 1929–30, 'Note on Bishop Andrew', *Proceedings of the Orkney Antiquarian Society*, VIII, 45
Mooney, J, 1924–5, 'Discovery of relics in St Magnus Cathedral', *Proceedings of the Orkney Antiquarian Society*, III, 73–8
Owen, O and Smith, B, 'Kebister, Shetland: an armorial stone and an Archdeacon's teind barn' (in press)
Orkneyinga Saga, 1981, Translated by H Palsson and P Edwards (Penguin edition)
RCAHMS, 1946, Royal Commission on the Ancient and Historical Monuments of Scotland, *Orkney*

CHAPTER 9

The Architectural Context of the Romanesque Cathedral at Kirkwall

Eric Cambridge

This paper will concentrate on two main aspects of the architectural context of St Magnus Cathedral: its similarities to, and contrasts with, the design of Durham Cathedral and the group of churches influenced in some degree by that great church, and, in a broader perspective, its relationships to contemporary work in Scotland and Scandinavia.

Begun in 1137, St Magnus Cathedral is probably the latest in the series of Durham-inspired designs, started after the completion of Durham itself in 1133, and at a time when the other related churches were well under way.[1] Its particular significance in this context is that substantially more of its eastern parts survive compared to the others, enabling its relationship to Durham to be evaluated unusually comprehensively.

The particular indebtednesses to Durham repay close inspection. They are present at all levels of the design, from aspects of the basic layout and proportions down to the smallest architectural details. The cylindrical columns of the arcades,

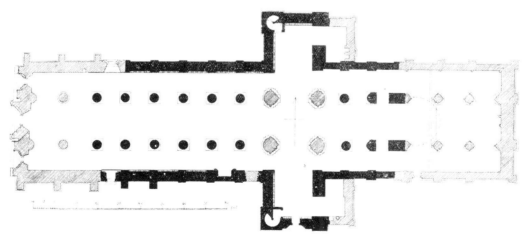

FIGURE 12   St Magnus Cathedral, ground plan (MacGibbon and Ross, 1896, fig. 225).

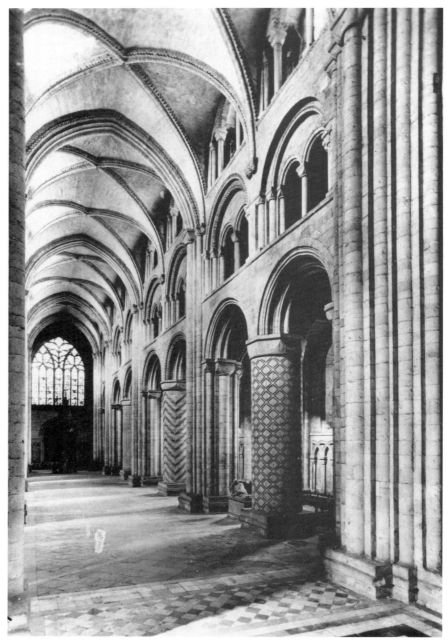

PLATE 14   Durham Cathedral, nave, northside looking west. (Photo. J R Ellis, probably
*c.*1915; Courtesy of Dean and Chapter of Durham).

with their octagonal scalloped capitals (pls. 3, 14), are perhaps the most frequently cited example; yet it is worth recalling that such features are not exclusive to Durham. They also occur in North-East England in a contemporary context (and one apparently independent of Durham), at Tynemouth priory, Northumberland. What makes the ultimate indebtedness of the Kirkwall piers to Durham clearer are the taller, more slender proportions, compared to the stubbier Tynemouth examples (Knowles, 1910, pl. V, 3).

Several smaller details at Kirkwall betray the unmistakable fingerprints of the Durham designer: the remarkably prominent transept stair turrets for example, protruding uncomfortably inwards into the church (fig. 12); the enrichment of the outer order of the choir arcades with billet, clearly derived from a similar moulding in this position on the Durham nave arcades; or the use of intersecting wall arcading, both divided into bays in the east parts of the nave, and in longer runs on the west walls of the transepts.[2] Though the profiles of these arcades are more varied than at Durham, some, notably on the west wall of the north transept, are reminiscent of the latter.

On a larger scale, the elevation of the end walls of the transepts, with a single window placed centrally in each of the lower two stages (a form of Romanesque facade less common than one might suppose) probably reproduces the form which originally obtained at Durham, though only one Romanesque window, in the lowest stage of the south transept, now survives there.[3] The elevation of the transept west walls (allowing for the lesser projection at Kirkwall) is also strikingly similar; and the intended design of the aisle walls must have been much closer than their present appearance suggests. There is clear evidence that the nave and choir were to be provided with high galleries above the aisles, instead of the present lean-to roofs (see Fawcett, this volume, above). The aisle walls were therefore almost certainly intended to have been carried up higher, and to have been pierced by an upper row of small windows above the existing ones, each possibly surmounted by a small transverse gable, as was the case with the nave of Durham before the fourteenth century (Billings, 1843, pl. VIII; James, 1983, 142, fig. 11 and 144–5, n. 11).[4]

The contrasts with Durham are equally instructive. Most obviously, there is no evidence of any intention to provide high vaults. The system of alternating circular and compound piers has also gone, and with it, apparently, the primary system of articulation into double bays (but see below, p. 121). Instead, the elevation at Kirkwall reverts to the 'aqueduct' principle, particularly favoured in midland and western England, where the three vertical stages are emphasized by string courses unbroken by any vertical element. More fundamentally, the proportional system, both in plan and elevation, differs in several major respects. For example, the central vessel of St Magnus is much higher in proportion to its width than at Durham: $c.1:2.7$ compared to $c.1:2.3$.[5] It also slightly less than half the total internal width, a much more unusual circumstance in terms of Romanesque principles of design. In the elevations, the relative proportions of three stages are more similar than is apparent at first sight: the Romanesque vaults of Durham and the heightening of the walls and inserted vaulting at Kirkwall alike produce a misleading impression of the actual proportions. Nevertheless, there appear to be some subtle differences, the gallery being proportionally a little higher—its lack of subdivision making it appear more prominent still—and the clerestorey a little lower at Kirkwall (figs. 13, 14 and pl. 14). The design of the latter, with a single window in each bay, owes more to the Durham choir clerestorey (though with the addition of a wall passage) than to the tripartite forms used later in its transepts and nave (Billings, 1843, pls. X–XI, XV).

The similarities and contrasts between the two churches need to be seen in the context of the selection and rejection of aspects of the design of Durham made by others among its followers. In particular, the abandonment of vertical articulation in the elevation involves the rejection of a fundamental principle of the Durham design. This should not be taken to imply a lack of contact with Durham masons, however, as it is paralleled (and almost certainly anticipated) in the nave of Lindisfarne priory, a church which must have been built under the direct patronage of the Durham monks, and surely by masons in charge of the cathedral. The parallel is the more striking in that Lindisfarne nevertheless retains alternation in the design of its arcade piers. Nor should it be assumed that the rejection of vertical articulation at Kirkwall was merely the consequence of the decision not to erect high vaults, as Lindisfarne combines horizontal articulation with high vaults; while, in contrast, the more southerly members of the group, Selby, Waltham, and (probably) Kirkby Lonsdale, retain vertical articulation and alternating pier forms, yet have no provision for high vaults in their surviving parts (Fernie, 1985, 66, n. 46). Like the cylindrical piers with octagonal cushion capitals, horizontal articulation had already been anticipated in the north in the nave of Tynemouth (Knowles, 1910, pl. V, 3).

But by far the closest and most significant comparison with any of the followers of Durham lies, of course, with Dunfermline abbey (pl. 15) (RCAHMCS 1933, 106–13). It has been suggested that the Durham-inspired features of Kirkwall's design were derived indirectly, via Dunfermline (Cruden, 1977, 88), and though there is no reason to dispute the general truth of this, the relationship appears to be in some respects more complex. In spite of the fact that the early build at the former breaks off almost exactly where the surviving parts of the latter start (i.e. the second bay of the nave), it is clear that the two churches have in common many of the distinctive features in respect of which Kirkwall diverges from Durham; the presumption must therefore be that these developments had already taken place c.1128, when the design of Dunfermline was formulated.

Dunfermline shares with Kirkwall the exclusively columnar arcades, with no alternation of pier forms, the layered elevation with no vertical elements, and the unsubdivided triforium (the south choir triforium at Kirkwall, with its unarticulated rectangular piers, being especially similar).[6] Further, they share unusually narrow proportions, both of width to height of the central vessel and of its width in proportion to the total width. And, exactly as one might expect, Dunfermline stands a little closer to Durham in its details, having incised decoration on its eastern piers, and compound responds punctuating the bays of the aisle arcades, features alike abandoned at Kirkwall. The moulding profile of its main arcades is generally

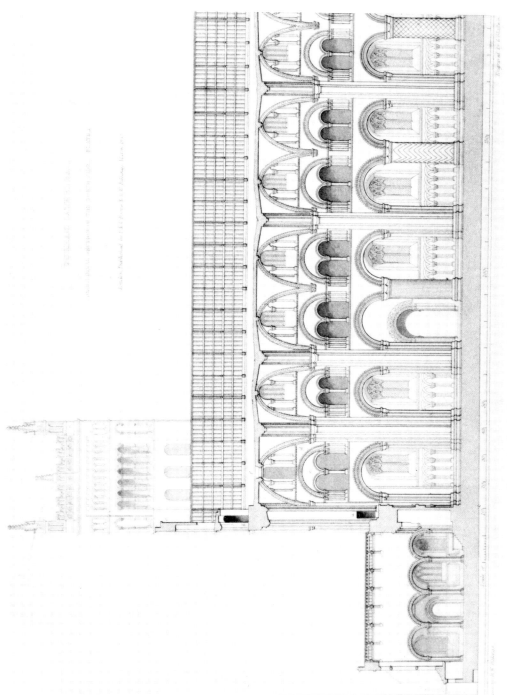

FIGURE 13   Durham Cathedral, nave north elevation (after Billings, 1843, pl. x).

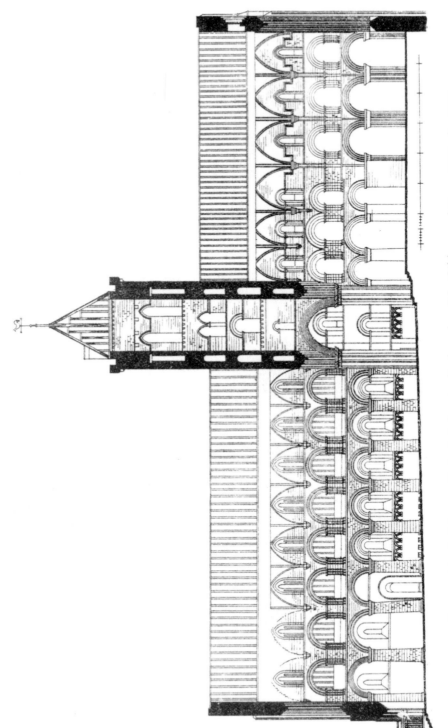

FIGURE 14   St Magnus Cathedral, longitudinal section (MacGibbon and Ross, 1896, fig. 226).

PLATE 15   Dunfermline Abbey, nave (Crown copyright RCAMS).

similar to Durham's, and in particular, the billet-moulded outer order is, like the Durham nave arcades, without a hood-mould, whereas one was adopted at Kirkwall; here the arcade mouldings, though evidently from the same stable, have a distinctive profile of their own.

Close though these similarities are, the two designs also differ in important respects. For example, none of the existing wall arcading at Dunfermline is intersecting(though the paired shafts may indicate that it was originally intended to be so), whereas at Kirkwall intersecting arcading is exclusively employed. Also, the columnar piers are much less slender than at Dunfermline. Now, it is possible that these features were present in the eastern parts of Dunfermline, and that the apparent contrast with Kirkwall is entirely a consequence of their subsequent

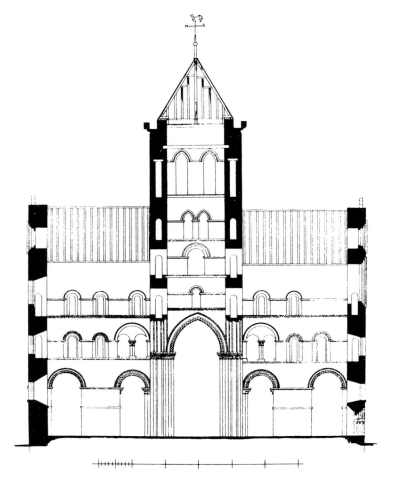

FIGURE 15   St Magnus Cathedral, section through transept (MacGibbon and Ross, 1896, fig. 227).

destruction. It may well be significant, however, that both are also found at Durham; only intersecting arcading is employed there, and the proportions of the Kirkwall piers are most closely paralleled in its nave. In contrast, the proportions of the Dunfermline columns are clearly derived from the Durham transepts, as is the plan of the inner face of its aisle walls (Billings, 1843, pls. XV, IV); the billet moulding alone betrays the influence of the nave of Durham. These differences between the two churches, some, apparently, deriving from different parts of the Durham design, suggest a certain independence on the part of the Kirkwall master, and a direct knowledge of the great cathedral itself.

The unusual plan of the east sides of the transepts at Kirkwall (figs. 12, 15; pl. 16), with chapels opening out from the extreme north and south ends of the walls, and separated from the arches to the choir aisles by large chunks of blank walling, may strengthen the case for a degree of independence in the formulation of its design. Again, we cannot now know whether that form was already present at Dunfermline. On the other hand, nor can it be paralleled in the surviving parts of any of the other churches in the Durham group, finding its closest parallel instead at the (otherwise unrelated) collegiate church of Southwell in Nottinghamshire (Clapham, 1934, 44, fig. 13).[7]

The design of Kirkwall thus suggests that there may be features which betray influences from outside the Durham group, as well as features which suggest that its designer may have looked back directly to Durham itself, and was not content to derive everything at second hand from Dunfermline, even though that church remains a powerful influence on the design. This mixture of extraneous and Durham-inspired features (however they were transmitted) is familiar from other members of the group, most notably Waltham (Fernie, 1985, 66–73).

Before leaving the Durham connection, it is worth considering the functional parallels between it and St Magnus. After all, uniquely among churches of the Durham group, they were designed to house both a bishop's chair and the relics of a saint. Mr Cruden has suggested a direct connection between form and function in seeking to explain one of the oddest features of the design of Kirkwall, the east bay of the choir arcades, which is narrower and lower than the others, and is cut straight through the wall instead of having cylindrical columns or other responds (fig. 12; pl. 3). This was, he suggests, intended to accommodate a processional way leading behind the high altar to the shrine of St Magnus at the east end (Cruden, 1977, 91 and above).[8]

This interpretation is perfectly possible; indeed, the method of supporting the inner order of the arches of the east bay on pairs of head corbels, exactly like the transverse arches of the choir aisles, could be held to emphasise their function as the points of access to the aisles from the east end. And it may be further elaborated by supposing that the desire to maximize space for altars against the flat east ends of the choir aisles may also have been an influence on the plan at this point. Further, it must be admitted that comparison with Durham is of little immediate help in evaluating this problem as we know nothing for certain of its original liturgical arrangements. One recent (though entirely hypothetical) reconstruction has, indeed, suggested a passage between high altar and shrine similar to Cruden's

PLATE 16   St Magnus Cathedral, interior of south transept, showing the area of blank walling dividing the eastern chapel from the transept. (Crown copyright, HBM Directorate).

proposal for Kirkwall (Klukas, 1984, 163–5, fig. 11). The circumstantial evidence for the early liturgical arrangements does not support this view, however. There is a long stretch of solid walling c.30 ft (9.14m), between the shrine of St Cuthbert (which seems always to have stood in the same position as the saint's grave does now, that is, in the main apse of the Romanesque church), and the east responds of the choir arcades. This seems to imply that, whether or not the shrine platform was originally joined to the high altar, or, as in the later Middle Ages, provided with its own small altar at the west end, the high altar standing a few feet west of that, the shrine and high altar can never have been been separated by an ambulatory.[9]

The Durham evidence thus raises potential difficulties for the proposal that the east bay of Kirkwall gave access to an ambulatory between shrine and high altar. Given the direct connection between shrines and altars in this period (Wilson, 1977, 5) it is likely that the church's principal relics would have been associated with its principal altar, particularly as St Magnus's bones were presumably accommodated in a reliquary of much more modest size than that which contained Cuthbert's incorrupt body. If we envisage shrine and high altar juxtaposed in the east end, the east bay would have fallen between these and the bishop's throne and choir stalls, and would presumably then have accommodated the *ostia presbyterii*, that is, the gates between choir and sanctuary which allowed processions (and doubtless also pilgrims) to circulate round the church. The unusual length of the Durham choir arm would have meant that, unlike Kirkwall, the *ostia presbyterii* could be accommodated in the eastern bay of the arcades (where they still are) without needing to make any specific provision for them architecturally. This may seem a less convenient arrangement for pilgrims seeking access to the shrine; but convenience may be a misleadingly anachronistic notion in this context, given that it seems to have persisted at Durham for at least the first century and a half of its existence, and was probably also adopted for the principal Scottish shrine-church, St Andrews, a generation after Kirkwall was begun (see also below, n. 13).

Whether or not this alternative explanation of the function of the east bay of Kirkwall choir is accepted, the fact of its peculiar architectural expression clearly still requires explanation on its own terms. It is, perhaps, misleading to consider this problem exclusively functionally; architecturally at least, the treatment of the other two bays of the choir may be no less significant. In elevation, the east bay appears as if cut through a solid wall terminating to the west in a semi-circular respond, from which the middle arcade arch springs (see pl. 3); presumably the third arch sprang from a matching impost at the west end of the arcade before the Gothic recasting of the crossing. It is possible that these two fully articulated western bays were intended to be read as a double bay, and therefore that the Durham system of articulation did have some effect on Kirkwall after all, though in a much modified form.[10] The plan of the eastern arm should therefore perhaps be read as a half version of Durham's, with the second double bay eliminated, and the eastern arch conceived of as a piercing of the solid wall in the equivalent position to the unusually long expanse preceding the main apse at Durham, rather than as an integral part of the arcade.[11] If so, all traces of double bay articulation were abandoned at an early stage, not only in the setting out of the nave, but in the superstructure of the choir itself, where the thoroughgoing rejection of any vertical articulation in the elevation must, in any case, have made it virtually impossible to express. Whether or not any of these suggestions is right, the important point is that the idiosyncratic features of the eastern arm of St Magnus require explanation in terms of the influences determining its design, and not just in terms of the particular purpose they may have served.

What of the more general context of the building? First, what can be inferred from its actual size? Though the intended original form of the church cannot be known with certainty, the reconstruction proposed by the Royal Commissioners (RCHMS 1946, 113, fig. 159) seems not unlikely in essentials, especially as the ratio between the distances from the nave west wall to the transept west wall, and from the nave west wall to the chord of the apse, is as the side of a square to its diagonal (that is, one to the square root of two), which is the most commonly found ratio in the larger Anglo-Norman churches (Fernie, 1979, 2). This plan gives an original internal length of c.188 ft (57.3 m) and a width across the transepts of 90.5 ft (27.58 m).[12] Given the church's close links with Anglo-Norman Romanesque, initial comparisons must be to English work. There can be little doubt that, from this perspective, St Magnus is on a lesser scale: almost exactly a half-scale version of Durham (the whole length of the church could be fitted comfortably inside the Durham nave), smaller than all but the smallest English cathedrals, smaller even than a middling Benedictine house like Selby Abbey (Hodges, 1893, pl. V). A more exact comparison would be with a modest collegiate establishment such as Waltham Abbey (Fernie, 1985, 51, fig. 4).

It should be remembered, however, that some of the largest buildings ever erected in medieval Europe were built in Anglo-Norman England; and that none of the other progeny of Durham ever attempted to match the considerable dimensions of their distinguished parent. Comparison with those areas with which the earls of Orkney had direct contact, in particular Scotland and Scandinavia, may, therefore, be more appropriate. So far as we can tell, Kirkwall was probably only a little smaller than Dunfermline. This, though modest by English standards, was probably the most prestigious monastic foundation of its generation in the Scottish kingdom, in addition to housing the mausoleum of its ruling house. Its only serious rival, Kelso, was rather larger, to judge from the scanty remains, though still of middling size by English standards (Tabraham, 1984, 40). Not until the foundation of St Andrews cathedral in 1162 would Scotland witness a project conceived on the scale of the great churches of Anglo-Norman England.[13]

More revealing still is a comparison with contemporary Romanesque churches in mainland Scandinavia. Here again Kirkwall compares favourably, in linear dimensions if not in area, with the greater churches, such as the (roughly contemporary) Danish cathedral of Ribe, and is not greatly inferior to the metropolitan cathedral itself at Lund (Andersson, 1968, 51, 39; Cinthio, 1957). Only the rebuilding of Trondheim involved a somewhat larger-scale conception, to judge by the surviving transepts (Fischer, 1965, 43–108, pls. I–IV). What is particularly significant is that Kirkwall ranks alongside churches of the first rank, and not with the smaller contemporary Norwegian cathedrals like Hamar or Stavanger (Andersson, 1968, 163–4, 155–6; Hohler, 1964; Lidén, above).

Dimensions are, however, a crude indication of context. Equally important in considering the Scandinavian perspective is the up-to-date nature of the work stylistically. Though stone churches had been present in the Scandinavian world from the later eleventh century, high Romanesque forms seem to have made their appearance only from about the second decade of the twelfth century with the reconstruction of major buildings such as Lund (Cinthio, 1957, 59, fig. 20). Even at Trondheim itself, if the conventional building sequence is accepted, the first Romanesque building only began to be extended *c.*1150, when work on Kirkwall must have been well advanced (see Lidén, above). It must, of course, be admitted that this avant-garde aspect of the design may be, in some degree, accidental. Durham, the most influential cult centre of northern Britain, had been graced with one of the most outstanding churches ever built in the high Romanesque style. It was the most obvious place for the patrons of Dunfermline to seek for masons. Even by the time Kirkwall was begun, there were not yet many alternative workshops in existence in the north, though there were some: Kelso, for example.

Apart from its size and style, the design of Kirkwall is also significant in the way it sets out to reproduce the characteristic features of an Anglo-Norman great church, albeit on a modest scale: the cruciform plan; three story elevation; aisled choir and nave; central tower; and (if it was intended to follow Dunfermline in this respect as in so many others), twin western towers. This immediately establishes the aspirations of its patrons to erect a first-rank building, especially when considered in contemporary Scandinavian terms. Lund, for example, stands in a precisely similar relationship to the great Rhenish cathedrals on which it is modelled, particularly Speyer, as Kirkwall does to Durham and the Anglo-Norman tradition. There is, again, a marked contrast with the smaller Norwegian cathedrals, like Stavanger or Hamar, the latter of which reproduces (on a slightly more generous scale) features characteristic rather of churches serving important parochial centres.

Kirkwall is also typical of major contemporary Scandinavian churches in the length of time it took to translate intentions into reality. Lund, and especially Trondheim, were also unusually long in the building by the standards of the twelfth-century European architectural mainstream: an eloquent comment upon the extent to which ambition outstripped resources (doubtless human as well as financial) at even the highest levels of patronage in the Scandinavian world.

The presence of so many components of a great church in the design of St Magnus enables us to speculate on its iconography: not just intended as an appropriate setting for a dynastic cult centre-cum-mausoleum and a bishop's seat, but perhaps also a quite deliberate attempt on the part of the earls of Orkney to express how they themselves perceived both their considerable standing and their independence in the northern world. From this perspective, it is surely not coincidental that nothing like Kirkwall is to be found in any of the other Norse colonies and, equally, that its comparanda are to be found exclusively among the greatest contemporary Scandinavian churches, erected under royal patronage.

Politics and the church seem to have been intermingled more overtly in Scandinavia than almost anywhere else in contemporary Christendom; and in a society which historical circumstances had left distinctly short of local cults well into the twelfth century (see Jexlev below), the canonisation of murdered rulers and dynastic scions is certainly a conspicuous phenomenon; St Olaf of Norway being only the earliest and best known of them.[14] It may well be significant that Magnus is the only example in this category who was not royal. Is it too rash to speculate that the deveopment of his cult, together with its material presentation, is tantamount to a claim on the part of the Orkney earls to quasi-royal status? For a previous generation, the acquisition of a bishop had perhaps been an adequate expression of a ruler's importance and independence.[15] But, as the twelfth century advanced, the rules of the status game were changing, and it is a measure of their (typically Viking) capacity for catching on fast that the earls of Orkney realised not only the importance of developing an indigenous cult, but also of giving both it and the bishopric an appropriate material embodiment.

St Magnus Cathedral, then, was intended to be a powerful status symbol: no mere passive reflection of the material-cultural contacts of the earldom at this period, but the chief manifestation of the earls' determination to be considered in no way inferior to their neighbours the kings of Scots, nor to the kings of the Scandinavian mainland. This granted, it is harder to believe that a Durham school design was selected entirely from lack of choice. The resonances of Durham, centre of a great cult, and of Dunfermline, housing a great dynastic mausoleum, may rather have been sought out and cultivated quite deliberately. The intrinsic quality of those designs may have been no less significant a factor; it would do less than justice to the patrons of this splendid cathedral to suppose that they were incapable of appreciating a good building when they saw one.

NOTES

1. They are: Dunfermline Abbey, Fife (1128–c.1150); Kirkby Lonsdale church, Westmorland (?early twelfth century); Lindisfarne priory, Northumberland (1120s–?1140s); Selby Abbey, W Yorkshire (c.1100–late twelfth century); and Waltham Abbey, Essex (c.1110–60). Piers decorated with incised designs which may owe something to Durham are also found at Lenton, Castle Acre, and Norwich.
2. This feature is curiously absent from the east parts of the church, where one would most have expected such enrichment.
3. For a reconstruction of the original elevation of the transept facades, see Curry, 1986, 37, fig. 3, a, c, and 38 fig. 4 where, however, documentary evidence suggests that the clerestorey stage probably originally contained an oculus.
4. Disturbances in the west wall of the south transept above the junction with the nave aisle wall may be the result of patching up following the removal of the return of such a gallery wall.

Dunfermline abbey nave has a gallery, much altered later. The third bay from the east on the north side externally retains the clearest evidence for the original fenestration: a single small window in each bay. There is no visible evidence as to whether or not these were originally surmounted by transverse gables.

5. Changes in floor levels and alterations to the original wall heads make precise measurement impossible in the case of either building.

6. The design of the triforium piers at Kirkwall was later modified to a stepped plan, corresponding to the orders of the arches which they carry.

7. The similarity in plan to the slightly later transepts at Trondheim cathedral (Fischer, 1965, pls. I–IV) suggests a common English model, such as Southwell, rather than any direct influence from Kirkwall.

8. It is a reasonable guess that the choir terminated in an apse originally, but there is, as yet, no archaeological evidence to demonstrate this.

9. For the relationship between Cuthbert's grave, the later medieval context of the shrine, and the Romanesque apse, see B.A.A. 1980, fig. facing p. 3. The exceptional length of the eastern arm at Durham probably also implies that the choir screen has always been positioned where it has certainly been since the later Middle Ages, between the east crossing piers with the stalls located in the eastern arm, rather than following the more common arrangement in this period of having the stalls in the crossing or the east bays of the nave. The comparatively modest size of the monastic community in the first half century or so of its existence, starting with 23 monks in 1083 and increasing to about 40 by the mid twelfth century, tends to support this view. I am grateful to Alan Piper for his advice on this point.

10. The predominantly cylindrical plan of the compound piers at Waltham shows a comparable scheme of retaining an alternating system without recourse to strongly contrasting forms for the major piers (Fernie, 1985, 71, fig. 17).

11. Cruden's point that the arch of the east bay is lower and narrower than the other two as part of a deliberate architectural effect (1977, 91) needs to be considered in the context of both the irregular setting-out of the choir arcades at Kirkwall, and the notable (though not easily explicable) variations in the widths of the bays at Durham.

12. The scale of the plan in RCHMS 1946, pl. 25, facing p. 120, is inaccurate; the plan in MacGibbon and Ross, 1896, 261, fig. 225, is to be preferred. I am most grateful to Miss Beverley Smith for her assistance in checking the width of the transepts.

13. I hope to show elsewhere that there are aspects of the plan and dimensions of St Andrews which may indicate that it was explicitly modelled on Durham.

14. For Olaf, see Andersson, 1968, 20; and cf. Cnut (ob.1086) and Cnut Lavard (ob. 1131, canonised 1169) in Denmark (ibid., 24–5 29–30); and Erik Jedvardsson in Sweden, characterised by Andersson as '. . . un saint politique, fondateur d'une dynastie et patron du royaume de Suède' (ibid., 29). Cnut Lavard is a particularly instructive parallel to the case of St Magnus, as the canonnisation was at first opposed by Archbishop Eskil of Lund. See also Dr Jexlev, this volume, below.

15. For the correlation between the legitimation of a ruler and his possession of a bishop, see Crawford, 1983, 106–11.

BIBLIOGRAPHY

Andersson, A, 1968, *L'Art Scandinave*, II (La Nuit des Temps, xxix, Zodiaque)

B.A.A. 1980, Medieval Art and Architecture at Durham Cathedral: (Br. Arch. Assocn Conference Trans for 1977)

Billings, R W, 1843, *Architectural Antiquities and Description of the Cathedral Church at Durham*

Cinthio, E, 1957, *Lunds Domkyrka under Romansk Tid* (Bonn and Lund)

Clapham, A W, 1934, *English Romanesque Architecture*, II, *After the Conquest*

Crawford, B E, 1983, 'Birsay and the Early Earls and Bishops of Orkney', *Orkney Heritage*, II, 97–118

Cruden, S, 1977, 'The Cathedral and Relics of St Magnus, Kirkwall' in M Apted, R Gilyard-Beer and A D Saunders, eds, *Ancient Monuments and their Interpretation:* Essays presented to A J Taylor, 85–97

Curry, I, 1986, 'Aspects of the Anglo-Norman Design of Durham Cathedral', *Archaeologia Aeliana*, ser. 5, XIV, 31–48

Fernie, E C, 1979, 'Observations on the Norman Plan of Ely Cathedral', in *Medieval Art and Architecture at Ely Cathedral* (Br. Arch. Assocn Conference Trans for 1976), 1–7

Fernie, E C, 1985, 'The Romanesque Church of Waltham Abbey', *J. Br Arch. Assocn* CXXXVIII, 48–78

Fischer, G, 1965, *Domkirchen I Trondheim Kirkebygget*, I, *Middelalderen* (2 parts, forlaget Land og Kirke) Oslo

Hodges, C C, ed, 1893, *Coucher Book of Selby*, II (Yorks. Archaeol. and Topographical Assoc., Record Ser., xiii)

Hohler, C, 1964, 'The Cathedral of St Swithun at Stavanger in the Twelfth Century' *J Br. Arch. Assocn*, ser. 3, XXVII (1964), 92–118

James, J, 1983, 'The Rib Vaults of Durham Cathedral' *Gesta*, XXII/2 135–45

Klukas, A W, 1984, 'The Architectural Implications of the *Decreta Lanfranci*', *Anglo-Norman Studies*, VI, 136–71

Knowles, W H, 1910, 'The Priory Church of St Mary and St Oswin, Tynemouth, Northumberland', *Arch. J*, LXVII, 1–50

MacGibbon, D, and Ross, T, 1896, *The Ecclesiastical Architecture of Scotand . . .*, I

RCAHMCS, 1933, The Royal Commission on Ancient and Historical Monuments and Constructions of Scotland. *Eleventh Report* with *Inventory of Monuments and Constructions in the Counties of Fife, Kinross, and Clackmannan*

RCAMS, 1946, The Royal Commission on the Ancient Monuments of Scotland. *Twelfth Report* with an *Inventory of the Ancient Monuments of Orkney and Shetland*, II, *Inventory of Orkney*

Tabraham, C J, 1984, 'Excavations at Kelso Abbey', *Proc. Soc. Ant. Scot.*, CXIV, 364–404

Wilson, C, 1977, *The Shrines of St William of York*

CHAPTER 10

Norwegian Influences in the Design of the Transitional and Gothic Cathedral

Ronald Cant

As envisaged in 1137 St Magnus Cathedral was to be a Romanesque church of the first rank worthy to be the seat of a major bishopric and a setting for the veneration of its own distinctive patron saint. One would also expect it to be provided with a body of clergy capable of maintaining all the customary services of the medieval church, probably in the form of a community of Benedictine monks or Augustinian canons regular. Such a community might indeed already have been associated with Earl Thorfinn's 'stately minster' at Birsay and may well have been expected to transfer thence to Kirkwall once the new building was sufficiently advanced to permit of this.

In normal circumstances a decision on such a matter would rest with the bishop, that is, William I 'the Old', so consistent a supporter of Magnus' rival Earl Håkon that his authority had been challenged by another promoted by his opponents (Watt, 1969, 248–9) but who in the final conflict of 1136 between Håkon's son Paul and Magnus' nephew Rognvald seems to have been persuaded to support the latter and his plan for a memorial minster at Kirkwall. It would thus be with his approval (even if perhaps proposed by the Earl)[1] that it was designed on a monastic plan with a relatively short structural choir and provision for the customary monastic buildings to the south of the nave.

In detail, the earliest parts of the fabric bear a marked resemblance to the nave of Dunfermline Abbey, itself constructed by masons from Durham (see Cruden, Fawcett, Cambridge and pl. 15 above). But in the completion of the clerestorey stage of the north transept, perhaps in the early 1190's, a transitional (though still round-arched) style was employed similar to that in the corresponding stage of the transept side walls of Nidaros Cathedral at Trondheim (Fischer, G. 1965, i, 106–7). In the remodelling of the great arches of the crossing, however, a Gothic form was introduced, continued in the replacement of the transeptal *apsidioles* or 'altar-niches' by fully-developed chapels, in a new doorway cut through the south transept gable, and in the three portals of the nave west front. And although round-arched elements were included in the three-bay extension of the choir, its character was otherwise emphatically Gothic.

What circumstances or considerations lay behind these changes? Most important, one may suggest, is the fact that from 1153 the diocese of Orkney came to form part of an ecclesiastical province comprising Norway and its overseas dominions, with the bishop of the national cult-centre of St Olaf at Trondheim raised to the dignity of archbishop and metropolitan. This development greatly strengthened the ties between the island territories and the ancient homeland, especially Orkney during the episcopate of Bjarne Kolbeinsson from 1188-90 to 1223 (Watt 1969, 251). He himself belonged to a family of considerable influence on both sides of the Norwegian Sea, his father being Kolbein Hruga, an important landowner in western Norway, and in Orkney builder of the remarkable castle on Wyre still known by his name (RCAHMS 1946, ii, 235-9). In the great conflict, early in his episcopate, between the 'island beardies' and King Sverre (1194-6), he pursued a diplomatic middle course and became something of a national celebrity as church-man, statesman, and *skald* (*NBL*, i, 554-6).

As a leading dignitary of the Norwegian church Bishop Bjarne would be familiar with the developments in diocesan and cathedral organisation in this and the imme-diately preceding period. In his own diocese of Orkney and Shetland (to give it its full title) there must then have been, in both archipelagoes, a wide distribution of churches and chapels grouped in parishes (*soknar*) and priests' districts (*prestegjelder*), supported by tithes (*tiundar*) in accordance with the ecclesiastical provisions (*kristenrett*) of the Norwegian legal codes (Cant, 1972, 8-11; 1984, 171-8). For their regulation an archdeacon (*erkediakon*) was appointed for Shetland by at least 1215, but with Orkney remaining (until about 1300) under the immediate supervision of the bishop who of course had his principal residence there beside the Cathedral (Watt, 1969, 259, 261).

In certain Scottish dioceses of the period (late twelfth and early thirteenth century) the archdeacon presided over a body of 'synodal character' which participated in the election of the bishop (Watt, 1969, 5, 101). In Norway, however, episcopal appoint-ments were made by the king with a minimum of consultation (Kolsrud, 1958, 186-202).[2] But when the English Cardinal Nicholas Breakspear came (in 1152) to prepare for the creation of the new province he prescribed that they should be elected by chapters of secular canons associated with their cathedrals. He may even have set up a body of this kind at Trondheim in the course of his visit and persuaded King Inge to grant it a right of free election[3] (Johnson, 1945; Edwards, 1949).

In the Trondheim archdiocese, which extended from South Møre to north of the Lofoten islands, there were three archdeacons, each with a separate area. For this reason, or perhaps simply by following the example of England, the head of the Nidaros chapter was a dean (*decanus, dekan*). At Oslo there was an archpriest (*archipresbyter, erkeprest*). At Bergen, however, the archdeacon presided, an arrange-ment likewise to be found at Stavanger, Hamar, and Kirkwall.[4] Under the Car-dinal's plan each cathedral chapter (*domkapitel*) was to consist of twelve canons (*kanniker*) supported by the tithes of particular parishes of the diocese.[5] This figure was adhered to at Bergen but at Nidaros and Oslo it was raised to twenty-four and twenty respectively while at Stavanger and Hamar, and apparently also at Kirkwall, there were sometimes fewer than the prescribed number (Kolsrud, 1958, 191-5; Cowan, 1960, 39-40, 46).[6]

The first confirmation of the existence of a body of this kind at Kirkwall is in 1247 when Henry, 'canon of Orkney', was its unanimous choice as bishop in succession to Jofrey who had occupied the see since the death of Bishop Bjarne (this apparently occurring quite suddenly while attending an important council meeting at Bergen in 1223) (Watt, 1969, 250). In the circumstances King Hákon IV Hákonsson had filled the vacancy there and then by the promotion of the provost of his own collegiate church at Tunsberg. Bishop Jofrey was thus a stranger to Orkney. More seriously, by 1237 he was said to have been incapacitated by paralysis 'for many years' and under pressure to resign or accept a coadjutor (DN i, no. 13). Although this never happened there is a distinct impression that Bishop Henry might, as a canon of St Magnus', have been in virtual charge of matters there during much of his predecessor's episcopate and before he was elected bishop in 1247. It is noteworthy that the papal dispensation to him (as the natural son of an ecclesiastic) was made on the special recommendation not only of the Archbishop but of the King and the Cardinal Legate William of Sabena (DN i, no. 42).[7]

In this context it seems most likely that the decision that St Magnus Cathedral should be served by secular canons rather then by monks or canons regular was taken by Bishop Bjarne, and perhaps at a relatively early date in his episcopate. The principal change brought about by such a decision was quite clearly the extension of the choir, this occasioned by the general preference of secular canons to have the stalls for their corporate services east of the crossing rather than within it as in most monastic churches.[8] At Kirkwall, however, Bjarne had inherited a building of which little more than the three-bay choir and apse seem to have been available for use and his primary obligation was quite obviously to complete the crossing and transepts together with the six bays of the nave on which work had begun under his predecessors.

For most of this he was committed to the Romanesque style employed by the first builders. Yet he himself, and some at least of his senior masons, seem to have been familiar with the Transitional and Gothic design being introduced, from the 1180's, into the hitherto Romanesque Nidaros Cathedral at Trondheim (Fisher, G. 1965, i, 95 foll.). At Kirkwall, as has been noted, the first appearance of Transitional forms is in the north transept and of Gothic in the reconstruction of the pillars and arches of the central tower (Meyer 1906, Fig. 78), also of the arches opening from the transepts into the nave aisles (RCAHMS 1946, ii, Figs. 182–3). The pillars with their square bases, composite shafts, and 'water-leaf' caps, have affinities with those in the 'crossing' of the Nidaros chapter-house c.1180 (Fischer, G. 1965, i, 114–5). The Kirkwall arches, however, with their dog-tooth and chevron ornament, seem to be built of voussoirs originally intended for a Romanesque design similar to that of the choir aisles but re-cut to a Gothic form before being placed in position (RCAHMS 1946, ii, 114, Figs. 182–3).[9]

From here Bishop Bjarne and his builders moved into the nave and its aisles of which six bays were completed to a temporary wall two bays short of the intended west front. To provide access from the town meantime a doorway was included in the final bay on the north side, of advanced Transitional design but round-headed like the two rather more conservative Transitional windows adjoining it to the east

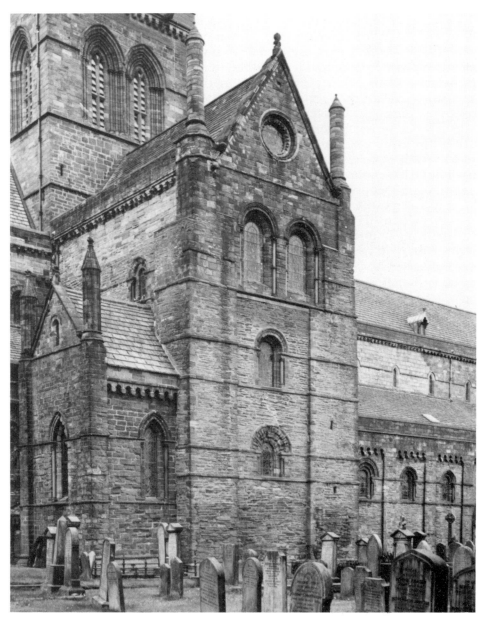

PLATE 17   St Magnus Cathedral, north transept, showing the projecting chapel. (Crown copyright, HBM Directorate).

(RCAHMS 1946, ii, Figs. 165, 8). While a beginning may have been made with the vaulting of the aisles, working westwards from the transepts, it does not seem to have been brought to a conclusion until work on the new transeptal chapels (see below) had been completed. The vaulting of the central nave appears to be even later, and it is indeed difficult to believe that it would have been given priority over that of the central choir. If, as seems evident, this had hitherto had no more than a timber roof (between vaulted aisles) how much more likely that a similar initial covering would have been regarded as adequate for the central nave, and quite possibly at no more than triforium level.[10]

In all this Bishop Bjarne was completing—albeit with some variation of style— what had been planned by his predecessors. In the two chapels projecting from the

PLATE 18   St Magnus Cathedral, window on north side of nave with masonry of the late twelfth century building period above contrasting with earlier masonry. (Crown copyright, HBM Directorate).

east side of the transepts in place of the original *apsidioles* he made his first actual addition to the fabric (pl. 17). In plan as in location resembling those attached to the Romanesque transepts at Nidaros (Fischer, G., 1965, i, 43 foll.), their windows are Gothic lancets while the lateral wallheads are carried on corbelling of a type well represented in the upper parts of the Nidaros octagon and choir (Fischer, G., 1965, i, 189; RCAHMS 1946, ii, 118-9, Fig. 173). Particularly striking are the pinnacles surmounting the angle buttresses, repaired and in part replaced in Victorian times yet virtually identical with the ones on the eastern corners of the extended choir and all bearing a striking resemblance to those flanking the gablet of the 'bishop's entrance' to the Nidaros octagon (Fischer, G. 1965, i, 140-1). The entire construction—elegantly vaulted within—is of the most beautiful red sandstone ashlar (Kirkwall's counterpart to Trondheim's grey-green *klebersten*) contrasting with the vernacular *rumble* masonry hitherto employed in most of the external walling of St Magnus'.[11] (pl. 18)

In addition to these chapels Bishop Bjarne was probably responsible for the doorway in the gable-end of the south transept (Meyer, 1906, Fig. 91) (thereby implying the abandonment of the earlier plan for claustral buildings here) and for the three doorways in the 'definitive' west front (RCAHMS 1946, ii, 115-6, 118,

PLATE 19   St Magnus Cathedral, doorways of the west front. (Crown copyright, HBM Directorate).

Figs. 162, 164, 166–7, 174). All are of early Gothic design with dog-tooth and chevron ornament similar to that in the arches of the central tower (pl. 19). But in the caps of the supporting shafts (the latter modern replacements) the foliaceous ornament is mingled, in the central and south portals of the west front, with tendrils and zoomorphic elements oddly reminiscent of Norwegian ecclesiastical wood-carving of the period (Meyer 1906, Figs. 110a, 111 and Fawcett, above). But the only part of the Kirkwall design suggesting any strong analogy with Trondheim is the provision of ornamental pinnacles in a more robust variation of those on the 'bishop's entry' designed to flank the gablet of the principal portal where their bases may still be seen (RCAHMS, 1946, ii, 116; Meyer, 1906, Fig. 110a).

A remarkable feature of this work is the use made in the voussoirs of the portals, as also in the lower courses of the buttresses on the left side of the west front, of alternating blocks of red and white stone. Despite suggested Italian models (Meyer, 1906, 62–4), this may simply have been an expedient arising from the introduction of white stone from Eday to supplement the red sandstone from the Head of Holland hitherto employed in the main structural elements of the building and so distinctive a feature of its architectural character. They had in fact already been employed in this way in parts of the internal walling of the transepts (RCAHMS 1946, ii, 122) and, as Douglas Simpson observed, in the nearby Bishop's Palace to which he assigned an approximately contemporary date and Norwegian provenance (Simpson 1961, esp. 68–72; see also below).

The one remaining part of the fabric of St Magnus' directly attributable to Bishop Bjarne comprises the vault in the two western bays of the choir, the ribs of which spring from wall-shaft capitals quite different from the remainder and rather like those of the Gothic arches leading into the chapels of the Nidaros octagon (Meyer, 1906, Fig. 90; Fischer, G. 1965, i, 154). As this splendid composition was quite clearly intended to complete, in an appropriately dignified manner, the most important part of the original design, it ought logically to have preceded the four Gothic portals and could well be dated accordingly on stylistic grounds. Yet even if the materials for its construction were prepared at this time they do not seem to have been placed in position until the decision had been taken to roof the entire extended choir at a somewhat greater height than that of the pristine structure (RCAHMS, 1946, ii, 124).[12]

This extension of the choir was quite probably envisaged by Bishop Bjarne, who may even have taken the first steps towards its planning and construction (see below). For the most part, however, the work was of later date and markedly different character. Hence it may be appropriate to sum up the argument to this point. As has been said, the analogies between the Transitional and early Gothic design of St Magnus' and Nidaros Cathedral are so numerous as to suggest the possibility of a direct link. Although the evidence of masons' marks can be as fallible as stylistic similarities it is, once again, remarkable how many to be found throughout these phases at Kirkwall are identical with those of the corresponding phases at Nidaros. (Fischer, D., 1965; Thomson, 1954).

When the Norwegian architect Johan Meyer contributed his study of St Magnus Cathedral to Lauritz Dietrichson's *Monumenta Orcadica* (Meyer 1906) he mentioned some of these resemblances. However, in his concern to associate the original structure with the mainstream of 'Norman Romanesque architecture' coming from France by way of England and Scotland, against the view of it as 'practically a Norwegian edifice' advanced by the Scottish architectural historians David MacGibbon and Thomas Ross (1896-7, i, 267-9) he tended to extend this interpretation—with much less justification—into the immediately succeeding period.

After the west front of the cathedral had been carried up to just above its three portals, work here was brought to a halt, perhaps on account on the death of Bishop Bjarne (1223). More probably, however, it derived from the desire of the canons—and quite possibly of himself—to proceed with the enlargement of the choir. In any event, with the bishopric reduced to prolonged ineffectiveness under Bjarne's successor Jofrey and the earldom diverted by external problems under the heirs of Harald II Maddadson, the canons would be in virtually undisputed control of the building.[13] In a strictly constitutional sense their affairs should have been directed by the archdeacon (of Shetland) but nothing is known of Nicholas who held this position in 1226 (Watt 1969, 254-5, 261) and, as already suggested, the future Bishop Henry may well have been in charge of matters for a prolonged period beforehand (Watt 1969, 250). Thus he and his fellow canons may have pursued their ambition to extend the choir for their corporate services before completing the west end of the nave.

As built, the choir extension virtually doubled the length of this part of the cathedral by the removal of the central apse and aisle gables and the addition of three bays with a rectangular east end.[14] What is particularly interesting about the design is that while the pillars of the arcades are of fully-developed Gothic form many of the other features are of what seems to be a deliberately conservative character. In particular, the arcade and triforium arches are of semi-circular form as if to match the earlier work, and although the aisle and clerestorey windows are of Gothic form this seems to be of a calculated simplicity. The only use of tracery is in the great east window which has evidently been of a less elaborate character than its Victorian reconstruction (RCAHMS, 1946, ii, 119-20, 123-4).

In view of the powerful identity of St Magnus' imparted to it by its original designers—and of which all who see it for the first time are made instantly aware—it is understandable that those concerned with its later development should have felt an obligation to conform. What is rather more surprising about the choir extension, deriving as it did from the close ties of Orkney with the Norwegian church, is the limited extent of Norwegian architectural allusions in its design, especially by comparison with the immediately preceding period. Such allusions are indeed identifiable in the south aisle which appears to be the earliest part of the work and might well have been begun in Bishop Bjarne's time, rising as it does from a base-course similar to that of the transeptal chapels and with door and window openings of early Gothic form (RCAHMS 1946, ii, 119).[15]

Beyond this, however, there is a change, discreet but emphatic, deriving from an architectural director apparently more familiar with French and English Gothic design than that of Norway but with his own independent concept of what would be most appropriate here. In explanation of this MacGibbon and Ross suggested, albeit very tentatively, that it might reflect the influence of Frenchmen previously engaged at Uppsala and Trondheim 'brought over to work at St Magnus' (MacGibbon and Ross, 1896–7, i, 280). However, the French work at the former was of later date and different character, while the design of the Gothic nave at Trondheim was of English derivation (Fischer, G. 1965, i, 334–40) and also quite unlike that of the choir extension at Kirkwall.

When, however, one considers the scale and the skill of the work undertaken here from the 1190's to the 1220's it is clear that it could only have been achieved by a relatively large, well-organised, and resourceful professional group. Initially it may well have depended on experienced masons of the Trondheim school but their successors, though obviously aware of external developments, seem to have had their own notions of how the building should be completed. And if Bishop Bjarne is to be regarded as the effective director of building operations during his episcopate, the next phase can almost as certainly be attributed to Bishop Henry whose background and associations were Orcadian rather than Norwegian.

In the construction of the outer walls of the choir extension a distinct change is apparent in what seems to be the second phase, from the north-east corner of the old choir to the south-east corner of the new. Here French influence is particularly in evidence—in the large untraceried Gothic windows and formidable dimensions of the wall-shafts and ribs of the aisle vaults. The pillars of the arcades are of composite form with powerful keel-shaped main members projecting from plane faces linked by twin lesser shafts of curvilinear section.[16] The boldly detailed capitals include crocketed foliage of French type though there is also a stiff form of trefoil foliage not uncommon in early English and Scottish Gothic. Mingled with these, however, are human and animal grotesques which might have been contributed by a Norwegian carver or one trained in that tradition (RCAHMS, 1946, ii, 123, Figs. 186–9, 192).[17]

The relationship of the new work to the old is particularly felicitous. As was both structurally and aesthetically desirable, the side walls framing the original apse were left in position with their five string-courses continued eastwards, all but one at the same level as before. Thus the arches of the main arcade, triforium, and clerestorey are in continuity throughout, the first two of semi-circular form and the new triforium of identical scale with the middle member of the Romanesque sequence. And if the new clerestorey takes a pointed form, this, with the two phases of the surmounting vault, has been deliberately designed to produce the most exemplary architectural harmony. Externally, too, the east facade is of great distinction in itself and masses well with the (later) central tower and spire (RCAHMS 1946, ii, Fig. 161) (pl. 5).

The latter effect owes much to a heightening of the choir wallhead in the course of the work as a consequence of the decision to lift the vaults within above the level intended earlier. The transepts were raised slightly higher (to achieve the same ridge elevation) and it would seem that the roofing of the nave—at a somewhat lower level—took place in the same period (c.1250) and likewise in association with the vaulting of its central element. This vault is carried on plain chamfered ribs similar to those in the aisles but springing from conoidal corbels (some with dragon carvings) at the level of the Gothic clerestorey and meeting in foliaceous bosses not unlike those in the choir extension but executed by masons of rather less skill[18] (pl. 12). This same 'secondary group' was probably also responsible for the decorative corbelling supporting the parapet of the six eastmost bays of the nave north aisle—an adaptation of the earlier and much more delicate 'Trondheim' version in the transeptal chapels (RCAHMS, 1946, ii, Figs. 168, 173).

In all this work—of such commendable architectural quality in itself—the one regrettable feature is the random use of white Eday stone in the clerestorey exterior at variance with the rich red sandstone of the remainder. It may simply be that at the period in question the latter was not obtainable in sufficient quantity. Fortunately, however, when work began on the belfry stage of the central tower—the crowning feature of the whole design—this was entirely in red stone. With twin pointed openings on each face, mullioned and transomed and vigorously moulded throughout, this is a majestic composition reasonably well completed by the modern parapet and spire and impressively related, in form and scale, to the remainder of the building (RCAHMS, 1946, ii, 120–1, Figs. 161, 179). If, as would seem, it dates from the early fourteenth century, this might associate it with the episcopate of Bishop Dolgfinn 1286–1309, quite probably a Norwegian (Watt 1969, 250), yet the design follows the same independent eclectic formula as the choir extension with allusions of a French and English rather than a Nordic character.

One further task alone remained—the completion of the west front and its integration with the nave by the addition of two bays to the six constructed so far. As originally planned, St Magnus Cathedral was apparently to have twin western towers as well as a central tower over the crossing (RCAHMS 1949, ii, 110–4). This also seems to have been the intention of the builders of the early Gothic portals, but by the time that the central tower was complete the great days of medieval Norway were drawing to a close. The death of King Håkon V Magnusson in 1319 marked the beginning of the end of an independant Norwegian monarchy and as this happened Norwegian control of the island territories gradually weakened.

Well before Orkney and Shetland were absorbed in the Scottish kingdom and church (1468–9, 1472) Scotsmen were established in positions of influence there. By the 1360s both archdeacons were Scots (Watt 1969, 254, 261) and after a period of confusion extending from 1383 to 1418 the Scot Thomas Tulloch emerged in possession of the bishopric (Watt 1969, 252–3).[19] Thus when the west end of the cathedral was eventually completed it was under Scottish auspices and in a more modest form than intended earlier (RCAHMS, 1946, ii, 115-7, Figs. 162, 164). Yet the continuing influence of this remarkable church on all its builders is reflected in the care taken, once again, to match the new work with the old.

NOTES

1. Like a good many other medieval churches—but unusually for a cathedral—St Magnus' was a 'proprietory church' pertaining to the founder and his successors in the Earldom of Orkney (Moonie, 1947).
2. Similar powers appear to have been exercised by the Earls of Orkney, at least until 1196.
3. In practice the Kings of Norway continued to control appointments to bishoprics.
4. As head of the cathedral Chapter the Archdeacon had the status of Provost (*domprost*), but in some cases this became a separate post. In the Orkney diocese, where the Archdeacon of Shetland continued to preside over the Chapter (despite the later emergence of an Archdeacon of Orkney) a functional and financial distinction was recognised between the two responsibilities though it was not until 1542 that this assumed a constitutional form with the creation of a separate Provost (Watt, 1969, 255).
5. The term *Korbrøder* ('choir-brother') was also in use and seems to have been, initially at least, virtually interchangeable with *kannik*. At a later period, however, some at least of the former may have been, to use a Scottish parallel, 'chaplains of the choir'.
6. Among the island cathedrals of the Trondheim province Kirkwall alone seems to have developed a chapter of canons with a clearly established right to conduct episcopal elections. In Man the chapter associated with the cathedral at Peel (*c*.1231) was apparently of 'synodal character' (Watt, 1969, 207). In the Isles (Sodor) the canons of Snizort involved in an episcopal election in 1326–31—apparently representing a 'separatist trend' of Hebridean and Scottish character (Watt, 1969, 207–8)—may have had no more than an intermittent existence. In Faroe (Kirkjubøur), Iceland (Skalholt and Holar), and Greenland (Garðar) the cathedrals appear to have had no formal chapters, the right of episcopal election being claimed by the chapter of Trondheim, and in the case of Faroe at least occasionally by Bergen (Kolsrud, 1958, 192).
7   In view of this it is at least conceivable that the 'ecclesiastic' might have been Bishop Bjarne, though there is no suggestion of this in the fairly comprehensive genealogies of the period.
8. A parallel of slightly later date in mainland Norway was the replacement of the short Romanesque chancel of Stavanger Cathedral, after a fire in 1272, by the handsome six-bay vaulted Gothic choir still to be seen there—though both opened directly from the Romanesque nave without interposition of a crossing or transepts (Fischer, 1963, 49–81). There is also some evidence of Trondheim influence, likewise to be seen, more strongly, in the Swedish cathedral of Linköping (Lindblom, 1944–6, i, 188).
9. Although it has been suggested that the change of design may have been brought about by a collapse of the central tower this seems unlikely. In the earlier building phase construction may well have been limited to the piers.
10. This seems to have been so in the case of the St Magnus' transepts, also those of Nidaros (Fischer, 1965, i, 59), but not of the original St Magnus' choir which had a timber roof at clerestorey level. In the nave, however, the upper walls, windows, and vault seem to be of a single, and rather late, 'early gothic' form.
11. Although the northern term *rumble* has much the same meaning as rubble, in the case of Orkney, where naturally well-shaped slabs are readily available, the resulting masonry may be of quite high quality.
12. The evidence is provided by the remains of a corbel course on the south side of the original choir, likewise on the north side of the extension.
13. While the Cathedral had been founded by Earl Rognvald and remained the property of the earldom there is no evidence that his successors exercised much control over building operations, or that these depended on their continued financial support. Although the west end remained

incomplete, the extension of the choir was an appreciably greater undertaking, funded from revenues and constructed of materials, in part at least, under the control of the Chapter.

14. It is even possible that the lower part of the construction might have been put in hand before the completion of the transeptal chapels, the vaults of which are of quite a well-developed gothic form.

15. As all medieval churches were essentially 'functional' in design there would be a clear concept beforehand of how the additional space was to be used. One might envisage the two bays (of the old choir) east of the crossing as containing the canons' stalls, beyond them on the south side the bishop's throne, most probably (as at Elgin) originally against the blank wall at the junction of the old work with the new rather than one bay farther east as later (Billings, 1845–52, iii, pl. 47). The high altar, with associated *sedilia* on its south side, would be in the penultimate bay, and behind its reredos, in the final bay, would be a 'reliquary chapel' containing the shrines of St Magnus and St Rognvald.

16. The unusual bulk of the pillars in proportion to their height recalls those of the nave at Wells (*c*.1190) and of the outer chapels of Bourges Cathedral (*c*.1200) though there is no evidence, as in the case of Nidaros, of any direct connection with St Magnus'.

17. Lidén has noted certain resemblances to this work at Kirkwall in the west portal of Dale church at Lyster in western Norway. Paradoxically, this work has been traditionally ascribed to Scots masons (conceivably masons who had worked on the 'Scottish' or western side of the Norwegian Sea?)

18. A comparable discrepancy may be seen in the vaulting of the sacristy and vestry towers flanking the east end of the Gothic choir of Stavanger Cathedral (see Note 8), the former being carried on moulded ribs and the latter on ribs with plain chamfers (Fischer, 1963, 58–9).

19. The primary cause of the confusion was the Great Schism (1378–1418) when competing 'provisions' were made by the Popes based at Rome (and supported by, among others, Norway and England) and those in the Avignon succession (supported by Scotland).

BIBLIOGRAPHY

Billings, R W, 1845–52, *Baronial and Ecclesiastical Antiquities of Scotland*, 4 vols

Cant, R G, 1972. 'The Church in Orkney and Shetland and its relations with Norway and Scotland in the Middle Ages., *Northern Scotland*, i, 1 (1972) 1–18

Cant, R G, 1984, "Settlement, Society, and Church Organisation in the Northern Isles', in A Fenton, and H Palsson, eds, *The Northern and Western Isles in the Viking World*, 169–79

Cowan, I B, 1960, 'The Organisation of Scottish Secular Cathedral Chapters', *Records of the Scottish Church History Society*, xiv (1960), 19–47

DN, *Diplomatarium Norvegicum*, I–XX, 1847–1915, Christiania/Oslo

Edwards, K, 1949, *English Secular Cathedrals in the Middle Ages*

Fischer, D, 1965, 'Stenhuggarmerkene' in Fischer, G. 1965, ii, 529–48.

Fischer, G, 1963, *Domkirken i Stavanger: Kirkebygget i Middelalderen*, Oslo

Fischer, G, 1965, *Domkirken i Trondheim: Kirkebygget i Middelalderen*, 2 vols. Oslo

Johnsen, A O, 1945, *Studier verdrørande Nicolaus Brekespeards Legasjon til Norden*, Oslo

Kolsrud, O, 1958, *Noregs Kyrkja Historia*, Oslo

Lindblom, A, 1944–6, *Sveriges Konsthistoria*, 3 vols. Stockholm

MacGibbon, D, and Ross T, 1896–7, *Ecclesiastical Architecture of Scotland*, 3 vols.

Mayer, J, 1906, 'Description of St Magnus Cathedral and its Architectural History' in L Dietrichson, and J Meyer, *Monumenta Orcadica*, 47–71

Mooney, J, 1947, *The Cathedral and Royal Burgh of Kirkwall*

NBL, Norsk Biografisk Leksikon, 19 vols., Christiana/Oslo 1923–83

RCAHMS, 1946, Royal Commission on the Ancient and Historical Monuments of Scotland: *Inventory of Ancient Monuments...of Orkney and Shetland,* 3 vols. vol. ii, Orkney

Simpson, W D, 1961, *The Castle of Bergen and the Bishop's Palace at Kirkwall* (Aberdeen University Studies, 142)

Thomson, A, 1954, 'Masons' Marks in St Magnus Cathedral', *Orkney Miscellany*, i, 57–71

Watt, D E R, 1969, *Fasti Ecclesiae Scoticanae Medii Aevi*, 2nd draft

CHAPTER 11

The Church of St Magnus, Egilsay

Eric Fernie

INTRODUCTION

The *Magnus' Saga* records that when Earl Magnus arrived on Egilsay to meet his rival Earl Hakon he 'went ashore with all his men up to the church, where he passed the night' and that the place where he was killed the next morning 'was rocky and overgrown with moss, but soon God revealed how worthy he was in His eyes, for the spot turned into a fair meadow and he himself won the beauty and greenness of Paradise, which is called the Land of the Living. Afterwards a church was built there' (*Magnus' Saga*, 1987, 29, 32). The surviving remains of the church on the island have been associated with these events of *c*.1116 and given varying dates and significance in consequence. In what follows I wish to ask three questions concerning this building:

1. What is its date?
2. What was its function? and
3. What were its sources?

All three are aspects of the single question 'Why does the church look the way it does?', so it will be best to begin with a brief description (figs. 16a–c). It consists of a rectangular chancel, a nave and a cylindrical western tower arranged on an east–west axis with an overall length of 62 feet 9 inches (19.12 m). The chancel is barrel-vaulted with a chamber above reached through an arched entrance in its west wall. The nave is a short rectangle with a doorway towards the end of each side wall, while the tower has three doorways one above the other on its eastern face.

DATE

The Orkneys were in pagan Norse hands from 876 until the conversion of Earl Sigurd in 995, and since towers built in conjunction with small churches are extremely unusual anywhere in Europe before the middle of the ninth century our building must almost certainly have been built after 995. Indeed its form and parallels make it extremely unlikely that it was erected before the late eleventh

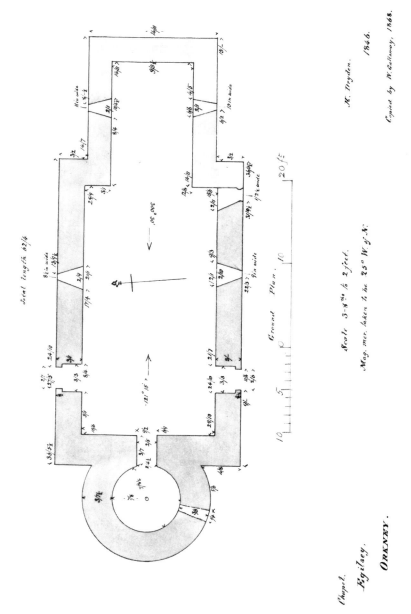

FIGURE 16a   St Magnus, Egilsay, plan (Sir Henry Dryden, 1848, redrawn 1868; Crown copyright RCAMS).

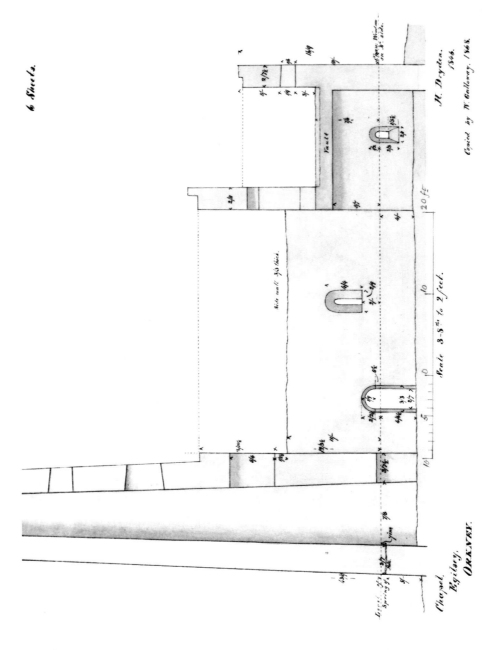

FIGURE 16b   St Magnus Egilsay, longitudinal section to north (Sir Henry Dryden, 1848, redrawn 1868; Crown copyright RCAMS).

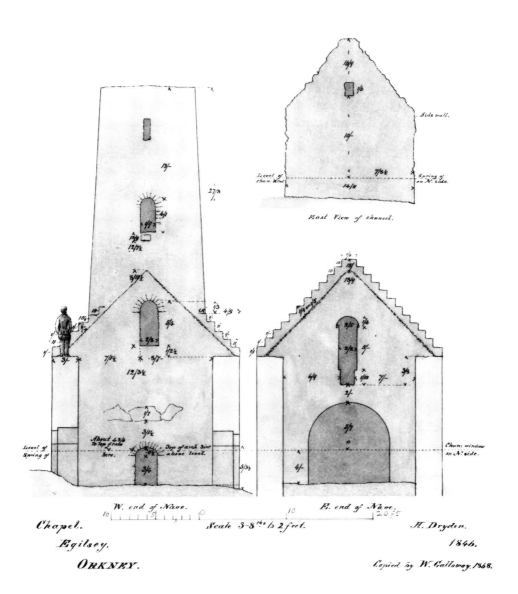

FIGURE 16c   St Magnus, Egilsay, cross-sections (Sir Henry Dryden, 1848, redrawn 1868; Crown copyright RCAMS).

century, when the Romanesque style first appears in Scotland and in Norway, or after the early thirteenth century, when it ceases to be in fashion. Although the dedication to St Magnus can only be traced back to the sixteenth century (*Orkneyinga Saga*, 1873, xcii), it is not unreasonable to assume both that it is much older and that the structure is one of the two churches mentioned in the Saga, that in which St Magnus prayed before his death, or that built to mark the site of the event itself. Of these two possibilities it is more likely that it is the special, purpose-built church which has survived. (Tradition conflicts with this conclusion in placing the location of the martyrdom a quarter of a mile from the church, at a place—HY470300—marked by a stone set up by the vicar of St Magnus in London on the occasion of the octocentenary celebrations in 1937—Marwick, 1951, 172; Ritchie, 1985, 100—but this may well enshrine the facts behind the miraculous transformation of the site 'rocky and overgrown with moss' into a 'fair meadow'—*Magnus' Saga*, 1987, 32—namely that the actual place of the killing was not quite prominent enough for what was required for the successful prosecution of the cult of the saint).

PLATE 20   St Magnus, Egilsay, nave to east. (Crown copyright, HBM Directorate).

This would place the most likely date of construction in 1136 as the Saga says that it was 'twenty years after the killing of Earl Magnus' when Bishop William finally recognised Magnus' holiness and agreed to translate his bones from his grave in the church at Birsay to a shrine before the altar there (*Magnus' Saga*, 1987, 36). The events which convinced him:—the change in the wind on his return from a visit to Norway (almost certainly to deliberate with Rognvald, Magnus' nephew and claimant to the earldom), and his blindness on arrival at Birsay (*Magnus' Sage*, 1987, 35–6), are exquisitely apposite examples of the miracle as political symbol, with William changing his allegiance from the ruling Earl Paul to the party of Rognvald. William's estrangement from Paul would explain his frequent visits to Egilsay at this time and consequent absence from Birsay, where the earl had his palace (*Orkneyinga Saga*, chapters LX, LXVII?, LXX and LXXI, 1873, 95, 104–5, 109, 113, though it should be noted that they are not mentioned in the earlier *Magnus Saga*), and there is in fact reason to believe that the bishop had a residence on the island (Radford, 1983, 26–7; Crawford, 1983, 109–11). When Rognvald came to power he lost no time in pressing acceptance of his uncle's cult, building the cathedral at Kirkwall and transferring the relics to their new setting there (Dietrichson and Meyer, 1906, 24–8; Wainwright, 1962, 189).

FIGURE 17   St Magnus, Egilsay, as in 1822 (Hibbert, 1822, 609).

The simultaneous establishing of three sites to commemorate the saint and the construction of new churches on at least two of them may sound unlikely, but it conforms to the standard practice of capitalising on whatever aspects of a saint's life were available. The arrangements made for St Thomas at Canterbury, for example, offer a close parallel with those just suggested, with the separate points of pilgrimage at the places of his martyrdom and burial and at his shrine being equivalent to the churches at Egilsay, Birsay and Kirkwall respectively. While the points at Canterbury are all in one building they themselves are analogous to the martyria in the Holy Land marking events in the life of Christ, such as the sites of the Crucifixion, the Entombment and the Ascension.

FUNCTION

Apart from the possible significance of the whole church as a commemorative building, the eastern arm would as usual have housed the sanctuary, altar and celebrants, and the broken lower parts of the jambs of the chancel arch (visible in pl. 20) indicate screens which would have separated off the eastern arm and restricted the laity to the nave. The functions of the tower and the eastern upper chamber (also visible in pl. 20) on the other hand are less obvious.

The tower is cylindrical and is entered through a low arch in the west wall of the nave. The drawbar hole in the south doorway to the nave suggests that the floor level at the west end must originally have been nine inches to a foot lower than it is at present, which would increase the restricted height of the opening (4 feet 8 inches (1.42 m), to the crown) to a reasonable size. The ground floor chamber could not have been a porch as there is no western doorway, and as it is too small to have functioned as a meeting place or baptistery (with an internal diameter of only 7 feet 8 inches, 2.34 m, not 10 feet as recorded by the Royal Commission, 1946, 229), its most likely function was simply to house the stairs or ladders to the upper floors. Above this is a doorway with its sill about 1 foot 9 inches (0.53 m) above the level of the eaves of the nave roof. It could not, however, have led into a roof-space, as the opening in the east wall above the chancel arch has a sill which originally lay the same distance *below* eaves level, with the result that a flat ceiling would have cut directly across it (fig. 16c; pl. 20). The western arch must instead have led onto a wooden gallery across the west end of the nave, with its beams resting on the wall-heads and necessitating the raised position of the sill. The provision of a first-floor gallery for an ecclesiastical or lay magnate can be paralleled in numerous structures such as the tenth-and eleventh-century parts of the Anglo-Saxon church of St Mary at Deerhurst (fig. 18) (Knowles, 1927, 152; Taylor and Taylor, 1965, s.v.; Fernie, 1983, 101-6), or, tucked up into the roof-space in a manner very like that at Egilsay, in the late twelfth-century church at Toft Monks in Norfolk.

The next arch in the tower opens onto the exterior above the roof (fig. 16c; pl. 21). It has parallel jambs, indicating that it is a doorway and not a window, though it is unclear why its sill lies some 3 feet (0.91 m) above the ridge, onto which one would otherwise have assumed it gave access. Above that are four windows with

PLATE 21   St Magnus, Egilsay, from south east. (Crown copyright, HBM Directorate).

inward splays, one at each of the cardinal points. The tower was originally some 15 feet (4.57 m) taller than at present, including a cap-like roof as shown in Hibbert's early nineteenth-century engraving (Hibbert, 1822, opp. 608; see fig. 17) making a total of some 63 feet (19.20 m), or about 55 feet (16.76 m) without the roof. Since the overwhelming majority of medieval ecclesiastical towers were built to house bells, it is reasonable to assume that this was the case at Egilsay unless there are good grounds for thinking otherwise. The sound holes could have been situated in the lost storey above the present wall-head. No such holes are shown in Hibbert's engraving, but neither are the extant windows, all openings presumably having been blocked to improve stability. The gap in the north-east quadrant of the present wall-head sits at an odd angle, cuts down into a ring of putlog holes, is not shown in Dryden's elevation of 1848, and hence probably belongs to a modern consolidation.

The tower could not have been built to provide a seriously defensible position. Any determined attacker could have gained relatively easy access via the nave roof to the doorway at its apex, or, if he wished to avoid the attentions of a defender at the window above, via either of the large doors in the nave walls (out of the line of sight of those in the tower) and thence to either of the interior openings in the west wall.

Chancels with chambers above them are most unusual, and seldom of unambiguous purpose. The chamber at Egilsay has been described as a prison (reported by Dryden in MacGibbon and Ross, 1896, I, 131), a dwelling (Muir, 1885, 115; Ritchie, 1985, 100), and a refuge (Marwick, 1952, 32). Nothing supports the notion that it was designed as a prison, but there are a number of instances of early churches with roof-spaces used as dwellings: at Deerhurst, again, the doorway from the tower into the nave roof has the most worn sill in the building, implying traffic of a domestic intensity (figs. 18a, b) (Taylor and Taylor, 1965, s.v.). At Eilean Mor in the Sound of Jura there are remains of a fireplace and chimney in the roof-space of the nave, though this appeared in the nineteenth century to be relatively modern (Muir, in MacGibbon and Ross, 1896, I, 89), and the roof-spaces of numerous Irish churches were used for similar purposes. Most if not all of these examples are however over the nave rather than the chancel. The suggestion that it is a refuge is based on the label 'grief house' applied to it locally in the nineteenth century (Dryden, in MacGibbon and Ross, 1896, I, 131), which has been derived from Old Norse *grið*, a place of safety (Marwick, 1952, 32; DOST, s.v. girth), though again it seems unlikely that it would have been built specifically for such a purpose. Another etymology for 'grief' which may recommend itself is Old Scots *graith* (DOST, s.v.), meaning furnishings, as in 'Ane alter . . . with . . . buke and chalice of silver and al uthir grath belangand tharto' (1454), or 'For carrying the chapell graytht to Lythgow'(1488). This explanation would suggest that the chamber was used as a treasury-cum-sacristy, and, since sacristies were often used for the reservation of the Sacrament (Cross, 1958, 1201), as a form of sanctuary, that is for primarily religious and liturgical purposes.

This hypothesis is supported by the presence of the western gallery, which often occurs in conjunction with a sanctuary of some sort above the eastern chancel. At Deerhurst, Glos. (figs. 18b, c), an opening originally led between an eastern upper chamber and a wooden gallery, the latter provided with the same supports as those still surviving for a gallery at the west end of the nave. Melbourne in Derbyshire has a Romanesque version of the same arrangement, built entirely of stone. In ground plan the crossing appears as a standard element which one would expect to carry a lantern tower. Instead, almost perversely, the arches of the crossing rise no higher than those of the nave arcade, and support a wall passage which runs eastwards into the chamber above the chancel and westwards into clerestorey passages which lead to a tribune gallery at the west end of the nave, providing access to every part of the church at the upper level. This arrangement is like a longitudinal version of centralised palace chapels built for the needs of emperors and bishops such as Charlemagne's palace chapel at Aachen of around 800 or that of the archbishop of Cologne at Schwarzrheindorf consecrated in 1151 (Kubach, 1972, 335, 355). Nor is this surprising, as the church at Melbourne was almost certainly built by a bishop primarily for his own use. In the first place, it is situated on the edge of the village between the manor house and the tithe barn, not at all where one would expect to find a parish church. In the second place, in 1133 Henry I gave the church and manor of Melbourne to Aethelwulf bishop of Carlisle, and as he was driven from his diocese in 1136 and spent the rest of his episcopate until his

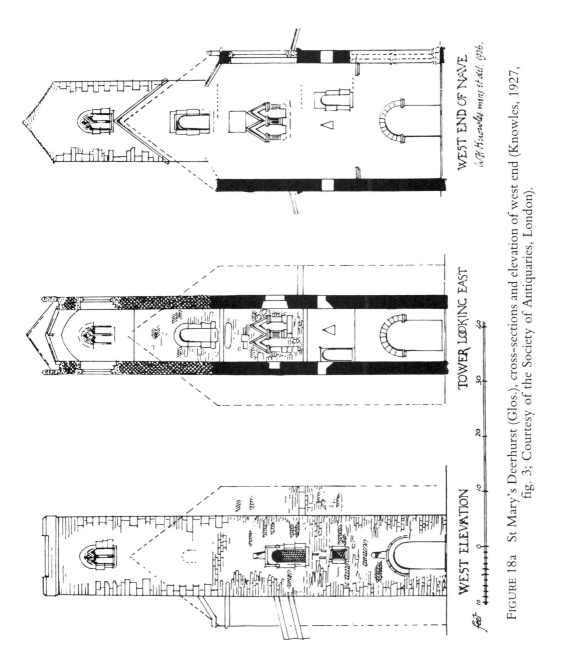

WEST END OF NAVE

W. H. Knowles mens et del. 1926.

TOWER LOOKING EAST

WEST ELEVATION

FIGURE 18a St Mary's Deerhurst (Glos.), cross-sections and elevation of west end (Knowles, 1927, fig. 3; Courtesy of the Society of Antiquaries, London).

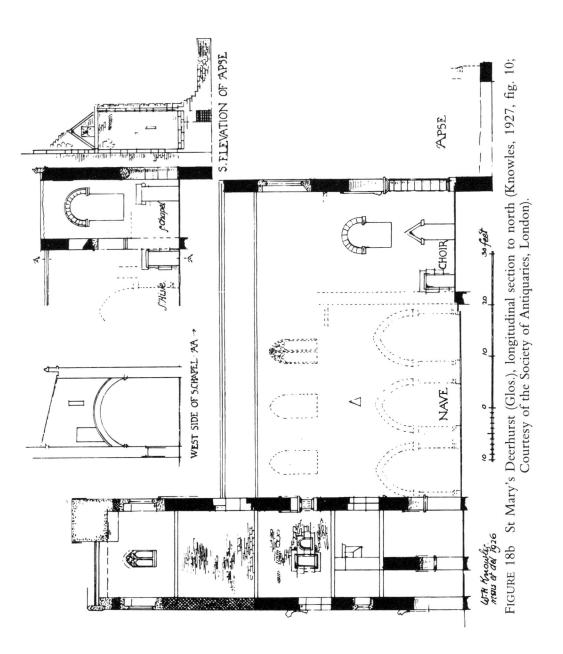

FIGURE 18b St Mary's Deerhurst (Glos.), longitudinal section to north (Knowles, 1927, fig. 10; Courtesy of the Society of Antiquaries, London).

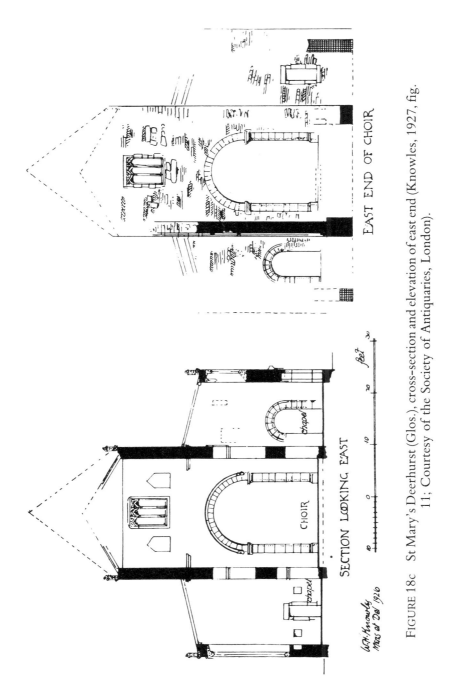

FIGURE 18c St Mary's Deerhurst (Glos.), cross-section and elevation of east end (Knowles, 1927, fig. 11; Courtesy of the Society of Antiquaries, London).

death in 1157 in exile, it is likely that he passed a good deal of time at Melbourne (Barman, 1974, 8, 9, 18–19).

One is reminded of the possibility that Bishop William may have had St Magnus built as part of an episcopal residence on Egilsay, a connection which combines with the commemorative function of the church to explain the high quality of the masonry, the techniques of construction and the layout. Despite the intractable nature of the material the church is neatly disposed and regularly built, the plentiful putlog holes running right through the wall indicating both care in construction and an intention to maintain the fabric in good order thereafter (pl. 21). The measurements show a similar attention to detail, with the length made up of four units of just under 15 feet (4.54 m), one for the chancel, two for the nave and one for the tower, while the chancel and tower have widths of the same unit.

SOURCES

The three-cell plan of chancel, nave and west tower is a popular one for small churches throughout the British Isles and northern Europe from the tenth century to the sixteenth. Egilsay can thus, in general terms, be placed in the same group as later Saxon buildings like St Benet's in Cambridge, Saxo-Norman ones of around 1100 like Kirk Hammerton, and buildings of the first half of the twelfth century such as Wharram-le-Street and St Rules at St Andrews, as well as examples closer to home like those on Eynhallow and the Brough of Birsay (assuming, that is, that their western chambers originally carried towers).

Attempts to be more specific have produced three propositions: that the design comes from Ireland, that it comes from East Anglia, and that it is *sui generis*. The third (Sharratt and Sharratt, 1985, 317) is an unhappy solution in that it evades the questions posed by the clear similarities with other churches, if indeed this can ever be an explanation for something as dependent on its cultural and material context as a building. It only makes sense if it is taken as shorthand for the notion of a local school, which certainly has an important part to play in an understanding of St Magnus. Of the two main contenders, Ireland has been supported by Wilson (1863, 386–7), Dryden (in MacGibbon and Ross, 1896, I, 127–35), Boase (1953, 150), Radford (1962, 183 and 1983, 27), Bailey (1971, 86, 222), Laing (1974, 196–8), Ritchie and Ritchie (1978, 68), Fawcett (1985, 34), and Cruden (1986, 11), and East Anglia only by Donaldson (1986, 3), though one can add Dietrichson and Meyer (1906, 23) in that they argue for a 'non-Celtic' source. Despite the weight of opinion in favour of Ireland I believe that East Anglia has the stronger case as the source, the source that is of the design, which has been executed entirely in local Orcadian techniques, of masonry, roofing and tower building.

The Irish case rests on four factors. The overall length of nearly 63 feet (19.2 m) corresponds closely to the traditional Irish figure of 60 feet (of unknown length) (Dryden, in MacGibbon and Ross, 1896, I, 133–5); the masonry and attendant techniques are similar, from the manner in which the stone is laid to the lack of an external chamfer on the windows and the provision of an off-set in the thickness of the gable wall to take the roof; the chamber over the chancel can be paralleled in Cormac's Chapel at Cashel and in many other places; and finally the round tower is ubiquitous in Ireland.

Against these the following points can be made. As to size, numerous examples of the three-cell type approach 60 English feet (18.29 m) in length, such as, among those mentioned above, Kirk Hammerton at 54 feet (16.46 m) and Wharram-le-Street at 66 (20.11 m). Next, the materials and techniques of Egilsay church are local and virtually timeless. The stone-work of the nave is difficult to distinguish from that of the sixteenth-century earl's palace at Birsay, and that of the tower from the equally late parts of the palace at Kirkwall, while the method of roofing is found in the farm buildings near the pier on the island. Just as churches in this sort of masonry are found in the thirteenth century in Norway, after the introduction of good ashlar techniques at places like Trondheim Cathedral, so there is nothing to prevent Egilsay from post-dating Kirkwall, though it might be a little surprising if it were being erected at exactly the time when masons skilled in cutting ashlar were at work on the cathedral in the ten or fifteen years after 1137. In the case of the chamber over the chancel, the Irish examples at places like Glendalough and Cormac's Chapel, or the chancel at Eilean Mor (which may be taken as of Irish type), appear to arise from a technique of roof construction rather than from the specific wish to have a room over the chancel, as is clearly the case at Egilsay with its separate vertical sections of wall between floor and roof. In this regard it is also noteworthy that there is no corbelling in the roof of the chamber (fig. 16b; pls. 20, 21), the commonest method of roofing in stone in Ireland.

As far as round towers are concered, the Irish examples differ from that at Egilsay in their shape, their proportions and in their position in relation to the church. Egilsay tower curves before tapering whereas the Irish towers have a straight taper, and it has a cap-shaped roof rather than a cone (pl. 21; fig. 17). Taking the examples without their roofs, Egilsay (at $c.15 \times 55$ feet, 4.57×16.76 m) has proportions of a fraction over 1:3.5, the round tower of Irish type at Abernethy (at 16×72 feet, 4.87×21.95 m) 1:4.5, and those at Brechin (Brash, 1862, 189), Antrim (Hare and Hamlin, 1986, 136) and Glendalough (Henry, 1970, pl 67) 1:5.

As regards their position, the great majority of the Irish examples are free-standing. In only a few instances are they attached to the church and in all of those, with one exception, they are attached as if at random around the circumference, as in the twelfth-century church of Temple Finghin at Clonmacnoise (Henry, 1970, 158-9, pl 66). By contrast, Egilsay and the only other two Orcadian churches with round towers, those at Deerness and Stenness, both destroyed in the eighteenth century, have symmetrical arrangements (Low, 1879, xxiii, 53-4. The churches of Tingwall, Ireland and Burra in Shetland are reported as having had towers, but neither their position nor their form is known: Low, 1879, 77-8, 188, 189). The only example of an Irish tower on the centre of the facade is that at Trinity church, Glendalough, of uncertain date and largely destroyed, but of which there is an early engraving (Dunraven, 1875, 99) which has provided the basis for a reconstruction (Leask, 1955, fig. 41) (figs. 19a and b). Despite the fact that it is a unique example, its similarities to Egilsay are so strong that the Irish case might appear unanswerable

FIGURE 19a   Trinity Church, Glendalough (Wicklow), engraving (Dunraven, 1875, 99).

FIGURE 19b   Trinity Church, Glendalough (Wicklow), reconstruction (Leask, 1955, fig. 41).

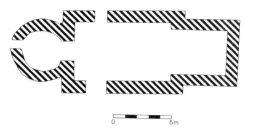

FIGURE 20   Bowthorpe Church, Norwich (Norfolk), plan of excavated church (Courtesy of Norfolk Museums Services).

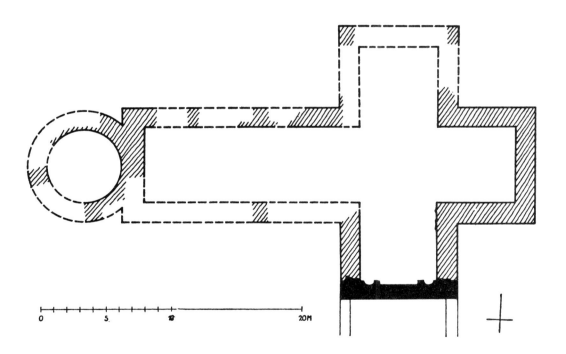

FIGURE 21   St John's, Johannisberg (Hessen), plan (Oswald, *et al.*, 1966, 132).

on this basis alone. Any such parallel is however vitiated by at least two factors. First, only the upper part of the tower is round, sitting uncomfortably on a rectangular base. Secondly, the rectangular base is itself an addition to the church, an addition which blocked the original western entrance so that a doorway had to be inserted into the south wall of the nave, removing another apparent parallel with Egilsay. Indeed the arrangement of the west end of Trinity church is so piecemeal that one is tempted to see it as the conversion of a standard Irish plan into the form of a building such as Egilsay, if not in reality then at least in Leask's reconstruction.

In sharp contrast there are over a hundred churches in East Anglia with a round tower attached to the axis of the facade, and dozens of examples which in plan are

PLATE 22 St Magnus, Egilsay from the south west. (Crown copyright, HBM Directorate).

PLATE 24   Ratekau Church (Schleswig–Holstein) from south-west. (Courtesy of Orkney Museums Service).

PLATE 23   Hales Church (Norfolk) from the south west. (Photo. S Heywood).

virtually indistinguishable from Egilsay, such as the recently excavated church of St Michael at Bowthorpe in Norwich (figs. 16a, 20) (Ayers, forthcoming), or, among standing churches, St Julian's in the same city, and the parish churches of Hales (pl. 23), Colney and Cranwich (Taylor and Taylor, 1965, s.v.). Most of these towers are regular cylinders with wooden roofs, so that in these respects Egilsay differs from the East Anglian examples as much as those from Ireland, suggesting once more the use of local building techniques.

Links between the Orkneys and East Anglia may at first glance appear more difficult to establish than those with Ireland, though one may begin by at least pointing to the possibility that St Magnus himself had English origins. William of Worcester, in his *Itinerary*, claims that the saint 'was conceived near London Bridge' (Sanctus Magnus, rex et comes de Orkenway, . . . fuit conceptus prope pontem Londiniarum', 1778, 356-7). William wrote in the fifteenth century and thought Egilsay was the main island of the Orkneys, but his source for this extraordinarily precise piece of information may well be reliable, as he claims to have heard it from one Sinclair, who could be Sir John Sinclair, a canon of Kirkwall Cathedral in the fifteenth century. The reference to London Bridge is explained by the fact that in the Middle Ages the Scandinavian quarter, with its church of St Magnus, was situated near its north end. (Dickens, 1935, 51-2). There are in addition other and more compelling reasons, concerning architectural links and patterns of trade across the North Sea, for looking to the south-east rather than the south-west in a search for the sources of Egilsay church.

The origins of the round-towered churches of East Anglia have themselves been extensively discussed, all scholars until recently concluding that the type was a local invention in response to the lack of good building stone. Stephen Heywood has however pointed to the similarities between these buildings and the round-towered churches of north Germany and what was in the period southern Denmark (1977, 25; 1988, 169-77). Those in the area around Bremen and further south are circular inside and out, they are numerous, and they are documented from the late tenth century. The abbess Hathui (973-1013), for example, is recorded as having built a church of stone at Heeslingen, where a round western tower survived until the late eighteenth century (Oswald, *et al.*, 1966, 410); at Johannisberg near Hersfeld excavations have revealed the round western tower of the church founded in the early eleventh century (fig. 21); Ratekau in Schleswig-Holstein offers a close external comparison with East Anglian towers such as those at Hales and Roughton (pls. 23, 24).

For an explanation of this transfer of types across the North Sea one need look no further than the ancient links between the Anglo-Saxons and both Schleswig and Saxony, the presence of bishops of apparently German origin in East Anglia in the tenth century (Whitelock, 1972) and the great prestige of the Holy Roman Empire in the tenth, eleventh and twelfth centuries. In addition, there are at least some grounds for thinking that Egilsay might depend directly on the continental source rather than on the English intermediaries, when one considers both the physical similarities of the buildings (pls. 22, 23, 24) and the close links of Orkney with the archbishopric of Hamburg-Bremen, both at the time of Adalbert (archbishop 1042–72) and in the late eleventh and early twelfth centuries (Adam of Bremen: in Tschan, III, 24, 75; IV, 35, and in Dietrichson & Meyer, 344, 366, 384; Watt, 1969, 247–8; Crawford, 1983, 105–9). Indeed, if one considers the geographical relationship between Bremen, East Anglia and the Orkneys from a northern rather than the more conventional southern perspective (fig. 4), then the North Sea appears more like a lake than a barrier, with our three areas forming three corners of a rectangle and Norway and Sweden the fourth, where other examples of round-towered churches can be found. Whether Egilsay church is more closely affiliated with East Anglia or North Germany remains an open question, but that its design should be seen in the context of the North rather than the Irish Sea seems to me to be indisputable.

CONCLUSION

To the three questions posed in the introduction to this paper I would, then, answer as follows.

1. St Magnus at Egilsay was built between the late eleventh century and the late twelfth, probably after the murder of the saint in 1116 and perhaps in 1136 when his sanctity was recognised by both the bishop and the future earl.
2. If it was constructed after 1116 then the church's primary function was to mark one of the sites associated with the martyrdom, either as a replacement of the old church in which he prayed beforehand or as a new building at the place of the killing itself, with the balance of probability pointing to the latter. The chamber above the chancel is likely to have had a religious function as a treasury or sacristy-cum-sanctuary, which, taken in conjunction with gallery at the west end of the nave, gives it the appearance of a bishop's church.
3. Its design belongs to a family of buildings originating in North Germany and linked by the North Sea.

I cannot conclude this paper without referring to a nineteenth-century parallel to this last point. In January 1986 Dr Mark Dilworth, Keeper of the Scottish Catholic Archives, presented to the Dining club of the Society of Antiquaries of Scotland a brief account of the Prefecture of the Arctic, established by Pope Pius IX in 1854 to care for the souls of the Roman Catholic inhabitants of the northern regions (Dilworth, forthcoming). The jurisdiction of the Prefect Apostolic of the North Pole, to give him his full rather curious title, included Caithness, the Orkneys, the Faroes, Lapland, Iceland, Greenland and even part of Hudson's Bay, with the prefecture centred first at Wick and then at Copenhagen. It is a suggestive coincidence, if no more than that, that Copenhagen is only a little further from Schleswig than Wick is from Egilsay.

ACKNOWLEDGEMENTS

I would like to record my thanks to Mark Dilworth for allowing me to refer to his paper on the Prefecture of the Arctic in advance of its publication, to John Higgitt for his suggestions concerning the meaning of the term 'grief', to Graham Ritchie and Raymond Lamb for their help with the procuring of illustrations, and to Ian Fisher, Hans-Emil Lidén, Kenneth Nicholls, Harry Gordon Slade, Barbara Crawford and others for helpful comments at the Conference. The many examples of upper chambers not discussed here will be considered in a subsequent paper.

BIBLIOGRAPHY

Adam of Bremen, *History of the Archbishops of Hamburg-Bremen*, edited and trans F J Tschan, New York, 1959; *Monumenta Germaniae Historica*, Scriptores, VII, Hannover, 1846, 267–389
Ayers, B, forthcoming, Excavation Report on Bowthorpe Church. Norfolk Archaeological Unit
Bailey, P, 1971, *Orkney*
Barman, R J, 1974, *A History and Guide to the Parish Church of Melbourne*
Boase, T, 1953, *Oxford History of English Art, 1100–1216*
Brash, R R, 1860, 'The round tower of Abernethy, with drawings', *Proc. Soc. Antiq. Scot.*, iii, 303–19
Brash, R R, 1862, 'Notices, historical and architectural, of the round tower of Brechin', *Proc. Soc. Antiq. Scot.*, iv, 188–211
Crawford, B, 1983, 'Birsay and the early earls and bishops of Orkney', in *Birsay: A Centre of Political and Ecclesiastical Power* (Orkney Heritage, 2)
Cross, F, 1958, *Oxford Dictionary of the Christian Church*
Cruden, S, 1986, *Scottish Medieval Churches*
Dickens, B, 1935, 'St Magnus and his countess', *Proc. Orkney Antiq. Soc.*, xiii, 51–2
Dietrichson, L and Meyer, J, 1906, *Monumenta Orcadica*
Dilworth, M, forthcoming, in Review of Scottish Culture
Donaldson, G, 1986, 'Scotland's earliest church buildings', in *Scottish Church History*, 1–10
DOST: *Dictionary of the Older Scottish Tongue*
Dunraven, Earl of, 1875, *Notes on Irish Churches*
Fawcett, R, 1985, *Scottish Medieval Churches*
Fernie, E, 1983, *The Architecture of the Anglo-Saxons*
Hare, M and Hamlin, A, 1986, 'The study of early church architecture in Ireland: an Anglo-Saxon viewpoint', in L A S Butler and R K Morris, eds, *The Agnlo-Saxon Church*, 131–45
Henry, F, 1970, *Irish Art in the Romanesque Period 1020–1170 A.D.*
Heywood, S, 1977, *Minor Church Building in East Anglia during the Eleventh and Twelfth Centuries*. M.A. report, University of East Anglia
Heywood, S, 1988, 'The round towers of East Anglia', in J Blair, ed., Minsters and Parish Churches, the Local Church in Transition, 950–1200.
Hibbert, S, 1822, *Description of the Shetland Islands*

Knowles, W H, 'Deerhurst Priory Church: including the result of the excavations conducted during 1926', *Archaeologia*, lxxvii, 141–61

Kubach, H, 1972, *Romanische Kirchen an Rhein und Maas*

Laing, L, 1974, *Orkney and Shetland: an Archaeological Guide*

Leask, H G, 1955, *Irish Churches and Monastic Buildings*, I, Dundalk

Low, G, 1879, *A Tour through the Islands of Orkney and Shetland*

MacGibbon, D and Ross, T, 1896, *The Ecclesiastical Architecture of Scotland*

Magnus' Saga, 1987, trans and with an intro by H Pálsson and P Edwards

Marwick, H, 1951, *Orkney*

Marwick, H, 1952, *Orkney Farm Names*

Muir, T S, 1885, *Ecclesiological Notes on Some of the Islands of Scotland*

Orkneyinga Saga, 1873, ed. J Anderson; 1978, trans H Pálsson and P Edwards

Oswald, F, Schaefer, L and Sennhauser, H, 1966, *Vorromanische Kirchenbauten*, Munich

Radford, C A R, 1962, 'Art and architecture: Celtic and Norse', in Wainwright, 163–87

Radford, C A R, 1983, 'Birsay and the spread of Christianity to the north', in *Birsay: a Centre of Political and Ecclesiastical Power* (Orkney Heritage, 2)

RCAHMS, 1946: Royal Commission on the Ancient and Historical Monuments of Scotland, *Orkney and Shetland*

Ritchie, A, 1985, *Orkney and Shetland*

Ritchie, A and Ritchie, G, 1978, *The Ancient Monuments of Orkney*

Sharratt, P and Sharratt, F, 1985, *Ecosse Romane*

Taylor, H M, and J, 1965, *Anglo-Saxon Architecture*

Wainwright, F T, 1962, *The Northern Isles*

Watt, D, 1969, *Fasti Ecclesiae Scotticanae Medii Aevi ad Annum 1638*

Whitelock, D, 1972, 'The pre-Viking Age Church in East Anglia', *Anglo-Saxon England*, i, 1–24

William of Worcester, 1778, *Itineraria*, ed. J Nasmith

Wilson, D, 1863, *Prehistoric Annals of Scotland*

GLOSSARY OF ARCHITECTURAL TERMS

BILLET MOULDING   A continuous moulding incorporating a regular series of small rectangular projections.

CHEVRON   A V-shaped decoration, usually applied in a continuous zig-zag pattern.

CLERESTOREY   An upper tier of windows, above the level of flanking aisles, casting light into the central space of a church

CORBEL TABLE   A row of projecting blocks carrying a cornice or parapet

CROCKET   A projecting carved ornament, usually of leaf form, and generally applied repetitively at salient angles.

FREESTONE   A finely grained stone that can be freely cut in any direction.

JAMB   The vertical flank of an opening in a wall

LABEL MOULDING   A salient moulding around the head of a wall opening, designed to throw off water

LANCET WINDOW   A single window with a sharply pointed arched head.

MULLION   A vertical bar sub-dividing the lights of a window

OCULUS   A circular window, or a circular opening within a window

OGEE   A double-curved line, resulting in an S-shape. In an ogee arch the arcs are first concave and then convex

ORDER   In a medieval arch of more than minimal width, strength was ensured by composite construction with concentrically built half-rings set out to a stepped profile. Each half-ring is known as an order

PLATE TRACERY   Decorative openings at the head of a window, in which the openings are cut through a flat plate of stone

REREDOS   A carved or painted panel behind an altar, which might be decorated with biblical themes or with scenes from the life of the saint to whom the altar was dedicated

RESPOND   A half-pier carrying one side of an arch, and often at the end of an arcade

REVEAL   The external part of the vertical flank of a window or, less frequently, of a doorway

SPANDREL   The approximately triangular area between an arch or arches and the adjacent horizontal and vertical mouldings

STRING COURSE   An extended horizontal moulding built into a wall

SYNTHRONON   Benches provided for the clergy either in an apse or the chancel area of a church; usually applied only to Early Christian and Byzantine churches

TRIFORIUM   In churches of three (or four) internal storeys the triforium is the stage below the clerestorey. It is usually in the form of an arcaded passage in the wall thickness, but the term can be more loosely applied to a space which stretches back into the space above the aisle roof, with an arcade towards the main space

VESSEL   One of the major contained spaces within a church

VOLUTE CAPITAL (OR CAP)   A capital with spiral scrolls at the angles; ultimately inspired by the Corinthian capitals of the Greeks and Romans

VOUSSOIR   One of the wedge-shaped stones which make up a true arch and which, by its shape, makes the arch self-supporting

WATER-LEAF CAPITAL (OR CAP)   A capital with broad flattened leaves which usually curl up at the corners

SECTION III: CULTURE

Literary, Artistic and Musical Achievements of the Age.

Much of medieval 'culture' was associated with the 'cult' of saints (and the two words are both derived from latin 'colere' = to worship). The need to provide adornment for a saint's resting-place, to create visual images of him and his life and death, to compose music for the liturgy and religious ceremonial necessary for keeping his memory alive, all stimulated the production of works of art and culture which typify the Middle Ages, and the twelfth century more than others. A large and unknown proportion of this fragile material has gone, due to the passage of time and the turbulence of history, so that we are left with a very limited impression of the richness of object and colour and sound which once filled our great churches. But we can be quite certain that the Cathedral of St Magnus would have been richly decorated with gifts from the earldom family and donations from the pious worshippers and pilgrims who visited the shrine of the martyred saint. Once again the written sagas of these northern lands give us incidental comments about such matters. When Bishop William led the grand procession taking the holy relics from Birsay to Kirkwall they were carried in a reliquary (which most probably survived until the Reformation although we know nothing more of it). Many of the miracles recorded in St Magnus Saga as happening to pilgrims to the shrine at Kirkwall resulted in sums of money and in one case 'a great deal of money' being given to the shrine; while two men 'stole some gold' from the shrine and suffered in consequence (*Orkneyinga Saga* ch. 57). Presumably the rest was 'stolen' at the Reformation although the remarkable fact that the saint's relics were preserved and hidden high up in the large south pillar of the choir suggests that reverence for the patron saint continued to exist at that time (pl. 1). There seems to be little doubt that these bones are those of St Magnus, while the opposite pillar held another skeleton which could hardly belong to anyone other than Earl Rognvald, the founder of the Cathedral, whom we know from the Saga was buried there after his murder in 1158 and soon came to be venerated and called 'the Holy' (*Orkneyinga Saga*, ch. 104, 109; Mooney, 1935, 253–5). The extension of the choir, most probably under Bishop Bjarni (see Cant, above), may well have been stimulated by the need to provide space for two saintly tombs; in this case Bishop Bjarni was the moving spirit, for he is said to have had Rognvald's relics translated (moved from grave to shrine) with papal permission.

So the cults were there in plenty, and as a result the Cathedral became the central focus of a cultural movement, attracting pilgrims and transmitting inspiration from the life and death of St Magnus out into the northern world. One of the most revealing contributions to the Conference was that lecture which demonstrated the extent to which St Magnus appears in sculpture and art throughout Scandinavia (see Blindheim, below). In this respect we benefit from the remarkable preservation of religious figures in Scandinavia. The poverty of collections of medieval religious sculpture surviving in England was dramatically obvious at the recent 'Age of Chivalry' exhibition in London where the best wooden religious sculpture by medieval English craftsmen had been brought over from churches and museums in Scandinavia because so little has survived in this country. Statues and representations of St Magnus in Norway, Denmark and Iceland show how popular and widespread his cult was, alongside the martyred kings Olaf and Edmund and the murdered archbishop, Thomas à Becket. Moreover, several of these representations are from the late Middle Ages, some of the Icelandic ones even post-Reformation in date, showing how long the memory of St Magnus was cultivated in northern lands. The survival of the cult in Iceland into the late Middle Ages is further demonstrated by the remarkable discovery of several fragments of a St Magnus hymn incorporated into the binding of old Icelandic MSS (see De Geer, below). Whereas there are only three certain medieval church dedications to St Magnus in Orkney today, and five in Shetland there are ten in Iceland. Evidence also suggests that the cult spread into eastern Europe for the Cathedral Church at Prague is said to have had a relic of St Magnus (Mooney, 1935, 255), and his name even appears in a Russian list of saints. This evidence for the widespread nature of the cult symbolises the earldom's involvement in European culture, which must have helped to make Orkney a known and integral part of the international ecclesiastical network.

This involvement of Orkney and its ruling caste in the two worlds of the Scandinavian north and the European south is further shown by the studies of the literary relics of the age. Both the saga of the earls (*Orkneyinga Saga*) and the skaldic poetry attributed to Earl Rognvald are foremost examples of the literary skill attained by the cultivated writers and poets of twelfth-century Scandinavia (in particular Iceland). But clearly these writers also drew inspiration from more southerly culture as is demonstrated remarkably in the verses written in Provence by Earl Rognvald which incorporate elements of the newly-fashionable 'courtly-love' songs and poems. These 'constitute a case-study in cultural links' (see Bibire, below). Rognvald was of course on his way to the Holy Land, fulfilling the pilgrimage never undertaken by his uncle Magnus. But Earl Hakon had done it before him and Earl Thorfinn had been to Rome before *him*. As widely-travelled as their Viking ancestors, although with more peaceful intent, these Orkney earls brought back ideas and inspiration from southerly lands which they wished to incorporate into their northern culture. They were patrons of the arts in the best tradition, and the Cathedral dedicated to the martyred member of their family is the most supreme example of that patronage put into effect. It preserves a glorious memorial to Orkney's place in the wider European world of the twelfth century.

BIBLIOGRAPHY

Mooney. H, 1935, *St Magnus*

CHAPTER 12

St Magnus in Scandinavian Art

Martin Blindheim

Magnus Erlendson was enshrined twenty years after his death, in 1136 or 1137. He thus became one of the earliest national saints of the Norse world. Norse is here used for Norway and the Norwegian setttlements in the west and the north-west. St Olav had been enshrined about one hundred years before Magnus, Halvard of Oslo a little less than a hundred years before and the Irish St Sunniva and her brother Albanus (if they ever lived) and the Selja-men, some time in the eleventh century.

It is said in the *Longer Magnus Saga* that Magnus' *Vita* and the lectionaries were composed twenty years after his death by a Master Robert. They were necessary for the feasts of 16 April when he died and 13 December when he was enshrined. If Master Robert is Robert of Cricklade, he is supposed to have written about Thomas Becket too (*KHL sub* Magnus). The different sagas, hymns and breviaries are in great debt to Master Robert.

How popular did St Magnus become? Dedications of altars and churches ought to give us a fair picture of his fame, although we have to remember that only a few of the former dedications are known to us today, (possibly with the exception of Iceland). About 1300 Bishop Erlend of the Faeroe Islands began building a cathedral to St Magnus in Kyrkjebøur. It was never finished but got a relic of the saint from Kirkwall. Ten churches and altars in Iceland were dedicated to St Magnus, and the church diaries, the *máldager*, mention in some places St Magnus statues (Larusson, 1962; *KHL sub* Magnus).

St Magnus fame ought to have reached Norway very early, but today only one altar dedication is known. That is in the ecclesiastical centre, Trondheim Cathedral, where he certainly ought to be. In the fifteenth century an altar and later a choir is mentioned (Engelstad, 1936, 203). The original dedication was probably much older.

One would not have expected much interest for this Atlantic saint in medieval Denmark, but four altar dedications are known: one is mentioned as early as 1304 in the cathedral of Lund in Scania County, another in Torhamn church in Blekinge County to the east, one in the cathedral of Viborg in Jutland and one in Tating-Eiderstedt, possibly in southern Jutland (see fig. 4). The last three were first mentioned in the fifteenth century. All four may of course be earlier (Jørgensen, 1909). The main reason for the Danish dedications to St Magnus may have been the

PLATE 25a   Statue of St Magnus from the Cathedral, Kirkwall (730mm high × 200mm wide). (Courtesy of Orkney Museums Service).

PLATE 25b Statue of St Olav from the Cathedral, Kirkwall (640mm high × 240mm wide). (Courtesy of Orkney Museums Service).

presence of a small colony of Scots in Copenhagen at the end of the Middle Ages. They had a St Ninian guild or society and a St Ninian altar in Our Lady's Church, where a St Magnus relic was also found (Liebgott, 1982, 179). In Sweden no churches or altars dedicated to Earl Magnus appear to have been known.

We do not know how early the St Magnus feast days entered the Norwegian church calendars. In Orkney it naturally happened in 1135 for the two church feasts (16 April and 13 December). Usually the day of death (16 April) became the more important of the two, but in Iceland it was the opposite (Larusson, 1966). Already before the end of the Middle Ages painted or carved calendars were produced for people to know the Sundays and the more important saints' days or they risked being fined (*Nordisk Kultur*, 1934). From post-Reformation times about a thousand wooden calendars or clogs have been preserved in the Scandinavian countries proper. In modern Norwegian printed calendars 16 April was marked with St Magnus name. A few years ago all the saints' names were dropped for economic reasons.

It is an interesting question as to how St Magnus was depicted in art. How should we recognise him in the very great crowd of European saints? By his attributes if they still are there, or by special characteristic traits. Magnus Erlendsson was not a king but a *jarl* or earl which in Scandinavia was a title next to a king. In 1237 King Hakon of Norway introduced the German title 'hertug' or duke for his father-in-law earl Skule, and bestowed it later on his sons. The princes were allowed to wear a ribbon or a garland, a ribbon with flowers on it, around their head.[2] When Saint Magnus is depicted with a ribbon or a garland it means that the Church accepted that this was right despite his lower rank. In pictorial art this could hardly have happened before the end of the thirteenth century at the earliest. In Scandinavian and European art some heads and whole figures with garlands or ribbons around the head have been preserved from the thirteenth century onwards. As a rule they are beardless but exceptions exist in European art. They are supposed to depict dukes despite general difficulties of identification. They must not be confused with beribboned angels. Magnus died at the age of about 30 to 35 years old, and according to the fashion of the day he should have a full beard. But he was described by Master Robert as a youthful and beardless man. The sources do not agree on the weapon with which Magnus was killed, whether a sword or an axe. Consequently both weapons may be his attributes, or only one of them.

Starting at the centre of his cult in Kirkwall there is a relief made of sandstone representing a beardless man standing with an upright sword in his right hand and with a ribbon about his head (pl. 25a). His left hand is playing with his cloak-string and according to dress and style it should date from the beginning of the four-teenth century. On this worn relief one cannot expect to see smaller details such as flowers on the ducal garland. The details mentioned make it very probable that the relief, represents St Magnus himself as concluded already by Ludvig Daae in 1879. (Daae, L., 1879, 204). From the Cathedral also comes a St Olav relief of exactly the same size, appearance and material as the St Magnus relief (pl. 25b). St Olav's dress, crown and halberd make it clear that the date of this relief can hardly be earlier than *c.* 1400, probably somewhat later. Consequently the two reliefs must either be of different periods, or, what is more reasonable, the carver of the St Magnus relief had an earlier model to copy, which would explain the difference of style.

We may, however, have a fragment of an older representation of the saint which has not previously been recognised. In spring 1987 I made a visit to Trondheim and explained to Torgeir Suul, architect and head of the Cathedral's Restoration Office how one would expect St Magnus to look in medieval art. After having heard my quest Mr Suul pointed to a fragment of a more than life-sized head in his office (pl. 26). The fragment is the very top of a head carved in soapstone. The size, *c*.28 cm from temple to temple (*c*.10 cm more than life-size) makes it very probable that it once belonged to one of the big lost statues from the cathedral's west front.[3] Many fragments and a few almost complete statues are on display in the Cathedral Museum. They were carved from *c*.1260 (in Archbishop Einar's period) till the great conflict with the royal power in the beginning of the 1280s, when works of this kind probably stopped. Seen from the front the fragment is carved with curling hair and with a garland with three flowers around the forehead.

PLATE 26   Fragment of head *c*.28 × 13cm. Trondheim Cathedral. (Photo. M Blindheim: Courtesy of Restoration Office, Trondheim).

PLATE 27   Statue of St Magnus from altarpiece originally in Torhamn Church, Blekinge.
(Photo. courtesy ATA, Stockholm).

It must once have been part of a statue on the west front and no earl/duke saint other than Magnus is known. If the fragment came from a head somewhere else on the cathedral, garlanded heads might possibly represent princes of the royal family who were titled dukes. Garlanded heads without known individuality and dated to about 1300 are preserved from the cathedrals in Oslo and in Stavanger. But in my opinion the size of the Trondheim head makes this possibility unlikely.

In Denmark better preserved sources than in Norway give us four church or altar dedications. But only from Torhamn church, a coastal town of county Blekinge, do we have sculptural evidence for this dedication. An altar-piece from the latter part of the fifteenth century passed via another church to Fridlevstad church in the interior of the county (pl. 27). The central group is a crowning of the Virgin as Queen of Heaven by God the Father. On her right side is placed her Son, and on the right flank is possibly St Thomas Becket standing, and on the left flank of this celestial group is the young St Magnus. He is in late medieval armour like St Olav of this period and has a big cloak over his shoulders. The right forearm and all the colours are lost. His left hand has been holding something which is lost too. He is beardless and his hair is long and curling while around his forehead is a ribbon or circlet adorned with a great round jewel of some kind. That could be a local late

PLATE 28   Mural painting at St Mary's Helsingbörg, Scania. (Courtesy of National Museum, Copenhagen).

medieval way of making a ducal garland. It is probable that this saint really is St Magnus as has been proposed (with some reservations) (Tuulse, 1961, 46, fig. 31).

At two other churches in Scania two murals of our saint have been preserved under layers of chalk. One was discovered in the ambulatory of the chancel of St Mary's in Helsingbörg in Scania, north of the archbishop's seat at Lund (*A Catalogue of wall-paintings*, II, 1976, 188, 189; Borelius, 1954, 111, 116–22). It was the second layer of murals at this place and has been dated to *c*.1500 (pl. 28). Two saints are standing side by side. According to inscriptions one is Sanctus Brandanus, i.e. the Irish monk Brendan who was said to have crossed the Atlantic Ocean in a curragh. The other is 'Sanctus Mangnus', a spelling which was rather common. He is in full armour, a short axe in his right hand and a long two-handed sword in his left. Over his shoulders hangs a short cloak. The details of the head may have been very

PLATE 29   Mural painting at Brunnby Church, Scania. (Courtesy of National Museum, Copenhagen).

PLATE 30a   Altarpiece from Onsøy Church, Østfold, Norway with St Magnus in the very top right hand niche. (Courtesy Universitets Oldsaksamling).

PLATE 30b   Figure of St Magnus from the Onsøy altarpiece. (Courtesy Universitets Oldsaksamling).

unclear when the conservator tried to restore them, but there is no garland and the young saint has got a full beard.

The nave of Brunnby church, again in Scania, got new murals about the same time as St Mary's in Helsingbörg. Here too an inscription says 'Sanctus Mangnus' (Pl. 29). At his side is St Olav. St Magnus is in armour with a cloak, and a heavy sword in his left hand and a short axe in his right. The details of the head are unclear and may count for the loss of the garland here too. The chin is beardless as it should be (*A Catalogue of wall-paintings*, 54–8).

The three Norwegian late medieval St Magnus sculptures are far spread, from the very south of Norway to almost the very north. They are still in place on their old altarpieces, which are made of oak with much of the original colours preserved, and they were all probably carved outside Norway. An All Saints altar-piece from Onsøy church, south in Østfold County (pl. 30a), (now in Universitetets Oldsaksamling in Oslo)[4] was, according to a lost church diary, bought in Oslo during the Reformation period (Engelstad, 1936, 211–13, pls. 134–7). It was probably made in Odense in Denmark *c*.1520 by a German master-carver called Claus

PLATE 31   Altarpiece from Lurøy Church, Nordland, Norway with figures of St Thomas, St Olav, St Edmund, and on the right St Magnus. (Courtesy Historical Museum, Bergen).

Berg for an altar in St Halvard Cathedral in Oslo (Engelstad, 1936, 112–24). The church diary of Onsøy said that the donor was a lady Gro Gyldenhorn, widow of Knut Knutson Baat, a renowned member of the Norwegian Council who was beheaded in 1519. St Magnus is one of 24 figures placed around God the Father receiving His dead Son from angels (pl. 30b). The 43 cm high St Magnus has no visible armour under his long cloak. His face is beardless, his long hair in curls and he is alone in having a ribbon around his head. With both hands he is holding the handle of a sword on the left side, of which the blade is lost.

In the Bergan Historical Museum collection is the central part of an altarpiece from Lurøy church in Nordland County in Northern Norway (Engelstad, 276–77, pl. 35).[5] The colours of the four figures are fairly well preserved. Their names are painted below their feet (pl. 31). Centrally placed are Olavus Rex and Edmund Rex. On their right side is Thomas, probably Thomas Becket who was very popular in Norway and is depicted with unhurt head. On the other side is St Magnus (Colour plate 3). Both of his attributes are lost, but on the garland there are remnants of flowers. This altar-piece is filled with North Sea saints, which has suggested a provenance from an English workshop c.1435. (Bugge, 1932), although it is more likely to be a late fifteenth century work ordered from Lübeck via the Hanseatic merchants in Bergen (Engelstad, 1936).

According to long established rules and laws fish from Northern Norway and from districts north of Bergen had to be brought to this town and sold there. The main buyers were the German merchants of this very important Hanseatic Station. They were mainly from Lübeck. (Helle, 1982, 378–9). One of the articles brought from Northern Germany and especially from Lübeck was church art. The old Norwegian workshops in this field could not compete. That is why the Norwegian churches, and especially churches on the West coast and in Northern Norway, were filled with art from Lübeck and other Hanseatic towns during the fifteenth and sixteenth centuries, till the trade was stopped by the Reformation. In Bergen and a few other towns buyers could discuss details of their orders with representatives of the German workshops. Without doubt the late medieval representations of saints, even of St Olav, were created outside Norway. Generally-speaking the types were uniform all over Scandinavia and in North Germany. Only details differed. Without doubt the spread of art and the iconographical change of figures ought mainly to be seen against this background of trade where the main product in question was dried fish for Europe. Among these saints St Magnus had his place.

One of the most remarkable altar-pieces in Norway came from Andenes church to the Museum of Tromsö.[6] Andenes was and still is one of the most important fishing centres of Norway. The altar-piece has its doors and colours fairly well preserved (Engelstad, 1936, 286–8, pls. 77–9). What makes it unique in the whole of Scandinavia is that when shut the doors show the passion of St Olav, and when opened at Easter the real passion of Christ along with three saints, is revealed (Reuterswärd, 1980, 21–5; Blindheim, M, 1981, 53–68). (Colour plates 6–7) St Olav's passion is based on a Low German passional of the end of the fifteenth century, printed in Lübeck in 1505. In the centre of the open altar-piece is placed God Almighty with His naked, dead Son in his arms. At his left side St Olav in armour with a dragon under his feet. To the right of God the Father is standing a bishop, perhaps Thomas Becket and to the left of St Olav our youthful saint Magnus of Orkney (Colour plates 8–9). He is in gilded armour and cloak with a red lining. The handle of the long sword in his left hand, whose blade is lost, is red, as is the cap or garland with two gilded flowers. The gloves were gilded in another way (not all gilding is real gilding). His beardless face is white with rosy cheeks and red lips and blue eyes. This very interesting altar-piece has been dated to c.1500 as a Lübeck product (Engelstad). With the printed passional of 1505 in mind I believe this dating cannot be much off the mark.

St Magnus became very popular in Iceland. But no sculpture, nor any paintings

PLATE 32 Altarfrontal from Draflastadir Church, Iceland. (Photo. Gisli Gestsson:
Courtesy National Museum of Iceland).

have been preserved. Iceland is singularly rich in embroidered hangings and other
embroidered textiles from the end of the Middle Ages up to the eighteenth century.
Some of them were embroidered in the same technique as the Bayeux tapestry, five
hundred years earlier, called in Icelandic 'refilsaumur'. From Draflastadir church
in northern Iceland comes an altar-frontal with the Virgin and child as main motif.[7]
In the lower left corner two youthful saints are facing each other. The one on the
left has got a sword in his left hand and a ribbon around his head and is supposedly
St Magnus (pl. 32). The other with an arrow in his hand would be St Halvard of
Oslo who became fairly popular in Iceland. The date of this hanging is supposed
to be the second quarter of the sixteenth century (Gudjonsson, 1985, 14–16, fig.
6; idem, 1986, fig. p.5).
    Another charming Icelandic frontal came from Skard church in western Iceland.[8]
It is made in a related technique although damaged, and is dated to the first half

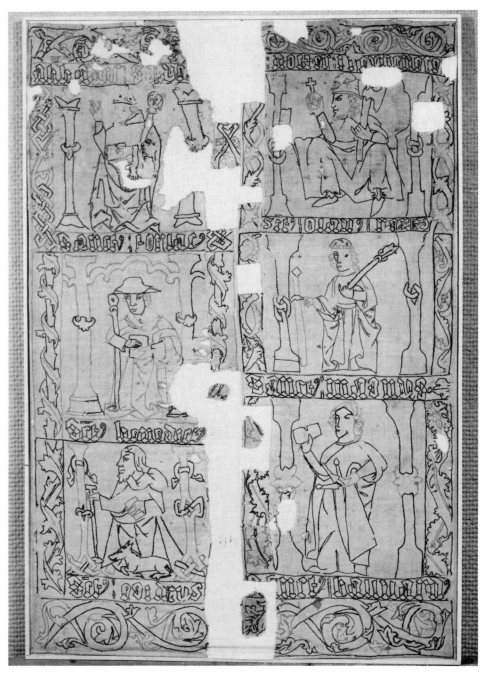

PLATE 33   Altarfrontal from Skaard Church, Iceland. (Photo. Gisli Gestsson: Courtesy
National Museum of Iceland).

of the sixteenth century (Gudjonsson, 1985, 48–50, fig. 50; idem, 1986, fig. p.11). Below the six figures are embroidered their names (pl. 33). On the top right is St Olav, in the middle St Magnus and at the bottom St Halvard. St Magnus has got the garland around his head, a big sword near his right hand and over his left shoulder possibly a palm branch, the general attribute for saints.

In my search for figural St Magnus representations in medieval Scandinavian art I have succeeded in bringing together examples in painting, sculpture and textile, although the soapstone fragment from Trondheim Cathedral is only possibly from a St Magnus statue. With the exception of this fragment and the relief in Kirkwall from *c*.1400 all the other eight representations have been dated to the end of the medieval period, i.e. the last half of the fifteenth and the first half of the sixteenth centuries. The two Icelandic textiles are native productions, whereas the three Norwegian altar-pieces were made by Germans, probably in Lübeck and in Odense. The two murals in Scania and the altar-piece in Blekinge were certainly executed under strong North German influence in the artistic language of the period. It is characteristic that the St Magnus figures produced in Lübeck and other Hanseatic towns (or influenced by their art) are, with the exception of the Onsøy figure, rendered in full armour. Among all the figures found in Scandinavian art of this period only the royal national saints, St Magnus and occasionally St George got this warlike dress. They were defenders of the true faith, and of their realms. The popularity of St Magnus in Denmark and especially in Scania is not easily explained. It may be that the North German merchants who in spite of prohibitions sailed onto Orkney and the North Atlantic islands, took St Magnus as their patron.[9] It might be a parallel to the Lübecker Bergen merchants whose patrons was St Olav. In this way St Magnus's fame may have spread to Danish towns, greatly helped by Scots and possibly Islanders who settled in Danish towns at the end of the Middle Ages. Scots and especially people from Shetland and Orkney moved over to Norway too, not least because of the many strong ties which for centuries had bound the Norwegian provinces north of Scotland to the motherland. Despite missing church and altar dedications in Norway it should not be unreasonable to suppose that long before the end of the Middle Ages the cult of St Magnus was well known in Norway and hardly needed support from the outside world in the late Middle Ages. The many pilgrims to the shrine of St Olav in the Metropolitan church of Trondheim had ample opportunity to see and to follow the service at St Magnus's altar when entering the Cathedral.

In Denmark one altar-dedication preceded the late Middle Ages. A St Magnus altar was mentioned in the Metropolitan church of Lund in 1304. This dedication needs another explanation than the Scots immigrants of the fifteenth and sixteenth centuries. The reason may be that from 1104 to 1153 Lund was the ecclesiastical centre for the whole of Scandinavia. The archbishop certainly claimed to be the head of the churches of the North Sea and the Atlantic too. If so, an altar for the popular Earl and Saint Magnus would be as natural in the Cathedral of Lund as it later became in the Cathedral of Nidaros (Trondheim).

It is interesting to observe that in the preserved North German altar-pieces or in works of art influenced from these towns—Andenes, Lurøy and Fridlevstad—

PLATE 34 St Magnus, west front Trondheim Cathedral. (Courtesy of Trondheim Restoration Office).

St Magnus is placed as a flanking figure to God the Father and Christ or to royal national saints. It looks like an elevation above the great crowd of saints of both sexes.

The fame of St Magnus today is mainly based on a sort of romantic nationalism expressed in art by painted windows in the cathedrals of Kirkwall and Trondheim. Today the west front of the original metropolitan Cathedral has again been filled with more than life-sized sculptures of soapstone, and quite naturally the young St Magnus has his place among all the other saints (pl. 34).[10]

NOTES

1   If Master Robert composed the *Vita* of St Magnus for the church feasts of 1135 and also wrote about Thomas à Becket (who was murdered in 1170) he must by then have been *c*.70–80 years of age.

2   *KHL* sub Krona.

3   I want to thank architect Torgeir Suul for kind helpfuless. On J Maschius's engraving of 1661 almost all the figures of the first row are preserved, although he shortened the front and left out a flanking niche on each side of the west front. In the second row only two statues are still in their niches (Fischer, G, 1965, 308). Today it is impossible to tell where on the ruined front national saints were placed.

4   Universitetets Oldsaksamling, nr. C 9896. The architecture of the central part of the Onsøy altar-piece is destroyed. The original arrangement of the figures is unknown. Height 200 cm; width 272 cm; height of small figures *c*.40–50 cm.

5   Historical Museum, Bergen nr. B. 21; height 113 cm; width 119 cm.

6   Historical Museum, Tromsö nr. TS. K9; height 118 cm; width 138 cm.

7   Þjoðminjasafn Islands (National Museum), Reykjavik, nr. 3924. Photo: Gisli Gestsson.

8   Þjoðminjasafn Islands (National Museum), Reykjavik, nr. 2028. Photo: Gisli Gestsson.

9   As the historian Arnvid Nedkvitne has suggested to me.

10   St Magnus on the west front of Trondheim Cathedral has been sculptured by Stinius Fredriksen. For kind assistance I want to thank Dr Elsa Gudjonsson and Margret Gisladottir (Þjoðminjasafn Islands, Reykjavik). Bjørn Kaland (The Conservation Department, Historical Museum, Bergen). Dr Søren Kaspersen (Kunsthistorisk Institut, København Universitet). Phil Dr Mereth Lindgren (Riksantikvarieämbetet, Stockholm), Photographic Department, Tromsø Museum and last but not least Photographic Department, Universitetets Oldsaksamling, Oslo.

BIBLIOGRAPHY

A catalogue of wall-paintings in the churches of medieval Denmark, 1100–1600. Scania-Halland-Blekinge, II, Copenhagen 1976

Beveridge, J, 1938–9. 'Two Scottish thirteenth century songs', in *Proc Soc Antiq Scotland*, LXXIII

Blindheim, M, 1981, 'St Olav–ein skandinavischer Oberheiliger, St Olav–Seine Zeit und sein Kult', *Acta Visbyensis*, VI, Uddevalla

Borelius, A, 1954, *Skånes medeltida monumentalmåleri*, Linköping

Bugge, A, 1932, 'Kunsten langs leden', *Foreningen t.n. fortidsminners bevaring*, Årbok

Bull, E, 1912–13, 'The cultus of Norwegian saints in England and Scotland,' *Saga-Book of the Viking Society, VIII*

Daae, L, 1879, *Norske helgener*, Christiania/Oslo

Engelstad, S, 1936, *Senmiddelalderens kunst i Norge*, Oslo

Fischer, G, 1965, *Domkirken i Trondheim*, I–II, Oslo

Gudjonsson, E, 1985, 'Traditional Icelandic Embroidery', *Iceland Review*, Reykjavik

Gudjonsson, E, 1986, 'With a shining needle', Exhibition catalogue, Reykjavik

Helle, K, 1982, *Bergen Bys Historie*. I

Jørgensen, E, 1909, *Helgendyrkelsen i Danmark*, København

KHL   Kulturhistorisk Leksikon for nordisk middelalder, vol. iv, Hertig; vol. ix, Magnus, *Magnus Saga*

Künstle, K, 1928, *Iconographie der christlichen Kunst*, II, Fr.i.Br. In handbooks about saints St Magnus is either forgotten or the passage about him is full of errors

Larusson, M, *Sct Magnus Orcadensis Comes*, Saga 1962

Liebgott, N-K, 1982, *Hellige mænd og kvinder*, Højbjerg

Nordisk Kultur, Tideräkning, Stockholm 1934, Lit.

Orknøyinga Soga, 1929, *Norrøne Bokverk*, Nr. 25, Oslo

Paasche, F, 1923, *Norges og Islands litteratur, Norsk Litteraturjistorie*, I, Christiania/Oslo

Petersen, H, 1888, 'Et Bilde af Hellig Knud Hertug i Jydsk Kirke,' *Aarbog for Nordisk Oldkyndighed*, 98–106

Reuterswärd, P, 1980, *De dubbla passionerna, Den Iconographiska Post*, Stockholm

Svanberg, J, 1987, *Furstebilder från Folkungatid* (Stockholm)

Tuulse, A, 1961, *Kyrkor i Blekinge, En konsthistorisk Øversikt*, Stockholm

Undset, S, 1937, *Norske helgener*, Oslo

CHAPTER 13

The Cult of Saints in Early Medieval Scandinavia

Thelma Jexlev

The cult of saints arose partly from the classic 'agape', the yearly commemoration at the hero's burial place. The early Christians gathered in the catacombs, where their martyrs were buried, and as miracles occurred at the graves, martyrs were supposed to be saints functioning as mediators between man and God. During the years of persecution the merits acquired by being a Christian hero enabled the martyr to be near God and with his prayers intercede for both living and dead. The cult was described by *St Augustine* as a religious ceremony aimed at inspiring people to follow the martyrs' example, share in their merits and be helped by their prayers.

At first the Roman church opposed the cult of saints and especially the veneration of relics. But Christianity needed its heroes, so the church had to accept the cult as important to the Christian congregation. As the persecutions actually stopped in the fourth century a call arose for new saints; so as well as martyrs we find confessors—well-earned merit, but who died peacefully. The hierarchy of the saints: God the father, Christ, his mother Mary, the apostles and evangelists, martyrs, confessors and virgins, is listed in the litany for Easter Saturday

As Christianity spread throughout Europe the Roman and Eastern martyrs soon had the company of missionary saints and other local saints. Bishops, abbots and a few virgins similar to the virgin martyrs of the early church came first, but were soon followed by martyrs of royal blood. Some local saints were just local, that is their cult was restricted to a few monasteries, a diocese or maybe an archbishopric. We know of many such Irish and Anglo-Saxon saints. Others were known in a wider area, their cult for instance spread to the newly christianised Nordic countries, but very few became universal saints like those of the Gregorian and Gelasian sacramentaries. Later on when history gave the Scandinavian countries their own saints some of those from Western Europe disappeared from the liturgy but remained in the calendars, and thus might be remembered from their continued use in the dating of documents.

The monastic orders, both the old ones (Benedictines and Cistercians) as well as the later mendicant orders (Dominicans and especially the Franciscans) were very important both in the development of hagiography as well as in the propagation and upholding of a saint's cult. With few alterations the Franciscan calendar was

183

adopted by the universal Roman missal. The youngest Scandinavian order, the
Bridgetines (*regula sancti Salvatoris*), were characterised by double institutions: convents for nuns and convents for monks combined. They took local Swedish saints
into their liturgy and extended knowledge of them abroad.

Modern studies on the origin of the worship of saints follow different trends.
Some researchers emphasise the heritage from the Hellenistic cult of heroes,
whereas others prefer to stress that the loan and inspiration from heathen rites have
contributed much to the cult of Christian saints. Certainly the development has
been marked by a tension between official liturgy and popular belief. Figurative
art as well as the legends incorporate on the one hand a lot of popular belief, while
on the other hand the narrative both of picture and oral history influenced people's
concept of the saints. This interaction has to be considered when using the various
sources illustrating the saints' lives and the worship of them.

Already during the missionary period the Scandinavian countries had their own
saints, and in the eleventh and twelfth century history gave them their national
saints. The biggest number of local saints is to be found in Sweden. First there are
the missionary saints Botvid, David, Eskil, and Sigfred, later in the twelfth century
Helena of Skövde, Bishop Henric and King Eric.

Botvid from Södermanland was christened in England and went back to Sweden
to propagate the Christian faith. His legend is supposed to be the oldest one of
Swedish origin. It tells us that he was killed by a former slave on a journey to Gotland
about 1120. A local cult in Södermanland is known of in the twelfth century and
later spread to many places in Sweden. His translation took place in the 1170s,
when a stonechurch (Botkyrka) was built near his former home. In several Swedish
mural paintings he is shown with an axe and a fish referred to in the legend.

The other (and older) 'apostle' for Södermanland is Bishop *Eskil* of whom we
first hear in Ailnoth's biography of King Canute. Eskil came from England to
preach among the heathens; he was stoned at Strängnäs and buried at Tuna, where
he had been bishop. A town and a convent grew up and was called Eskilstuna. He
became patron of Strängnäs diocese, and around 1300 Bishop Brynulf of Skara was
asked to write an *officium* in his honour. A chapel in the cathedral was named after
him, and iconographically he is shown as a bishop with a stone in his hand.

Bishop *Sigfred* of Växjö came from England also, as Adam of Bremen tells us.
In one of the legends he is even said to have been archbishop of York, before he
went to Denmark and from there to Sweden. Several parts of the liturgy in his
honour have survived. In the fifteenth century he was made a national saint, and
a Danish bishop who had been in Växjö and later came to Roskilde brought the
cult of Sigfred along and built a chapel named after him—still existing in Roskilde
Cathedral.

The last of the missionary saints, *David*, was of noble English blood and was
urged by Sigfred to go to Sweden where he died and was buried at Munktorp. His
legends are late and stereotyped. They have miracles in common with St Olav, St
Ethelreda and the Danish local saint, Andrew (Anders) of Slagelse.

The noble widow *Elin (Helena)* contributed much to the building of a church in
Skövde. She had visions, went to the Holy Land, came back and was soon after

killed by her son-in-law's kin, supposedly in the middle of the twelfth century. The facts about her are scarce, and her history in some ways resembles that of the Danish local saint, Margaret of Roskilde. Both of them gained martyrdom for economic reasons, their kin disliking their generous gifts to the church. An early popular cult of Helena was supported by the said Bishop Brynulf, who wrote an *officium* for her worship as he did for Eskil. A number of indulgences was given throughout the middle ages for visits to the churches of Skövde and Götene (where she was killed) and to a chapel beside the nearby fountain bearing her name, where people came to be cured of their diseases.

Henric, the apostle of Finland, is said to have made a pilgrimage from England to Rome, and from there he followed Nicolaus Breakspeare (the later Pope Hadrian IV) when he was sent as a papal legate to the Nordic countries. According to the legend Henric took part in the Swedish King Eric's so-called 'first crusade' to Finland and was killed in Satakunta 1151—or thereabouts. The legends of both Henric and Eric were written long after their death and seem entirely made for religious use giving very few historical facts. Henric must have been venerated as a saint quite soon after his death, as his name is to be found in the Vallentuna calendar of 1198. Later he became patron of Abo (Turku) diocese which covered most of medieval Finland.

The Finland expedition was probably more a raid than a crusade, and no expeditions are known from historical sources during King Eric's reign. *Eric* himself is said to have been very devout and helpful to the church. He was killed (1161) in a feud, rivalry among princes being a common feature of the twelfth century. His shrine is still to be seen in the cathedral of Uppsala, but there has been much discussion about its contents. The cathedral clergy worshipped Eric in many ways, although his cult was not very popular outside Uppsala and Stockholm until the Bridgetines and the Kalmar union of the Scandinavian countries made him patron of all Sweden.

Although from a later period the most famous of all Scandinavian saints must be mentioned: that is the noble widow *Birgitta* (named after the Irish Saint Bridget), who had her first revelation at Bishop Brynulfs grave. She went on pilgrimage to both Compostella and Jerusalem and stayed for many years in Rome, where she died (1373) in her house, which is now a modern Bridgetine convent and guesthouse. Her social position as an aristocrat made it possible for her to take part in the politics both of Sweden and Denmark, and in Rome she made great efforts to call the popes back from Avignon to Rome. She was also a mystic, and her many revelations—both mystic and political—were written down by the two Swedish priests who had followed her to Rome. These revelations are among the most important contributions from Scandinavia to the Latin literature of the middle ages. Birgitta was canonised a few years after her death and as a founder of the Bridgetine order became a universal saint. Her type of saint is not to be found in the early or high middle ages.

Throughout the middle ages new saints were created in Sweden, among them Bishop Brynulf of Skara, the Dominican nun Ingrid of Skänninge and Saint Bridget's daughter Catherine; but the popular cult of the earlier saints seems to have lived on as we can see from pieces of art existing from the later middle ages. Naturally the influence of the Bridgetine movement, which amoung other things put a stress on national saints, was stronger in Sweden than elsewhere. The well-kept Vadstena archives, together with a reasonably big fund of liturgical sources from most dioceses, as well as many pieces of late medieval art enable us on the whole to draw a more elaborate picture of the cult of Swedish saints—and saints in Sweden—than can be done for Denmark or Norway.

A characteristic of Danish saints is that (apart from the royal saints) most are not martyrs, but confessors. That may mean nothing for the official cult, but as martyrs have a greater appeal to the public their cult is more easily spread and leaves the worship of confessors—whether miracle-working or not—more restricted and more easily forgotten.

Thøger (Theodgar) was German by birth. After staying in England he went to Norway as a chaplain to King Olav. When the king died Thøger went to Denmark and built a church in the northern part of Jutland, where he died after having done a lot of good things. Light was seen above his grave, so his successor had his body translated to the altar, which both king and bishop opposed. Miracles occurred, however, and forced them to acknowledge his sanctity. Different years for the translation have been given but 1067 is most likely as Vaestervig, the place of his cult, was at that date a bishops see, being abandoned for Børglum in 1120, when Vestervig became a convent of Augustinian canons. There are a number of parish churches in northern and western Jutland dedicated to Thøger, and his name was used frequently as a personal name in the same region. Iconographical sources are rare and very late.

Keld (Ketillus) was leader of the Augustinian chapter at Viborg, but was expelled by his companion brothers due to his bestowing gifts and benefits on the poor. He went thence to Rome with a request to be sent on mission to the heathen Slavic tribes along the south Baltic coast. However the pope sent him back to take up his former position at Viborg where he died peacefully in the year 1150. A biography accompanied by 23 miracles was sent by Archbishop Absalon to Rome and accepted by Pope Clement III, so a solemn translation took place on 11 July 1189. Keld's shrine was burnt and melted down in the big fire of 1726. His feast, the day after King Canute, was celebrated with processions and big markets every year until the Reformation, and his cult was popular all over Jutland as can be seen from the many legal documents dated by his feast day. His legend is also found in a manuscript from Vadstena, and his feast is included in a Norwegian calendar of the fifteenth century.

Abbot *Wilhelm (William)*, a French nobleman by birth, was a canon of Saint Victor, when he was summoned by Bishop Absalon to reorganise the monastery at Eskilsø, which was moved to AEbelholt (Paraclitus). Wilhelm built a big monastery, of which ruins can still be seen, but the church was not completed, when he died in 1203 (only one year after Archbishop Absalon). Besides organising and building up a big monastery he found time to write a treatise on Saint Genevieve, the patron saint of Paris, and three volumes of letters, a few trying to comfort the wretched Queen Ingeborg, (wife of King Philip August) who was put away in jail just after her wedding. Wilhelm in a way was responsible for her sufferings, as he had played an important role in arranging the fatal marriage. On the other hand however he did a lot of good things, and soon after his death rumours arose of wonders at his grave. His *vita et miraculi* was sent to Rome and papal canonisation initiated in 1224, whereas the translation did not take place until 1238. Liturgically he was worshipped all over the Danish church province, but a popular cult was very local. The cathedral of Roskilde had an important relic, one of abbot William's arms, which was celebrated by a special feast 'translatio bracchii s. Vilhelmi' on 30 November—the same day as Saint Andrew's feast.

Margaret of Roskilde was a real martyr, killed by her husband, who pretended her death was suicide, so she was buried on the beach instead of in the churchyard. In her we have the example of a saint supported by the supreme clerical authorities for she was of Bishop Absalon's kin. Her story included elements for a vivid popular cult, which however did not continue to thrive. She lived and died in a period when the call for new saints was still urgent, and yet it all came to nothing. Why? We have not yet found an answer. At her grave light appeared, and miracles happened, so her husband was questioned and had to confess. Bishop Absalon had her transferred to the parish church of Our Lady in the southern part of Roskilde in 1177, where a Cistercian nunnery had been founded a few years earlier. In 1257 the nunnery had all its possessions and privileges secured by a papal bull, among them the rights to money collected at St Margaret's chapel near the coast. But later on we hear nothing of her, no feast and no liturgy is known, although we have a few sources from the diocese of Roskilde. Her history is known from a contemporary writing by Herbert of Clairveaux, the monastery where the former Archbishop Eskil spent his last years. Another short story of Danish origin possibly dates from the 1190s, and the so-called 'Annales Sielandie' tell us of her death and burial. Her shrine in Roskilde is mentioned in an Icelandic itinerary for pilgrims of the thirteenth century, but after that time we have no trace of any cult.

The stories of the two Norwegian virgin saints also show that the worship of saints can be rather inconsistent during the middle ages. Of *Brictiua* very little is known, as no legend has survived. Her name indicates that she might have been Anglo-Saxon, and a church in Trøndelag dedicated to her locates her cult in the Nidaros diocese. Her feast on 11 January is well known from old written sources, both calendars and lawbooks, and it was used for dating documents throughout the middle ages, but she is not mentioned in the Nidaros missal and breviary, both printed in 1519.

The legend of the supposed Irish princess *Sunniva* and her companions landing in Norway on the isle of Selja, where merchants sailing past saw a column of light, sounds more like fiction than fact. King Olav Tryggvason and the local bishop are said to have found her incorrupt corpse in a cave and had it buried in the church of Selja. Nearly 200 years later a historical translation took place, when Bishop Paul had her moved to the cathedral in Bergen, as the Benedictine priory in Selja was in decline. After the translation Sunniva became an important person and the younger legend has borrowed features from the Rhenish Saint Ursula and her 11,000 virgins, whereas most calendars stuck to the old name 'festum sanctorum in Selis'. In documents written in the Norse language the day is often called 'Thridia voku' (the feast of the three i.e. Sunniva and her two companions). In the late Norwegian breviary a rhymed officium is found and also some prayers, but the older ordinary has no special texts. She is known in some places in Sweden.

The genuine Norse saints are only *Olav* and *Halvard*. Like the supposed relation between Bishop Henry and King Eric in Sweden there should be some sort of kinship between King Olav and Halvard, who was killed only few years after the king, maybe 1043, (his death is mentioned by Adam of Bremen). Halvard was worshipped all over Norway, including Iceland, but especially in the diocese of Oslo whose patron he came to be later on. The neighbouring Swedish diocese of Skara venerated him in the thirteenth century, and the Bridgetines brought him to Denmark.

If we look at the middle ages as a whole *King Olav Haraldson*, killed in the battle of Stiklestad 1030, was by far the most popular saint. He is the first Scandinavian example of the making of a saint more from political than from religious reasons, the same pattern as known from Britain in earlier centuries. The cult of Olav spread rapidly, a lot of parish and town churches, especially in coastal towns are dedicated to Olav throughout Scandinavia as well as in Northern Germany and Britain. A big variety of liturgical texts, legends and lay literature is known, the oldest manuscripts of which are found in England (pre-1100). Anyone who could afford to undertake the long journey wished at least once in a lifetime to go on pilgrimage to Saint Olav's shrine in Trondheim. Relics such as pieces from his banner or from the stone he fell on were precious; King Eric of Pomerania donated an arm-relic to the cathedral of Lund. The story of Saint Olav's life is a favourite theme for mural paintings, and wooden statues come next in number to those of Our Lady and her mother Anne all over Scandinavia.

Saint Olav was already a well-known and beloved saint, when the Danish King *Canute* was killed (1086) in St Alban's Cathedral in Odense by revolting peasants from Jutland, who had grown tired of going on unsuccessful expeditions to England. Of course it was sacrilege that he was murdered in church, and he certainly had been favouring several church institutions, for instance the very big donation of landed property to the cathedral of Lund the year before his death. To strengthen the bond of church and kingship Canute was made a saint. In the 1090s his brother Eric summoned monks from Evesham to found a Benedictine abbey in Odense functioning as chapter to the cathedral. King Eric and his queen Bodil were bound for the Holy Land, when they passed through Rome and managed to complete the canonisation of Canute, and to loosen the Scandinavian churches from the Hamburg-Bremen supremacy, establishing a new church province at Lund for all Scandinavia. The translation of Canute took place in 1101; his shrine together with that of his brother Benedict, who was killed defending the king, are still kept in the undercroft of Saint Canute's Cathedral. The first biography was written by Ailnoth, one of the monks from Evesham. There are other sources, both liturgical and historical—nearly contemporary. They picture the king in very different ways, and the historical debate is still going on, as can be seen in the publication from last year's celebrations of the 900 years' anniversary of his death (*Knudsbogen*, 1986).

King Eric's son *Canute* was a small child at the time his father died abroad, so Niels, another of Sven Estridsson's many sons followed on the throne and his reign lasted more than 30 years, not all of them peaceful. Just after New Year 1131 Niels' son Magnus killed his cousin Duke Canute in the woods near Ringsted, and another royal martyr came into existence. This political murder due to rivalry can be compared to the killing of Earl Magnus in Orkney. King Eric Emune founded a Benedictine abbey at Ringsted (1135), but it took many years for the canonisation to get through; finally in 1170 the translation of *Knud Lavard* was celebrated by his son King Valdemar at the end of the civil war. For some years King Canute might have come under the shadow of his nephew Duke Canute, but he soon regained his popularity and became a national saint. Iconographically and as patrons for merchants' guilds the two Canutes melt together, and even the Åbo missal confuses them by putting King Canute on the 7 January, the date of Duke Canute's death.

After 1154 the sees of the Atlantic Isles belonged to the archbishopric of Nidaros and venerated the Norse saints; but they also had local saints of their own, Bishop Thorlak for instance in Iceland. The Orkneys acquired their saint, when Earl Magnus was killed on Egilsay *c*.1117 by his cousin Earl Hakon. There are quite a few examples of Norwegian documents dated according to Saint Magnus's feast on 16 April, particularly when you consider that the feast is just two days after the traditional change from winter to summer in Norway (where the first week of summer nights and the first week of winter nights in October were favourite fixed points for dating). Also the Easter period's supreme celebrations might often interfere with Saint Magnus' feast.

The oldest example of this seems to be from 1315 'a Maghnus messae dagh', the same expression being used several times during the period 1354 to 1474. In Latin documents he is usually named as *comes Orcadie* or as a martyr *in festo s. Magni martiris* (which outside Norwegian regions normally means the universal saint Bishop Magnus from the Gelasian sacramentary). Latin examples from 1396 to 1548 use the exact date, numerous examples both Latin and Norse are to be found for the days between 10 and 21 April in the year 1333 and onwards. It is characteristic of Norwegian documents—in contrast to Denmark and Sweden—that they use the days close to a saint's feast for dating purposes as well as the feastday itself. As the day of Saint Magnus' translation is 13 December, the feast of the universally and highly worshipped virgin Saint Lucia, one would not expect the translation to be used outside Orkney, but a testimonium exists in Norway which was written by two lay judges on 12 December 1396 '*j prestogonne a Vanghe tysdaghen neste firir Magnus messo firir jol*' (at Vang, the Tuesday before St Magnus's day before Christmas).

NOTE

Editions of annals, chronicles and and liturgical texts used are to be found in the Bibliography. Most relevant documents have been printed in *Diplomatarium Danicum, Diplomatarium Norvegicum* and *Diplomatarium Suecanum.*

Documents dated according to Saint Magnus feastdays are to be found in *Dipl. Norv.* vol. I, 179, 223, 374, 712, 829, 847, 877: vol. II, 351, 656, 730, 760 and 856; vol. IV, 291–92, 418, 449, 481, 500, 592, 665, 863 and 1125; vol. V, 61, 89, 216, 218, 358, 466 and 505; vol. XI, 93–94.

BIBLIOGRAPHY

Only principal works published before 1950 are mentioned.

Acta Pontificum Danica I–VII, 1904–43, L Moltesen, A Krarup, J Lindbaek, eds, Copenhagen

Acta Visbyensia VI, 1981, articles by M Blindheim, U Haastrup, M Lingren, T Nyberg, Uddevalla

Albrectsen, E, 1974, *To normanniske Krøniker*, Odense

Arentoft, E, Brandt, V & Grandt-Nielsen, F, 1985, *Albani kirke & Torv* (Fynske Studier 14), Odense

Braun, J, 1971 (reprint), *Die Reliquiare des christlichen Kultes und ihre Entwicklung*, Osnabrück

Breengaard, C, 1982, *Muren om Israels hus. Regnum og sacerdotium i Danmark 1050–1170*, Copenhagen

Bø, O, 1955, *Heilag-Olav i norsk folketradisjon*, Oslo

A Catalogue of Wall-Paintings in the Churches of Medieval Denmark 1100–1600. Scania-Halland-Blekinge I–IV, Copenhagen, 1976–82

Gad, T, 1971, *Helgener. Legender fortalt i Norden*, Copenhagen

Gad, T, 1961, *Legenden i dansk middelalder*, Copenhagen

Gertz, M Cl, 1907, *Knud den helliges Martyrhistorie* saerlig efter de tre aeldste Kilder. Festskrift udgivet af Kjøbenhavns Universitet, Copenhagen

Haastrup, U,1985, 'Danske kalkmalerier 1375–1475', *Danske kalkmalerier l. Gotik 1375–1474*, Copenhagen

Hald, K, 1981, *Personnavne i Danmark. II. Middelalderen*, Copenhagen

Jexlev, T, 1981, 'Lokalhelgener og middelalderlige nordiske brevdateringer', *Middelalder, metode og medier*. Festskrift til Niels Skyum-Nielsen, 223–60, Copenhagen

Jorgensen, E, 1909, *Helgendyrkelse i Danmark*. Studier over Kirkekultur og kirkeligt Liv fra det 11. Aarhundredes Midte til Reformationen, Copenhagen

Knudsbogen, Studier over Knud den Hellige, 1986, Fynske Studier XV, articles by C Breengaard, E Albrectsen, T Jexlev and others, Odense

Koch, H, 1936, *Danmarks Kirke i den begyndende Højmiddelalder*, Copenhagen

Koch, H, 1961, 'Kongemagt og Kirke 1060–1241', *Danmarks Historie*, vol 3, J Danstrup and H Koch, eds, Copenhagen

Kulturhistorisk leksikon for nordisk middelalder, Copenhagen 1956–78, vol. 1–22. Articles about the different saints, calendars, liturgy, etc.

Legender från Sveriges medeltid illustrerade i svensk medeltidskonst, 1917, E Fogelklou, A Lindblom and E Wessén, eds., Stockholm

Libri antiquiores ecclesiae et capituli Lundensis, 1985, Lunds domkyrkas äldsta liturgiska böcker, a catalogue by P Ekström, Lund

Libri Memoriales Capituli Lundensis, 1884–89, reprint 1971, Lunds Domkapitels Gaveboger ('Liber Datici Lundenses'), C Weeke, ed., Copenhagen

Liebgott, N, 1982, *Hellige maend og kvinder,* Højbjerg

Ljungfors, A, 1955, *Bidrag till svensk diplomatic före 1350*, Lund

Lundberg, K-E, 1978–79, 'Helgon och helgonkult. Essä om S : t Sigfrid och Västergotland', *Skara Gilles Arsbok 1978–79*

Manuale Norvegicum (Presta Handbók), 1962, O Kolsrud(+) and H Faehn, eds., Oslo

Necrologium Lundense, 1923, Lunds domkyrkas Nekrologium (Monumenta Scaniae Historica, L Weibull, ed.) Lund

Olrik, H, 1893–94, *Danske Helgeners Levned*, Copenhagen

Ordo Nidrosiensis ecclesiae (Ordubok), 1968, L Gjerløw, ed., Oslo

Pellijeff, G, 1962, 'Sancti Knuds dag. En medeltida datumformel', *Namn och bygd*, 9–54, Uppsala.

Riising, A, 1969, *Danmarks middelalderlige praediken*, Copenhagen

'Sanctuarium Birgerianum eller Erkebiskop Birgers Fundatz paa Gudstienesten i Kraften i Lunde-Domkirke', *Samlinger til den Danske Historie* I : 3, 1780, P F Suhm, ed., Copenhagen

Schück, H, 1959, *Ecclesia Lincopensis*. Studier om Linköpingskyrkan under medeltiden och Gustav Vasa, Stockholm

Svanberg, J, 1985, 'Rex et dux. Kung och hertig i svensk och norsk stenskulptur under 1200-talet', *Kongens magt og aere*. Skandinaviske herskersymboler gjennom 1000 år, 79–92, M Blindheim, P Gjaerder, D Saeverud, eds, Oslo

Thordeman, B, 1954, *Erik den Helige*. Historia, kult, reliker, Stockholm

Vellev, J, 1981, 'Helgenskrinene i Sct. Knud i Odense, Opdagede og undersøgte 1582, 1696, 1833, 1874 og 1981', *Fyens stiftsbog 1981*, 15–44, Odense.

Vitae Sanctorum Danorum, 1908–12, M Cl Gertz, ed., Copenhagen

Vogel, C, 1975, *Introduction aux sources de l'historie du culte chrétien au Moyen Age* (Studi Medievale), Spoleto

Wallin, C, 1975, *Knutsgillena i det medeltida Sverige*. Kring kulten av de nordiska helgonkonungarna (Kungl. Vitterhets Historie och Antikvitets Akademien. Historiskt arkiv 16), Lund

Weibul, L, 1946, 'Skånes kyrka . . . till 1274', *Lunds domkyrkas historia I*, 141–356, Lund

Ælnoths Krønike, 1984, translated and annotated by E Albrectsen, Odense

CHAPTER 14

Observations on *Orkneyinga saga*

Peter Foote

Orkneyinga saga has been intensively studied for a century or more by many admirable scholars, Orkney men, Scots and Icelanders in particular. If I differ from them at all, it will be only in some slight shift of emphasis, a shift, as it happens, towards an unremarkable medieval norm. I wish to note a few points in the saga which seem to me to give some indication of what may be called, rather grandly, the mentality and moral stance of the author. I shall inevitably neglect many other considerations that a full characterisation of his engrossing narrative would require. It seems desirable to begin, however, by saying something about the saga's literary setting.

Orkneyinga saga was written in Iceland about 1200—I think probably a bit before that date, others thinks a bit after it, but we do not have more than a decade or so either way in mind. In Orkney eyes it may well appear a great, solitary monument, like the Old Man of Hoy, but it is obviously proper to consider it alongside other Icelandic writings of the same generation. It is natural in particular to look at two notably entertaining works from that period, *Jómsvíkinga saga* and *Færeyinga saga*, which resemble *Orkneyinga saga* in dealing with the fringes of the Norwegian past. The history of Norway, remote and recent, was of course always the chief preoccupation of the Icelandic recorders.

Jómsvíkinga saga has a Danish setting but culminates in a famous sea-battle in a Norwegian fjord. It begins with an elaborate series of omens, one of them forecasting the arrival of Christianity in Denmark, and early on in the story we are told of the mission of Bishop Poppo, the conversion of the Danes through his preaching, and the ordeal by fire which he underwent to prove the superiority of the faith. Hákon Hlaðajarl from Norway, present there as an ally of the Danish king, is also forced to accept baptism: and this is the background to his apostasy, to events that lead to Norwegian-Danish hostility, and ultimately to the attack of the Jómsvíkingar. Hákon's defeat of this incursion meant a long lull in Danish intervention in Norway, as we know from other sources, and there were good times in the country under Hákon's rule. In the established Christian view of the early middle ages, however, Hákon the apostate was primarily the arch-pagan and he came to a bad end, murdered in a pigsty. Intrinsic interest in his success in the earlier part of his career sprang from patriotism and was bolstered by knowledge of much fine poetry composed in his honour. Icelandic literary interest in him at the end of the twelfth century, however, is probably rather to be seen in association with the current interest in the still greater success of the apostle of Norway, King Óláfr Tryggvason, who supplanted Hákon and was credited with the conversion not only of the Norwegians but of the people of Orkney and the Faroes and the Icelanders and Greenlanders as well. Latin lives of Óláfr Tryggvason were composed by two Icelandic Benedictines in just this same period, one about 1190, the other some ten years later; the first of them soon appeared in a vernacular version and is preserved only in that form; the second is known only in excerpts, again in Icelandic (Turville-Petre, 1953, 190–6).

In *Færeyinga saga* Sigmundr Brestisson is portrayed as a loyal retainer of Hákon Hlaðajarl, and he is given a prominent part to play in the defeat of the Jómsvíkingar. The jarl gives him a fateful bracelet, which he has obtained from his special deity, Þorgerðr Hölgabrúðr. When Sigmundr meets Óláfr Tryggvason after Hákon's death, he refuses to give up his personal attachment to the jarl but he readily gives up the old beliefs, accepts Christianity and imposes it on his Faroese countrymen, including Þrándr í Götu, his chief antagonist and finally the instrument of his destruction. Þrándr detests the new religion but his apostate adherence to the old ways is not directly attested in the story: instead he is shown as a master of magic arts, and the power of his cunning and witchcraft is fully acknowledged. The narrative takes us on through the reign of St Óláfr Haraldsson (1015–30) and into that of his son, Magnús the Good (1035–47). St Óláfr's claims on the islanders are not those of the missionary but of the political overlord: he wants to impose laws and take tribute. Þrándr staves him off—the author seems to admire his success without approving of his unscrupulous methods—but finally Þrándr's opponents in the islands destroy his henchmen, Þrándr himself dies, and Faroese existence settles into a subdued and peaceful course.

These sagas and what we know of the Benedictine works on Óláfr Tryggvason give the impression that the Icelandic authors, looking back two hundred years and more, knew little about paganism in Scandinavia, or were not prepared to write much about it if they did, but saw it theatrically as the black shadow dispelled by the bright and forceful Christian kings, Óláfr Tryggvason and Óláfr Haraldsson. They also seem to have found Norwegian overlordship over the Atlantic islands a well-established, perhaps even a natural, fact. The author of *Færeyinga saga* in particular appears to have been so confident of the basic Christian learning and orthodoxy of his audience that he allows Þrándr to twit an anxious mother, catechising her son, about the Creed and its apostolic originators (Foote, 1984, 188–98). His description of Hákon's heathen temple (with many glass windows!) is quite implausible, and the way in which Hákon approaches the statue of his goddess, Þorgerðr Hölgabrúðr, to obtain the bracelet for Sigmundr, reads like a parody of tales associated with images of the Blessed Virgin and other saints (cf. e.g. *Handwörterbuch*, iii, 243–4). The authors seem pretty confident that heathendom is a thing of the distant past, no more than fertile ground for the cultivation of sensational stories. Witchcraft on the other hand seems to remain real. From what we know of internal Norwegian propaganda in the twelfth century (Foote, 1984, 35–42) we may conclude that it was associated with Satan rather than with Óðinn (the two could of course be equated), even though such repugnant practices as *útiseta* were regarded as remnants of pre-Christian times. We may remember that the author of *Orkneyinga saga* (chs. 65–6) harps on Sveinn brjóstreip's addiction to that form of sorcery, evidently condemned as malignant though not demonstrated to be so in the narrative. The intention seems to be to make the slaughter of him by Sveinn Ásleifarson appear that much less reprehensible. The writer credits Bishop William with approval of the deed, saying he called it *landhreinsun*, a 'cleansing of the country', a conventional term for the extirpation of malefactors.

There are naive, exaggerated and conventional elements in these early sagas, but description of action is usually vivid and compelling. Direct speech is freely invented, sometimes stilted but often natural sounding. Rhetorical skills are evident in longer speeches, built on classical and homiletic formalities learnt at school but on native practice too: speechmaking must have played a large part in public and social life. The authors and their audiences are keen on conflict, violence and daring, cunning and stratagem: sometimes conveyed in a framework of such consistent implausibility that we are tempted to think that the narrators expected their audiences to relish watching them sail close to the wind. The material may be varied, even miscellaneous, but the writers were capable of linking parts: by ominous presage, by repetition and reminiscence, by contrasts in appearance and personality between generations or within the same generation, by elements that acquire a leitmotif character. Sometimes there are long intervals between such repeats and variations, and the author's grasp of the threads seems remarkably confident. Sometimes episodes or dialogue end in a way that leaves a reader teased and wondering. There is humour too.

I have spoken of authors and audiences but they can hardly be differentiated in their primary milieu. The authors had varying and sometimes innovatory skills as storytellers, and we can see that they had particular ways of looking at the past and manipulating the record—but this does not mean that we are meeting thoroughgoing individualists and original thinkers. We may rather take it that the attitudes we can read out of their sagas are an articulation of what was generally accepted. Relying on their audience, they could play down the norms or allow them to remain merely implicit; starting with different preconceptions, a modern reader may miss the inferences altogether. The primary audiences lay among circles of prominent Icelanders; the leading families of the late twelfth century provided the collective establishment whose attitudes are reflected in these sagas. It may be worth recalling that the Icelanders were not a poor and isolated community but a substantial and self-confident nation, with little experience of major strife in the near two hundred years of their Christian existence, and certainly nothing on the scale of twelfth-century conflict in Norway, Denmark and Orkney. Some Icelanders were well connected abroad, and relatively many of them in the twelfth century were widely travelled. Their bishops, abbots and clergy were native to the country, some schooled at home, some both at home and across the sea. The sagas I have mentioned were composed in just the age when official national sanction was given to the cults of Icelandic saints, Þorlákr of Skálholt in 1198, Jón of Hólar in 1200, both of them—typically—bishops and confessors, not rulers and martyrs like the best known of the early saints of continental Scandinavia and Orkney. The Icelanders had an extensive and independent legal tradition, and a native tradition both of storytelling and of history writing, the one ageless, the other, both in Latin and the vernacular, about a century old. Both storytelling and history writing were supplied and maintained by the practice of poetry, and further prompted by the acknowledgement throughout the Scandinavian world at the end of the twelfth century of the status of the Icelandic poets as authorities on the Nordic past (Halvorsen, 1958).

The writers, and the patrons who encouraged and commissioned their work, may well also have had remotor audiences in mind: the court of King Sverrir in Norway, circles of leading men in Bergen and Tønsberg, the households of Earl Haraldr Maddaðarson and Bishop Bjarni Kolbeinsson in Orkney.[1] And both in Iceland and abroad there were partisan views of the past to be borne in mind. The famed objectivity of Icelandic saga-writers may partly result from pragmatic prudence as they addressed themselves to audiences, present or prospective, on whose unanimity of opinion they could not rely.

Orkneyinga saga shares the characteristics of the contemporary *Jómsvíkinga saga* and *Færeyinga saga* briefly described above. It differs from them in its much greater scope in time and space, and differs again in the nature of its Christian history. Conversion and the struggle it generated are matters of concern in the two shorter sagas, bound up as they were with national and international politics. They show a militant interest in the death-throes of paganism, but Christianity, the true faith, was bound to win, and their authors are not concerned to display it in further action, in the practical or ethical sphere. In *Orkneyinga saga*, on the other hand, perfunctory deference is paid to the claim that Óláfr Tryggvason forced Earl Sigurðr Hlöðvisson to accept baptism (ch. 12), but there is nothing else on the conversion of the islanders. Presumably there were in fact no stories to tell, understandably if, as seems likely, gradual and uneventful transfer to Christianity had gone on from the time of the settlement, under the influence of the surviving native population in Orkney and their Scottish neighbours. What the author of *Orkneyinga saga* did have to fit into his history was the life and martyrdom of Magnús Erlendsson. That made a dramatic centrepiece to show Christian conviction in action; it could also offer a perspective under which other acts and actors in the narrative might be viewed.

The literary history of *Orkneyinga saga*, like that of other early sagas, is complex and in part obscure. It seems to be generally accepted, however, that in its first form it began with the rule of the sons of Rögnvaldr Mœrajarl and in all probability ended with the death of Sveinn Ásleifarson, tentatively put in 1171 (*The Orkneyinga Saga*, 1938, 407–8). The writer knew some good stories about Torf-Einarr and had a lot to tell of Þorfinnr the Mighty, who died in the early 1060s. The latter part of the eleventh century is largely a blank, but the rest of the saga, a good two-thirds of the whole narrative, then concerns the history of the Orkney dynasty and prominent men associated with it from about 1090 onwards. The author had a wealth of information, from men of Orkney and Caithness as well as Icelanders; he had probably met some of the people who figure in his account; and it has been suggested that he was personally familiar with some of the Orkney and Caithness landscape. He knew a good deal of scaldic verse and evidently enjoyed both the poetry and the anecdotes that went with it. He was knowledgeable about Norwegian history and apparently took Norwegian suzerainty over the islands for granted. His knowledge of the remoter Scottish background seems to have been almost as hazy as mine. Among written sources we may be sure he turned to was a *Vita* of St Magnús, known to him in Latin or perhaps already in a Norse version, perhaps in both.

The sources are multifarious and are sometimes reproduced with details bordering the irrelevant—though even these may sharpen the impression of immediacy and hence of authenticity. In spite of that, it is clear that the author had an overview and saw large themes in his history. He prepares the ground, already in ch. 9, for the rivalries and bloodshed to come—particularly the death of Magnús the martyr—by introducing the doom of *ættvíg*, 'kindred killing, family slaughter', laid on the dynasty, almost casually, when no heed is paid to a warning to do with day-choosing and nephew kills uncle for the sake of an evil woman and the earldom, both of which he then, as an appropriate irony, fails to obtain. The author sets a stamp on the narrative by bringing in a good many more ominous signs, some just in advance of the event or catastrophe they forecast, some at longer removes. We may also safely look for the author's art and intention in the speech he attributes to his characters and in the emphatic qualifiers he uses in describing them.

He is in general notably consistent in his presentation of Sveinn Ásleifarson, the outstanding problem-character who looms large in the narrative over a span of some thirty-five years. We get the impression that he admired Sveinn's daring exploits, his resource and ruthless ability to survive. We do not get the impression that he approved of him. In ch. 77 Sveinn is characterised as *ójafnaðar-maðr*; and so is Þorbjörn klerkr, who one day is to kill Rögnvaldr, earl and saint. The compound is often translated 'overbearing man', but Dasent's 'unfair overbearing man' (*Icelandic Sagas*, iii, 138) is nearer the mark. Literally it is 'man of iniquity', with the abstract in its archaic sense, 'want of equity, injustice'. It is used not uncommonly in Icelandic stories of men assertive, grasping and self-willed, who readily trample on the rights of others.[2] It is not a laudatory term, but it does not imply disrespect. The author then uses the same term to describe Sveinn on some further significant occasions. In ch. 82 Earl Rögnvaldr gives his telling opinion: in response to a complaint, he says that that would not be the only time that it would be discovered that Sveinn was no *jafnaðarmaðr*, and adds, 'but the time will come when he will meet retribution for his *ranglæti.*' *Ranglæti* is 'injustice, unrighteousness' (cf. Walter, 1976, 104), just the opposite, we may note, of St Magnús's merit, whose *réttlæti*, 'justice, righteousness', was seen as the cause of his death (ch. 51). It can hardly be doubted that through Rögnvaldr's remark the author is looking forward to Sveinn's distant deathday and the requital he can expect in the next life. Sveinn suffers some setbacks in this world but none seems sufficient to justify Rögnvaldr's words; and indeed the author himself appears to make the link plain in his description of the circumstances of Sveinn's end. In ch. 106, before his last foray, Sveinn gets some good advice from Earl Haraldr Maddaðarson, who uses a suitably modified version of *omnes enim qui acceperint gladium gladio peribunt* as his argument. He says Sveinn should give up raiding: 'You know that you have long supported yourself and your people by that: but it happens to most *ójafnaðarmenn* that they perish in warfare if they do not give it up of their own accord.' Sveinn replies with good humour and a grin, but sardonically points out, with refined litotes, that there are some people who complain that Earl Haraldr himself is not much of a *jafnaðarmaðr*. The earl's prognostication proves right, of course, and Sveinn goes off to meet his death in Dublin (ch. 107). And there, so the author tells us, the townsmen plan their treachery because they did not relish the prospect of surrendering to Sveinn, the man known to be the greatest *ójafnaðarmaðr* in the western lands.

On the other hand, the writer is adroit in using Sveinn as a foil to Earl Rögnvaldr, whose reputation for sanctity he obviously knew and endorsed. Rögnvaldr's prestige is enhanced by the author's emphasis on Sveinn's constant and immaculate regard for him, in spite of tension and differences between them. In ch. 83 the author alleges that Sveinn told King David in Edinburgh that he would turn down his good offers and return to Orkney because he had always been best content when he was on good terms with Rögnvaldr. This impresses the king who says, in effect, that this mere earl must be quite a chap. The impact made on Sveinn by Rögnvaldr's personality, as conveyed by the author, does credit to the earl and saint-to-be— whether at some cost to the credibility of the portrayal of Sveinn himself will be a matter of opinion. But in any case a ray of saving grace is also shed on Sveinn by it, as the author evidently intended it should. This intention comes out clearly in the words he puts into Sveinn's mouth as he is the last to be butchered in the Dublin trap: 'Let all men know, whether I die today or not, that I am the retainer of Saint Rögnvaldr, and I look for help now to where he stands with God'.

The author ends, quite rightly, with an epitaph which says that men reckon Sveinn was the most able and active man of all untitled men in the western lands ever—*at hann hafi mestr maðr verit fyrir sér í Vestrlöndum bæði at fornu ok nýju þeira manna, er eigi höfðu meira tignarnafn en hann* (ch. 108). That opinion did not affect his judgment of him as *ójafnaðarmaðr* or his doubt as to whether his lodging in the next world would be a good one. If there was hope for him, it lay in his devotion to Rögnvaldr the earl and his appeal, in his last words, to Rögnvaldr the saint. Faith in such a possibility was commonplace orthodoxy: even on his last day the righteous can fall to perdition, the sinner be saved.[3] When we see how the author of the saga sustains his stylised presentation, we may doubt whether it brings us at all close to the 'real' relations between Rögnvaldr and Sveinn (but cf. Ciklamini, 1970), or between Sveinn and King David, any more than the *Vita* of St Magnús tells us much about the 'real' relations between the martyr and Hákon, his cousin. But as a calculated advertisement for the sanctity of Rögnvaldr it could, in the circumstances, hardly be more skilfully pursued; and it is tempting to find its immediate background in the preparation for the translation of Rögnvaldr's relics in 1192. The formal institution of his cult seems to have got nowhere in the time of Bishop William II but rapidly came to pass after the election of Bjarni Kolbeinsson in 1188.

Sveinn's response to Earl Haraldr's admonition to give up his rapine, mentioned just now, is a good example of the way in which the Icelandic author may take an opportunity to deepen and round the impression of a character. He shares with numerous other saga-writers a marked reluctance to paint only in black and white. We find something similar in the episode which foreshadows Hákon Pálsson's killing of Magnús. In ch. 36 we are told that Hákon, in exile in Sweden, is strangely impelled to seek out a soothsayer to discover his destiny. The account is quite elaborately staged against a not implausible background. Allegations of long-lived heathendom among the Swedes seem to have been popular among their prejudiced Norwegian neighbours. They were not entirely baseless for, as we know from *Orkneyinga saga*, ch. 35, and other sources, a brief pagan reaction at the end of the eleventh century had put Sacrifice-Sven in control in central Sweden and caused King Ingi Stenkelsson to withdraw to Västergötland. The soothsayer is given a long speech, in which he makes sour mockery of Óláfr the Portly—St Óláfr as he is usually and more respectfully known—and of the fasts and vigils of Christians, which they suffer but are none the wiser in consequence. He claims in contrast that men like him take no hardships on themselves but never fail to discover what their friends think it important to know. He welcomes Hákon as a free-thinker, with apostate leanings, and tells him to come back in three days' time to learn what he has found out about his future. On Hákon's return he finds a weary soothsayer, who lets him know what great exertions he has had to make in order to discern his destiny. He tells him he will be sole ruler in Orkney one day and his descendants will live there after him, but he will commit a heinous crime (*glœpr*, cf. Walter, 1976, 93) for which atonement to the God Hákon believes in will be scarcely possible, if at all. Hákon's tracks, he says, go wider in the world than he could see, but he thought he would rest his bones in the North. In Hákon's rather dubious and truculent reply the author strikes a convincing note. Despite the artificiality, there is a boldness and urgency in this episode that help to convey the suggestion that Hákon is both a flawed and a starcrossed character. On the other hand, the author, though free with his imaginings, certainly does not sell himself. He is clearly confident that no one will take the shaman's woeful misunderstanding of Christian asceticism seriously. The disdainful reference to Óláfr the Portly has a background in a certain coolness towards Norway's patron saint which seems to have existed in some perfectly respectable circles in late eleventh- and twelfth-century Iceland (Björn Þorsteinsson, 1987, 53), and it was likely to be found amusing rather than blasphemous. After the soothsayer's taunts about Christian fasts and vigils, the author's irony is plain when he smoothly slips into the conventional description of the exhaustion of such wizards after their psychic ordeal and makes the shaman moan about the severity of his trials (Strömbäck, 1935, 182-6). Finally, Rome and the Holy Land are beyond the range of his visionary powers. As we know, Hákon was to visit them as a penitent and pilgrim soon after Magnús's death. His voyage is briefly described in ch. 52 and from it, we are told, he returned to settle down to a year or two of wise and popular rule. Some people have found this all too perfunctory to be plausible, but from an orthodox point of view there was no need for elaboration. The efficacy of pilgrimage and penance and papal absolution was unquestionable. Hákon could make a fresh start, could be a changed man. The author had been equally eager to give Þorfinnr Sigurðarson, that mighty and bloodstained earl, a similar chance (ch. 31).

As we know, no complete text of the *Vita S. Magni comitis* is extant and no confident reconstruction of it can be made from the various sources we have. When it was first composed is not at all certain: perhaps in 1137, and obviously in time for the author of *Orkneyinga saga* to adapt some of it for his own ends some fifty or sixty years after that date. It is attributed to a Master Robert—the conjecture that he was Robert of Cricklade, prior of the Augustinian house of St Frideswide's, Oxford, has yet to be substantiated (*Orkneyinga saga*, 1965, xlvi–xlvii). He apparently addressed his *Vita* in sermon form to an audience local to the Kirkwall shrine, but neither his name nor the information he provides suggests he was a native of the islands.[4] As far as we can tell, he saw Hákon as the more or less unrelieved opposite of Magnús who, once he became earl, turned into a perfect example of Christian virtue. Hákon is harsh and unjust, rapacious, envious and perfidious. Any political consideration is reduced to 'glory in dominion' and 'lust of sovereignty', the bare bones of motivation recognised by St Augustine in his examination of the story of Romulus and Remus alongside that of Cain and Abel (*The City of God*, 1945, ii, 64, 67 [XV, v, vii]). The author quotes the Lucan tag (*Pharsalia*, i, 93–4), *Nulla fides regni sociis, omnisque potestas / Inpatiens consortis erit . . .*, a fact of life which Matthew Paris a century later was also fond of acknowledging, though with his own refinement (e.g. *Chronicles*, 1984, 126, 185, 227). The conventionality of the author's *passio* pattern and general interpretation is matched by the stock nature of his lauds of Magnús, though his wide range of biblical allusion may appear as a more individual characteristic. He, and other churchmen after him, made much of the claim that Magnús preserved his and his wife's chastity in their ten years of marriage, presumably based on the fact that no children of theirs were known.[5]

Since prophecy of one kind and another is common in saints' lives it is possible that the *Vita* contained some presage of Hákon's great crime. If it did, we may doubt whether it took a form anything like that of the Swedish episode sketched above. That episode is undeniably integral to the saga, for not only does it fit in a specifically Icelandic storytelling convention, it is also recalled by a specific echo in the account of events leading up to the capture of Magnús. On passage to Egilsay (ch. 47) Magnús's men marvel at a wave which breaks over them in calm weather and deep water. The author says that Magnús told them it was not strange that they should marvel at it—'but my notion is that this is an omen of my death; maybe the prophecy that the son of Earl Páll will commit a very great crime (*glœpr*) will be fulfilled ...'[6] Both the more distant reminiscence and the more immediate portent are so much in keeping with the habit of the author (who here gives Magnús a share in his omniscience) that it is surely his art we are observing, not that of the *Vita*.

There is another episode which again appears integral to the saga but whose preexistence in the *Vita* must be counted uncertain and even, it may be argued, unlikely.[7] It is true that the kernel of the anecdote can be readily paralleled in works of hagiographic and related kind, but that also means it was a motif readily available to any educated writer of the twelfth century. The message conveyed also appears to be slightly unusual in such a context, but it squares rather nicely both with the saga-writer's balanced realisation of character and with his views on *ójafnaðarmenn*.

The episode is the one in which Magnús refuses to fight alongside King Magnús Bareleg in the famous battle in which Hugh earl of Shrewsbury was killed, fought in the Menai Strait in 1098. Young Magnús of Orkney made no preparation to fight and, when asked why, said that he had no cause of quarrel with any of their opponents—*Hann lézk þar við engan mann sakar eiga*. His royal namesake tells him to get below deck if he does not dare to fight—'for I think it is not faith that prompts you'—'*því at ek ætla þér eigi trú til ganga.*' Magnús's response is to stay on deck and chant from his psalter through the heat of the battle; he comes to no harm.

The situation described provokes recollection of a variety of associations, some more problematic than others. We may be reminded of the non-combatant holy man who stands by and invokes divine aid, like Moses during Joshua's battle with Amalek (Exodus 17.9–13; cf. e.g. *The Life of Bishop Wilfrid*, 1985, 28). We have a striking modification of the theme in *Sverris saga* (Foote, 1984, 129–31, 138). In the midst of the battle of Nordnes in 1181 Sverrir the pretender, who had taken priest's orders as a young man, 'went for'ard on the deck and put aside his weapons and knelt and lifted his hands to heaven and sang the sequence *Alma chorus domini* right through and did not protect himself meanwhile.' The *Alma chorus domini* contains fifty-six names of God: you were bound to catch the Almighty's ear with one of them, and Sverrir's victory at Nordnes comes as no surprise. There may be some link between the story told of Sverrir and the story told of Magnús, but the point is not the same.[8] Another theme, that of the Christian who resigns from armed service, is familiar from *passiones* of early soldier-saints and other sources (Cadoux, 1925, 584–92). The best-known example of all is that of St Martin (cf. *Hrafns saga*, 1987, xxii, n. 3), of whose story there is a verbal echo in the account of Magnús in *Orkneyinga saga*.[9] In these instances, however, Christian profession and the military profession are found simply incompatible: a solid form of conscientious objection on good Gospel grounds (cf. Stancliffe, 1983, 139–41). This kind of pacifism is not Magnús's response.

The problem of the man dedicated to God's service but involved in warfare against fellow-Christians was of course also recognised as of moment in the middle ages. It was not always solved as cynically as it may appear to have been by Philippe de Dreux, count and bishop of Beauvais, who after a lifetime in arms seems at last to have had some qualms of conscience. He went into the battle of Bouvines in 1214 armed only with a club so as to avoid effusion of blood—and then more or less completed the French victory with it by swatting the English commander, the earl of Salisbury, off his horse and into captivity (*Nouvelle biographie générale*, 1852–66, xiii, 757–8). Just four years before St Magnús was killed, Gaudry of Touillon, *miles inclitus*, persuaded to take monastic vows by his nephew Bernard, soon to be first abbot of Clairvaux, asked his lord, the duke of Burgundy, for permission to retire from the siege of Grancy in order to do so. The duke would not release him from his feudal bond. Gaudry was incensed and said he could not retaliate against him— '*sed scitote quod ab hodie in collo meo clipeus non pendebit*' (Chompton, 1895, 196); he apparently continued to do his duty at the siege but not under arms.

The difficulty of the man of God in relation to physical force may have been felt not least acutely in early Christian Scandinavia, where notions of personal and family honour and shame were still often paramount. The problem is eloquently voiced in the laws of Gotland, probably not later than about 1220 in origin. There an aggrieved cleric is told to appeal to the assembly for justice and say, 'I am a priest consecrated to God's service—I cannot stand amid strokes or in battle—I would take atonement if it were offered, but shame I would not willingly suffer' (Foote and Wilson, 1980, 429). Of course, in a vengeful age anyone might be faced with choice between obeying the traditional code and obeying Christian command; and the dilemma is sometimes made explicit in the histories that describe twelfth- and thirteenth-century events in Iceland. It is caught in this fragment from some Icelandic sermon notes made about 1250: '. . . overbearing men speak ill of the patience of the meek, those who drive out the spirit of wrath from their hearts, and they say that it is not because of their faith but because of their cowardice that they will not avenge themselves on their enemies . . .' (*Hrafns saga*, 1987, xxiii). A more measured response is offered by the Norwegian author of *Konungs skuggsiá*, of about the same date (*Konungs skuggsiá*, 1983, 6, 66). An offence must be weighed and the truth estabished. If vengeance is appropriate, it must be so calculated as to ensure that only the guilty suffers. Retribution is accepted as reasonable but it must be just.

And that may take us back to St Magnús and his reply to King Magnús. He will not fight, he says, because no one on the other side has done him wrong: he has no just retribution to exact. Magnús refutes the king's charge of cowardice by his cool psalm-chanting conduct through the battle, and that clearly had divine approval. The moral courage he showed, to the extent of renouncing his allegiance[10] and refusing to fight at all, might also be recognised by strict thinkers as having sound doctrinal warrant. The brief explanation the author credits him with is, after all, simply grounded on Christendom's simple definition of just war, formulated by St Augustine and made common property by St Isidore: *Justa bella definiri solent quae ulciscuntur injurias . . .; Nam extra ulciscendi, aut propulsandorum hostium causam, bellum justum geri nullum potest* (Regout, 1935, 42, 46).

The author of the saga presents a profile of Magnús's early life quite different from that of the *Vita* (cf. n. 7). He introduces Magnús with Erlingr his brother and Hákon his cousin in ch. 34. The two latter grow up very obstreperous (*gerðusk þeir ofstopamenn miklir*); Magnús was the quietest (*kyrrlátastr*) of the three. In the dissension between the families that is then described Magnús receives no independent attention; his existence is merely subsumed in expressions like *synir Erlends, þeir feðgar, þeir bræðr*. Then suddenly, in this Anglesey episode, he takes the centre of the stage and plays the part of a quietly determined young man, whose strength of conviction is on a par with that of heroes of the faith. But it is not the conviction of all-embracing Christian charity, meek and forgiving, it is more like the conviction of the rigorously just and righteous. The saga-writer puts no overt supernatural gloss on Magnús's safe survival in the battle, and the means by which he then escapes from King Magnús's retinue are not at all miraculous: first the universal adventure-story stratagem of a dummy in the bed and then a well-aimed cudgel thrown at a bloodhound. The narrative that follows is bare and rapid until Magnús has returned to Orkney and his share in the earldom has been confirmed by King Eysteinn of Norway. Then ch. 45 consists of a lengthy encomium, some of it doubtless corresponding to matter that was in the *Vita*, though we cannot tell whether it is a close version or not:

> Holy Magnús, earl of the Isles, was a man of the utmost excellence, big in stature, manly and frank of feature, moral in behaviour, victorious in battles, sagacious in wit, eloquent and a ruler by temperament, generous with money and munificent in mind, shrewd in counsel and the most popular of men, affable and fair-spoken to men peaceable and good but hard and unmerciful to robbers and pirates and he had many men put to death who harried householders and common people. He saw to the capture of murderers and thieves and he punished mighty and petty men alike for robbery and theft and every misdeed. He showed no partiality to friends in his verdicts; he respected divine justice more than distinction of rank.

A passage of similar length is then devoted to his charity and asceticism. In the next chapter (46) the author tells of two great men, one a kinsman, who were destroyed by Magnús and Hákon in alliance. Since he refers to a poem as his authority, though without citing any lines from it, it is unlikely that this information was in the *Vita*. He adds no comment but it is natural to infer that these examples are meant to illustrate the stern rectitude of Magnús's rule. That is how the fourteenth-century Icelandic editor of the *Magnúss saga lengri* took it, for he reserves description of Magnús's just government until after the account of the destruction of these magnates, when he says:

> St Magnús undertook these acts not as a bandit or robber, but as the lawful governor of the realm and the upholder of the laws, a lover of peace, to chastise men's wicked ways and punish wrongdoing . . .[11]
>
> (*Orkneyinga saga*, 1965, 352; cf. *Hrafns saga*, 1987, xxvi).

This emphasis on Magnús as the typical *rex justus* of medieval theory follows in a straight line from the import the author of the saga attached to his refusal to fight in the Menai Strait. As ruler in Orkney, Magnús's violence is visited on the guilty and is in the service of peace and protection. The violence of the aggressive King Magnús or of the *ójafnaðarmaðr*, Sveinn Ásleifarson, is visited on the innocent and is in the service of this world's glory and greed. They died, the king, as everyone knew, in an ambush while stealing cattle in Ulster, Sveinn, according to the saga, in a mantrap after an unprovoked raid on Dublin. Magnús died too, at the hands of his cousin Hákon, another man of blood, but he died as a sacrificial victim and became the mighty martyr on whose invocation men could rely, enshrined in Kirkwall's great cathedral, patron of another cathedral in the Faroes and of no fewer than ten churches in Iceland, three of them quite possibly dedicated to him in the generation which saw the composition of *Orkneyinga saga*.

Ǽettvíg and *ójafnaðr*, murder in the family and injustice, 'the brute and boisterous force of violent men', with right-minded Magnús and sunny-tempered Rögnvaldr their victims. I have met people, Orcadians among them, who have come away from reading our saga feeling rather confused and depressed—finding in it what Thomas Carlyle found in all Scottish history (before the advent of John Knox, of course): 'continual broils, dissensions, massacrings . . . Hungry fierce barons, not so much able as to form any arrangement with each other *how to divide* what they fleeced . . . "Bravery" enough, I doubt not; fierce fighting in abundance: but not braver or fiercer than that of their old Scandinavian Sea-King ancestors; *whose* exploits we have not found worth dwelling on'. But if we respond to the saga in such a way, it may be because we have failed, for varying reasons, to perceive and appreciate, within the discreet artfulness of the narrative, the conventional political ideals and the orthodox sacramental understanding—and hope and expectation—of the author and his contemporaries.

NOTES

1. In *Jómsvíkinga saga*, 1969, 27 Ólafur Halldórsson plausibly suggests that the poet of *Jómsvíkingadrápa* used an early recension of the saga that was not exactly the same as the oldest extant version known in AM 291 4to. On the other hand, he also has some justifiable reservations about the attribution of the poem to Bishop Bjarni Kolbeinsson, so we must not hastily conclude that an Icelandic saga-text had reached Orkney by about 1200.

2. Typical instances are Óspakr Kjallaksson, *Eyrbyggja saga*, 1935, 157; Egill Skúlason (so termed by Ófeigr Skíðason), *Bandamanna saga*, 1981, 30; Hrafnkell Freysgoði, *Austfirðinga sögur*, 1950, 99. Cf. also the quotation and comment offered by Lúðvík Ingvarsson, 1986, i, 110. Walter, 1976, 95 n. 4, notes, however, that Lat. *iniquus* is nowhere conveyed by *ójafn* or *ójafnaðarmaðr* in his material, and asks: 'Waren Etymologie und Bildung von *iniquus* nicht durchsichtig genug . . .? Oder war der Charakter der Wertung so verschieden?' It would be interesting to see someone attempt an answer based on a thorough study.

3. Ezekiel 18 and 33 gave prime scriptural warrant. The doctrine finds plain expression in the influential Pseudo-Augustinian *De vera et falsa poenitentia*, from about 1100 (cf. e.g. *PL*, xl, 1118, 1128; *KL*, ii, 182). Casually noted instances of the idea in Norse versions of works as varied as *Vita Antonii abbatis*, *Visio Tnugdali* and Aelfric's *De auguriis* are at *Hms.*, i, 64/1–4, 339/6–9, and *Hauksbók*, 1892–6, 168/3–11. For Norse citation of Ezekiel 33.11–16 see Kirby, 1976, 109–11.

4. Robert does not appear in Norwegian-Icelandic native name-giving before the thirteenth century, Lind, 1905–15, 583. Other names made popular by the Normans occur earlier, William in Norway in the first half of the twelfth century, Henry in Iceland in the late twelfth century; the earliest example of Richard is from Orkney *c*.1130; see Lind, 1905–15, 1110, *Hrafns saga*, 1987, 87, *Orkneyinga saga*, 1965, 21. If Bishop William I, consecrated 1112 (rather than 1102, cf. *DN*, xvii: B, 297) and presumably born not later than *c*.1080, was an Orkney local, he was given a Norman name surprisingly early, and it may be easier to think he was an incomer. (It may be noted though that King Duncan II, died 1094, had a son called William.)

5. Like Edward the Confessor and other saintly rulers, Magnús is said to have plunged into cold water to combat urges of the flesh. A word of warning on the practice has been offered by Professor Meyer (*The Life and Death of Saint Malachy*, 1978, 132): 'I believe that modern physiology has proven that cold baths are more apt to urge lustful feelings as a reaction once the warm blood flowed [*sic*] back.'

6. This follows the readings cited in *Orkneyinga saga*, 1965, 106 n.6. The staple text of the edition, from Flateyjarbók, has a simplified form of the sentence which is clearly inferior.

7. *Magnúss saga lengri* contains substantial passages specifically attributed to Master Robert, but they are expository rather than narrative. Contents of the *Vita* can otherwise be partially established by comparing *Msl.* with the so-called *Legenda de sancto Magno* (known in two copies representing different sources), the lections of *Breviarium Aberdonense* and of *Breviarium Nidrosiense*, and the liturgical composition based on the *Vita*, for which *Brev. Aberd.* is the chief source. *Msl.* and *Leg.* are printed *Icelandic Sagas*, i, 237–80, 299–302, iii, 302–4, and *Orkneyinga saga*, 1965, 335–83, 303–8; the *Brev. Aberd.* office is in *Icelandic Sagas*, iii, 305–22; the *Brev. Nidr.* office is on kk.vj. of the 1519 print. For a full survey of the liturgical material see De Geer, 1985, 118–37. Page references to the short Latin texts are not given in the following; *Msl.* is referred to by chapter. Main considerations that prompt doubt about the existence of the Anglesey episode in the *Vita* are then these:

    (i) The *Vita* describes Magnús as a pious and amiable child, with use of the *puer senex* topos and other commonplaces, who then in his youth turns into a pirate and manslayer (*Leg., Msl.* chs. 4 and 8, *Brev. Aberd., Brev. Nidr.*). But once accepted as earl in Caithness, after having escaped from the following of the Norwegian king, he underwent a swift spiritual transformation: Ok því næst án dvöl gerðist inn heilagi Magnús jarl Paulus af Saulo, predikari af manndrápsmanni . . . (*Msl.* ch. 12); Saulus ecce Paulus fit, prædo fit patronus . . . (*Brev. Aberd.*). If the *Vita* had contained the refusal-to-fight anecdote, we might expect less of a sharp contrast between Magnús's state before and after his acceptance as earl; but the coincidence of conversion and accession is consonant with the *Leg.* text, discussed under ii(b) below, which tells a different story. It is true that the editor of *Msl.* was prepared to live with such an inconsistency, but he obviously took his Anglesey episode in ch. 9 from the saga, not the *Vita*. He spells out there the miraculous nature of Magnús's preservation in the battle, but that can easily be read as his own gloss (cf. the independent expansion of the exchange between Magnús and the king in *Magnúss saga skemmri* , ch. 3, *Orkneyinga saga*, 1965, 313), although he may have been influenced by the Latin of ii (c) below, which is otherwise rendered in his ch. 11. As noted on p. 201 above, the saga-writer has nothing on Magnús's childhood and youth comparable to the matter of the *Vita*. Einar Ól. Sveinsson, 1937, 31–2, suggested the author omitted his viking activities for reasons of chronology. The argument is not compelling. The *Msl.* editor saw and overcame the problem with a sentence (ch. 8); the author of the saga found no difficulty in fitting in the narrative of Hákon's exile, and he could have located Magnús's banditry as an episode before or during that time. As an alternative explanation Einar suggested the author perhaps had an abridged *Vita* that lacked the matter of Magnús's early years; he pointed to its absence in the *Brev. Aberd.* lections. It seems unlikely however that so truncated a version ever existed outside an office, and in any case the responses and verses to the *Brev. Aberd.* lections make emphatic reference to Magnús's piratical adolescence. Altogether it may seem more likely that the saga-author's preferred interpretation of Magnús's character led him to reject all reference to Magnús the viking. His restrained description of Magnús as the 'quietest' of the young kinsmen points in the same direction.

    (ii) The refusal-to-fight anecdote is embedded in narrative most probably drawn from some written account of Magnús Bareleg (*The Orkneyinga Saga*, 1938, 67–72), which could not itself have provided matter for the *Vita*. Various discrepancies show that the *Vita* in fact purveyed a tradition independent of sources represented in the saga:
        (a) *Leg.* and *Msl.* ch. 8 contain the following parallel sentences, the latter at the end of a passage attributed to Master Robert by name. The sentences come after the description

of young Magnús's piracy but *Leg.* omits the intervening reflections of Robert supplied in *Msl.*

> Denique cum beatus Magnus hujusmodi sceleribus implicaretur, ad hoc tandem ventum est, ut patrem et germanum comitatus Hatlandiam applicaret.
> Sé um síðir, sem inn heilagi Magnús í vafðist slíkum syndum, þá kom þar, at hann af létti þessu starfi ok fylgdi feðr sínum ok bróður ok lendum mönnum í Orkneyjum.

Here the reference to Shetland and use of the unambiguous verb *applico* in *Leg.* were probably original in the *Vita*, while the curious *fylgdi feðr sínum . . . í Orkneyjum* ('stayed in the company of his father . . . in Orkney'?) probably betrays an unhandy improvement by the editor of *Msl.*, who found no mention of this move to Shetland in saga sources (and who may have misunderstood *comitatus*?).

(b) *Leg.* goes on to say that the earl and his sons were seized (in Shetland is the natural inference) by the king of Norway. He was under way *cum infinita navium et armorum multitudine, utpote exteras nationes invasurus*, and he forced them to fight against his enemies, *inimicis secum resistere coegit* (understandably preferred to the variant reading, *multos secum residere coegit*).

(c) One of the two *Leg.* copies continues with a text which ends defective but which can be made good from *Brev. Nidr.*:

> Sed omnipotens Deus, cui proprium est misereri semper et parcere, electum suum a talibus voluit mercimoniis suspendere et ostendere illi, quanta oporteret eum pati pro nomine ipsius, ut qui sanguinem innocentem multotiens fuderat ipse quandoque Spiritus Sancti victima fieret, ut proprium sanguinem Christo libaret. Unde contigit, ut de manu violenti regis et prædatoris eva . . .

In *Brev. Nidr.* the last sentence reads complete: Unde contigit eum de manu violenti regis et prædatoris evadere et Cathaniam adire, ubi honorifice susceptus est. The *Msl.* version of the whole passage is in ch. 11, with the reference to Magnús's arrival in Caithness and his acceptance there at the opening of ch. 12—which then continues with the *Paulus af Saulo* theme discussed in (i) above.

(d) *Leg.*, *Msl.* ch. 13, and *Brev. Aberd.* report that Hákon killed an official introduced by the Norwegian king to superintend the half of the earldom that was Magnús's by right.
     Of these points in which the *Vita* was at odds with the saga, (b) and (c) may suggest a context similar in outline to the saga narrative, though clearly different from it in detail. Severe abridgment may be assumed in *Leg.* and the lections, but even with that taken into account, it seems hard to believe that Magnús's resolute refusal to fight would find no mention anywhere in the liturgical prose and verse if it had in fact been described in the *Vita* in the first place. It may seem rather more likely that the *Vita* had a text like that of *Leg.*, and possibly it was its *inimicis secum resistere coegit* which spurred the saga-author to include his anecdote. The episode was doubly useful to him, since it both illustrated Magnús's character and motivated the king's displeasure, which in turn led to Magnús's escape.

(iii) If any weight is attached to the possibility that rumour of Sverrir's behaviour in the battle of Nordnes in 1181 had some formative influence on the Magnús anecdote, then the author of *Orkneyinga saga* was clearly the first to record it. Cf. n. 8 below.

8. The anecdote about Sverrir is thought to be original in *Sverris saga*, a work begun 1185-8 and finished after 1202, but the rumour or report which gave rise to it presumably had some

independent currency. That extraordinary stories about Sverrir were in wide circulation in his lifetime is shown by the account of his decisive Fimreite victory of 1184 given by William of Newburgh (1884, 230–1) some 10–15 years after the event. Sverrir triumphed because of his magical arts—*Habebat enim secum quandam filiam diaboli, potentem in maleficiis*—and most of his opponents' ships were swallowed up by the sea. (Perhaps there was some conflation here with the story of Þorgerðr Hölgabrúðr, who might well be described as *filia diaboli*, and her part in the defeat of the Jómsvíkingar 200 years earlier, *Jómsvíkinga saga*, 1969, 185–6.)

9. *Vita Martini*, ch. 4: 'Hactenus', inquit ad Caesarem, 'militavi tibi; patere ut nunc militem Deo. Donativum tuum pugnaturus accipiat; Christi ego miles sum: pugnare mihi non licet.' Tum vero adversus hanc vocem tyrannus infremuit dicens eum metu pugnae, quae postero die erat futura, non religionis gratia detractare militiam. At Martinus intrepidus, immo inlato sibi terrore constantior: 'Si hoc,' inquit, 'ignaviae adscribitur, non fidei, crastina die ante aciem inermis adstabo et in nomine Domini Iesu, signo crucis, non clipeo protectus aut galea, hostium cuneos penetrabo securus (*Vita di Martino*, 1975, 14–16). Cf. with the central passage *Hms.*, i, 555/28–30: '. . . ek em Crists ríðeri, ok er mér eigi lofat at berjask.' Þá reiddisk konungr ok kvað Martinum fyrir hugleysi vilja ráðask frá orrostu en eigi fyrir trú . . .' The Icelandic translation is doubtless twelfth-century work, since the oldest copy is that in AM 645 4to, a manuscript from *c.*1220; for other versions see *Hms.*, i, 576, 610. Schei, 1987, 57, makes the appealing suggestion that Magnús's 'act of defiance could also have been a political protest': King Magnús is holding his father, Earl Erlendr, hostage in Norway, and that is why he refuses to take part. Faced with this proposal, we may find the literary parallel with the *Vita Martini* one cause of reservation. There are others. The author of the saga nowhere shows any sign of interest in the relations between Magnús and his father except insofar as Erlendr backs his sons in their disputes with their cousin Hákon (just as Páll backs Hákon against them). (This is in some contrast to the portrayal of relations between Rögnvaldr kali and his father, which the author sees in a very amiable light.) Given the author's silence, we are presumably to take it that before getting to North Wales young Magnús had played his part in the conquest of the Hebrides: but that of course was a campaign in which King Magnús was justifiably reasserting his hereditary right. The author reports that the king made Magnús his *skutilsveinn* (cf. n. 10), which hardly indicates that he thought their relations could have been much soured by the enforced retirement of Earl Erlendr. The author has the king suppose before the battle that Magnús does not dare to fight (*ef þú þorir eigi at berjask*) and has him reckon after the battle that he had behaved *ódrengiliga*: these expressions seem to stamp Magnús's refusal as an act of cowardice in the king's view, rather than an act of defiance.

10. If Magnús became the king's *skutilsveinn*, he must have been *handgenginn*. We do not know the exact status of such a (junior?) dapifer about 1100, but it was an honorific position; the title came to denote a rank next below *lendr maðr*, cf. Fritzner, iii, s.v., *NgL*, v, s.v., *Heimskringla*, 1941–51, iii, 205–6 and 205 n. 6.

11. The opening of this passage perhaps reflects the stress, in the *Vita* and *Msl.*, on the early career of Magnús precisely 'as a bandit or robber'; cf. n. 7 above.

BIBLIOGRAPHY

Augustine, St, *The City of God*, 1945, trans by J Healey, revd by R V G Tasker
Austfirðinga sǫgur, 1950, Jón Jóhannesson, ed., Íslenzk fornrit, xi, Reykjavík
Bandamanna saga, 1981, H Magerøy, ed.
Björn Þorsteinsson, 1987, *Thingvellir*, Reykjavík
Breviarium Aberdonense, extracts in *Icelandic Sagas*, iii
Breviarium Nidrosiense, 1519, Paris; repr in facsimile, 1964, Oslo

Cadoux, C J, 1925, *The Early Church and the World*

Chomton, L, 1895, *Saint Bernard et le Château de Fontaines-lès-Dijon*, iii, Paris

Chronicles of Matthew Paris, 1986, R Vaughan, ed. and trans

Ciklamini, M, 1970, 'Saint Rǫgnvaldr and Sveinn Ásleifarson, the Viking', *Scandinavian Studies*, xlii, 50–7

De Geer, Ingrid, 1985, *Earl, Saint, Bishop, Skald—and Music*, Uppsala

DN, xvii : B = Kolsrud, O, 1913, 'Den norske Kirkes Erkebiskoper og Biskoper indtil Reformationen', *Diplomatarium Norvegicum*, xvii : B, 177–360

Einar Ól Sveinsson, 1937, *Sagnaritun Oddaverja*, Íslenzk fræði, i, Reykjavík

Eyrbyggja saga, 1935, Einar Ól Sveinsson, ed., Íslenzk fornrit, iv, Reykjavík

Foote, P, 1984, *Aurvandilstá. Norse Studies*, Odense

Foote, P, Wilson, D M, 1980, *The Viking Achievement*, 2nd edn

Fritzner, J, 1883–96, *Ordbog over Det gamle norske Sprog*, Christiania; repr 1954, Oslo

Færeyinga saga, 1978, Ólafur Halldórsson, ed, Íslensk úrvalsrit 13, Reykjavík

Halvorsen, E F, 1958, 'Theodricus Monachus and the Icelanders', *Þriðji Víkingafundur . . . 1956, Árbók Hins íslenzka fornleifafélags, Fylgirit*, 142–55

Hauksbók, 1892–6, Finnur Jónsson and Eiríkur Jónsson, eds, Copenhagen

Hms. Heilagra manna søgur, 1877, C R Unger, ed., Christiania/Oslo

Heimskringla, 1941–51, Bjarni Aðalbjarnarson, ed., Íslenzk fornrit, xxvi–xxviii, Reykjavík

Hrafns saga Sveinbjarnarsonar, 1987, Guðrún P Helgadóttir, ed.

Handwörterbuch des deutschen Aberglaubens, 1927–42, E Hoffmann-Krayer and H Bächtold-Stäubli, eds, Berlin and Leipzig

Jómsvíkinga saga, 1969, Ólafur Halldórsson, ed., Reykjavík

Kirby, I J, 1976, *Biblical Quotation in Old Icelandic-Norwegian Religious Literature*, Reykjavík

Konungs skuggsiá, 1983, L Holm-Olsen, ed., 2nd edn, Oslo

KL = Kulturhistorisk Leksikon for nordisk middelalder, 1956–78, L Jacobsen *et al.*, eds, Copenhagen

Icelandic Sagas, i, 1887, *Orkneyinga saga and Magnus saga*, Gudbrand Vigfusson, ed.; iii, 1894, *The Orkneyingers' Saga*, trans by G W Dasent

The Life and Death of St Malachy the Irishman [by Bernard of Clairvaux], 1978, trans by R T Meyer, Kalamazoo

The Life of Bishop Wilfrid by Eddius Stephanus, 1927, B Colgrave, ed. and trans; pb. 1985

Lind, E H, 1905–15, *Norsk-isländska dopnamn och fingerade namn från medeltiden*, Uppsala

Lúðvík Ingvarsson, 1986, *Goðorð og goðorðsmenn*, Egilsstaðir

NgL, v = Hertzberg, E, *Glossarium*, 1895, in *Norges gamle Love indtil 1387*, v, Christiania/Oslo

Nouvelle biographie générale, 1852–66, J C F Hoefer, ed., Paris

Orkneyinga saga, 1965, Finnbogi Guðmundsson, ed. Íslenzk fornrit, xxxiv, Reykjavík

The Orkneyinga Saga, 1938, trans with intro and notes by A B Taylor

PL = Patrologia Latina, J-P Migne, ed., Paris

Regout, R, 1935, *La doctrine de la guerre juste de Saint Augustin à nos jours*, Paris

Schei, Liv Kjörsvik, 1985, pb. 1987, *The Orkney Story*

Stancliffe, C, 1983, *St Martin and his Hagiographer*

Strömbäck, , D, 1935, *Sejd. Textstudier i nordisk religionshistoria*, Stockholm

Turville-Petre, G, 1953, *Origins of Icelandic Literature*

Vita di Martino . . ., 1975, C Mohrmann *et al.*, eds, Verona

Walter, E, 1976, *Lexikalisches Lehngut im Altwestnordischen*, Abh. der sächs. Akad. der Wissenschaften zu Leipzig, Phil.-hist. Kl. 62 : 2, Berlin

William of Newburgh, 1884, *Historia rerum Anglicarum*, R Howlett, ed

CHAPTER 15

The Poetry of Earl Rǫgnvaldr's Court

Paul Bibire

Rǫgnvaldr Kali, St Ronald, Earl of Orkney 1137–1158/9, maintained the tradition of court poetry in Old Norse, skaldic poetry, which appears to go back to the early period of the Viking Earldom. The bulk of the poetry attributed to him is preserved in or associated with the texts which we know as *Orkneyinga saga (Íslenzk fornrit* xxxiv, *Orkneyinga saga*, ed. Finnbogi Guðmundsson, Reykjavík 1965; all chapter, page and verse references in this discussion are made to this edition). The saga as it stands is a modern compilation of passages, mostly from *Flateyjarbók*, a very large Icelandic manuscript written *c.*1387. This contains an expanded cycle of the sagas of the Kings of Norway, largely derived from Snorri Sturluson's *Heimskringla* but enlarged by addition of much material dealing with, inter alia, the Orkneys and Faroes. From this material the present texts known as *Orkneyinga saga* and *Færeyinga saga* have been reconstructed. In the case of *Orkneyinga saga*, there also exist three manuscript fragments (bound together in AM 325 4to), and various collections of excerpts, most importantly that of excerpted verses with prose narrative explanations preserved in Uppsala Isl. R: 702. A more or less complete translation of what was then clearly a single coherent text of the saga was made into Danish ca. 1570 (preserved in Stockholm Royal Library, Cod. Isl. Papper 39 fol.). On the basis of this translation, it may be assumed that the modern reconstruction of *Orkneyinga saga* is likely reliably to represent a medieval version of the saga.

The eighty-two verses in *Orkneyinga saga*, as it is presently reconstructed, all fall into three groups: firstly, the group dealing with Torf-Einarr (numbered in the *Íslenzk fornrit* edition of the saga as 1–6), secondly, that dealing with Earl Þorfinnr and his associates (7–29, 33), and thirdly, that dealing with Earl Rǫgnvaldr Kali and his associates (30–32, 34–82), i.e. fifty-two verses. Of this last group, forty-five verses can actually be attributed to Rǫgnvaldr himself and the poets of his retinue. Verses 30–32 37, 40–41, 82 are attributed to other authorship. Verses 34–82 are given, with translation and where necessary commentary, at the end of this paper.

Earl Rǫgnvaldr Kali was himself an accomplished poet; thirty-two verses are attributed to him in *Orkneyinga saga*, and there are a further three versus, one strophe and two half-strophes, attributed to him in or associated with *Snorra Edda*; these are also appended at the end of this paper. A further major poem, *Háttalykill*, is attributed jointly to Earl Rǫgnvaldr and one of his court poets, Hallr Þórarinsson (*Orkneyinga saga* lxxxi). This was identified in the seventeenth century with a text, extremely imperfectly preserved, which presently consists of fragments of eighty-two strophes; this identification is plausible but far from certain (see Jón Helgason and Anne Holtsmark, edd., *Háttalykill* especially pp. 13–14, 19).

Oddi inn litli Glúmsson, Þorbjǫrn inn svarti and Ármóðr are specifically listed in *Orkneyinga saga* lxxxv, together with an otherwise unknown Þorgeirr safakollr, as the earl's poets. They are given pride of position amongst the 'lesser men', who accompanied him on the pilgrimage to the Holy Land 1151–1153. Of Rǫgnvaldr's court poets, Hallr Þórarinsson is further represented by a single separate verse (42), Oddi inn litli Glúmsson by five verses (52, 58, 65, 73, 74), Ármóðr by four (50, 54, 57, 71), Sigmundr ǫngull Andrésson by two (62, 76), and Þorbjǫrn inn svarti by one (72). Hallr, Oddi and Ármóðr are explicitly said in the saga to be Icelanders; Þorbjǫrn is listed with them, but his place of origin is not given. Sigmundr ǫngull's family was from the south-west (*suðrríki*, the Norse-influenced areas around the Irish Sea), and he is reportedly associated, at least initially, with the earl's turbulent retainer, Sveinn Ásleifarson. But unlike Sveinn he accompanies the earl on the pilgrimage to the Holy Land and comments on Sveinn's absence in v. 76. One other poet is associated with the earl: Bótólfr begla, who lived at Knarrarstaðir (Lingro, just south of Kirkwall), but whom we are specifically told was an Icelander and a good poet; according to *Orkneyinga saga* xciv he gave the earl lodgings in a sudden storm, and them misdirected his enemies away from the house in a verse (82). One verse (41) is also attributed to another Icelander, Eiríkr, who is associated with the household of Sveinn Ásleifarson. Other than Rǫgnvaldr Kali and Hallr Þórarinsson, these poets and their work are only recorded in *Orkneyinga saga*.

The distribution of verses attributed to Rǫgnvaldr Kali and his court poets in *Orkneyinga saga* is as follows (verses are attributed to Rǫgnvaldr unless otherwise indicated; page references are given in this table to indicate approximate distribution relative to the prose text of the saga as printed in the *Íslenzk fornrit* edition):

Rǫgnvaldr Kali's youth:
34 Accomplishments of a gentleman: introduction and description of Rǫgnvaldr Kali (p. 130).
35 Verse on pleasures of seafaring on return from Grimsby to Bergin (concludes narrative of visit to England at age of 15) (p. 131).
36 Caving on Dolls (p. 133).

Rǫgnvaldr's accession to power:
38 Verse mocking monks on Westray (p. 163).
39 Verse criticising Kúgi on Westray (p. 165).

Hallr Þórarinsson:
42 Verse introducing Hallr Þórarinsson (Hallr) (p. 183).
43 Verse mocking Ragna when she introduces Hallr to Rǫgnvaldr (p. 184).

Shipwreck on Shetland:
44–48 The shipwreck and condition of folk (pp. 195–198).
49 Fishing in disguise (p. 200) (NB. only in ms. Uppsala R: 702 4to.).

Other court poets (Ármóðr and Oddi):
50 Ármóðr thanks the earl for a gift (Ármóðr) (pp. 201–202).
51–52 Verse contest between Rǫgnvaldr Kali and Oddi (Rǫgnvaldr, Oddi) (pp. 202–203).

A madman:
53 Verse about a madman (p. 203) (NB. only in ms. Uppsala R: 702 4to.).

Pilgrimage to the Holy Land:
54 Verse on sailing in the North Sea (Ármóðr) (pp. 208–209).
55–58 The attractions of Queen Ermingerðr of Narbonne (Rǫgnvaldr x2, Ármóðr, Oddi) (pp. 210–212).
59–63 Attacking a castle in Galicia for Ermingerðr's sake (Rǫgnvaldr x4, Sigmundr ǫngull) (pp. 215–219).
64–67 Sailing at Gibraltar (Rǫgnvaldr x3, Oddi) (pp. 219–222).
68–70 Attacking a Saracen dromund (pp. 226–227).
71–72   Reaching the Holy Land (Ármóðr, Þorbjǫrn svarti) (p. 229).
73–74 Death of Þorbjǫrn from plague at Acre (Oddi) (pp. 230–231).
75–78 Pilgrimage to the Jordan and Jerusalem (Rǫgnvaldr x3, Sigmundr ǫngull) (pp. 231–233).
79–80 Sailing to Byzantium (probably in reverse order due to misunderstanding of a place-name) (pp. 234–235).

Rǫgnvaldr's subsequent political difficulties:
81 Verse criticising the Orcadian Noblemen for oath-breaking and treachery at home while Rǫgnvaldr was abroad (p. 238).
82 Verse in which Bótólfr misdirects Rǫgnvaldr's enemies (Bótólfr) (p. 258).

The distribution of verses attributed to Rǫgnvaldr Kali and his court poets is not uniform within the saga, as is demonstrated by the distribution table given above. Verses tend to occur in groups. Yet they do not seem to be derived from longer lays. Instances of dismembered lays occur fairly frequently in other texts. Lays could be remembered and recorded as separate literary entities, and can frequently be reconstructed, at least in part, from their fragmentary components. In contrast, all the verses cited in the saga are presented as *lausavísur*: individual verse usually associated with specific, discrete narratives. Sometimes the relevant passage only appears to have been included in the saga for the sake of the verse, which requires narrative explanation provided by the rest of the passage. The best example is the verse (36) quoted in association with a caving-trip (lxi); this anecdotal passage seems to have no function within the saga other than to provide a narrative commentary on the verse, which itself seems at first sight merely to be included on account of its poetic interest.

Such an uneven distribution has interesting implications for the sources of the saga. As argued more generally above, the distribution-pattern probably demonstrates that the verses were not composed for the saga itself, either as ornament or

6   Altarpiece from Andenes, Nordland, with doors closed. Lübeck work *c*.1500.
     (Courtesy of Historical Museum, Tromsö).

7   Altarpiece from Andenes, Nordland, with doors open. (Courtesy of Historical
     Museum, Tromsö).

8   Altarpiece from Andenes, Nordland, showing the central figures (from left to right) St Thomas, God the Father holding the dead Christ in his arms, St Olav and St Magnus. (Courtesy of Historical Museum, Tromsö).

as spurious corroboration of the historical events recounted in the prose. If this had been the case, a more even distribution of verses would have been expected, and these would be associated in particular with the political career of Earl Rǫgnvaldr, the account of which requires historical documentation but in fact contains very few verses. Indeed, there is no reason whatsoever to question the authenticity of any of this poetry (despite the comments of Jan de Vries, 'Jarl Rǫgnvalds Lausavísur', 1960, 133–141). Further, if the individual verses had merely been transmitted through generalised oral tradition as part of the common repertoire of skaldic performance, outwith the structured framework of a lay, their distribution in the saga would be expected to be approximately random, as opposed to even or coherently grouped.

It would therefore seem probable, in contrast, that specific sections of the narrative material of the saga have been transmitted in association with the verses: as oral or written commentary on the poetry. This suggests that the author of the saga had access to an annotated collection of poetry associated with Earl Rǫgnvaldr Kali. Such a collection could have been orally made and maintained, for instance by one of the earl's Icelandic poets. It is perhaps also likely to have been kept in writing from the beginning, as is suggested by the preservation of the verses as coherent groups of *lausavísur*. Rǫgnvaldr himself claims to be literate, and in his first verse (34) he associates literacy with his other skills, including poetry; there is no good reason to disbelieve this. He certainly also had literate clerics, including the bishop, as permanent members of his court. Since he clearly valued his own poetic skills, he is likely to have recorded his own poetry or caused its record. If, unlike King Sverrir some forty years later, he did not actually commission his own saga, he is likely at least to have ensured the written survival of its subject-matter in verse-form. The uneven distribution of the verses relative to the historical events of his earldom may thus even reflect the circumstances of their recording, as well as circumstances of transmission: instances where Earl Rǫgnvaldr had the opportunity of ensuring their survival. These must include the Shetland group (44–49), the group involving Rǫgnvaldr's court poets in Orkney (42–43, 50–52), and above all the group involving Rǫgnvaldr's pilgrimage to the Holy Land (54–80). It is difficult also to avoid the conclusion that one or other of Rǫgnvaldr's Icelandic poets had a hand in the preservation of this poetry, given the elaborate poetic introduction presented for Hallr Þórarinsson (42–43), and the equally elaborately described verse-contest between Oddi inn litli and the earl (51–52). In these two passages these two poets are presented with the same emphasis as the earl himself, and the passages have little other immediate function in the saga than to show the importance and excellence of the poets and their poetry. They also had an interest in recording and transmitting this poetry.

It is less clear whether written prose accompanied any early written text of the verses. The word *imbólum* (79,8) may in fact be a street- or quarter-name in Byzantium (so R. Meissner: Gk. *embolos/embolai*); if so, then it has undergone later reinterpretation as the name of a place visited by Rǫgnvaldr on the way to Byzantium (and so the order of vv. 79 and 80 has been reversed). If this view is correct (and alternatives have been put forward), then no substantial written narrative is likely initially to have accompanied these two verses. Written annotation would only have been added to these verses later when personal knowledge of the events themselves was no longer available in memory: i.e. either after living memory in Orkney, or when a copy of the verses was taken somewhere else. Since a version of the account of Earl Rǫgnvaldr Kali in *Orkneyinga saga* itself is likely to have been composed only some forty years after Rǫgnvaldr's death (in all probability before the translation of his relics in 1192), such prose annotation is likely to have been added to the verses when a copy of them was taken elsewhere, probably to Iceland. However, since these annotations sometimes seem to contain information not reconstructible from the verses alone, such as that of the caving expedition already mentioned, they are perhaps unlikely simply to be composed by the author of the present saga on the basis of the verses. The prose narrative commentaries on Earl Rǫgnvaldr Kali's poetry, now incorporated into *Orkneyinga saga*, are likely thus to represent Icelandic scholarly activity on skaldic poetry in the second half of the twelfth century. (For further discussion of such scholarly activity, see my 'Few know an earl in fishing-clothes', 1984, 82–98).

Only one of the poets around Earl Rǫgnvaldr and his retinue is known not to be Icelandic (Sigmundr ǫngull), while Þorbjǫrn inn svarti is of unknown origin; the four or five others are all specifically Icelanders. This emphasis on Icelandic poets in the earl's retinue may of course be authorial, since *Orkneyinga saga* was in all probability composed in Iceland. It could also be due to circumstances of transmission of material. It is also, of course, likely to be historically accurate, or any combination of these.

Skaldic poetry, Norse court poetry, was fairly exclusively a West Norse literary form; while it may have been appreciated and even understood elsewhere in the Viking world, there is little or no evidence for its composition in Sweden, Denmark or the eastern or southern colonial Norse settlements. Its earliest known instances are attributed to poets of about the middle of the ninth century, or perhaps a little earlier. Skaldic poetry is characterised by great elaboration of metre and diction. It is mostly attributed to named poets, and the vast bulk of surviving earlier poetry, from the pagan period, is assigned to professional poets working for specific, named Norwegian patrons: kings and noblemen. This is not exclusively the case, however, and it could be attributed to named and unnamed individuals, if normally within an aristocratic milieu. The functions of skaldic poetry were various. Much of the surviving poetry is in conventional praise of the martial glory of kings and chieftians now otherwise long forgotten. But it praises them in diction which looks beyond them to the gods and to the heroes of a further, legendary past. Some skaldic poetry may have had religious or magical function, and its diction may be in part derived from tabu. This poetry may act as worship, invocation, or incantation. Equally, and not unconnectedly, skaldic poetry was the prime medium for *níð*: often translated as 'slander' but with connotations of cursing. Indeed, some of the very words for poetry involve this notion, and the Norse word for poet, *skáld*, was borrowed into English and gives Modern English *scold*. A pleasing parallel is old English *scop* 'poet', which is related to ON *skop* 'mockery'. Further, at least in later literary convention, the intricate rhythms and riddling words of skaldic poetry enabled the Icelanders' otherwise tight-lipped Viking ancestors to comment on emotion or event. Doubtless life imitated art in this instance as in others.

It was normally considered that the composition of skaldic poetry died out in Norway in the first half of the eleventh century, and that therefore the very large amounts of surviving poetry of the twelfth to fourteenth centuries was Icelandic. Certainly the last major Norwegian professional poet who is named is Eyvindr skáldaspillir (d. *c.*990). But historical texts continue sporadically to attribute skaldic poetry to Norwegians, e.g. the kings Haraldr inn harðráði (reigned 1046–1066) and Magnús berfœttr (reigned 1093–1103). After the eleventh century instances are much rarer but verses are attributed to King Sigurðr jórsalafari (reigned 1103–1130), and other men of rank, i.e. isolated verses attributed to Ingimundr af Aski (d. 1134) and Sigurðr slembidjákn (d. 1139). An isolated verse in *Sverris saga* is attributed to a Norwegian (?—Nefari) for the year 1168. Subsequent to the reign of Sigurðr jórsalafari, only the verse attributed to Nefari is actually skaldic in metre and diction; the others are in simpler and less ornate forms. However, the Bergen rune-finds of 1960 included one very competent verse of skaldic poetry, datable archaeologically to ca. 1330 (see Liestøl, Krause and Helgason, 1962, 98–108). It is a love-verse, and is coupled in the same inscription with a runic Latin quotation from Virgil, *Eclogues* 10, again dealing with love. It must therefore be seen as a scholarly exercise in both the traditions of scholarly antiquity available to a learned Norseman at a centre open specifically to late Icelandic influence: Bergen was the main Norwegian port for trade with Iceland. Interestingly, such Icelandic influence has also been reported in more recent finds at Trondheim.

It is therefore not possible to state that composition of skaldic poetry ceased in Norway after the early eleventh century. However, it is clearly the case that after that time there are no longer any known professional Norwegian court poets. Thereafter, instead of hiring permanent court poets, Norwegian kings and noblemen continue themselves to attempt to practise the composition of such poetry during the 11th and 12th centuries though to a steadily diminishing extent. Of these, only Haraldr inn harðráði proves himself a competent poet. Significantly, Earl Rǫgnvaldr himself lists the nine 'accomplishments of the gentleman' in a verse, and after knowledge of chess, runes and books, dexterity in making things, skiing, shooting and rowing, in last position he places harp-playing and poetic composition.

Long-term employment of professional Norwegian poets at Norwegian courts thus ceases more or less with the Conversion to Christianity, and thereafter poetic composition seems to become simply the accomplishment of the nobleman himself. It is tempting to associate this change in practice with the Conversion itself, and to conclude that the court poet might have fulfilled quasi-sacral functions in paganism, whch did not continue thereafter. This is a large subject, and can hardly be discussed in any detail here; however, quite apart from the sacral quality of much skaldic diction, and of some terminology associated with it (e.g. *þulr, þula, þylja,* cf. v (78) in *Orkneyinga saga*), poets in paganism fulfilled a very obvious and specific function. They ensured the immortality of a man's fame, which may (according to *Hávamál* 76–77) have been his only immortality. At the Conversion, with Christian assurance of eternal life after death, this function of poetry loses its significance.

Further, as literacy is introduced following Christianity, writing provides another, seemingly more permanent record of praiseworthy deeds, and the saga-man, instead of possibly supplementing the skáld, supplants him.

However, professional skaldic poets continued to be welcome at Norwegian courts, and possibly at courts elsewhere in continental Scandinavia, even if they now apparently ceased to be permanently resident there. They continued to praise their patrons, though to a gradually diminishing degree as writing emerged as an alternative medium of record; praise seems now simply the conventional content of this poetry, rather than its purpose. The poets seem depicted in the literary sources more as travelling experts, engaged to demonstrate their craft; they doubtless instructed their patrons in poetry, and the playful poetic contests depicted between, for instance, Haraldr inn harðráði and his poets may in part reflect pedagogic techniques.

In Iceland there was no monarchy. Instead a constitution was devised and maintained with much ingenuity: an organised but not unified oligarchy of sacral chieftains, each theoretically balanced against each. Internal, individual violence could still, normally, be contained by the older equipoise of the feud, formalised and commuted within the law. In a society too poor to afford war, and too remote to be threatened by it, there was thus no need for a central authority unbalanced by any other. Each chieftain, therefore, was not only a local farmer, but fulfilled for his followers the sacral and social functions of a Norwegian nobleman. These involved poetry. Such constitutional features therefore give one reason for the unusual Icelandic cultivation of skaldic poetry, already striking during the late pagan period and dominant thereafter. Further, far from being courtly in any continental sense, this Icelandic cultivation of skaldic poetry should be seen in the context of a free peasant aristocracy. An Icelandic farmworker could appropriately claim descent from the gods and invoke the heroes of ancient legend in the intricate and courtly metres of skaldic poetry, just as he could worship, and could invoke the divine authority of the laws, without the mediating authority of a king.

Further, of course, the Icelanders formed a colonial society in want of a past. Skaldic poetry formed a major medium of transmitting tradition, and sometimes of manufacturing it. Here, therefore, antiquarian interests and those of literary composition converged. Also, the circumstances of the Conversion of Iceland involved no hostility to the pagan past and the vehicles of its traditions. Hence the study and composition of skaldic poetry throve in Iceland, both before and continuingly after Conversion. Indeed, apparently only in Iceland, this strange medium was applied to Christianity itself; some of the finest surviving late poetry was composed in praise of the Virgin and the saints.

These broad generalisations, as is usual, are distortions. The conventional view that skaldic poetry became more or less exclusively an Icelandic pursuit in and after the eleventh century, described and discussed above, totally disregards the Earldom of Orkney.

According to Orkneyinga saga, court poetry had been practised and valued in the earldom almost from its foundation. Some of the earls were considered to have been poets in their own right, in particular the second earl, Torf-Einarr. In the early eleventh century, the earldom seems to have been a particularly important centre of poetic activity; major poets such as the Icelander Arnórr Þórðarson jarlaskáld practised for much of their careers at the courts of the earls. Such apparent earlier poetic activity is well represented in *Orkneyinga saga*, but is unlikely to be an artefact of its author, since as discussed above, the distribution and variety of poetry is strikingly uneven, and major sections of the text wholly lack poetry, whether adduced as corroboration or as ornament. Correspondingly, there is no evidence for poetic activity in the Earldom of Orkney for long continuous periods, most strikingly from the death of Earl Þorfinnr, ca. 1065, until 1137, when Rǫgnvaldr Kali came to power. It is, of course, wholly uncertain whether this distribution–pattern reflects historical reality, or is governed by the nature of the sources for the saga, as discussed above, or, most probably, is caused by some combination of the two.

Earl Rǫgnvaldr Kali was not himself Orcadian. His family was from Agðir in south-western Norway, and his genealogy is given in *Orkneyinga saga* xxix. It is there taken back to Þorleifr inn spaki at the time of the Conversion of Norway, who is explicitly linked with the Icelandic poet Hallfreðr Óttarsson van-dræðaskáld. Rǫgnvaldr Kali's grandfather, Kali Sæbjarnarson, is described there as 'a very wise man, and dear to the king (Magnús berfœttr), and he composed (poetry) well'; this is demonstrated by verses 31–33. As recompense for Kali's death from wounds received on Magnús's campaign in the Irish Sea area (1098), the following spring (1099) King Magnús gave in marriage Gunnhildr, daughter of Earl Erlendr (and so sister of Earl Magnús Erlendsson, St. Magnús), to Kali's son, Kolr. Gun-nhildr's dowry included estates in Orkney. However, Kolr and Gunnhildr accom-panied the king back to Norway, and settled down on Kolr's ancestral estate in Agðir. They had two children, a son Kali (the future Earl Rǫgnvaldr Kali) and a daughter, Ingiríðr; their dates of birth are unknown, but are presumably shortly after 1100. Kali's formal introduction in the saga (lviii) includes the verse cited above (34), which describes his poetic and other skills. The saga reports a visit to Grimsby in England when Kali was fifteen years old (lix), when he is specifically said to have met people from Orkney, Scotland and the Hebrides, but he is not said to have gone to Orkney in childhood or youth. Instead, Kali was brought up at home and, as a young man, with his kinsman Sǫlmundr Sigurðarsonar sneisar in East Agðir and at Túnsberg in the Oslo-fjord. At Túnsberg, Kali will certainly have come into contact with north German merchants, since this is the period of the beginnings of the Hanseatic League. He might even have come into contact with courtly French there, since Túnsberg was also a royal seat. According to the saga (lxi), Kali's acquisition of the name Rǫgnvaldr, and any association with the earldom of Orkney, did not come about until 1129, when the name and half the earldom were granted to him by King Sigurðr jórsalafari in partial settlement of a feud. Thus Rǫgnvaldr Kali's interest and skill in poetry cannot be seen as Orca-dian, but as originally Norwegian, and the saga seems to indicate that this interest and skill was transmitted from his paternal grandfather and namesake, Kali Sæbjar-narson. This is not at all improbable, as poetic training seems often to be passed on from father to son; the Icelander Arnórr jarlaskáld, the most important poet associated with Earl Þorfinnr, was himself the son of another major poet, Þórðr

Kolbeinsson. There is no evidence for poetic skills on the maternal side of Rǫgnvaldr Kali's family. Rǫgnvaldr Kali must therefore be added to the small number of known Norwegian noblemen practising poetry in the twelfth century, and his skill is evidence for the survival of skaldic poetry in Norway at this period.

Probably in the summer of 1137, the foundations of the Cathedral of St. Magnús were laid out. Kolr had instructed his son Rǫgnvaldr Kali to invoke St Magnús for the power which is his inheritance (lxviii), and to make a vow to him to build a *steinmusteri* in Kirkwall as his shrine and the bishop's seat. Then the saga explicitly states (lxxvi) that Kolr was the person who took most thought for the building and was most in charge. But the actual masons who undertook to build the cathedral were gathered from far and wide, and more specifically from southern Scotland and northern England (see Fawcett, Cambridge above). Despite the political and personal preoccupations of the saga, therefore, this gives some evidence for the cosmopolitan interests of the Earldom. The saga had already discussed on many occasions the political relationships of the Earldom with Scotland, and we may recollect Rǫgnvaldr Kali's visit to England at the age of fifteen, when he also met Scots and Hebrideans. The cult of St Magnús will thus, doubtless, be interpreted as a political phenomenon, invoked in order to justify Earl Rǫgnvaldr Kali's authority. This is made virtually explicit in the words which the saga puts into Kolr's mouth when he instructs his son to make a vow to St Magnús. The martyr's blood sanctifies the political power which Magnús had himself held, and which he spiritually grants to his nephew. As a correlate to this, Rǫgnvaldr constructs a physical and outward form for the sanctity of St Magnús, for his shrine and for his cult. The cathedral will consequentially be seen as the physical expression of this political justification: an utterance in a political discourse of power, just as the palaces of the later, Stewart earls must be seen as expressions of political power. Thus the cathedral and Earl Patrick's palace, side by side, expressed the spiritual and temporal authority of the earldom at the end of the Middle Ages.

I do not doubt that this interpretation is correct as far as it goes, but it does not go far enough. Later in the chapter which describes the foundation of the cathedral (lxxvi), the earl was apparently obliged to sell land-rights to the farmers in perpetuity in return for a fixed fee, in order to raise money for continuing to build the cathedral. In the same terms of political discourse, therefore, the cathedral can be seen as embodying the freedom of the land and people of Orkney. Further, the cult of St Magnús must already have existed in order to be put to political ends. The cathedral has cultural, artistic and, above all, spiritual significance beyond any political purpose.

It is, I think, possible and desirable to draw useful analogies between the cathedral which Rǫgnvaldr built, and the poetry which he commissioned and composed. Rǫgnvaldr and his father brought masons for the cathedral from Scotland, since there was evidently small native Orcadian skill in dealing with the new architectural modes. Similarly, it would seem, Rǫgnvaldr employed poets from Iceland, because there was apparently little native tradition in the Orkneys. The cathedral may be seen as expression of the authority of the Earldom, and similarly court poets express that authority in words. The poetry is as fine and lasting an artistic achievement as the building. But the parallel may be extended further, in the wider context of Rǫgnvaldr's pilgrimage to the Holy Land. The cathedral, the pilgrimage and the poetry show not only the magnificence of Rǫgnvaldr's court, but also its enterprising and cosmopolitan culture, and, at its heart, its foundation and aspirations in Christianity.

But the poetry also has other functions. Earl Rǫgnvaldr Kali comes through as considerably more vigorous and intelligent personality in his verses than in the rather bland and anodyne presentation of the prose. A surprising number of verses cited in the saga show a sharp and sardonic sense of humour, which is not apparent in the characterisation of Rǫgnvaldr as depicted in the prose. Such verses as 38 and 43 must be seen in the tradition of *níð-vísur*, 'slander-verses', and both have potential religious significance in a number of ways. The same rather startling sense of humour can be found in the obscure obscenity of the first verse (44) associated with the shipwreck in Shetland, and, more gently, in the verse which imitates the chattering teeth of a serving-maid (47). Elsewhere in his poetry, there is a continuing sparkle of wit, which gives the poetry something of a biting edge. This wit involves a certain detachment, as the poet stands back and disengages himself from his subject-matter. Both in the humorous verses and elsewhere, we sense here the presence of a detached and self-aware intelligence, which ironically considers both the poet's subject-matter and his potential audience. Awareness of an audience is of course appropriate to skaldic poetry in general, which originated as a public art-form. But, as argued above, Rǫgnvaldr is unlikely so much to be composing for a present and immediate audience, as for the potential audience of a future readership. Since this readership includes ourselves, there is thus an unusual degree of conscious interaction on both parts between this poet and the present-day reader.

This wit must be associated with the technical brilliance of many of Earl Rǫgnvaldr's verses. The verse-contest between Rǫgnvaldr and Oddi (51–52) constitutes virtuoso display on both parts. The actual content is trivial: both poets describe the elaborate wall-hangings on the earl's hall, and thus the magnificence of his court. But the real and lasting magnificence of Rǫgnvaldr's court lies in the brilliance of its poetry. The glory of the earl's court does not only involve his own poetic skills, but those of the poets whom he employs and with whom he can compete as their equal at their own craft. Even beyond this, there is an inherent intellectual exhilaration in the riddling and punning exuberance of this poetry, and of the two men who sport, like dolphins, in its dangerous and uncertain waters. Just such an exhilaration is expressed in the leaping of Rǫgnvaldr's ship across the North Sea in verse 35, or into the Mediterranean in verse 64.

Much of Rǫgnvaldr Kali's poetry, as cited in the saga, falls into this category. It is produced and valued for its own sake, as art, and its content and context are often only important for understanding and appreciating the poetry itself. In terms of 'political discourse', as discussed above, it simply constitutes a statement of the earl's intellectual power and magnificence. This is not entirely true of all the politically significant poetry, however. In particular, Rǫgnvaldr complains in his last cited verse (81) at how the Orcadian chieftains have broken their oaths to him while he was on pilgrimage. Here his self-awareness involves a wittily wry admission of his own political weakness as well as of his continuing political resolve: 'Let's walk lightly (even) on short legs, while I (can) hold up my beard'. These are the last words which we hear from Rǫgnvaldr's own lips before the account of his murder, which, by cruelly appropriate irony, involved a sword-stroke which struck off the lower part of his face.

Of the poetry attributed to Earl Rǫgnvaldr Kali and his poets in *Orkneyinga saga*, the most important group has been left to last. Verse 54–80 deal with the earl's pilgrimage to the Holy Land (1151–1153). He was by no means the first Norseman to make this pilgrimage: indeed, it had become so frequent that by the end of the 12th century Icelandic scholars were producing guide-books for pilgrims, one of which survives (ed. Kålund 1908; see Hill, 1983 175–203, and references there). After the First Crusade (1096–1100), the capture of Jerusalem and the foundation of the Crusader Kingdom, the way was open for such pilgrimage. The first Scandinavian known to have attempted it is probably Skopti Ogmundsson (1101–1103). The Danish king Eiríkr eygóðr died in Cyprus on the way to the Holy Land in 1103, and the Norwegian king Sigurðr jórsalafari (reigned 1103–1130) acquired his nickname by such a pilgrimage (1108–1111). The pretender to the Norwegian throne, Sigurðr slembir (or slembidjákn), also made a pilgrimage to Rome and the Holy Land, mentioned in *Orkneyinga saga* liv, at an uncertain date. The primary source for this is the poem *Sigurðarbǫlkr*, vv. 2–3, composed by Ivarr Ingimundarson ca. 1140, but this gives neither chronology nor motivation. According to *Heimskringla*, the pilgrimage was undertaken in youth, before about 1127, but according to *Morkinskinna* and *Orkneyinga saga* it took place some years later. Further, in *Orkneyinga Saga* the implication is fairly clear that this pilgrimage was undertaken in penitence for the slaying of Þorkell fóstri, a close kinsman of St. Magnús killed as a consequence of the martyrdom of Magnús. Sigurðr slembir's pilgrimage should therefore be seen as a parallel to that of Earl Hákon.

Most strikingly, however, St Magnús Erlendsson himself offered to make a pilgrimage to Rome and the Holy Land (il), 'and pay recompense (*bæta*) for the soul of each of the two of us'. This was the first of three alternatives which he offered to his cousin Earl Hákon Pálsson, prior to his own martyrdom, that swifter pilgrimage to the Holy Places of which Palestine is merely a temporal image. Further, Earl Hákon subsequently himself made a similar pilgrimage in penitence, *c.*1120 (*Orkneyinga saga* lii, as also both the sagas of St. Magnús, which all here clearly use the same material); he received absolution from the Pope in Rome on the way to the Holy Land, where he bathed in the River Jordan. All these texts imply that Hákon was thereafter reformed by this penitential experience.

The saga does not actually give Rǫgnvaldr's reasons for undertaking his pilgrimage. It depicts him (lxxxv) as being persuaded by Eindriði ungi, and the reason put into Eindriði's mouth is simple tourism. Doubtless this is not untrue, but more is likely to lie behind the pilgrimage than this. The earl was no longer a young man by this date, and ran considerable personal and political risks in undertaking the enterprise. Quite apart from the probability of violence and disease on the journey, his political position in the Orkneys would be (and was) threatened by so long an absence from his earldom. The saga does not mention that Rǫgnvaldr Kali ever had wife or child, but he certainly had descendants (see below) and in one verse preserved in *Snorra Edda* he speaks of having to watch in grief over his sick wife for a long time (see Appendix to this paper). However, the saga mentions the unfulfilled possibility of marrying Ermingerðr in Narbonne. Rǫgnvaldr may therefore have been a widower at this stage. Genuine piety, the wish to pray for his wife's soul and to prepare himself for death, cannot therefore be dismissed as his possible motive for pilgrimage.

Beyond Rǫgnvaldr's actual motivation, the pilgrimage undoubtedly completes a literary triad in the saga. The pilgrimage which St Magnús offered to undertake, and which Earl Hákon and Sigurðr slembir actually performed, are both dismissed in one or two sentences, but are both emphasised by their positions in the text by their historical importance. Description of such a pilgrimage is, however, deferred at those points in the saga, and is not presented until Rǫgnvaldr. He fulfils his uncle's intention, and is thereby set in parallel with St Magnús within the saga. But he also follows the examples of Earl Hákon and of Sigurðor slembir, and is presumably therefore presented as undertaking the pilgrimage in penitence for the acts of violence and injustice in his own career. These have been largely associated in the saga with Sveinn Ásleifarson. Strikingly, both Rǫgnvaldr and Sigmundr ǫngull refer to Sveinn when crossing Jordan (vv. 76–77). Sveinn himself is the first (and only) individual in the text to acknowledge Rǫgnvaldr's sanctity as he cries out at his own violent death in Dublin (cviii): 'Let all men know, whether I die today or not, that I am a retainer of the holy Earl Rǫgnvaldr, and I look now for trust where he is with God'. Pilgrimage fulfils for Rǫgnvaldr the aspects both saint and of penitent within the structure of the text.

Apart from the actual visit to the Holy Land (described in vv. 71–78), the saga describes a number of incidents, all with verse-comments, which took place on the way to and from the Holy Land. These are: a visit to Narbonne in France (55–58), an attack on a castle in Galicia (59–63, an attack on a Saracen 'dromund' (mediter-ranean merchant-ship) (68–70), and a visit to Byzantium (79–80). Most scholarly discussion has concentrated on the sojourn at Narbonne, probably for the winter of 1151–1152, perhaps visited on the pilgrim-route from Toulouse to St Gilles.

The Narbonne-poetry, as has long been recognised, shows 'courtly love' in its content and choice of motifs; this has been fully discussed by Jan de Vries, (1938-1939, 701-735) and by Theodore M. Anderson, (1969, 7-41); further references are given by Andersson, ftn. 17, p. 13).

Here Rǫgnvaldr, Ármóðr and Oddi all use skaldic poetry for the purposes of troubadours. These verses are the first certain instances of 'courtly love' appearing in a Scandinavian language, and of course they are fairly precisely datable. Composed probably in late 1151, they will have been kown in Orkney by 1153 and in Iceland by, at latest, the earl's death in 1158/9. It is thus possible to state that courtly love and the literary motifs associated with it were known and available in Scandinavia by 1160. These verses constitute a case-study in cultural links.

In v. 55 Rǫgnvaldr praises Ermingerðr's golden hair, yellow and silky; in 56 he claims that his pilgrimage to the Jordan is actually a knightly quest, undertaken at Ermingerðr's wish (!). In 57 Ármóðr declares the impossibility of fulfilment in courtly love—many a man is stricken with sorrow for a lady—he would have been blest to spend one night with her; the lady has a beautiful forehead. Oddi claims in 58 that 'we' are unworthy of the lady, who may be called 'king of women' (possibly a reference to the romance motif of the 'maiden king'). Also in 58 Rǫgnvaldr contrasts the beauty of Ermingerðr, and wine-drinking at her court, with the violence of war, and in 63 says that through warlike endeavour 'we' are worthy of Ermingerðr.

Praise of a woman's (golden) hair, compared to silk, and of her forehead; military adventure as a quest undertaken for the lady and to show that the lover is worthy of her; the lover's lament; the lover as unworthy of his lady: these motifs appear here mostly for the first time in safely attested and datable Norse poetry. Further, they entered Norse early. Troubadour poetry, even in Provencal, is not attested much before 1100, with figures such as Guilhem IX, Count of Poitiers and Duke of Aquitaine (b. 1071, reigned 1087–1127), who took part in the disastrous crusade of 1101 to the Holy Land, and whose daughter was Eleanor of Aquitaine. Troubadour poetry was, like skaldic verse, a wholly courtly art-form, practised by kings and noblemen or at their courts, and was again often of great elaboration, even though its content was wholly distinct from that of skaldic verse. Rǫgnvaldr in verse 55 juxtaposes the two worlds to sharp effect; beside the courtly beauty of the lady, shining with golden tresses, he contrasts the older, harsher, but no less vivid world of Viking warfare: 'I reddened the greedy eagle's claw': gold set off against scarlet. The saga-author participates enthusiastically, and depicts the whole episode as a miniature from a romance. Ermingerðr (ruled 1143–1192, died 1197) was probably a widow, or had married for the second time, and was aged about thirty at this date; still some twenty years later the troubadour Peire Rogier sang of her beauty. However, Rǫgnvaldr was by now about fifty years old. Thus this poetry may be little more, as such, than literary exercise. Prompted by exposure to the new poetry of the south, these Viking poets rise to the technical challenge, and do so with complete success. Yet Eleanor of Aquitaine married Henry II of England in 1152. Perhaps courtly love, and even a suggestion of marriage between a countess of Narbonne and an earl of Orkney, was not so implausible in 1151.

However, it is most striking how easily and effortlessly these Viking skálds seem to be able to assimilate the new material to the older conventions of their own poetry. These verses are hardly the fumbling first attempts at the poetry of courtly love, but are easily and fully achieved examples. The skálds have some assistance within their own tradition: elaborate and ornate woman-kennings were already available, largely due to the convention of presenting a woman as formal audience of skaldic poetry. This is reflected in v. 62, where Sigmundr ǫngull says that 'these words', describing his martial prowess, will be carried back to the woman in Orkney. Cf. 69. Whether or not any native tradition of love-poetry also existed is much debated, though undoubtedly there was sex-poetry. The ease and effectiveness of the Narbonne-poetry, however, suggests that even at this early date,

Rǫgnvaldr and his poets may have had some prior acquaintance with the ideas and literary conventions of courtly love.

It has been suggested (by P G Foote) that Rǫgnvaldr Kali could have met the conventions of courtly love in his youth at Túnsberg. It could also be suggested that he had become acquainted with them on his visit to England at the age of fifteen. However, neither of these is particularly probable: both are rather early for this material to have reached Norway or England, and as mentioned, at Túnsberg the main southern influences will have been northern German rather than southern French, while at Grimsby we are specifically told that the young Kali met Scots, Hebrideans and Orcadians. Moreover, it is not likely that the earl himself understood French or Provencal at this date, since he is said specifically to have requested Bishop William to accompany the pilgrimage as an interpreter because he had been educated in Paris (lxxxv).

Bishop William himself could have set up the cultural link which enabled the ideas and literary conventions of courtly love to reach Orkney. To judge from his name, he is likely at this date to have been of Norman or Anglo-Norman origin, and so his native tongue was probably French. He died in 1168 and was said to have been bishop of Orkney for 66 years, thus taking up office in 1102, presumably as a very young man on immediate arrival from Paris. It is just possible that he could have been acquainted with the earliest troubadour poetry at that stage. It is much more probable, however, that (like his contemporary John, bishop of Glasgow ca. 1118–1147), William maintained direct contacts with France during his long episcopacy, and perhaps, for instance, sent students to his own old school. Indirect contact through known contemporary Franco–Scottish ecclesiastical connections is also plausible.

Of the other poetry of the pilgrimage, the verses dealing with the siege of a castle in Galicia, and with the attack on the 'dromund', are fairly conventional, as are the episodes themselves. The attack on the castle is reminiscent of accounts in *Haralds saga Sigurðarsonar* in *Heimskringla* of various stormings of cities in the area of the eastern Mediterranean, there also accompanied by verses. This was manifestly the Done Thing for a Scandinavian lord, on reaching southern lands, and doubtless the literary convention represents conventional military behaviour. Here, however, the attack is given some slight moral justification in the prose: Guðifreyr (Godfrey), the lord of the castle, is a foreigner (probably Norman), who is tyrannising the local population. This justification is not found in the verses, which contrast this warfare with peaceful life at court in Orkney or Narbonne, mostly in symmetrical half-strophes. The attack on the 'dromund' is of importance in showing Rǫgnvaldr as a crusader: his pilgrimage is not otherwise directed against the infidel. But although this point is explicit in the prose, the verses are fairly straightforward battle-poetry; only in verse 70 Rǫgnvaldr states that God has brought about their victory. In 69 the woman again serves as conventional potential audience—but now she is the lady at Narbonne.

The central section of the episode and central group of verses deal with the actual pilgrimage in the Holy Land. It is introduced by a fairly conventional seafaring verse (71). It is notable how the account of the whole pilgrimage is structured and punctuated by such verses, occurring at the beginning (54), at entry into the Mediterranean (64–67), here, and at the end (80). Þorbjǫrn svarti is then assigned a verse (72), directly comparable with the Galicia-poetry, which contrasts courtly life in Orkney with his present exotic activity, landing at Acre. The verse is not particularly interesting, but is immediately followed by the statement that plague struck the pilgrims and that Þorbjǫrn died. Oddi composed two memorial verses for him (73–74). These verses, in a simpler metre, are very touching, and their emotional weight translates the text to an altogether more serious level. Then three verses (75–77) describe how the earl and Sigmundr ǫngul bathed in the Jordan and swam across it, while in verse 78 Rǫgnvaldr presents himself as a palmer at the descent of the Mount of Olives into Jerusalem.

Verse 75 is particularly interesting, for it summarises almost all aspects of Rǫgnvaldr's poetry, It states that he swam across Jordan and set a marker, knots in bushes, on the far side; it makes the comparison with others who do not come. Its content is very reminiscent of the description which Sigurðr jórsalafari gives of his own pilgrimage, in an abusive comic debate with his brother, *Heimskringla, Magnússona saga* xxi (expanded from a much briefer account in *Morkinskinna*, ed. Finnur Jónsson, p. 383). Here also Sigurðr swam across Jordan and set a knot in scrub-woodland on the other side. *Heimskringla* adds the details that Sigurðr lays on the knot an explicit but unfortunately unreported *formáli* directed against his absent brother if he did not come to untie it. Unhappily, this elaboration in *Heimskringla* is rather likely to be modelled upon the passage in *Orkneyinga saga*, and if so would merely represent the interpretation which Snorri Sturluson placed upon Rǫgnvaldr's actions.

At the literal level, verse 75 shows that Rǫgnvaldr's sense of enterprise is undiminished. The wit of the verse reminds its audience of the earlier verses of mockery; it invokes the unnamed wise woman who will remember these things in winter-time, and it calls up the warlike imagery of the blood-stained battle-field.

But this verse has much more literal meaning, both for Rǫgnvaldr himself and within the wider structure of the text. It is virtually identical in form and narrative context with verse 36 from far earlier in the saga's account of the earl's career. There, as discussed above, the young Rǫgnvaldr Kali had swum across an underground lake on the island of Dolls and raised a cairn for the hard-hearted, cave-dwelling *draugr* on the far side. There seems to be something of a play here on the notion of the cave-dwelling troll or giant, and that of the animated corpse, *draugr*, the walking dead, who normally occupies a cairn or barrow, though these two notions, probably originally distinct, become increasingly difficult to distinguish in later popular tradition. Correspondingly, Rǫgnvaldr ties a knot in bushes across Jordan, for a stay-at-home (*heimdrǫgum* v. 75,8) wretch (*kauða* v. 77,1), certainly referring to Sveinn Ásleifarson. Here, finally, verse 36 and its prose narrative is given a function in the text, for it is now seen to prefigure the earl's baptismal and penitential bathing in Jordan.

In contrast, verse 78 is quiet and pious. Instead of a corslet on Rǫgnvaldr's breast, there hangs a cross; instead of a shield slung at his back, a palm. Here also Rǫgnvaldr invokes his own poetry, describing himself as a *þulr*. He has cast aside his warlike attributes, and enters Jerusalem as a pilgrim and palmer—yet his poetry remains as a vehicle also for this. Just as it can express romantic love at Narbonne, so it can follow Christ down the Mount of Olives. Rǫgnvaldr cannot of course be claimed as an innovator in composing Christian skaldic poetry, but the immediate and personal tone here is not usual. The self-awareness which Rǫgnvaldr normally employs for ironic purposes is here wholly serious. As he light-heartedly cast himself in the role of romantic lover at Narbonne, now, more seriously, he sees himself as simply a pilgrim.

The last two verses of the pilgrimage (79–80) revert to the light-hearted exuberance to which we are more accustomed in Rǫgnvaldr Kali. As mentioned, verse 80 is another sailing-verse, while 79, probably transposed, mocks Erlingr skakki for falling into an open sewer in Byzantium when drunk.

Earl Rǫgnvaldr Kali left a heritage of skaldic poetry for his successors, and it is clear that skaldic poetry continued to be composed in the Earldom with considerable vigour after his time. Bishop Bjarni Kolbeinsson (bishop from 1185 until his death in 1223) was the bishop who translated Earl Rǫgnvaldr's relics and thereby acknowledged his sanctity in 1192; he also continued the building of the cathedral on an enlarged scale (see Cant above). He had close personal connections with Iceland, and may have provided some of the material and motivation for the composition of a version of *Orkneyinga saga*, probably in the last decade of the twelfth century. He was also, however, an accomplished poet, and there survives one major poem attributed to him: *Jómsvíkingadrápa*. This lay of some 45 surviving verses recounts the heroic story of the Jómsvikings, particularly Vagn Ákason, and their battle with Earl Hákon the Mighty of Norway (which took place between about 974–980), but it does so within the context of the poet's own unhappy love for a (married) lady (especially vv. 3–4 and the refrain). The poem recounts its warlike content with a light, even ironic, touch which is most unusual in poetic treatment of heroic subject-matter. In both these respects Bishop Bjarni must be seen as Rǫgnvaldr's poetic heir. However, Bjarni's interest in legendary history was a new feature in Orcadian poetry, and of course this had close parallels in contemporary Iceland, in particular the *Búadrápa* of the Icelandic poet Þorkell Gíslason, which also deals with the Jómsvíkingar but concentrates upon the figure of Búi digri. *Jómsvíkingadrápa* is also closely related to various prose versions of the story, Norwegian and Icelandic, especially that in *Fagrskinna* (ed. Finnur Jónsson, 87–103); for a discussion of how these may be related, see Blake(ed.), *The Saga of the Jomsvikings*, xv–xix.

It has also been suggested that Bishop Bjarni composed the poem known as *Málsháttakvæði* (*Griplur*), now of some 30 verses and preserved with *Jómsvíkingadrápa*. This is likely to be an Orcadian poem (on grounds of language and vocabulary, as discussed by Finnur Jónsson, *Litteraturs historie* II, 47). Hermann Pálsson presents arguments for composition of the poem in the middle of the thirteenth century (1984, 258–264); if so, it must at the least be regarded as influenced by Bishop Bjarni. It is a collection of proverbs, and of proverbial examples drawn mostly from Norse legend and history. But it is largely concerned with unhappy love, especially in its refrain, and it mentions the poet's own love for a lady called Rannveig (v. 18). In its combination of amorous form and heroic content, it is a fairly close and striking parallel to *Jómsvíkingadrápa*. Such a structural use of love-poetry, *mansöngr*, was to become a rigid convention in the Icelandic *rímur* (and is already parodied in *Skíðaríma*, late fourteenth or early fifteenth century). These Orcadian examples of the thirteenth century therefore show at least an early stage of a major literary convention of the later Icelandic *rímur*, and possibly even provide a route whereby the *minnesang* of courtly love can become the *mansöngr* of the *rímur*. Rǫgnvaldr Kali composed troubadour poetry of courtly love; the poetry of courtly love was used by Bishop Bjarni and the poet of *Málsháttakvæði* to structure poems of heroic content; the poetry of courtly love is used in the *rímur* to introduce and contain narratives of romance, the heroic or mock-heroic.

A third poem is normally attributed, on grounds of language and content, to twelfth or thirteenth century Orcadian authorship: *Krákumál*, a poem now of 29 verses listing heroic deeds of legend or history, supposedly associated with the legendary Viking hero Ragnarr loðbrók. It supports the antiquarian interest in heroic Norse antiquity shown in the *Jómsvíkingadrápa* and *Málsháttakvæði*.

By a final, happy chance, the last glimpse of Orcadian poetry in Norse is seen in *Hákonar saga Hákonarsonar* (ed. M. Mundt, p. 110), where a verse is attributed to Snækollr Gunnason for the year 1239. He was not Norwegian, as Finnur Jónsson erroneously calls him, but was a great-grandson of Earl Rǫgnvaldr Kali (ed. p. 86). He witnesses to continuing poetic activity West over Sea in the Norse Earldom of Orkney. Earl Rǫgnvaldr left an enduring legacy.

BIBLIOGRAPHY

Andersson Theodore M, 1969, 'Skalds and Troubadours', *Medieval Scandinavia* ii, 7–41

Bibire, P, 1984, 'Few know an earl in fishing-clothes', in *Essays in Shetland History*, B Crawford, ed.

Blake N F, ed., 1962, *The Saga of the Jomsvikings*

Fagrskinna, Finnur Jónsson, ed., 1902–1903, Copenhagen

Hákonar saga Hákonarsonar, M Mundt, ed., 1977, Oslo

Helgason Jón and Holtsmark Anne, eds, *Háttalykill enn forni, Bibliotheca Arnamagnæana* I, 1941, Copenhagen

Hill Joyce, 1983, 'From Rome to Jerusalem: An Icelandic Itinerary of the Mid-Twelfth Century', *Harvard Theological Review* lxxii, 2, 175–203

Jónsson Finnur, *Litteráturs historie* I–III, 2nd ed., 1920–1924, Copenhagen

Kålund Kr, 1908, *Alfræði íslenzk* i, Copenhagen

Liestøl, A, Krause, W, Helgason, J, 1962, 'Drottkvaett fra Bryggen i Bergen', *Maal og Minne*, 98–108

Orkneyinga Saga. ed. Finnbogi Guðmundsson, *Íslenzk fornrit* xxxiv, 1965, Reykjavík

Palsson, H., 1984 'A Florilegium in Norse from Medieval Orkney' in *The Northern and Western Isles in the Viking World*, ed., A Fenton & H Palsson, 258–264

Vries Jan de, 1938–39, 'Een skald onder de Troubadours', *Koninklijke Vlaamsche Academie: Verslagen en Mededeelingen*, 701–35, Gent

Idem, 1960, 'Jarl Rǫgnvalds Lausavísur', *Folkloristica. Festskrift till Dag Strömbäck*, Uppsala, 133–41

APPENDIX TO THE POETRY OF EARL RǪGNVALDR'S COURT

Paul Bibire

The text of the verses given here is based where possible upon *Flateyjarbók*. Translations are fairly literal, and have little pretension to literary merit. No attempt is made to reproduce alliteration, internal rhyme, or other metrical features, but sometimes the sentence-structure of the original is reflected in the translations. Kennings are not resolved; they are explained in commentaries on individual verses.

(34) Tafl em'k ǫrr at efla,
íþróttir kann'k níu,
týni'k trauðla rúnum,
tíð er mér bók ok smíðir,
skríða kann'k á skíðum,
skýt'k ok rœ'k, svá't nýtir,
hvárt tveggja kann'k hyggja
harpslǫtt ok bragþǫttu.

Chess I am keen to play, I know nine skills, I scarcely forget runes, book and handicrafts are usual for me, I know how to ski, I shoot and row serviceably, I know how to evaluate both harp-playing and poetry.

(35) Vér hǫfum vaðnar leirur
vikur fimm megingrimmar,
saurs vara vant, er vórum,
viðr, í Grímsbœ miðjum.
Nú'r þat's mós of mýrar
meginkátliga lǫtum
branda elg á bylgjur
Bjǫrgynjar til dynja.

We have waded the mud-flats five mighty-grim weeks, there was no want of filth, when we were in mid Grimsby. Now we let the bowsprit's elk crash across the gull's fens, mighty-glady, to Bergen.

Kennings: *branda elgr*, 'bowsprit's elk': ship; *mós mýrar*, 'gull's fens': sea.

(36) Héf hef'k hávan reistan
harðgeðjuðum varða
Dolls í døkkum helli
draug, leita'k svá bauga.
Eigi veit'k, hverr ýta
unnskíða ferr síðan
lenga braut ok ljóta
leið yfir vatn it breiða.

Here I have raised a high cairn for the hard-hearted Dolls-zomby in (his) dark cave; so I seek riches. I don't know, which wave-skis' thruster will go afterwards (such) a long and ugly way over the broad water.

draugr: 'walking corpse', normally buried under a cairn; more generally 'troll-like being' (see discussion in text). *bauga* 'rings', hence 'riches'. Kenning: *ýtir unnskíða*, 'wave-skis' thruster', 'urger of ships', 'seaman'.

(38)   Sextán hef'k sénar
     senn ok topp í enni
     jarðar elli firrðar
     ormvangs saman ganga.
     Þat bǫrum vér vitni,
     vestr, at hér sé flestar,
     sjá liggr út við élum
     ey, kollóttar meyjar.

I've seen sixteen (women) at once, with forelock on forehead, stripped of the old age of the serpent-field's land, walk together. We bear witness that most girls here—this isle lies out west against the storms—are bald.

Rǫgnvaldr is joking about monks, whose clothing and clean-shaven faces seem effeminate. Their (Celtic) tonsure gave a bald crown but left a forelock at the front of the head. Kenning: *elli jarðar ormvangs*, 'old age of the earth of the serpent-field': 'serpent-field' ie. 'gold' (since dragons/serpents legendarily lie on gold); the 'earth' of gold is a woman (since women wear twisted serpentine ornaments of gold, and 'earth' is grammatically feminine); the 'old age' of a woman is facial hair, of which these monks are shaved. The kenning therefore means 'clean-shaven', but in no complimentary way.

(39)   Liggja sé'k at leggjum,
     láss bannar þer rásir,
     kveldfǫrlustum karli,
     Kúgi, jarn in bjúgu.
     Eiguð aldri, Kúgi,
     aptr munt settr af prettum,
     nauðr er at nýta eiða,
     náttþing ok halt sáttir.

I see the twisted fetters lie on the limbs of the evening-wandering old fellow; a lock forbids your rushing, Kúgi; never, Kúgi—you will be put back from your tricks; one must hold oaths—hold night-meetings, but keep agreements.

Anonymous

(40)   Heyri'k hitt, en órir
     hafa dolgar skap folgit,
     þengill ríkr, af þingi
     þann kvitt búandmanna,
     at valdandar vildi,
     vargseðjandi, margir,
     at þú vigg á brim byggir
     brands, en Pál at landi.

I hear contrasting report, mighty lord—our foes have dissimulated—this decision of the land-owners from the meeting, that many lords wish that you, wolf-sater, should occupy the bows-steed at sea, but Paul on land.

Kennings: *vargseðjandi*, 'wolf-sater', ie. 'one who provides carrion for wolves', 'warrior'. *vigg brands*, 'steed of the bows', ie. 'ship'. Paul should continue to rule the land, but Rǫgnvaldr should be a landless 'sea-king'.

Eiríkr

(41)   Bœir eru brenndir,
     en búendr ræntir,
     svá hefr Sveinn hagat,
     sex í morgin.
     Gerði hann einum
     œrinn þeira,
     leigir þar kol
     leigumanni.

Farms are burnt, farmers robbed— so has Sveinn contrived—six this morning. He did enough for any one of them, rents out charcoal to the tenant-farmer.

Sveinn ironically takes over the role of landlord for the tenants, but in lordship he rents out only the burnt remains of their farms.

Hallr Þórarinsson

(42)
Senda'k son þinn, Ragna,	I sent your son, Ragna—true tales
sǫnn koma mǫl fyr bragna,	come to men; his was a noble task—
hans var hólig iðja,	to request residence at court for me.
hirðvistar mér biðja.	The hoard-diminisher, who controls
Hafa kvezk hodda rýrir,	greatest glory—he refused the
hinn er mestum veg stýrir,	sausage's neighbour—said that he
neitti hann grúpans granna,	had enough warlike men.
gnótt vígligri manna.	

Kennings: *hodda rýrir*, 'diminisher of hoards', ie. 'generous man', Rǫgnvaldr. *grúpans granni*, 'the sausage's neighbour', ie. 'Icelander'; it was a long-standing Norwegian joke that Icelanders lived off mutton-fat made up into blood-pudding, as indeed they largely did. Hallr wryly directs this joke at himself, and so contrasts himself with the generous and warlike court of the earl who had nonetheless refused him.

(43)
Aldr hef'k frétt þat's feldu	Always I've heard that all high-
framstalls konur allar,	ranking women clad their heads
verðrat menja myrðir	with kerchiefs—the ring-slayer does
mjúkorðr, hǫfuðdúkum.	not prove soft-worded. Now the
Nú tér Hlǫkk um hnakka	hawk-land's valkyrie manages to tie
haukstrindar sér binda,	a mare's tail around her neck; the
skrýðisk brúðr við bræði	woman puts on finery for the
bengagls, merar tagli.	wound-gaggle's feeder.

Kennings: *menja myrðir*, 'murderer of neck-rings', ie. 'generous man', Rǫgnvaldr. *Hlǫkk haukstrindar*, 'Hlǫkk' (valkyrie-name) of the hawk's land'; the 'hawk's land' is the arm upon which the hawk rests; its 'valkyrie' is the (noble) woman who goes hawking. The image is warlike, since the 'valkyrie's hawk' implies the raven, the carrion-bird of battle. *bræðir bengagls*, 'feeder of the wound-gaggle' is the raven, the bird that feeds on wounded carrion; the one who gives raw meat (*bræðir*) to the raven is the warrior, Rǫgnvaldr . All these kennings contain much barely suppressed violence, in comic constrast with the narrative context.

(44)
Hengi'k hamri kringðan	I hang the hammer-rounded hanged
hanga rjúpu tangar,	man of the tongs of the ptarmigan on
Grímnis sylg, á galga	the gallows of the serpent of the
ginnungs brúar linna.	hawk's bridge for Grímnir's drink.
Svá hefr glóraddar gladdan,	So has the tree of the gleaming voice
gagfellis, mik þella,	of the cave's Gautar gladdened me,
lóns, at ek leik við mínar	that I play with my bends of the
lautir, hellis Gauta.	bay's towering feller.

Kennings: *hangi rjúpu tangar*, perhaps 'hanged man of the tongs of the ptarmigan'. 'Ptarmigan' here probably means 'woman'; it is grammatically feminine, and is used elsewhere as a female personal name and nickname; its 'tongs' (claws) are the woman's hand, and that which hangs from the hand, as the hanged man from the gallows, is a ring. There may be two doubles entendres in this kenning: obscene puns on the bird-term *gás* 'goose'/'*cunnus*', and *hangi* 'hanged man'/'penis'. The use of 'tongs' echoes the image of the smith's tools already present in *hamri kringðan*, 'hammer-rounded'. *gálgi linna ginnungs brúar*, 'gallows of the serpent of the hawk's bridge'; the 'hawk's bridge' is the arm upon which the hawk rests; the serpent of the arm is the twisted spiral arm-ring; its gallows is, again, the hand of arm from which it hangs. Recurrence (of the image of the arm) in the second kenning is not uncommon; it gives a formal echo of the spiral arm-ring. These two kennings are unified by the Óðinn-image of the hanged man.

Alternatively read *linni ginnungs brúar*, 'serpent of the hawk's bridge': twisted ring worn on the arm; *gálgi tangar*, 'gallows of the tongs': hand; *hanga rjúpa*, 'ptarmigan of the hanged one': (obscenely) woman. The kenning-sequence would then read 'I hang the hammer-rounded serpent of the hawk's bridge on the tongs-gallows of the hanged one's ptarmigan'; it gives slightly more convential kenning-types but more difficult word-order.

Grímnis sylgr, 'Grímnir's (ie. Óðinn's) drink', 'poetry' (which in the cycle of myths of its origin was the supernatural mead which the god Óðinn drank). *Þella glóraddar hellis Gauta*, 'fir-tree of the gleaming voice of the Gautar of the cave'; 'Gautar (inhabitants of the region around mod. Gothenburg) of the cave' are giants, who conventionally live in caves; the 'gleaming voice' of giants is gold (since in a myth a giant filled his mouth with gold); the grammatically feminine 'fir-tree' of gold is a woman, laden with gold just as in winter a tree is laden with silver-shining snow. *lautir gagfellis lóns*, 'bends of the bay's towering feller'; 'towering feller of the bay' is an oar, that breaks upon the water from above; its *lautir*, 'bends', are the hollowed hands of the rower. Overall interpretation of the verse is uncontroversial, although the two major kennings in the first half-strophe are in any interpretation difficult. The whole verse therefore means: 'I hang the hammer-rounded ring of the woman's hand upon her arm, in return for poetry; so the gold-laden lady has gladdened me that I play with my hands'.

(45) Brast, þá's boði lesti,
bauð hrǫnn skaða mǫnnum,
sút fekk veðr it váta
vífum, Hjǫlp ok Fífu.
Sé'k, at sjá mun þykkja
snarlyndra fǫr jarla,
sveit gat vás at vísu
vinna, hǫfð at minnum.

Hjǫlp and Fífa were smashed when a billow struck; the wave threatened men; the wet weather gave women sorrow. I see that this voyage of bold-hearted earls will seem memorable; the crew certainly got wet work.

The *víf*, 'women' (l. 4) may playfully refer to the two ships, both grammatically feminine, Hjǫlp and Fífa; although storms at sea normally give women sorrow (through loss of their menfolk), here the shipwreck seems to have involved no loss of life.

(46) Skek'k hér skinnfeld hrokkinn,
skraut er mér afar lítit,
stórr er sá's stendr of órum
stafnvǫllr yfirhǫfnum,
nærgi's enn af úrgum
álvangs mari gǫngum,
brim rak hest við hamra
húns, skrautligar búnir.

I shake out a wrinkled leather cloak here; there's very little finery for me—much is the prow-field which stands around our cloaks—whenever yet we go finer-clad from the spray-swept steed of the eel-plain—surf drove the mast-head's stallion against cliffs.

Kennings: *stafnvǫllr*, 'stem-plain, prow-field', ie. 'sea-(water)'. *álvangs marr* 'eel-plain's stallion'; 'eel-plain' is the sea; its 'stallion' is the ship. *hestr húns* 'stallion of the mast-head', again 'ship'. The image which runs through these kennings is of horses running free across the land.

(47) Dúsið ér, en Ása
—atatata—liggr í vatni,
—hutututu—hvar skal'k sitja?
heldr er mér kalt, við eldinn.

You roast yourselves by the fire, but Ása—atatata—lies in water—hutututu—where must I sit?—I'm rather cold!

(48) Ala kvezk Einarr vilja
engan Rǫgnvalds drengja,
mér kemr Gauts á góma
gjalfr, nema jarlinn sjalfan.
Veit'k, at hratzk í heitum
hugþekkr firum ekki,
inn gekk'k Yggs, þar's brunnu
eldar síð á kveldi.

Einarr says he wants to look after none of Ronald's men except the earl himself; Gautr's flood comes to my lips. I know that this unpleasant man failed in his promises; I went in, where Yggr's fires burnt late in the evening.

Kennings: *Gauts gjalfr*, 'the (resounding) ocean of Gautr (ie. Óðinn)', 'poetry': a reference to the myth of the divine origin of poetry as Óðinn's drink. *Yggs eldar*, 'Yggr's (ie. Óðinn's) fires', probably 'shining weapons' or perhaps merely 'treachery'. An unusual and very striking kenning: Rǫgnvaldr enters a hall, where fires are burning in the evening, giving warmth and welcome. Further, these are Óðinn's fires in the hall of Einarr: Óðinn's hall is Valhalla, where the *Einherjar* ('chosen warriors', pl. of pr.n *Einarr*) fight and feast after heroic death until the final battle at Ragnarǫk. But Óðinn is also god of cunning treachery, and to enter his hall is to die by the sword and, in Christian terms, be damned. Rǫgnvaldr thus condemns Einarr in the strongest terms.

(NB. only in Uppsala R: 702 4to)
(49) Skelk aflar Sif silkis
svinn at umbúð minni,
hlær stórum mun meira
mær en fallit væri.
Fár kann jarl, en árla
ǫrlyndr, at sjá gǫrla,
hlunns dró'k eik af unnum
áðr, í fiskivǫðum.

The wise Sif of silk guffaws at my get-up; the girl laughs much more than would be fitting. Few know how to see clearly an earl in fishing-clothes; generous, I dragged the roller's oak from the waves earlier

Kennings: *Sif silkis*, 'Sif (goddess-name) of silk', 'well-clad woman' (who laughs at this ill-clad wretch). *hlunns eik* 'oak-tree of the roller', boat.

Ármóðr
(50) Eigi metr inn ítri
alvaldr gjafar skaldi,
Yggs, við aðra seggi
élstœrir, at fœra.

The glorious ruler, enlarger of Yggr's storm, does not compare with other men in bringing gifts to the poet; the keen guardian of the

Snjallr bar glæst með gulli
grundar vǫrðr at mundum,
buðlungr nýztr, it bezta
blóðkerti Armóði.

land, most excellent lord, bore the
best blood-taper, gold-gleaming, to
Ármóðr's hands.

Kennings: *Yggs élstœrir*, 'enlarger of Yggr's (Óðinn's) hail- or snow-storm'; 'Óðinn's storm' is battle, and its hail is flying weapons; its 'enlarger' is the war-leader, the earl. *grundar vǫrðr*, 'guardian of the ground', the earl. *blóðkerti*, 'blood-taper': that which shines and is in shape like a taper, but gleams with blood not flame, a weapon.

(51)   Lætr of ǫxl, sá's útar,
aldrœnn, stendr á tjaldi,
sig-Freyr, Svǫlnis Vára
sliðrvǫnd ofan ríða.
Eigi mun, þótt œgir
ǫrbeiðanda reiðisk,
blikruðr bǫðvar jǫkla
beinrangr framar ganga.

The aged victory-Freyr, who stands
further out on the tapestry, lets the
scabbard-wand of Svǫlnir's goddesses swing down by his shoulder.
Though the arrow-askers' terrifier
grows angry, the bandy battle-
icicles' gleam-bush will not go
forward.

Kennings: *sig-Freyr*, 'Freyr (god-name) of victory': warrior. *Svǫlnis Vára sliðrvǫnd*, 'scabbard-wand of Svǫlnir's (Óðinn's) Várs (goddess-name in pl.)': Óðinn's goddesses are valkyries, their scabbard-wand is a sword. *œgir ǫrbeiðanda*, 'terrifier of arrow-askers' (or possibly *Ægir ǫrbeiðanda*, 'Ægir (god-name) of arrow-askers'): 'arrow-askers' (or possibly 'eager askers'?) are warriors; their terrifier (or god) is another warrior. *blikruðr bǫðvar jǫkla*, 'gleam-bush of the icicles of battle': the 'icicles of battle' are swords, that are in shape and glint like swords, and drip with liquid'; the *ruðr/runnr* (masc.), 'bush' of swords is the warrior, gleaming with his weapons.

Oddi
(52)   Stendr ok hyggr at hǫggva
herðilútr með sverði
bandalfr beiði-Rindi
Baldrs við dyrr á tjaldi.
Firum mun hann með hjǫrvi
hættr; nú's mál, at sættisk
hlœðendr hleypiskíða
hlunns, áðr geigr sé unninn.

The belt-elf of the Rind that begs for
Baldr stands bent-shouldered by the
doorway on the tapestry, and thinks
of hewing with a sword. He will be
perilous to men with his blade; now
it's time that loaders of the roller's
leaping ski should be reconciled,
before harm is done

Kennings: *bandalfr beiði-Rindi Baldrs*, 'belt-elf of the Rind (goddess-name) that begs for Baldr': the goddess that begs for Baldr is his mother, Frigg, who beseeches on his behalf before and after his death at the hands of his brother, Hǫðr; *Frigg*, however, is not only a goddess-name but an island-name; the belt of an island is the sea that surrounds it; a poetic term for sea is *marr; marr* is also a poetic word for 'sword'; its 'elf' is thus a swordsman. This kenning thus involves twofold word-play, on *Frigg* as goddess- and island-name, and on *marr*, as sea- and sword-term. This technique is known as *ofljóst*, and it appears elsewhere in Rǫgnvaldr's poetry (eg. in the two verses attributed to him and cited as examples of the technique, associated with *Snorra Edda*; see below). *hlœðendr hleypiskíða hlunns*, 'loaders of the leaping skis of the roller'; the 'skis of the roller' are ships; their loaders are seamen.

NB. only in Uppsala R: 702 4to)

(53) Fekk í fylkis skikkju
fangramligr ótangi;
rekkr réð hart at hnykkja hildingi
fémildum.
Sterkr var stála-Bjarki,
staka kvóðu gram nǫkkut;
afl hefr eggja skýflir
orðvandr fyr hyggjandi.

The strong-grasping wretch grabbed at the lord's gown; the man tried hard to pull at the generous battle-lord. The steels-Bjarki was strong; they said the lord stumbled somewhat; the ill-mouth edge-skirmisher has force instead of thought.

Kennings: *stála-Bjarki*, 'Bjarki of steels': Bǫðvar-Bjarki was a legendary hero, a cross between man and bear; the Bjarki of steel (weapons) is thus a bearlike warrior. *eggja skýflir* 'skirmisher of edges', one who feints with sharp-edged weapons, warrior.

54) Hrǫnn's fyr Humru mynni
háleit, þar's vér beitum;
sveigir lauk, en lægjask
lǫnd fyr Veslu sǫndum.
Eígi drífr í augu
alda lauðri faldin,
drengr ríðr þurr af þingi,
þeim er nú sitr heima.

Steep is the surge before Humber's mouth, where we tack; the mast bends, but lands lower before Wall-send's sands. No foam-capped wave drives into the eyes of him who now sits at home; the fellow rides dry from the meeting.

Veslu: the identification as Wallsend is far from certain (and is topographically odd).

(55) Víst's at frá berr flestu
Fróða meldrs at góðu
vel skúfaðra vífa
vǫxtr þinn, konan svinna.
Skorð lætr hár á herðar
haukvallar sér falla,
átgǫrnum rauð'k erni
ilka, gult sem silki.

Truly your tresses, wise lady, surpass (the hair) of most women with locks of Fróði's milling. The hawkland's prop lets hair fall on to her shoulders, yellow as silk—I red-dened the greedy eagle's claw.

Kennings: *(skúfr) fróða meldrs*, '(tassel, lock of hair) of Fróði's milling': 'Fróði's milling', as recounted in *Grottasǫngr*, was the legendary milling of gold by two giantesses for the Danish king Fróði, and then of salt at the bottom of the Pentland Firth, which is why the sea is salt and why the tide-races between Orkney and Scotland are full of whirlpools. The kenning is unusual in being used adjectivally, 'gold-tressed'. *Skorð haukvallar*, 'hawk-plain's prop': the 'hawk-plain' is the arm on which the hawk rests; its (fem.) 'prop' is the noblewoman who practices falconry.

(56) Orð skal Ermingerðar
ítr drengr muna lengi;
brúðr vill rǫkk at rídim
Ránheim til Jórðánar;
en er aptr fara runnar
unnviggs of haf sunnan,
rístum, heim at hausti,
hvalfrón til Nerbónar.

The glorious warrior must long remember Ermingerðr's words; the noble lady wishes us to ride Rán-world to Jordan; but when the wavesteed's trees go back north across the sea, home in autumn, we shall score the whale's land to Narbonne.

Kennings: *Ránheim*, 'Ránworld': Rán ('robbery') is the sea-goddess who plunders men's possessions and lives; her 'world' is the sea. *runnar unnvíggs*, 'bushes of the wave-steed': the 'wavesteed' is the ship; its (masc.) 'bushes' are seamen. *rístum*, 'we shall cut': the image is of the ship's keel scoring the sea with its wake, as a knife cuts wood.

Ármóðr

(57) Ek mun Ermingerði,
     nema ǫnnur skǫp verði,
     margr elr sorg of svinna,
     síðan aldri finna.
     væra'k sæll, ef ek svæfa,
     sýn væri þat gæfa,
     brúðr hefr allfagrt enni,
     eina nótt hjá henni.

I shall never—unless Fate turns out otherwise—many a man nurtures grief for a lady—see Ermingerðr again. I would be blessed if I slept—clear grace it would be—the lady has a very fair forehead—one night with her.

Oddi

(58) Trautt erum vér, sem ek vætti,
     verðir Ermingerðar,
     veit'k, at horsk má heita
     hlaðgrund konungr sprunda,
     því't sómir Bil bríma
     bauga stalls at ǫllu,
     hon lifi sæl und sólar
     setri, miklu betra.

Scarcely are we, as I reckon, worthy of Ermingerðr—I know that the wise broider-ground may be called king of women—for altogether much better befits the Bil of the fire of the rings' stand; may she live blessed beneath the sun's seat.

Kennings: *hlaðgrund*, 'broider-ground': *hlað* is an embroidered strip or seam, used in feminine attire; its 'ground' is the woman. *Bil bríma bauga stalls*, 'Bil (goddess-name) of the fire of the rings' stand'; the 'raised floor, platform (*stallr*) of rings' is the arm upon which rings are worn; its 'fire' is gold; the goddess that wears gold is the woman. *sólar setr*, 'seat of the sun', sky.

(59) Vín bar hvít in hreina
     hlaðnipt alindriptar,
     sýndisk fegrð, er fundumsk,
     ferðum Ermingerðar.
     Nú tegask ǫld með eldi
     eljunfrœkn at sœkja,
     ríða snǫrp ór slíðrum
     sverð, kastala ferðir.

The fair-haired, pure broider-sister of the ell-drift bore wine, Ermingerðr's beauty was shown to men, when we met. Now bold folk do attack with fire—sharp swords swing from scabbards—the castle-men.

Kenning: *hlaðnipt alindriptar*, 'broider-sister of the snow-drift of the forearm': the 'snow-drift of the forearm' is silver; the embroidery-clad sister who wears silver is the woman.

(60) Muna mun'k jól, þau's ólum
     austr, gjaldkera hraustum,
     Ullr, at Egða fjǫllum,
     undleygjar, með Sǫlmundi.
     Nú geri'k enn of ǫnnur,
     jafnglaðr sem var'k þaðra,
     sverðs at sunnanverðum
     svarm kastalabarmi.

I'll remember Yules that we spent east at Agðir's fells, woundflame's Ullr, with the bold steward Sǫlmundr. Now during others, as glad as I was there, I make the sword's tumult at a southern castle wall.

Kennings: *Ullr undleygjar*, 'woundflame's Ullr (god-name)': the 'woundflame' is a sword; its god is a warrior, here addressed. *sverðs svarmr*, 'sword's tumult', battle.

(61) Unða'k vel, þá's vanðisk
      víneik tali mínu,
      gæfr var'k vǫlsku vífi
      vánarlaust, á hausti.
      Nú geri'k enn, þvít unnum
      áttgóðu vel fljóði,
      grjót verðr laust at láta
      límsett, ara mettan.

I was well content when the wine-oak grew used to my talk—I was doubtless welcome to the French woman—in the autumn. Now again I make, for we love the noble-born lady well—mortared stone must loosen—the eagle fed.

Kenning: *víneik*, 'wine-oak', (fem.) tree that bears wine, woman.

Sigmundr ǫngull
(62) Ér berið aptr, er várar,
      orð þau Skǫgul borða,
      fjallrifs fægiþellu,
      fleyvangs til Orkneyja,
      at engr, þar's slǫg sungu,
      seggr und kastals veggi,
      ár, þótt ellri væri,
      ítr drengr framar gengi.

Bear back, when Spring comes, these words to the Skǫgul of embroidery, the mountain-rib's polishing-tree, across the skiff-plain to Orkney, that no glorious warrior under the castle wall where blows resounded early, though he were older, went further.

Kennings: *Skǫgul borða*, 'Skǫgul (valkyrie-name) of embroidered strips', woman. *fjallrifs fægiþella*, 'polishing fir-tree of the mountain-rib': the 'mountain-rib' is a stone; the (fem.) 'fir-tree' that polishes stones (for adornment) is a woman. *fleyvangs*, 'skiff-plain', sea (gen. of place).

(63) Vǫn á'k, út á Spáni
      var skjótt rekinn flótti,
      flýði margr af mœði
      menlundr, konu fundar.
      Því erum vér, at vǫru
      væn hljóð kveðin þjóðum,
      valr tók vǫll at hylja,
      verðir Ermingerðar.

I look for—out in Spain the fleeing were swiftly driven, many a torc-tree fled in weariness—meeting the lady. So are we, for the splendid voices (of war) were spoken to nations—carrion covered the field—worthy of Ermingerðr.

Kenning: *menlundr*, (masc.) 'grove of the neck-ring', man wearing a neck-ring, man.

(64) Skal'kat hryggr í hreggi,
      Hlín, meðan strengr ok lína, svǫrðr
      fyr snekkju barði,
      svalteigar, brestr eigi;
      því nam'k hvítri heita
      hǫrskorð, er ek fór norðan,
      vindr berr snart at sundi
      súðmar, konu prúðri.

I shan't be sad in storm of the chill field, Hlín, while rope and cord, cable at the warship's prow, does not break; so I promised the white flax-prop, the proud woman, when I went south; wind bears the seam-steed swiftly at the sound (ie. the Straits of Gibraltar).

Kennings: *hregg svalteigar*, 'storm of the chill field', storm at sea. *Hlín* (goddess-name), woman. *horskorð* 'flax-prop', linen-clad woman. *súð-marr*, 'seam-stallion', ship.

Oddi

(65) Hafði hollvinr lofða,
hinn er mjǫð drekkr inni
sunda logs með sveigi,
sjau dœgr muni hœgri.
En ríklundaðr renndi
Rǫgnvaldr með lið skjaldat
hesti, halli glæstum,
hlunns at Nǫrvasundum.

The trusty friend of men who drinks mead indoors with the seafire's flexer had seven daytimes somewhat easier. But great-hearted Ronald, with a shield-bearing troop, galloped on the roller's stallion, gleaming with paint, to the Straits of Gibraltar.

Kennings: *sunda logs sveigir*, 'flexer of the flame of the sound': the 'flame of the sound' is gold, that shines like fire even under water; its 'flexer' is the generous man who bends it to break off part as a gift. *hestr hlunns*, 'stallion of the roller', ship.

(66) Vindr hefr vǫlsku sprundi
vetrarstund frá mundum,
út berum ás at beita,
austrœnn skotit flaustum.
Verðum vér at gyrða
vánar hart fyr Spáni;
vindr rekr snart at sundi,
Sviðris við rǫ́ miðja.

An east wind for a winter's hour has shot ships from the hands of the French lady; we put out the beam to tack. We have to fasten (the sail) to the middle of Sviðrir's sailyard somewhat firmly off Spain; the wind drives swiftly in the sea.

Kenning: *Sviðris rǫ́*, 'sviðrir's (Óðinn's) sailyard': 'Óðinn's sailyard' is Yggdrasill, the world-ash upon which he hung as his gallows; hence 'tree' in general, but 'tree', *(siglu)-tré*, is 'mast'. Paradoxically therefore the sailyard must be fastened to the middle of the mast, which is described as a 'sailyard'. The procedure is half-lowering of the sail, to avoid breaking the mast in stormy weather.

(67) Landi víkr, en leika
lǫgr tér á við fǫgrum,
síð mun seggr at hróðri
seina, norðr at einu.
Þenna ríst'k með þunnu,
þýtr jarðar men, barði
einum út frá Spáni
ǫfundkrók í dag hróki.

The land bends continuously north, but the sea sports on the fair timber; the man will be late to delay poetry. I score with slim prow out from Spain this envy-turn for a single fellow—Earth's neckring roars.

Kenning: *jarðar men*, 'Earth's neckring': Earth (possibly personified as a giantess, mother of Þórr) is surrounded by Ocean; hence its 'neckring' is the sea. The *ǫfundkrókr* and *hrókr* are references to Rǫgnvaldr Kali's increasingly tense relationship with Eindriði ungi, described in the prose text of *Orkneyinga saga;* here the earl deliberately turns south away from Eindriði.

(68) Erlingr gekk, þar's okkur,
ógnsterkr, ruðusk merki,

Erlingr, the renowned, terror-strong javelin-tree, went where our stan-

frægr, með fremð ok sigri,
fleinlundr, at drómundi.
Hlóðum vér, en víða
varð blóð numit þjóðum,
sverð ruðu snjallir fyrðar
snǫrp, blámanna gǫrpum.

dards were reddened, with valour
and victory, against the dromond.
We piled up—but widely were folk
deprived of blood; bold men reddened keen swords—champions of
the blackamoors.

Kenning: *fleinlundr*, (masc.) 'tree of the throwing-spear', warrior.

(69) Nennum vér at vinna,
      valfall má nú kalla,
      ár hefr drengr í dreyra,
      drómund, roðit skjóma.
      Þat mun norðr ok norðan
      naddregn konan fregna,
      þjóð beið ljótt of lýðum
      líftjón, til Nerbónar.

We're prepared to take the dromond
—you could call it killing now—a
warrior has early reddened his
sword in blood. The woman will
hear of that spear-storm from north
and south, to Narbonne—the people
suffered ugly life-loss from men.

Kenning: *naddregn*, 'spear-storm', battle.

(70) Gekk á drómund døkkvan,
      drengr réð snart til fengjar,
      upp með œrnu kappi
      Auðun fyrstr inn rauði.
      Þar nǫðum vér þjóðar,
      því hefr aldar guð valdit,
      bolr fell blár á þiljur,
      blóði vǫpn at rjóða.

Auðun the Red went first up on to
the dark dromond with sufficient
valour—the warrior was swift for
booty. There were we able to
redden—men's God brought it
about; a black body fell on the
planking—weapons in people's
blood.

71)   Eigum vér, þar's vági
      verpr inn of þrǫm stinnan,
      þann hǫfum vér at vinna,
      varðhald á skæ barða,
      meðan í nótt hjá nýtri
      námdúks hǫrundmjúkri
      lókr sefr, lind, inn veiki,
      lít'k of ǫxl til Krítar.

We keep watch, where the sea spills
in over the stiff gunwale—this have
we to do—on the prow-steed, while
tonight the feeble wretch sleeps with
the excellent, soft-skinned kerchief-
tree; I look over my shoulder to
Crete.

Kennings: *skær barða*, 'prow-steed', ship, *námdúks lind*, (fem.) 'tree of the kerchief', woman.

Þorbjǫrn svarti
(72) Var'k í hirð með herði
      hjǫrþeys í Orkneyjum,
      réð folkstara fœðir
      fyrr of vetr til styrjar.
      Nú berum rǫnd með reyndum
      raunsnarliga jarli
      ǫrt á úrga vǫrtu
      Akrsborg fríamorgin.

I was at court with the hardener of
the sword-rush in Orkney; the host-
starlings' feeder earlier, during
winter, decided (to go) to battle.
Now we bear shield boldly with an
experienced earl on to the spray-
swept watch-tower (?) of Acre on
Friday morning.

Kennings: *herðir hjǫrþeys*, 'hardener of the sword-rush', battle-leader, earl. *folkstara fæðir*, 'feeder of the host-starlings', feeder of ravens, warrior or battle-leader. The word *vǫrtu* appears nowhere else in Norse, and may be a Russian or German form with approximate meaning as given.

Oddi

(73) Bǫru lung
       lendra manna
       fyr Þrasnes
       Þorbjǫrn svarta.
       Trað hlunnbjǫrn
       und hǫfuðskaldi
       Áta jǫrð
       Akrsborgar til.

The ship of landowners bore Þorbjǫrn the Black before Freswick. The roller-bear trod Áti's earth beneath a chief poet to Acre.

Kennings: *hlunnbjǫrn*, 'roller-bear', ship. *Áta jǫrð*, 'Áti's earth': Áti was a legendary sea-king, and his earth is the sea.

Oddi

(74) Þar sá'k hann
       at hǫfuðkirkju
       siklings vin
       sandi ausinn.
       Nú þrumir grund
       grýtt of hǫnum
       sólu birt
       á suðrvegum.

There I saw him, friend of the prince, sprinkled with sand at a chief church. Now stony earth, sun-brightened, lies still over him in the south-lands.

(75) Ek hef lagða lykkju,
       leiðar þvengs, of heiði,
       snotr minnisk þess svanni
       sút, fyr Jórðán útan.
       En hykk'k, at þó þykki
       þangat langt at ganga,
       blóð fellr varmt á víðan
       vǫll, heimdrǫgum ǫllum.

I have laid a lock on the heath—the wise lady will remember this in grief of the path's thong—beyond Jordan. But I think that nonetheless it will seem a long way to go there—warm blood falls on the wide field—for all stay-at-homes.

Kenning: *sút leiðar þvengs*, 'sorrow of the path's thong': the 'thong of the path/road' is a serpent; its 'sorrow' is winter.

Sigmundr ǫngull

(76) Knút mun'k þembiþrjóti,
       þeim er nú sitr heima,
       satt's, at heldr hǫfum hættan
       hans kind, í dag binda.

I will tie a knot for the fat-bellied man who sits now at home—truly we have rather risked his child—today.

(77) Knút ríðum vér kauða,
       kem'k móðr í stað góðan,
       þann í þykkum runni
       þessa Lafranzmessu.

We tie this knot for the wretch—I come weary to a good place—in a thick bush this Laurence-day.

The *þembiþrjótr* 'fat-bellied man' (76,1) and *kauði* 'wretch' (77,1) are references to Sveinn Ásleifarson, as can be deduced from the prose.

(78) Kross hangir þul þessum,
      þjóst skyli lægt, fyr brjósti,
      flykkisk fram á brekkur
      ferð, en palmr meðal herða.

A cross hangs for this poet—uproar should be lowered—before my breast—men flock forward on to the hill-slope—but a palm-branch between my shoulders.

(79) Vill eigi vinr minn kalla,
      varð allr í drit falla,
      nær var í því œrin
      ógæfa, miðhæfi.
      Lítt hykk'k, at þá þœtti
      þengils mágr, er rengðisk,
      leirr fellr grár af gauri,
      góligr, í Imbólum.

My friend won't call out—he had all to fall in dirt; there was almost enough bad luck in that—"miðhæfi". Hardly I think that then the king's kinsman seemed, when he went astray, glad—grey filth falls from the fool—in Imbólar.

miðhæfi is not a Norse word; it has been plausibly argued that it is an approximately phonetic representation of a Greek word or phrase meaning 'Turn aside!' or (more probably) 'Don't cross!' For a brief discussion of the place-name *Imbólar*, see text.

(80) Ríðum Ræfils Vakri,
      rekuma plóg af akri,
      erjum úrgu barði,
      út at Miklagarði.
      Þiggjum þengils mála,
      þokum fram í gný stála,
      rjóðum gylðis góma,
      gerum ríks konungs sóma.

We ride Ræfill's steed—we don't drive the plough from the field but furrow with a spray-swept prow—out to Byzantium. We take the prince's pay, rush forward into the crash of steels, redden the wolf's gums, win the honour of the mighty king.

Kennings: *Ræfils Vakr*, 'Ræfill's Vakr': Vakr is the name of a legendary horse, and Ræfill of a legendary sea-king; the horse of a sea-king is a ship. *gný stála*, 'crash of steels', battle; *stál* is also a term for the foremost part of the keel of a ship, beneath the prow; *gný stála* in this context could therefore also mean 'crash of prows', in stormy weather or in a sea-battle.

(81) Nú hafa gœðingar gengit,
      goðfjón er þat ljónum,
      upp grafask ill róð greppa,
      œrit mǫrg á sœri.
      þat mun þeygi sjatna
      þeim, er svik viðr heima.
      Stígum létt á lágan
      legg, meðan upp held skeggi.

Now the lords have gone back—hateful to God is it for men; men's ill plans are uncovered—on enough oaths. It will never settle for him who practices treachery at home. We walk lightly on a low leg, while I (can) hold up my beard.

gœðingr is a specifically Orcadian term for nobleman of high rank beneath the earl.

Bótólfr begla

(82) Ferr at foglum harri,
     firar neyta vel skeyta,
     vǫn á heiðar hœna
     hnakkadytts, und bakka.
     Þar verðr almr, er ólmir
     undlinns stafir finnask,
     land verr lofðungr brandi,
     lynghœsn, dreginn kyngjum.

The lord goes fowling under the hill-slopes; men use their arrows well; the heath-hen can expect a neck-blow. There the bow will be drawn often, where the frenzied staves of the wound-serpent—the prince defends the land with his sword—meet grouse.

Kennings: *heiðar hæna*, 'hen of the heath', grouse or ptarmigan. *undlinns stafir*, 'staves of the wound-serpent': the 'wound-serpent' is a sword, and its (masc.) 'staves' are warriors, men.

SnE Hvat mun'k yðr eða ǫðrum
     ulfbrynnǫndum kynna,
     heiðs lofa'k hilmi blíðan
     háranns, nema goð sannan.

Of what shall I tell you or other wolf-waterers—I praise the glad lord of the cloudless high hall—other than true God.

Kennings: *ulfbrynnandi* 'wofl-waterer': he who causes a wolf to drink gives it blood, and is therefore a warrior. *hilmir heiðs háranns*, 'lord of the cloudlessly shining high hall': the 'cloudless high hall', with implications of brightness, is the sky; its lord is God.

SnE Akr verð'k opt fyr sjúkri
     eyfitja þó sitja,
     rjóð er mér in mæra
     menbrík, Njǫrun síka,
     heiðis fylgjask hauðri,
     hauk tíni'k svá, mínu,
     setrs leitandi sútar,
     slœgr, á hverju dœgri.

Yet I must often sit in my acre beside the sick goddess of the fishes of the island-watermeadows (red-faced for me is the table of the neck-ring), to accompany my falcon's land—so I, cunning, express hawk, seeking a seat for sorrow, in each day.

This and the following verse are cited in text appended to *Snorra Edda* as examples of word-play. *Akr* 'ploughed field' = *salr* 'soil', but *salr* also means 'hall'. *Njǫrun síka eyfitja*, 'Njǫrun (goddess-name) of the fishes of the island-watermeadows': 'fishes of meadows' are 'serpents', but among serpent-terms is *hringr*, which more usually means 'ring'; the kenning can thus be interpreted as 'goddess of rings', woman. *menbrík*, (fem.) 'table of the neck-ring', that which wears a neck-ring, woman. *heiðis hauðr*, 'falcon's land': where the falcon rests, 'arm' or 'hand'; this might be literal, or the poet may be playing on *armr* 'arm' and *harmr* 'sorrow' (see below). *haukr* 'hawk', but another word for 'hawk' is *harmr*, which more usually means 'sorrow'. 'Seeking a seat for sorrow' means 'seeking a resting-place for sorrow', seeking sorrow's end. The verse as a whole therefore means 'Yet I must often sit in my hall beside my sick wife—the woman is red-faced (with fever?) towards me—leaning on my arm (or 'to accompany my grief'?); so I in cunning express my grief, every day seeking a resting-place for sorrow'.

SnE Eigi veit'k, nær ægi
     óðflýtir má knýta,
     dýr er fiska fœra
     feigligt, þat's vér eigum.

I don't know, when the frenzied fleeter can knot the sea, the beast of fishing tackle, which we own, is likely to die.

This half-strophe is also cited, together with the preceding verse, as an example of word-play. *ægir*, 'sea': another term for 'sea' is *marr*, which also means 'horse'; the *óðflýtir*, 'frenzied fleeter' of a horse is its rider who makes it gallop; 'knot' here probably means 'bridle'. *dýr fiska færa*, 'beast of fishing tackle': 'fishing tackle' is also known as *taumar* (according to the passage which cites this verse), but this also means 'reins'; the 'beast of reins' is therefore a horse.

CHAPTER 16

Music and the Twelfth Century Orkney Earldom: A Cultural Crossroads in Musicological Perspective

Ingrid De Geer

The twelfth century marked a peak in Orkney earldom history. It prospered, materially and culturally, and there were many and differing contacts with surrounding areas and even with distant countries. Creative spirit and capacity permeated the earldom, and competent, gifted and ambitious earls, bishops and influential families were not adverse to spending time, labour and money on large-scale projects and donations. It was a society with room for art, in architecture, in literature, in poetry. Barbara Crawford expresses it well, when she remarks that the achievement of building the St Magnus Cathedral 'symbolises the new age of the 12th century and the full incorporation of Orkney into the European architectural and cultural heritage' (Crawford, 1983, 114). Let us not forget that the art of music, musical creativity, music in the church, outside the church, in the marketplace, in the castles, the bishop's palace and in the humble abodes was an important, an indispensable part of this cultural heritage.

No culture, past or present, without music is known to us. This is the common denominator. But when it comes to seeking to retrace the actual music of, e.g., twelfth-century West-European cultures, our possibilities differ from country to country, from region to region with regard to quantity, kind and quality of primary sources. Whereas the source material from, for instance, France and also England is comparatively abundant, Ireland, to take another example, is less fortunate in that 'the documentation of medieval music . . . is in inverse ratio to the fame with which its protagonists have endowed it [Ireland]' (Harrison, 1967, 74). And yet, no one would contemplate denying medieval Ireland music.

Turning to the twelfth-century Orkney earldom, the direct evidence is scarce, to say the least: A few instruments, instrument fragments and 'possible instruments'; a skald, who tells that he can play the harp—though it may not be a harp at all but some other string instrument; and a hymn, which is, strictly speaking, not a hymn and may or may not belong to the twelfth century. In short, a situation, which could at first sight seem almost fatal. However, when primary sources, i.e. in the first place notated music and instrument artefacts, fail, secondary sources, 'circumstantial evidence', become all the more important and may, and frequently do fill gaps, which would otherwise remain blank spots on the musicologist's map.

Slowly and laboriously, evidence and indications are accumulated and co-ordinated, and we begin to gain an impression of the 'musical situation' in the Orkney earldom; to an extent that makes the choice of subject for the present purpose a little problematic. The central theme of this conference is the St Magnus Cathedral, to the musicologist not least a place of music and inconceivable without song and maybe instruments. No functioning cathedral of this size and importance ever in music history existed without music or, for that matter, without church-goers, who shared in the music performed. It would have been appropriate to focus specifically on the Cathedral in Kirkwall, to join as a musicological commentator the discourses on church history and supplement with the aspect of ecclesiastical relations, ecclesiastical influence lines, as intermediates of musical style, of church music—and of secular music.

We have also heard about the subject of Earl Rognvald and his men visiting troubadour regions and leaving us poetry that bears witness to troubadour idiom. In all investigations and discussions caused by these verses, it has seldom been observed that in troubadour—and trouvère—art words and music generally went hand in hand, and that Rognvald and the skalds in his company could hardly have avoided being influenced by the musical component of this idiom. Likewise, we can turn to the *courtoisie*-influenced poems of Bishop Bjarni and possible musical implications, or discuss the Háttalykill, where several metres demonstrate northern influence, again with musical consequences.[1]

This list of subjects could be extended. However, it is not here the intention to present a résumé of the assembled results obtained so far,[2] but to concentrate on a few facets, where possible adding new dimensions. Of singular importance to the musicologist, as well as the most obvious to the non-musicologist, are sources with notated music, and it is this aspect, which will be the main theme of the following pages.

Unavoidably, the point of departure is the so-called St Magnus Hymn, *Nobilis humilis* (hereafter also *NH*), a two-part syllabic piece of music, to be termed *conductus* rather than hymn, and characterised by parallel movement in thirds. It is one of the very few sources of notated music that is relevant in an Orkney earldom context, if for no other reason then because its seven Latin stanzas, repeated to the same music, celebrate St Magnus of Orkney. The manuscript containing *NH* is today in the possession of Uppsala University Library (Cod. Ups. C 233 4°) and dates to the second half of the thirteenth century (col. pl. 10).

In music history writings *NH* has caused eager debates and several, often very far-reaching hypotheses have been launched. For a long time the dominating and eagerly maintained view has been that *NH*, with regard to its two-part texture and—in as far as taken into consideration—its melody, is a Norse music culture manifestation. This must be seen in the light of the question of the history of early polyphony, where we are still suffering to some extent from the protagon-ist/antagonist situation vis-à-vis the hypothesis that polyphony is of Nordic origin and originated independent of church music. The (major) third is by the

9   Detail of altarpiece from Andenes, Nordland, with figures of St Olav (left), and St Magnus (right) shown as a young and beautiful man in armour and cloak with the remains of a ?sword in his hand. (Courtesy of Historical Museum, Tromsö).

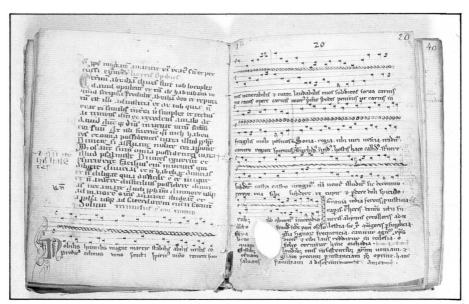

10 St Magnus Hymn, *Nobilis humilis,* in Cod. Ups. C233 4°, ff. 19v–20r, is a two-part syllabic piece of music with seven Latin stanzas, repeated to the same music, celebrating St Magnus of Orkney. The MS dates to the second half of the thirteenth century. (Courtesy of Uppsala University Library)

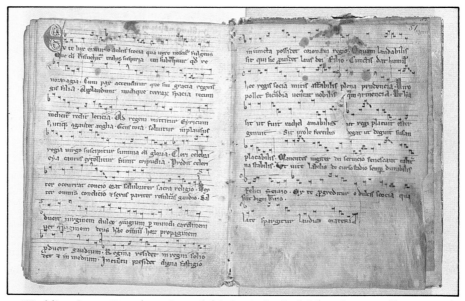

11 Wedding Song, *Ex te lux oritur o dulcis Scotia,* in Cod. Ups. C233 4°. ff. 50v–51r) late thirteenth century, for the marriage of Erik Magnusson (king of Norway 1280–1299) and Margaret, daughter of Alexander III of Scotland, which took place in Bergen in 1281. It is in the same hand as the St Magnus Hymn (colour plate 10).

protagonists regarded as typical Nordic and polyphony as of Nordic or at least Germanic origin. *NH* was here brought forward as evidence in the case. The antagonists, on the other hand, adhere more or less to the view that polyphony emanated from Gregorian chant, from music connected with the church or, at any rate, they are of the opinion that there is a linear evolution from (art) monophony to polyphony, governed by theory.

Intensified research in combination with a rapid increase of available source material, as well as recent achievements within the field of ethno-musicology, no longer offer a basis for such strict either/or hypotheses. Polyphony is no doubt a 'polygenetic invention' (Schneider, 1981, 137), and neither Western Europe nor the Norse area can claim the exclusive privilege of having 'created' polyphony or, more specifically, of having introduced the harmonic interval of the third. However, with these reservations there is no gainsaying that polyphony is, from an early time, a characteristic of West-European music, and it is a fact that the harmonic interval of the third characterises part of the notated music preserved in sources from north-western Europe, foremost Britain and to some extent northern France.

A close analysis of the two-part texture and of the melodic structure of *NH*, as well as investigations into the text, the MS, the historical context, relevant music sources, music theory writings, etc, brought the conclusion that an exclusive, indigenous Norse origin of *NH* could not be maintained (De Geer, 1985, 143–86). Naturally, this is a conclusion, which cannot be very popular to the protagonists, who regard *NH* as a demonstration of specific Norse musical originality and achievement. The present author can sympathise. Some twenty years ago she started out with similar ideas in favour of Norse origin, perhaps and not unreasonably, influenced by previous writings on the subject. However, the evidence failed to live up to and corroborate the expectations. In compensation, there was the satisfaction of reaching a result, congruent with the geographical, historical, cultural context and, not least, with the Orkney earldom's transcultural situation.

The inhabitants of the Orkney earldom should not be underestimated. They were no isolated tribe, thriving exclusively on local fares, literally and figuratively. They certainly had their Norse heritage, which should on no account be minimised, but they also had contacts with other areas abroad, were open to influences, had a gift of adopting and adapting. They served themselves freely, peacefully or by force, whenever it suited their purpose—also, we may safely assume, with regard to a fashionable manner of practising polyphony or in the case of a well-known and useful tune.

Figure 22 shows one way of transcribing *NH*. The melody is written out twice in the MS, with only one important—and generally ignored—difference, namely in the melodic unit 7a (cf. col. pl. 10). In this transcription (without rhythmic interpretation) the whole melody has been divided into units, demonstrating that *NH* is based on a short melodic formula, which varies a simple 'a'–'c'–'b'–('c') or –'d', except for the cadences (4b and 6 with the repetition 8) with the immediately preceding units. In unit 5a 'f'–'a' is transposed up a fifth.[3]

The melodic analysis showed that the basic structure of *NH* was formulaic and, further, that the (varied) formula employed could be identified in a number of

FIGURE 22   Transcription of *Nobilis humilis* with the text of the first verse. The melody is written out twice in the manuscript, the first version with the text for verses one and two, the second version with verses three and four. The variant in version two is here included together with the corresponding text of verse three.

pieces—*lais*, '*lai*-like', *conductus*—from foremost the northern French (Anglo-French) repertory. This short formula, then, was in all probability taken from a common stock and, considering its mnemotechnical character, presumably belonged to an older tradition, and preserved in sources referrable to these areas. In the examples that follow, the comparison refers mainly to the upper part of *NH*; in fact, the question whether *vox principalis*, as against *vox organalis* (the second voice), is in the upper or in the lower part makes no difference to the formulaic structure.

FIGURE 23a   *Rosula primula*, a music example in *Regulae* (*c*.1326) by the English music theorist Robertus de Handlo. Transcription in modern notation, with a division in units; no rhythmic interpretation.

Rosula primula is a short music example in *Regulae*, from about 1326, by the English music theorist Robertus de Handlo, where he comments upon a treatise by Franco 'of Cologne' (fl. *c*.1250–after 1280) and possibly identical with Franco 'of Paris'

(Coussemaker, i, 402). It may be the beginning of a *lai*, but we only have this fragment and thus know nothing about the continuation. The example (as far as it goes)
is identical with the upper part of *NH*, which, incidentally, could give, though not
necessarily, an indication as to the *vox principalis* of *NH*.[4] The transcription is, again,
in modern notation, with a division in units and without rhythmic interpretation.
A comparison with fig. 22 speaks for itself. If we, moreover, make the experiment
of adding a *vox organalis* as a lower part, in parallel movement in thirds—an experiment that is in no way unrealistic—the result is striking (fig. 23b; cf. fig. 22).

(Ingrid De Geer 1986)

FIGURE 23b   *Rosula primula* with an, experimentally, added lower part, cf. figs. 22 and 23a.

The next example is a transcribed extract of parts of the *conductus Natus est* from
the 'Feast of Fools', an office which was usually celebrated on 1 January. There are
five known MSS of this office, dating from the mid twelfth century to the fourteenth century and referrable to a primarily northern French tradition (Villetard,
1907; Beyssac, 1908; Arlt, 1970; De Geer, 1985, 197–201). *Natus est*, in the sources
designated *conductus* but having several of the characteristics of a sequence, is a
lengthy piece. It is divided in sections, which generally employ different melodic
material.

In fig. 24 we have a comparison of the relevant sections of three of the MSS,
where our formula is used (Sens Bibliothèque Municipale 46A (early thirteenth
century), London BL Egerton 2615 (*c*.1230/1240), Madrid Biblioteca Nacional 289
(probably mid twelfth century). It should be noted that it is not a question of an
incidental occurrence, but the formula is repeated, varied, time and again.[5]

The last example is a French lyric *lai*, attributed to Ernoul de Gastinois (fl. late
thirteenth century), who probably came from Gâtinais, a province between Seine,
Loire and Loing. It is called *Lai de l'ancien et du nouveau testament* and is contained,
uniquely, in the *Chansonnier de Noailles* from the end of the thirteenth century (Paris
Bibliothèque Nationale fr 12615 4°). This very long *lai* also employs different
melodic material for various sections. The transcription in fig. 25 of extracts from
the *lai* is in modern notation, with indications of the melodic units and without

Overleaf

FIGURE 24   *Natus est* from the 'Feast of Fools'. The transcription, in modern notation,
comprises extracts from three of the five known MSS of this office: S = Sens Bibl. Mun.
46A (early thirteenth century), L = London BL Egerton 2615 (*c*.1230/1240), M = Madrid
Bibl.Nac.289 (probably mid twelfth century). Melodic units are indicated; no rhythmic
interpretation.

Na- tus est, na- tus est,

Nec mi- nu- it quod e- rat,
as- su- mens quod non e- rat,

se- cu- la

Ut spon-sus e tha- la- mo,
pro- ces- sit ex u- te- ro,
Flos de Jes- se vir- gu- la,
fruc- tu re- plet se- cu- la.

(De Geer, 1985)

FIGURE 25a and b Transcription, in modern notation, of extracts from *Lai de l'ancien et du nouveau testament* by Ernoul de Gastinois (late thirteenth century). The *lai* is preserved, uniquely, in the *Chansonnier de Noailles* (Paris Bibliothèque Nationale fr 12615 4°, late thirteenth century). Melodic units are indicated; no rhythmic interpretation.

(De Geer, 1985)

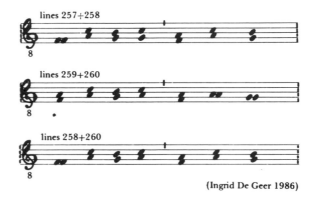

FIGURE 26 *Lai de l'ancien et du nouveau testament.* Transcription, 'telescoping' the lines 257–8, 259–60 and 258–60, respectively (cf. fig. 25).

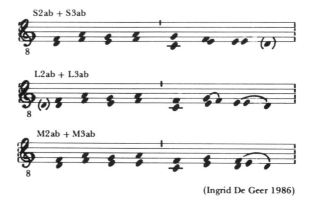

FIGURE 27 *Natus est.* Transcription, 'telescoping' units 2ab and units 3ab of the three MSS, respectively (cf. fig. 24).

rhythmic interpretation (transcription of the whole *lai*, with a rhythmic interpretation in Maillard, 1964). We are here concerned with lines 12–39 (partly reconstruction, cf. Maillard, 1964) and lines 257–65, giving another instance of the formula, with multifold repetition, with variants and transposition.[6] Of specific interest are the lines 257 and 258, as well as lines 259 and 260, respectively. On visualising a 'telescoping' of these two pair of lines, we immediately come very much closer to the parallel movement in thirds of *NH*. In addition and as a further illustration, also the lines 258 and 260 have been 'telescoped' (fig. 26).

We may do the same with *Natus est*, units 2ab and units 3ab of the three MSS, respectively (fig. 27; cf. fig. 24)—with a similar and in some respects even more interesting result (cf. NH, fig. 22).

This kind of 'simultaneousness' within the scope of melodic repetition may well have arisen quite spontaneously in actual performance practice, especially if the singers knew the formula well, had been singing it often to long texts, etc.

Concerning the melodic aspect of *NH* it seems fairly obvious that we have to do with melodic material, which can be considered as belonging to a common stock, available and used within a comparatively large area. This implies that we cannot regard the melody of *NH* as a unique melody, 'composed' at a certain date and place—in the sense of, for instance, a song by Schumann. It should be emphasised, though, that a formulaic structure, and the analysis of such a structure, in no way degrades or aims at degrading the entity of a single piece of music; the 'building' as such is not destroyed by analysing the elements that make up the construction. An examination of these elements may give important indications as to regional styles and distribution and may offer valuable hints regarding relations to older traditions. Varied or transposed recurrencies, or both, of motivic material, of melodic formulas, are of structural importance in, for example, much of plainchant or, for that matter, in any number of non-Western repertories. This music, these structures cannot be labelled 'primitive'. They are skillfully created entities, as are *Natus est, Lai de l'ancien et du nouveau testament*—and *Nobilis humilis*.

The pieces mentioned in connection with the melodic aspect of *NH*—and others could be included—all have in common traits that are characteristic of the *lai*, the sequence. Here is not the place to discuss the intricate questions of terminology, interrelations and origins of the lyric *lai*, the sequence, *conductus*, or likely further relations to the *chanson de geste* and the very plausible suggestions concerning roots in Celtic tradition. It must suffice to state that the melody of *NH* falls within the limits of this complex, regionally and stylistically.

Returning to the polyphonic aspect of *NH* and more specifically to the parallel movement in thirds, we again get a very similar picture: affinity with sources from an area comprising the British Isles and northern France. Preserved, known, sources containing polyphonic music—to say nothing of music notated in consecutive thirds—are missing in Scandinavian sources previous to the fifteenth century, with one exception (and not including *NH*): a late twelfth-century hymn to the Danish St Cnut Lavard, *Gaudet mater ecclesia*, most likely of English provenance (De Geer, 1985, 179, 190). In contrast, English sources show a predilection for, and an early and wide employment of this harmonic interval. However, not only has ethnomusicological research contributed greatly towards breaking the West-European 'monopoly of the third', but more thorough comparative analyses of continental, foremost northern French, and insular sources have also to some extent modified the (in a European context) English exclusiveness in this respect and has shown a considerably greater and freer use of the (harmonic) third throughout a wider area than had previously been suspected. It should be observed that some of the sources (English, French or otherwise) showing this preference for the third, are from the late twelfth and the first half of the thirteenth centuries, but that most belong to the second half of the thirteenth century or later.

The question regarding the situation in this respect specifically in Scotland is somewhat problematic, not least in view of the excessive losses of relevant material in that area (De Geer, 1985, 104–6). However, there is a tendency on the part of a number of musicologists to underrate the extent of music transmission between England (and France as well as Ireland) and Scotland—and inherently the Orkney earldom area. Evidence other than actual notated music, not least ecclesiastical sources, to mention but one aspect, indicates music connections, at times suggesting that 'English sources' should more correctly be referred to as 'British sources'.

We do have, though, one extremely valuable source, which provides us with an impression, and more than just an impression, of the kind of (ecclesiastical) music repertory that was 'en vogue' at least and presumably in St Andrews: the famous manuscript known as 'W1' and now in Wolfenbüttel (HAB Cod. Guelf. 628 Helmst. 4°). 'W1' is one of the most important, if not the most important, MSS with medieval polyphony that has been preserved. It consists of eleven fascicles, which foremost represent the Parisian polyphonic tradition and contains chiefly two-part, but also three- and four-part music as well as some monophonic pieces. In the seventh fascicle, f. 64r, is inserted an *ex libris*, which links the codex to St Andrews: 'liber monasterii S. andree apostoli in scocia'. The *ex libris* may be dated to the early fourteenth century (Roesner, 1976, 344), but the MS itself is no doubt of an earlier date.

The dating as well as the origin of 'W1' have been the subjects of discussion back and forth for close to a century. Several years ago Jacques Handschin argued that 'W1' originated in the British Isles, that the entire codex was written at, or at least for, St Andrews and suggested a mid- to late-thirteenth-century date (Handschin, 1933; 1951). Before as well as after that time the arguments and hypotheses have been manifold, and it is not here the place to go into detail. However, with some fairly recent and excellent studies, where *inter alia* palaeographic aspects are also considered, 'W1' seems to be back again, after many detours, to a mid-thirteenth-century date and to the St Andrews area (Roesner, 1976; Brown, *et al.*, 1981). This unique manuscript provides us not only with a fair idea of what the repertory was like in St Andrews and presumably also in a wider Scottish area. 'W1' also has some significance in relation to *NH*, as it contains examples of the kind of polyphony that is characteristic of that piece of music.

It is important to bear in mind that a music repertory, and the written evidence thereof, usually does not emerge out of nonentity. There is a 'prehistory', written or unwritten. The ground must be prepared, there must be not only the will and the wish to perform this kind of (for the time) quite advanced music, but also a certain performance practice and training; in short, the capacities as well—even if we make allowances for the ultimate result. It took time and effort to procure the notated music, and more effort and time still to train singers, to form a choir, however modest: it does today and it certainly did then, maybe some decades, a generation. It is reasonable to assume that polyphony was practised in the area already for some time previous to the event of 'W1'. And it would be surprising if polyphonic practices of the neighbouring south had not reflected on music performed in the Orkney earldom, especially in the St Magnus Cathedral. As yet we have no actual evidence for these suppositions, but we are, it would seem, at least justified in saying that there can be little doubt that polyphony as extant in 'W1' was known and executed in Scotland, or at any rate in St Andrews, at the time when *NH* was written down in Cod. C 233, i.e. close to the year 1281.

In that year King Erik Magnusson married Margaret, the daughter of Alexander III of Scotland in the Christ Church cathedral of Bergen. Cod. C 233, ff. 50v–51r, contains a wedding song to the couple, written by the same hand as *NH*, and, except for a minor rectification (f. 19v, which also has the beginning of *NH*), this hand occurs nowhere else in the MS. Both *NH* and the wedding song, *Ex te lux oritur o dulcis Scotia*, are inserted in vacant spaces in the MS (col. pl. 11).

Very little attention has been bestowed on *Ex te lux oritur* by musicologists. So observations regarding resemblances, especially concerning notation and rhythmic interpretation, to thirteenth-century trouvère songs and to contemporary songs for liturgical drama and pastoral plays have found but little reflection in musicological literature (cf., e.g., Elliott and Rimmer, 1973, 10–11).[7] Of non-musicologists, Knut Helle is one of the very few Scandinavian scholars, who has seriously considered this wedding song also from a musical standpoint. However, it is difficult to agree with Helle's unreserved statement that 'This is, in fact, the oldest piece of Norwegian secular music to survive in manuscript form' (Helle, 1980). A Norwegian, Scottish or even English provenance is equally conceivable. In this connection, it must also be realised that *Ex te lux oritur*, which has the form of a sequence, may well be, and probably is a *contrafactum*, though this has as yet not been possible to establish. Further investigations in this respect are needed and may throw some light on the question as well as, indirectly, assisting in the matter of *NH*.

It is rather surprising that *NH* has not been considered more closely in the context of this Scottish–Norwegian marriage, the missions, negotiations, persons and regions involved. After all, *Nobilis humilis* and *Ex te lux oritur* are the only pieces of music in Cod. C 233, written down by the same scribe, presumably on the same occasion. Could that occasion have been, for example, the final wedding negotiations, which took place in southern Scotland, close to the English border? The marriage contract was signed in Roxburgh, and co-signers were Frater Mauritius and Bishop Peter of Orkney. Whereas Frater Mauritius has turned up incidentally in *NH* literature, Bishop Peter has not. From a musicological viewpoint Frater Mauritius, Bishop Peter, and with them the whole entourage of these negotiations, including Princess Margaret's relations to religious houses and the like, are of considerable interest (De Geer, 1985, 144–5; see also Milveden, 1967).

Pending further investigations into these and other matters concerning *NH* and taking into account the evidence that we have so far, it may safely be assumed that, as to its melodic structure and also with regard to its two-part texture, *NH* belongs to the British/northern French influence sphere. There is at present little in favour of a twelfth-century, and much to support a thirteenth-century date for *NH*, probably the second half of that century. This is the time, when C 233 was written down. This is also the period to which most of the sources with a comparable two-part texture can be assigned.

There is, of course, the benefit of doubt. *NH* in C 233 may rely on an earlier source, having *NH* in the same 'shape'. Or, *NH*—in that same 'shape'—may have existed for a longer or shorter time in oral tradition. Such suppositions are acceptable and are sometimes probable. In fact, this reasoning is valid for a considerable number of sources from that time. We are still in a period—certainly in the twelfth century and also in the thirteenth century—when oral music tradition and written, notated music existed side by side to an extent not known in later centuries. We must always beware of *a priori* interpreting a piece of notated music from these early periods as a non-recurrent phenomenon, as a 'composition' in our sense of the word. It may be so, also in our sense. But it may be and very often is a 'frozen' performance version. Certainly once 'composed', but existing in oral transmission, not in notated form—until the day when, perhaps, somebody writes it down in the version he knows, he remembers. If we are very lucky, this notated piece may even have survived, possibly along with other 'frozen' versions of the same piece— which leaves the musicologist in quest of 'the original' with a complex and precarious task.

Perhaps it is not quite superfluous to point out, since experience has taught that otherwise matter-of-course circumstances are not always taken into account where music is concerned, that oral music tradition (transmission, 'composition') is not automatically identical with 'popular music tradition' (transmission, etc.). Terms like 'popular music', 'popular music making', 'folk music' are problematic, certainly when used as criteria concerning preserved music from seven or eight centuries ago. Labels like 'popular music' or 'art music' are extremely difficult to apply 'in retrospect'. It becomes a question of assumed social context, of presumed function and so on and so forth. Moreover, 'popular music' should not be confused with 'music with popular attraction'—so is also often a nineteenth-century *lied*, which may, incidentally, also make use of 'popular' material.

Nobilis humilis may very well have been 'popular' in the sense of 'attractive'. But *NH* as extant today was hardly 'popular music', neither as to the melodic structure, which is quite admirable, nor with regard to the Latin text, which indicates rather advanced literacy, though the two-part texture probably reflects 'popular practice'. *NH* incorporates melodic material with, presumably, ancient, perhaps Celtic roots. We do not know, however, if this material was ever really 'popular music material', whatever the definition. Speculations concerning the function of *NH* are, of course, permitted, and it would seem that a larger church or cathedral organisation, or a religious order, were the indicated settings for its performance. We have no certainty as to its place in liturgical or rather 'para-liturgical' context, except that its character as a *conductus* makes an introductory or processional function, or both, likely.

There is little doubt that many of the pieces of this period, including *NH*, were executed in different ways at different times and that, moreover, allowance must be made for improvisation. Text and music will normally have been performed as a whole, but even there we cannot be sure. *NH* may have been performed by voices only, but instrumental participation is probable, and almost any kind of combination is conceivable. An important aspect in the context is that *NH* as we now have it in Cod. C 233 can have been preceded by another version, or versions, with the same text and with the same, or approximately the same melody, possibly polyphonic, but more likely monophonic and perhaps in existence already in the twelfth century.

Provenance is seldom a simple matter in medieval music context, and where *NH* is concerned the issue has been and to some extent still is controversial. However, as was said above, *NH* belongs, as to melodic structure and two-part texture, to the British/northern French influence sphere. This is a question of regional style and regional diffusion. *NH* might, in fact, stylistically, have 'come about' almost anywhere within this sphere of influence and by almost anyone influenced by this regional style. But it is reasonable to keep to a fairly limited area, i.e. the area, where the cult of St Magnus was prominent, where he was a 'first class saint', not a 'secondary' one (De Geer, 1985, 118–42). Orkney was the heart of the St Magnus cult and had a tradition of learning, of culture. The sum total of extant evidence and indications allows us to regard *Nobilis humilis* as yet another exponent of the Orkney earldom as a cross-cultural centre, where a saint of Norse extraction was celebrated with music in accordance with prevailing fashion, style and traditions of north-western Europe.

This is about as far as we can come at present with regard to *NH*—short of letting free fantasy get the better of us. But well within the limits of admissible imagination lies the realistic expectation of new finds, of new evidence which may, for better or for worse, confirm or reject our hypotheses.

Great expectations do sometimes come true, as can be shown from our next piece of music, the sequence to St Magnus. For this, we have first to transport ourselves back in time, not 850 years as is the purpose of the present conference, but 'only' 550 years, to another anniversary, namely the tercentenary of the Translation of St Magnus—and thus well outside the period under discussion. Its presentation is nonetheless justified, since the case concerns St Magnus, the Orkney earldom and music, a rare combination. Besides, and equally important, it reflects the impact of twelfth-century Orkney earldom culture and achievement on subsequent centuries.

The sequence to St Magnus, *Comitis generosi militis gloriosi*, has been known for quite some time; that is to say, the text of the sequence. It was first published by Vígfusson and by Dasent in their edition and translation, respectively, of the *Orkneyinga Saga* (OSV, 1887, 303–5; OSD, 1894, 327–9). They had the text from MS AM 670f 4°, which contains, in the autograph of Árni Magnússon, a paper copy of the complete liturgy for the Mass of the Translation of St Magnus on 13 December (ff. 9r–12r), including the sequence *Comitis generosi*. At the beginning of the sequence Árni Magnússon wrote: 'Super totam hanc Sequentiam sunt lineae cum notulis cantoriis'. The lines are there, very neatly, but—and quite exasperating to a musicologist—the musical notation is not.

In his copy Árni Magnússon also wrote: 'Exscriptum ex libro Officiorum Sacrorum in grandi folio, qvem nactus sum Scardi Scardstrandensium in occiden-tale Islandia'. Magnússon's source was, thus, a *Missale Scardense* from Scard in the western part of Iceland and another item lost, or believed lost, until fairly recently. Further research, however, brought to light a vellum fragment in the Arnamagnean Collection (AM Acc. 7aα, ff. 28r–29v), which was published in 1968 in *The Sequences of the Archbishopric of Nidarós* (Eggen, 1968, i, 141–3; ii, 169). With the heading *in festo Magni ducis m[artiris]*, it contains the beginning of the same Mass as was copied by Árni Magnússon in AM 670f, including our sequence as far as the first words of the third verse—this time with at least part of the musical notation.

Now it could be established that *Comitis generosi* was in all probability a *contrafactum*, as the fragment turned out to have the melody of the sequence *Mane prima sabbati*. Presumably also the rest would have the same melody. This vellum was identified, with other fragments, as belonging to the *Missale Scardense* mentioned above and believed lost.

Eggen's publication was edited posthumously, and in a supplement the editors, more specifically Jón Helgason, refer to yet another vellum, removed from the binding of AM 1dα fol., having the beginning of the Mass already mentioned, with the heading *Translacio Magni m[artiris]* and the complete sequence *Comitis generosi*, now, at last, with musical notation throughout (Eggen, 1968, i, LI–LII). In a recent publication, Merete Geert Andersen ascertained that the sequence from Acc. 7aα belonged to *Missale Scardense*, whereas she identified the fragment from the binding of AM 1dα fol.—with other fragments—as part of a *Graduale Gufudalense*, from Gufudal Church in the northwestern part of Iceland. According to Geert Andersen, the *Missale Scardense* can be dated to *c.*1450–1478, the *Graduale Gufudalense* to *c.*1450–1470 (Geert Andersen, 1979).[8]

Comitis generosi occurs in yet another MS, AM 98 II 8°, from the end of the fifteenth century and probably intended as a supplement to AM 98 I 8°, a small Icelandic Missal from *c.*1200. The vellum fragment starts with the sequence, but without musical notation (Gjerløw, 1980, i, 29–31, 48–50). We are then at present in the possession of a total of four sources, all Icelandic, containing the only known St Magnus sequence, and but one of these sources has the complete musical notation.

Oluf Kolsrud in 1913 suggested that the sequence (only the text was known at the time) was written about 1435, since the third line of verse eight reads *ter centeno laureatus*. The recent datings of *Missale Scardense* and of *Graduale Gufudalense* do not gainsay Kolsrud's assumption (Kolsrud and Reiss, 1913, 18).

Plate 35a and 35b show the vellum leaf from the binding of AM 1dα fol. with *Comitis generosi*. The music is written in square notation on four black lines with F clef for verses one to two and C clef from verse three onwards. (The change from F clef to C clef occurs in Acc. 7aα shortly before the end of half verse 2a.) The vellum has been cut off at the margin, causing some damage.

In transcribing *Comitis generosi*, I have here made use of modern notation on five lines and with a G clef (fig. 28). The sequence has a total of nine verses, all of them written out in the manuscript. Verses one to eight consist of two parallel half verses, each half with exactly the same music with a few exceptions, which is the reason why verses three and seven are written out in full in this transcription. Verse nine consists of a half verse only, with the exact melody of verse eight, plus the additional *Amen*. The damage at the margin affects the half verses 7b, 8a and 9, and the reconstruction is marked by square brackets.

It has now finally been confirmed that *Comitis generosi* is indeed a *contrafactum*, with the St Magnus text set to the melody of the well-known Easter sequence *Mane prima sabbati*. This sequence had a very wide diffusion on the Continent, in the British Isles and also in Scandinavia from at least the early twelfth century. *Analecta hymnica* lists a very great number, but only comparatively few survive with music (AH, liv, 214–218). The Swedish musicologist, Carl-Allan Moberg, in his study *Über die schwedischen Sequenzen* from 1927, encompasses fourteen sources of the *Mane* melody, from the eleventh or twelfth to the sixteenth centuries (Moberg, 1927, ii, no. 8). Six sources are Swedish, most of them from the fifteenth and the sixteenth centuries. Some of the sequences with the *Mane* melody in Moberg have other texts as, for instance, a source from Lund (*Liber daticus Lundensis*) from the twelfth century, with the text *Ab arce siderea*. *Ab arce siderea* is also listed in *Analecta hymnica* (AH, viii, 13), but the Lund source is not included. *Comitis generosi* is not to be found in *Analecta* (which has only texts, no music), or in Moberg, who concentrates on the musical aspect—and the melody to *Comitis generosi* was not known in 1927.

There has been some discussions as to the origin of *Mane prima sabbati*. *Analecta hymnica* tends to favour English/British, possibly northern French provenance, as do most later scholars. There seems as yet to be no reason for a revision of this hypothesis.

Naturally, a close investigation of all existing sources employing the *Mane* melody may reveal further information concerning *Comitis generosi* and the circumstance of its turning up in fifteenth-century Icelandic sources. A preliminary comparison with the source material available to me has not disclosed any specific similarities of the St Magnus sequence as compared to one or more of the others, whether with the *Mane* text or with other words. All sources investigated differ more or less, and, besides, several sources have larger or smaller lacunae. *Comitis generosi* cannot as yet be placed in any specific variant group, nor is it especially close to another, single variant.

Except for the beginning and the end, the first verse is remarkably different from all sources so far considered. Moreover, this verse consists of two parallel halves, which is less usual for the introductory verse of a sequence, which more often has only a half verse. *Comitis* has this characteristic in common with another *Mane contrafactum, Gaude prole Graecia*, also in Moberg and presumably originating 'in Frankreich, 12.Jh., Adam v.St.Viktor (?), †1192' (Moberg, 1927, i, 67). These two sequences also share the peculiarity that verse nine is a melodic repetition of verse eight.

Overleaf

PLATE 35a and b. Leaf from the binding of AM 1dα fol., identified as belonging to *Graduale Gufudalense*, dated to *c.*1450–1470. The sequence to St Magnus, *Comitis generosi*, starts with line 12 of pl. 35a and ends with the last line of pl. 35b. (The Arnamagnean Collection, Copenhagen)

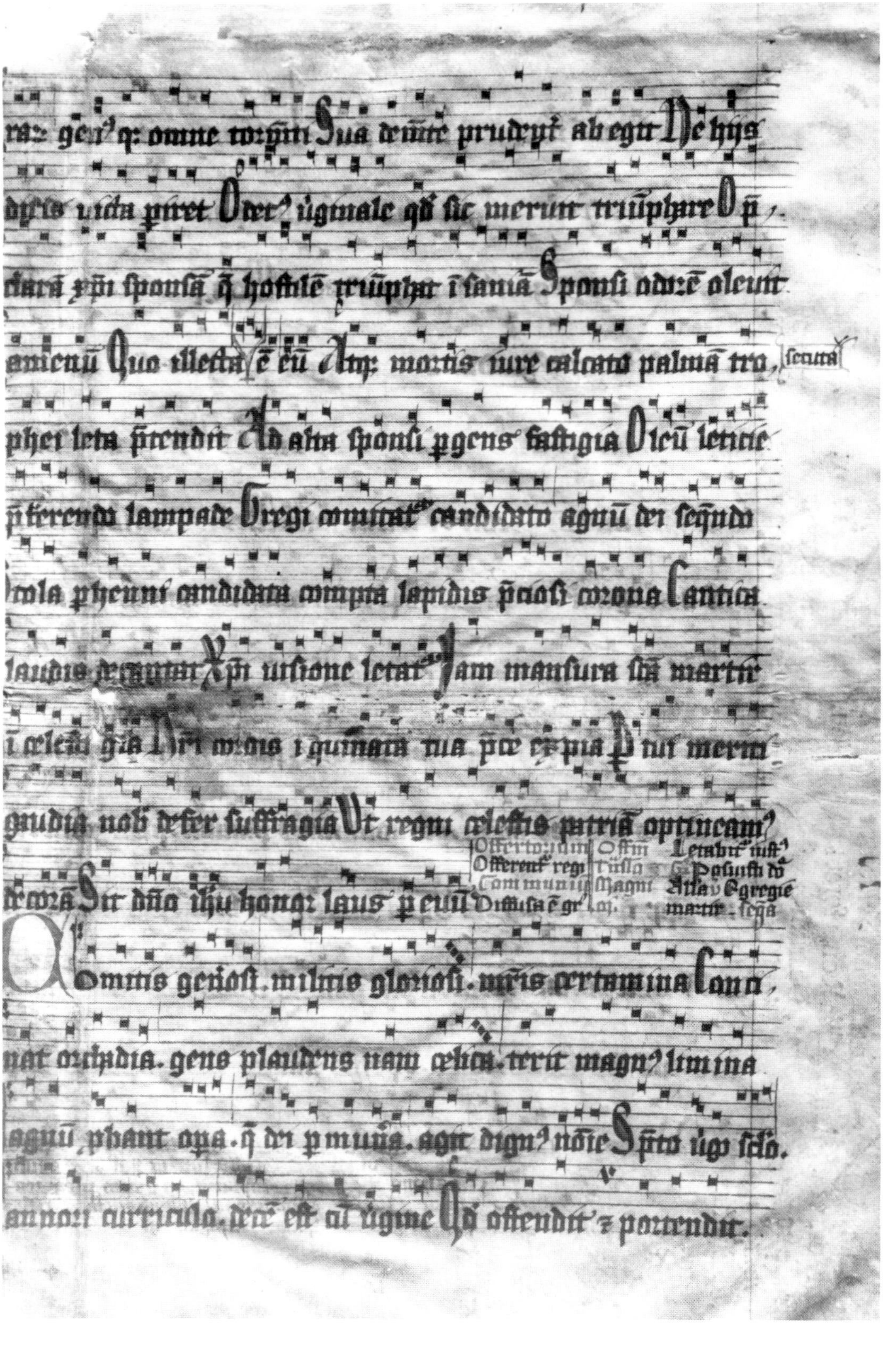

casu fract'oue nactus. puerili pmo Labens ita. erat uira ti

puer' eu' mestur. magni i fuencio Quia pado pmitt? resuer

mouit? eligit sagaci? illud qd e meli? Mox piusticia. optat

dei gra. suscept'ur gaudia. ditand? i gla In agone. spe corone.

martir sudat qd dniudit. sanguinis dispdio Deo grat? sola

strat? ñ i uir? ut predic? e celesti solio Mestis ris? impendit

cecis uis? agitur. ei? prociuio Presul erat. ut fauerir ? imple

rar. qd medetur. mox ipm ob sega Morbo lepre mediocri. uou

nis qd est tutam. ediutis languoribus. plebe amat uidetalibus

Tribulatos cunctos audit. pre uoto iustis plaudit. plen? miseria

dia. ñq; fugit dimonia Oqua martir hic beat? ergo fructu fol

lat? ? cuitepo laureatus: fruit palacio Quos nos esse te laud

utes. tuu festu celebrantes. pperuo magne tuo. impetres cele

quio Ut erepti tua pce. nos ab hostis seui nece. colletemi ? huic
guiduli pui Egi au Iust'ut pat Ad adune
Gla ? honor thome Gra refugiat choro stando pfequtes
Coiuuim... i au? fere uigilys ob suciuro Gla ?
gehenne supplicio Am Magna Egl of il pene... Magna egl die sci thom...

1.a Co - mi - tis ge - ne - ro - si mi - li - tis glo - ri - o - si mar - ti - ris cer -
1.b Con - ci - nat or - cha - di - a gens plau - dens nam ce - li - ca te - rit mag - nus

ta - mi - na. 2.a Mag - num pro - bant o - pe - ra que de - i per mu - ne - ra
li - mi - na. 2.b Spre - to uir - go se - cu - lo an - no - ri cur - ri - cu - lo

a - git di - gnus no - mi - ne. 3.a Quod os - ten - dit et por - ten - dit
de - cem est cum uir - gi - ne.

ca - su frac - tus o - uem nac - tus pu - er - i - li pre - mi - o.

3.b La - bens i - ta o - rat ui - ta ne pri - ue - tur cu - i me - de - tur

mag - ni in - ter - ven - ci - o. 4.a Qui - a pac - to pri - mi - tus re - si -
4.b Mo - ri pro iu - sti - ci - a op - tat

le - re mo - ni - tus e - li - git sa - ga - ci - us il - lud quod est me - li -
de - i gra - ti - a sus - cep - tu - rus gau - di - a di - tan - dus in glo - ri -

us. 5.a In a - go - ne spe co - ro - ne mar - tir su - dat quod de - nu -
a. 1) 5.b De - o gra - tus so - le stra - tus non in - ui - tus nunc pre - di -

dat sang - ui - nis dis - per - si - o. 6.a Mes - tis ri - sus im - pen - di - tur
tus est coe - les - ti so - li - o. 6.b Pre - sul o - rat ut sa - ne - tur

coe - sis ui - sus a - per - i - tur e - ius pa - tro - ci - ni - o.
et im - plo - rat qoud me - de - tur mox pre - cum ob - se - qui - o.

7.a Mor - bo le - pre me - di - ca - men nau - tis qui - dem est tu - ta - men e - di - uer -

sis lang - uo - ri - bus ple - bem cu - rat mor - ta - li - bus.

7.b. Tri - bu - la - tos cunc - tos au - dit pre - ce uo - to ius - tis plau - dit ple - nus mi -
se - ri - cor - di - a quae - que fu - gat de - mo - ni - a.

8.a O quam mar - tir hic be - a - tus uir - go fruc - tu fos - sus la - tus ter cen -
8.b Quos nos es - se te lau - dan - tes tu - um fes - tum ce - le - bran - tes per - pe -
9. Ut e - rep - ti tu - a pre - ce nos ab hos - tis se - ui ne - ce col - le -

te - no lau - re - a - tus fru - i - tur pa - la - ci - o.
tu - o mag - ne tu - o im - pe - tres col - lo - qui - o.
te - mur et pri - ue - mur ge - hen - ne sup - pli - ci - o. A - men.

(Transcription by Ingrid De Geer, 1986)

FIGURE 28   Transcription of *Comitis gerosi*, cf. pls. 35a and b. Annotations:
(1) The second and third notes of 5b are 'g' and 'a', not as in 5a 'a' and 'g'.
(2) The MS is damaged at this point of 7b, and a note is missing for the syllable *cor-* in *misericordia*. Presumably it should be 'a', here within square brackets.
(3) and (4) 8a and 9 are damaged here. The missing syllables and notes are placed within square brackets.

Whereas it is, of course, possible to find specific concordances like those mentioned above, none found so far forms a sufficient basis for further conclusions regarding *Comitis generosi*. There are still many question-marks, and we cannot, for example, be sure that the St Magnus sequence originated in the fifteenth century. It may have been in existence for a longer or shorter time before that, with the *Mane* melody, but with another or slightly different (Magnus) text. We do not even know for certain that *Comitis generosi*, as we now have it, is of Icelandic origin—though it probably is—, only that it was written down there.

One thing is certain, though: Research into the music of the Orkney earldom of the twelfth century, and of earlier and successive centuries will go on. And as the research proceeds, new indications, new evidence, new sources are bound to turn up—as the story of *Comitis generosi* indeed shows. More bits and pieces of the puzzle will be unearthed: a text as yet unknown to the musicologist, an instrument artefact, a vellum fragment with notated music. We may have to revise our hypotheses and conclusions along with future discoveries, within as well as outside the field of musicology.

Music is an elusive art, the more elusive the farther we trace it back through the centuries. We shall never be able to *hear* the Orkney earldom of the twelfth century; its sounds are irrevocably lost. The harp of Rognvald is forever silenced, the voices of the skalds left no record, Bjarni wrote down his 'songs', but—'without music'. No one can recall the market-place flutist, or the choristers in the Cathedral. Only faint echoes of the music once played and sung will ever reach us. But we do have the prospect and, indeed, the duty as musicologists of seeking to increase our knowledge of this integral part of Orkney earldom society; in other words, to give music its rightful place in the cultural pattern, alongside a Brough of Birsay, an Orkneyinga Saga, the poems of earls and bishop—the magnificence of a cathedral.

Some years ago I summarised my conclusions concerning music and the twelfth-century Orkney earldom in words that are as valid today as they were then. Since it is not only a conclusion but also in a sense a lodestar, I venture a reprise in this coda.

> The Orkney Earldom and the majority of its population was primarily Norse: in its language, to a great extent in its traditions and largely also in its dependency. Strong bonds connected the Northern Isles with the further Norse area—of which it was in many respects a part. However, the small crossroads realm of the Orkney Isles was also a bridge-head, a place where capacities and talents and traditions of the north and of the south met and amalgamated, and from where in turn impulses were likely to spread—to the north and to the south.
>
> Its background, its heritage was Norse, but the Earldom also reached out to the south, learning, absorbing, applying. It would be vastly to underrate the Orkneyman and the Orkneywoman to make them deaf and dumb to what was, literally, going on next door or in the same room, whether at home or abroad: a troubadour song, a lay with ancient roots, a new fashion of singing, a psalm sung in the church or in the Cathedral at Vespers, a Mass at Christmas, the liturgy on the day of the patron saint—or for that matter, a harp played at the court of a Scottish relation, a pipe in the hands of a Celtic servant.
>
> As a northern reflection of southern brilliance of the 'Rennaissance of the Twelfth Century', the Orkney earldom produced its poetry and saga, its saints and its cathedral, its pilgrims, crusaders, monks and bishops. The earldom had its court, its skalds, its bishopric, an élite as well as ordinary men and women—

and it had its music. It also had its strifes and warfare, cruelty and injustices—as had the south on the reverse side of the brilliance. Few would, in a twelfth-century music context, dream of drawing parallels between the St Magnus Cathedral in Kirkwall and the Notre Dame in Paris, or between the court of Earl Rognvald and the court of Ermengarde in Narbonne, or the Orkney Mainland and Sicily. The twelfth-century Orkney earldom was, however, no backwater. There was the space, the prerequisites and the capacities for a harp-playing earl, a singing skald, a bishop preoccupied with courtly love (and 'courtly music'?) and a saint, worshipped in words and songs in a cathedral that bore his name.

NOTES

1 Cf. van Eck, 1974, where these matters, including the influences of French *lais*, Celtic romances, etc. in the Earldom and further Norse areas are discussed from a musicological viewpoint. See also: de Vries, 1938; Helgason and Holtsmark, 1941; De Geer, 1985, 228-240.

2 General reference to De Geer, 1985, and literature listed there.

3 Concerning the relation text—music, it should be observed that units 2a, 4a, 5a, 6, 7 and 9 end with a full trochee, the others with a catalectic trochee.

4 It has been suggested that the *Regulae* fragment is 'secondary' to *NH*. If 'secondary' is to be interpreted as 'borrowed from', 'derived from', 'dependent on', it would be, it seems, greatly to overestimate the impact and diffusion of *NH*. If by 'secondary', 'later' (than the *NH* source) is intended, this certainly is so. But, the formula, the melodic 'phrase', was apparently alive and well throughout a longer period (see also below), and de Handlo—or Franco—more likely drew on another source or sources. Concerning similarities in connection with the rhythmic interpretation of *NH* and *Rosula primula*, see De Geer, 1985, 166, with references.

5 The two other MSS, not included in this example, have the same passages, basically corresponding but more elaborate. These MSS are: Cambridge, Trinity College B1 16 (*c.*1200) and Limoges Bibliothèque Municipale 217 (fourteenth century).

6 Judging from this example, it is the lower rather than the upper part in *NH*, which should be regarded as *vox principalis*. Such observations are, however, in no way conclusive—compare a similar remark above regarding *Rosula primula*—considering the frequent transpositions of this as well as other formulae (cf., e.g., lines 258 and 259 of this example and *Natus est*, section 2, fig. 24).

7 From considerations of space, a transcription of *Ex te lux oritur* could not be included here. Transcriptions can be found in e.g., Kolsrud and Reiss, 1913, 26-30; Elliott and Rimmer, 1973; Helle, 1980; De Geer, 1985, 144-6, 152, 154, 180.

8 I am most grateful to Merete Geert Andersen for having provided me with excellent photographs of the fragment from AM 1dα fol.

BIBLIOGRAPHY

Sources
Cambridge Trinity College B1 16
Copenhagen AM 1dα fol

Copenhagen AM Acc. 7aα
Copenhagen AM 98 I 8°
Copenhagen AM 98 II 8°
Copenhagen AM 670f 4°
Limoges Bibliothèque Municipale 217
London British Library Egerton 2615
Madrid Biblioteca Nacional 289
Paris Bibliothèque Nationale fr 12615 4° (Chansonnier de Noailles)
Sens Bibliothèque Municipale 46A
Uppsala University Library Cod. C 233 4°
Wolfenbüttel HAB Cod. Guelf. 628 Helmst. 4° (Heinemann Cat. 677)

List of references and abbreviations
AH = *Analecta hymnica medii aevi*, Blume, C, *et al.*, eds, 1886–1922, (55 vols), Leipzig
AM = Arnamagnean Collection, Copenhagen
Arlt, W, 1970, *Ein Festofficium des Mittelalters aus Beauvais in seiner liturgischen und musikalischen Bedeutung*, (2 vols), Köln
Beyssac, G M, 1908, 'L'Office de la Circoncision de Pierre de Corbeil', *Rassegna Gregoriana*, vii, cols. 304–22
Brown, J, Patterson, S, and Hiley, D, 1981, 'Further observations on W1', *Journal of Plainsong and Mediaeval Music Society*, 53–80
Coussemaker, C H E de, 1864–76, *Scriptorum de musica medii aevi nova series*, (4 vols), Paris
Crawford, B E, 1983, 'Birsay and the Early Earls and Bishops of Orkney', *Orkney Heritage*, ii, 97–118
De Geer, I, 1985, *Earl, Saint, Bishop, Skald—and Music. The Orkney Earldom of the Twelfth Century. A Musicological Study*, Uppsala
Eck, I van, (= De Geer, I), 1974, *Jarl Rognvald, Orkney en de muziek. Een bijdrage tot het belichten van de vraag oud-noordse muziek*, unpublished *doctoraal* thesis, University of Utrecht
Eggen, E, ed., 1968, *The Sequences of the Archbishopric of Nidarós*, (2 vols), Hafniae
Elliott, K, and Rimmer, F, 1973, *A history of Scottish music*
Geert Andersen, M, 1979, 'Colligere fragmenta, ne pereant', *Bibliotheca Arnamagnaeana, Opuscula*, vii, 1–35, Hafniae
Gjerløw, L, 1980, *Liturgica Islandica*, (2 vols), *Bibliotheca Arnamagnaeana*, xxxv–xxxvi, Copenhagen
Handschin, J, 1933, 'A Monument of English Mediaeval Polyphony: The Manuscript Wolfenbüttel 677', *The Musical Times*, lxxiv, 697–704
Handschin, J, 1951, 'The Summer Canon and Its Background', *Musica Disciplina*, v, 65–113
Harrison, F Ll, 1967, 'Polyphony in Medieval Ireland', *Festschrift Bruno Stäblein zum 70. Geburtstag*, Kassel
Helgason, J, and Holtsmark, A, 1941, *Háttalykill enn forni*, = *Bibliotheca Arnamagnaeana*, i, København
Helle, K, 1980, *A song for the royal wedding in Bergen A.D. 1281*, Bergen
Kolsrud, O, and Reiss, G, 1913, 'Tvo norrøne latinske kvaede med melodiar', *Videnskapsselskapets Skrifter. II. Hist.-Filos. Klasse*, v, Christiania/Oslo
Maillard, J, 1964, *Lais et chansons d'Ernoul de Gastinois*, Musicological Studies and Documents, xv, Rome
Milveden, I, 1967, 'Organum', *Kulturhistoriskt Lexikon för Nordisk Medeltid*, v, Malmö
Moberg, C-A, 1927, *Über die schwedischen Sequenzen. Eine musikgeschichtliche Studie*, (2 vols), Uppsala

OSD = Dasent, G W, 1894, *The Orkneyingers' Saga*

OSV = Vígfusson, G, 1887, *Orkneyinga Saga and Magnus Saga*

Roesner, E H, 1976, 'The Origins of W1', *Journal of the American Musicological Society*, xxix: iii, 337–79

Schneider, A, 1981, 'Orale Tradition, Musikgeschichte und Folklorismus in Irland. Das Kontinuitätsproblem und die historische Volksmusikforschung', *Musikethnologische Sammelbände*, v, 117–57, Graz

Villetard, J de, 1907, *Office de Pierre de Corbeil (Office de la Circoncision), improprement appelé Office des Fous*, Paris

Vries J de, 1938, 'Een skald onder de troubadours', *Verslagen en Mededeelingen der Kon. Vlaamsche Academie voor Taal- en Letter-kunde*, 701–35

Legends of Saint Magnus
Extracted from the thirteenth-century
Fornsvenska Legendariet

Translated by Evan MacGillivray

The venerated king and martyr Magnus was the king Saint Olaf's son, and steadfast in the Love of God. A gentle, clean-iiving man and humble, he ruled the land likewise after his father's death.

Because he had striven against God's enemies who had come to his kingdom, he was at last crowned a martyr, and lies in the Orkney Islands in the magnificent church built there in his honour.

After Saint Magnus died there happened a gracious miracle. There came pestilence to the land and many people died. When the dead were buried they stood up again with devils' power from their graves, and returned home to smit and threaten many men.

The people who lived there when this happened sought solace in Saint Magnus with fast, and with alms, and with humble prayer, and begged that he would free them from the dead mens' uprising. After this, on a day when the dead men appeared as they were wont to do, Saint Magnus mingled with them. He had on the golden crown, and the royal spear of gold was in his right hand. And he turned the golden spear against the dead and charged the evil spirits to depart hence. At once when he said this the dead men were confounded who before seemed as if alive.

That happened in the Orkney Islands where homage is paid to Saint Magnus. In his church there took place many miracles in God's name. The saint Pope Leo ordained a miracle to be recorded to the honour of Saint Magnus.

On Christmas Eve when the Light of the World was on high, twelve men in company came to a town called Kölbigk, to Saint Magnus Church there where the leading men held sword-play.

They had in mind to rape the parish priest's daughter. The priest was named Robert and his daughter Anna. The men remembered not that Our Lord followed them, nor Christendom's pure light; and not the Holy Church's command, nor God's praise which they heard being sung. They continued in the desire which they had begun with. Then they sent two virgin maids into the church to lure Anna to them. When she came out they started to dance wantonly and shamefully with her in the weapon-house. The leading sword-player began to sing this verse:

> Passion rode rough-shod
> through the verdant forest;
> And into lust's sinfulness
> trapped the fair young virgin.
>   O, why do we stay?
>   O, why do we not go?

That pleasure became for them sadness with God's judgment through the holy Saint Magnus: for, from the dancing and from the ballad singing they could not stop for almost a whole year.

The same men danced so that the clerk could not continue the service within the church. The priest who heard this went from the altar to the door of the church, where he called upon them by God's grace and Saint Magnus to go into the church to serve God. When they would not heed him, then he called on God and Saint Magnus to prevent them for a year from ceasing to dance, and that no-one was to be separated from the others.

Thereafter the priest sent his son, John, to bring in his sister Anna from the dancers—which was something that had slipped his mind. Following his father's wish, John hauled on his sister's hands—and then happened an unheard of miracle, because in his dragging hands one of her arms was drawn from her body at the armpit, and so that there was still no broken link in the dance. It was an even greater marvel that no blood flowed out where the arm separated from her body.

The son carried back to his father this grotesque gift: the arm from his daughter torn away like a branch from the tree, and with such torment. 'See, father, this is your daughter and my sister whom you asked me to bring back indoors.' They regretted sorrowfully the ban, and the priest buried the arm of the living daughter. Then came wonder upon wonder. The next day he found the buried arm upcast from the earth. Again he buried Anna's arm, and again the next morning found it upcast. For the third time the arm was buried and the same happened. Then the priest laid the arm within the church.

Still the same men danced without ceasing and still sang the same song:

>   O, why do we stay?
>   O, why do we not go?

They who had neither the strength to stay nor the will to go. As if in tolerating this they were aware of no human need. In truth, in the arena they did nothing other than dance. They did not eat, nor drink, nor sleep. They did not hunger nor thirst; nor have any bodily feeling to tell night or day, the heat of summer or the cold of winter, storm, rain, snow or hail; and in all weather conditions they could not tire of the irresistible dance. Their hair and nails did not grow and their clothes did not wear, so mild was the torture and so sweet the revenge on them through the gentleness of God and Saint Magnus.

What land did not get to know of this marvel? Who did not hurry to this wonderful sight?

When the Roman Emperor heard of this he ordered that a shelter be built so that snow and rain should not harm them. But the building never came into use, because all that was built during the day was broken asunder in the night. Three times they started to build, and as often it was broken down.

They danced the year around, and when Christmas Eve came they were released by the prayer of Saint Magnus. At the same time when they ceased their dancing and their pleasure, and when the priest had chided them, they separated at once so that no-one's breath was longer withheld. And they ran immediately into Saint Magnus Church and fell at once upon the floor, and after their long wakefulness they slept for three days. On the third day God, who from the dead arose, allowed them to get up.

Even Anna, who had lost an arm, and who had been with them in their long perplexity and pardoning, was there mortified. When the priest had flogged them with the birch-rod, and all had arisen, she alone lay in death so that the priest thought that she was asleep. And all who saw this marvelled thereat and were afraid, and saw expire she who had lost a limb so that she should not lose all; and with God's punishment was preserved from destruction, and escaped eternal death for the death of a pauper. Her father the priest was the first person to die after her.

The arm which the priest had been unable to bury, the Emperor had enshrined in gold and silver, and bade that it should hang as a token.

Also the men who had danced with Anna, aware of their guilt, did not turn again to leaping and jumping, and where they had been boisterously loud when together, they were now subdued when apart.

There was there a congregation of folk that had come in groups to see this wonder—as if it had just then happened. They saw there clothes, hair, nails and skin all collected as if to be proved and made white and whole.

For the dancers who had been separated, so changed one torment into another torment. They were not allowed to be together, but instead were distributed all over the land. And they promised to go out from the town which more than any other had become a sanctified place.

This was witnessed by one who was there called Theodoricus, both by word of his mouth and by witness brief. He had this to acknowledge that when he danced it befell him that deep within he was guided by Our Lady and Saint Magnus. On Our Lady's Fast-day he was left in the church when all the folk had gone out after their prayers, and he fell asleep. On awakening he stood up whole and strong as of old, and was preserved steadfast after faithlessness and given life after death. He signed himself and was amazed that the priest's hard sentence was so lifted. And he said 'See all that the Virgin Mary and Saint Magnus have given me who am upheld in faith.'

This took place to the glory and honour of Saint Magnus.

Commentary on the Legends of Saint Magnus

Ingrid De Geer

The 'Legends of Saint Magnus', here translated into English by Evan MacGillivray, are to be found in the so-called *Fornsvenska Legendariet* (The Old Swedish Legendary), a chronologically arranged collection of legends from the early Christian era until the mid thirteenth century. The collection, which also deals with popes and emperors, is written in Old Swedish and originated not later than the first half of the fourteenth century (cf. Jansson, 1934; 1959).

Essentially, the *Fornsvenska Legendariet* (*F.L.*) is a translation, largely based on Jacobus de Voragine *Legenda aurea* (1263-1288), Martinus Oppaviensis *Chronicon pontificum et imperatorum* (redaction from 1276) as well as other sources, for example *Sächsische Weltchronik*. The author of *F.L.* is unknown, but the collection is dedicated to St Dominic, and it is reasonable to assume that it is the work of a learned Dominican friar. By the end of the thirteenth century there were a number of Dominican friaries in Sweden (Sigtuna, Skänninge, Visby, Kalmar, Skara, Lödöse, Strängnäs). Probably *F.L.* was compiled in one of these places, most likely—on linguistic and stylistic grounds—in Östergötland.

The most important MSS containing *F.L.* are: 1) Codex Holmiensis A 34 ('Cod. Bureanus'), mid fourteenth century, defect. 2) Codex Upsaliensis C 528 ('Cod. Bildstenianus'), first half of the fifteenth century. 3) Codex Skokloster 3 4° ('Cod. Passionarius'), now in the National Archives, second half of the fifteenth century. 4) Codex Holmiensis A 124, first half of the fourteenth century, fragments.

Cod. Ups. C 528 ('Bildstenianus' after one of its former owners) is a parchment manuscript in large quarto, consisting of 170 leaves. This is the oldest MS that comprises the complete legendary, and the only one with the legend of St Magnus. (Cod. 'Passionarius', with more or less the same contents as 'Bildstenianus', includes Magnus in the *Index*, but the legend is missing in the text.) The main part (leaf 3r.–148r.) consists of the legendary proper, starting with the Virgin Mary and John the Baptist and ending with St Dominic (d. 1221) and Peter the Martyr (d. 1252). Then follows a section, which has the character of an appendix (leaf 148r.–158v.), devoted to Nordic saints: St Sigfrid, St Olav, St Magnus of Orkney and St Erik, in this order. These legends are fairly short, and only in the case of St Olav is a special feast day mentioned.

The legends of St Magnus comprise leaf 155v.(bottom)–157v.(top); i.e. the section translated here. The correspondence between these legends and those of the Orkneyinga Saga or other sources on the Orkney saint is slight. There are no dates, no feasts mentioned, no 'Magnus saga'. The all-dominating contents of the text relating to St Magnus in *F.L.* consist of the legend known as the 'Kölbigk dance'.

During the Middle Ages it was a popular custom in certain parts of Europe to have dances and games in the church-yard and at times even in the church itself. In religious, moralising and historical writings of the Middle Ages and later, we repeatedly encounter tales and legends, warning against these practices. The most well-known of such legends is the one of the miraculous year-long dance of Kölbigk. The legend relates the tragic fate of those, who on Christmas Eve danced in the church-yard of the St Magnus church in Kölbigk. The dance, which continued for a whole year, is supposed to have taken place around the year 1020 and is usually localised to the small town of Kölbigk in Sachsen-Anhalt (present East Germany). The Kölbigk occurrence probably reflects an outbreak of a very real disease, known to have existed in the Middle Ages. The legend, which has been preserved in several different versions, probably refers to an actual event, as can be seen from, for instance a note in the annals of the abbey of Hersfeld from *c*.1070, concerning a certain Ruthart, who is said to have participated in the notorious Kölbigk dance. There are three, Latin, main sources for the event all represented by MSS from the mid twelfth century, and all having their origin in a common account, dating from the mid eleventh century. One, widely diffused, version is known from William of Malmesbury *Gesta regum anglorum* (*c*.1125), later also related in Vincent of Beauvais (d. *c*.1264) *Speculum historiale* and elsewhere. In this version the dancers are delivered from their curse by Bishop Herbert of Cologne. The year is said to be 1021. Another MS from the twelfth century, in Bibliothèque Nationale in Paris, offers a different and in places quite realistic version. It is, however, a third, the so-called Theoderik version, which concerns us here.

It has been clearly shown by Dag Strömbäck that there is an intimate connection between the Theoderik version and the legend of the miraculous dance in 'Cod. Bildstenianus' (Cod. Ups. C 528), and there can be little doubt that this version served as the, Latin, original for the Old Swedish text (Strömbäck 1944; 1961). According to careful investigations by Edw. Schröder, the Theoderik version found diffusion only in the British Isles (Schröder, 1897, 126–130; 1933, 360f.; see also Baeseke, 1941). The oldest MSS containing the Theoderik version belong to the twelfth century.

In this version of the story of the Kölbigk dance, a certain Theoderik, one of the participants and still suffering from the aftereffects, reached England on his wanderings where he was miraculously cured at the time of Edward the Confessor at the grave of St Edith (d. 984) in Wilton. The version obviously arose in connection with a relation of the life of St Edith and the miracles at her grave. It was probably written down in the second half of the eleventh century, presumably by the monk Goscelinus (d. *c*.1100).

The version of the Kölbigk dance in the *Fornsvenska Legendariet* places the event, not in Kölbigk in Saxony, but in the Orkneys and connects it, not with the St Magnus in Kölbigk and a St Magnus church there, but with St Magnus of Orkney and an Orkney St Magnus church (the Cathedral?). The time is changed from *c*.1020 to about the mid twelfth century. The miraculous cure, which in the frame story of the Theoderik version happened at the grave of St Edith in Wilton, is also transferred to the Orkney Islands and the sanctuary of Earl Magnus. The greater part of the frame story concerning Theoderik has been removed in the *F.L.* version, but a residue remains, as, for example, the reference to Theoderik and to Pope Leo. The pope in question died in 1054. Further, whereas the original only mentions St Magnus in relation to the church in Kölbigk (as being dedicated to the saint) and in connection with God's curse on the dancers, the *F.L.* version repeatedly inserts the name of St Magnus, respectively replaces 'St Edith' with 'St Magnus'. In general, it seems that an effort has been made to cut out all elements unsuitable in a legend concerning the Orkney saint.

Throughout the dance, the participants sing a verse:

> Redh(u) kompana redhobono jwer thiokka skogha
> Oc gildo mz synd venisto jomfrw
> hwi standom vi hwi gangom vi ey.

On repeating the refrain in the text, the author/compiler(?) inserts 'swa', thus making a metrical improvement:

> hwi standom vi swa: hwi gangom vi ey.

This dancing song has given rise to some discussions, and at times the verse has been regarded as a fragment of a Swedish folk ballad. This is not the case. The fragment has proved to be a, very imperfect, translation of the dance song of the Theoderik version:

> Equitabat Bovo per silvam frondosam,
> Ducebat sibi Merswinden formosam.
> Quid stamus? cur non imus?

It is uncertain from where the Latin dance song derives: possibly a French carol or a Low German song.

The story of the Kölbigk dance is a fascinating one, and it is not surprising that for centuries it travelled far and wide all over Europe, in many differing guises. Fascinating is not least its transformation into a St Magnus of Orkney miracle. It is not known which St Magnus it was who was worshipped in the church of Kölbigk, though it can hardly have been St Magnus of Orkney (De Geer, 1985, 114f.). Presumably, the original connection with Saxony was soon lost, and there will have been few difficulties in exchanging the Kolbigk saint for the Orkney earl. Did this 'revision' take place in the British Isles or in Scandinavia? Dag Strömbäck argued convincingly in favour of an English/Scottish provenance of the 'Orkney version'. According to Strömbäck, the dance legend in the *Fornsvenska Legendariet* is in all probability a direct derivation from an Earl Magnus adapted variant of the Theoderik version, originating in England or Scotland. However, Strömbäck does mention the slight possibility that the revision of the Theoderik version was carried out by the author/compiler of *F.L.* and that the association with Earl Magnus was his idea (Strömbäck, 1944). In view of the otherwise practically nonexistent evidence for the cult of a St Magnus in Sweden, the latter possibility seems very slight indeed (De Geer, 1985, 118ff.). Hopefully, further research into the matter may give us the answer.

The fact remains, though, that someone, somewhere, presumably in the second half of the twelfth century, found it of great importance to link St Magnus, Earl of Orkney, to one of the most famous wandering legends of the Middle Ages: the Kölbigk dance, transplanting the events of a small German town to the distant Orkney Islands. Thanks to Evan MacGillivray we now possess, in English, yet another dimension to the Saga of the Orkney Saint.

REFERENCES

Baeseke, G, 1941, 'Der Kölbigker Tanz', *Zeitschrift für Kirchengeschichte*, lxxvii

De Geer, I, 1985, *Earl, Saint, Bishop, Skald—and Music. The Orkney Earldom of the Twelfth Century. A Musicological Study.* Uppsala

Jansson, V, 1934, *Fornsvenska legendariet. Handskrifter och språk.* Nordiska texter och undersökningar, iv. Uppsala

Jansson, V, 1959, 'Fornsvenska legendariet', *Kulturhistoriskt lexikon för nordisk medeltid*, iv

Legendarium Suecanum 'Fornsvenska legendariet'. E codice membr. Bibl. Univ. Upsal. C 528 ('Codice Bildsteniano'). Suecice et Britanniæ praefatus, ed. Valter Jansson. Hafniae 1966. (Corpus codicum Suecicorum medii aevi, xix)

Schröder, E, 1933, 'Das Tanzlied von Kölbigk', *Nachrichten von der Gesellschaft der Wissenschaften zu Göttingen*, Philol.-hist. Klasse

Schröder, E, 1897, 'Die Tänzer von Kölbigk', *Zeitschrift für Kirchengeschichte*, xvii

Strömbäck, D, 1944, 'Den underbara årsdansen', *Arkiv för nordisk filologi*, lix

Strömbäck, D, 1961, 'Kölbigk och Hårga I', *Arv. Tidskrift för Nordisk Folkminnesforskning*, xvii

In these works references to further literature can be found.

Index

WITHDRAWN

WITHDRAWN
READING ROOM